MINDS and HEARTS in Praise of God

Hugh T. McElrath

MINDS and HEARTS in Praise of God

HYMNS AND ESSAYS IN CHURCH MUSIC IN HONOR OF HUGH T. MCELRATH

Edited by
J. Michael Raley and Deborah Carlton Loftis

Providence House Publishers
PROVIDENCE PUBLISHING CORPORATION
FRANKLIN, TENNESSEE

Printed in the United States of America

10 09 08 07 06 1 2 3 4 5

Library of Congress Control Number: 2006933745

ISBN-13: 978-1-57736-307-1
ISBN-10: 1-57736-307-8

Cover design by LeAnna Massingille
Page design by Joey McNair

Frontispiece courtesy of Dr. Andrew Rawls, Director of Media Services, The Southern Baptist Theological Seminary

PROVIDENCE HOUSE PUBLISHERS
an imprint of
Providence Publishing Corporation
238 Seaboard Lane • Franklin, Tennessee 37067
www.providence-publishing.com
800-321-5692

Contents

Preface

On November 13, 2001, Professor Hugh Thomas McElrath celebrated his eightieth birthday. Just two weeks earlier, in late October, a number of his former students and colleagues attending The Southern Baptist Theological Seminary's (SBTS) fortieth annual Church Music Institute in Louisville had gathered to honor Professor McElrath. Church Music Professor Emeritus Carlton R. Young, Candler School of Theology, Emory University, delivered the McElrath Lectures that year, entitled "Christian Global Song: Missional and Musical Perspectives" (to be published elsewhere by the seminary). In the afternoon session on October 25th, devoted exclusively to honoring Professor McElrath, Professors Harry Eskew and Janelle Ganey presented their papers published in this collection. That evening, the Church Music Institute banquet honored both Hugh and Ruth McElrath for their years of service to Christ and to Southern Seminary. Dean Thomas Bolton and Music and Audio-Visual Librarian David Gregory provided words of welcome and introduction. A special slide presentation, entitled "'He Keeps Me Singing': Dr. McElrath's Fifty Years of Ministry," had been assembled by Director of Media Services Andrew Rawls and William Jeffrey Jones, whose biographical overview of Professor McElrath's life and career is published starting on page 13. This presentation chronicled Professor McElrath's life of Christian service in the fields of teaching, local church ministry, and foreign missions. On the one hand, it paid well-deserved tribute to the great man and servant of God whom we all knew so well; but at the same time, thanks especially to Ruth McElrath's input, it also provided a time of much fun and laughter.

Afterwards, at 8:00 P.M., we all gathered in Alumni Memorial Chapel for a hymn festival, appropriately entitled "To Our God We Lift Our Voices: A Hymn Festival of Praise and Proclamation in Gratitude for the Ministry of Hugh T. McElrath." Those involved in this program included SBTS Professors Sandra C. Turner, Ronald A. Turner, G. Douglas Smith, James W. Cox, and Esther R. Crookshank, as well as Southwestern Baptist Theological Seminary Professor Angela F. Cofer. We sang a mixture of new and established hymns and tunes, including Gene Winters's text, published herein, entitled "O God, in Your Word You instruct us to sing," sung to the tune, FOSTER HALL (not to be confused with FOSTER HALL III, published in this collection); Professor McElrath's hymns, "To our God we lift our voices," set to Donald W. Packard's tune, BEECHWOOD, and "Sound the Word and share God's love," set to his own tune, SAMOHT (THOMAS spelled backwards), arranged and harmonized by

Ronald A. Turner; "How lovely, Lord, how lovely," (Psalm 84, paraphrased by Arlo D. Duba), set to Hal H. Hopson's MERLE'S TUNE; Milburn Price's hymn, "God of past, Who by Your Spirit," with Gerald Chafin's tune, VISION; Joy L. Walker's text, "God Almighty, be our shelter," set to NETTLETON; and Esther Crookshank's hymn, entitled "Covenant of Love," sung to the tune MARYTON.

Out of this joyous celebration ultimately came the collection of hymn texts and tunes, as well as essays, included within the covers of this Festschrift. Although plans for the McElrath Celebration had been underway for several months when the hijacked airplanes struck the World Trade Center towers and the Pentagon on September 11, 2001, that event, naturally, transformed everything. The contributing hymnists, in particular, attempted to help fill the void in our hymnody that existed prior to this attack. Thus Rae Whitney penned her moving text, "When all the world is wounded," while Hal Hopson drafted a new tune, MCELRATH, for Fred Kaan's text, "For the healing of the nations." Carlton R. Young composed the tune OCTOGENARIAN in honor of Professor McElrath's eightieth birthday. At the same time, however, he set it to Carl P. Daw, Jr.'s insightful text, "God of grace and God of laughter," whose second stanza petitions God, "When our lives are torn by sadness, heal our wounds with tuneful balm."

Professor McElrath himself suggested two additional much-needed themes for new hymn texts. The first was a call for hymns that address the unique problems and challenges of aging, while the second was for new hymns dealing with the third Person of the Godhead, the Holy Spirit. Brian Wren's new hymn, "Good News!" addresses this latter concern, but focuses as well on the "good news" by which believers continue to be called into community with one another. Louis Ball and A. L. "Pete" Butler have fulfilled another request of Professor McElrath, namely, to set to music more of the unpublished hymns written by Fanny J. Crosby. (For 120 such texts, see Donald P. Hustad, editor, *Fanny Crosby Speaks Again: 120 Hymns* [Carol Stream, Illinois: Hope Publishing Co., 1977]).

Others have sought to honor Professor McElrath by setting one of his own texts or themes to new music. Thus Milburn Price composed the new tune SOUTHERN SEMINARY for Professor McElrath's text, "We praise You with our minds, O Lord," which forms the central theme of the collection, while Gene Winters has composed a new text on a similar theme, entitled "O God, in Your Word You instruct us to sing," set to his new tune, FOSTER HALL III. Carl P. Daw, Jr.'s text, "Because his life was threatened," recalls another theme repeatedly emphasized by Professor McElrath—the ever-present need among congregations today for hymns that both teach and interpret Scripture—while reminding us all of the continued relevance of God's Word. Finally, in reflection of Professor McElrath's own missions emphasis in his lifelong ministry, a theme echoed as well throughout many of the hymns included in this collection, Austin C. Lovelace's new tune, AUSTIPOL, sets to music Ted Wilde's text, "Christ, engage us in Your mission."

The essays contained in this volume reflect the broad scope of inquiry that Professor McElrath encouraged in his students and affirmed in his colleagues. In numerous music history and hymnology classes, students were encouraged to look carefully at the historical record. Five essays here reflect Professor McElrath's teaching in music history and hymnology, covering a wide historical span stretching from a study of medieval carol manuscripts by Paulette Catherwood to studies in eighteenth- and nineteenth-century British and American hymnody contributed by Harry Eskew, Mel Wilhoit, Paul Hammond, and Donald Hustad. Another focus of Professor McElrath's teaching was attention to Baptist studies. While they are also historical in perspective, the essays by Paul Richardson, Esther Crookshank, and Michael Raley focus their attention on Baptist hymnal compilers and a Baptist seminary professor. Janelle Ganey's study of Brazilian missions hymns and William McElrath's essay on his hymnic work as a missionary in Indonesia underscore Professor McElrath's appreciation for music in missions. Professor McElrath's own interests, reflected in his writing, have encouraged church musicians and congregations to deepen their corporate worship experiences through the singing of hymns. Thus the articles by Deborah Loftis and Michael Hawn explore theological and global themes in current hymnody that wield an influence upon today's diverse worship practices. Finally, the breadth and prolific output of Professor McElrath's research, teaching, and ministry can be seen in the bibliography of his works, compiled and annotated by David Gregory and Jeffrey Jones, found at the end of this volume.

While the impact that Hugh McElrath has exerted upon his colleagues and students will, no doubt, continue to produce new texts, tunes, and research in hymnody for many years to come, we offer this volume in celebration of a long and successful career and with deepest thanks to an outstanding teacher, colleague, and friend.

J. Michael Raley and
Deborah Carlton Loftis, editors
December 2005

MINDS *and* HEARTS *in* *Praise of God*

I.

Hugh T. McElrath: His Life and Work

A Brief Personal Word About "Bubba"

WILLIAM N. MCELRATH

It will come as a shock to many readers of this book to learn that the dignified and venerated Professor Hugh Thomas McElrath was once known as "Bubba." As one of only three living persons (his younger siblings) who have ever dared to call him that, I have asked for the privilege of adding a brief personal note to this Festschrift (as well as contributing the essay beginning on page 223). Others have written all the needful biographical data, yet perhaps I can add a unique perspective.

This brief foreword, like a traditional sermon, has three points and a poem:

1) My brother is a gifted teacher.

I was among the first to find this out. One wintry Sunday morning Mother was trying to get us all ready to go to church, and she left me in Hugh's care. At that time I was a toddler, and he was in middle school. Using a steamed-up window in place of a chalkboard, Hugh patiently taught me—one letter at a time—how to write my name. I've never forgotten that first lesson.

In seminary I had always intended to take Hugh's "sugar-stick" hymnology course, but only as an auditor since my own studies were mainly in the field of theology. However, I ended up needing those credits in order to graduate on time. To take the heat off both of us, I tried to be such a diligent student that no one could accuse him of family favoritism if he gave me a good grade. Apparently I succeeded. When Hugh returned my final exam paper, he remarked, "William, I guess you made a hundred on this; at least I couldn't find anything wrong with it."

Many friends have heard me list on the fingers of one hand the seminary professors whom I considered to be the most able classroom teachers of my time. My brother is on that short list.[1]

2) My brother, though not demonstrative, is loving and compassionate.

Hugh has always been the member of our family who has shown the least outward expression of his feelings. Even our parents used to tease him sometimes because he seemed so silent and unmoved. (Mother nearly killed him when he failed to tell her he had won an audition to sing in the high school boys' quartet.) Yet we all knew Hugh truly loved us; he just didn't express his emotions as much as some folks do.

In seminary, when I came down with an acute attack of appendicitis, I found out firsthand just how loving and compassionate my older brother really is. It was my first major illness away from home. At that time my sister-in-law was far advanced in pregnancy; my brother was unbelievably busy as usual. Yet Hugh made sure I got to the hospital safely for surgery and aftercare. I well remember drifting in and out of consciousness while feeling the reassurance of that somber figure in a dark suit sitting beside my bed; Hugh had come straight from a concert to check on me, and he stayed till I fell asleep.

3) My brother, though his academic credentials are impeccable, is intensely practical.

Sometimes the word "academic" can mean something (or someone) of no practical use. That could never be said of my brother. Many readers of this volume can testify to the usefulness of his teaching, whether practiced in a church, at a school, or in doing missions through music. When Hugh came to Indonesia (and I got to be his interpreter), he didn't just use rehashed lecture notes from America. No, he stayed up late preparing materials that would be of practical use in the Indonesian setting.

This practical side had also showed up much earlier, while I was still in seminary. Hugh wanted to give me voice lessons, and I wanted him to. Both of us had had the same beginning voice teacher in college; our voices had enough similarities that Hugh said he was sometimes tempted to sing a passage and just tell me to imitate him rather than helping me learn proper vocal technique.

The main reason I didn't enroll for regular voice lessons with my brother was financial. Both of us knew I did well to pay for room and board and regular fees and books without the extra cost of private lessons. Yet it wouldn't have been ethical for Hugh as a faculty member to use seminary facilities while giving me free lessons on the side.

Here's the practical solution he found: He maintained an updated list of where I could be reached and when I was out of class throughout the day.

When he had a last-minute cancellation or no-show, he would telephone me and I would hurry over to his studio. Thus I never knew just when my voice lessons might be, but I got in quite a few of them. To return the favor, I babysat for free with my eldest McElrath nephew.

And now for the poem:

In 1922, the year after my brother was born, a hundred thousand people gathered in Washington for the dedication of the new Lincoln Memorial. Two million more listened in on their state-of-the-art marvels: crystal radio sets. A Lincoln poem had been selected out of 250 entries, and the poet, Edwin Markham, had been invited to read his work aloud.

Many readers of this Festschrift will remember that the past half century has not been an easy time to be a seminary professor. My brother has encountered many difficulties and disagreements along the way. Yet he has continued to do what God called him to do. In doing this so faithfully, he has reminded me of Markham's memorable lines written about our Grandfather McElrath's personal friend, Abraham Lincoln:

He held his place—
Held the long purpose like a growing tree–
Held on through blame and faltered not at praise.[2]

NOTES

1. To satisfy the curiosity of fellow old-timers from the 1950s who may be wondering, here are the others on my list: Theron Price, Hugh Wamble, Findley Edge, and E. C. Rust.

2. Edwin Markham, "Lincoln, the Man of the People," © 1900 by the author and now in the public domain.

Hugh T. McElrath

An Appreciation

Paul A. Richardson

To identify Hugh T. McElrath as "a gentleman and a scholar," while entirely true, would tell too little, even about his gentility or his scholarship, not to mention his numerous other characteristics. His vocation has been as a "Christian teacher"; but, again, these words—taken separately or together—are not sufficient to reflect the many facets of his commitment to God as it has been reflected in his life's work with students.

Hugh's accomplishments and accolades are recounted in the biographical sketch by Jeffrey Jones; the details can be read there. It has been my good fortune to know him as teacher, colleague, mentor, and friend. In these overlapping relationships, I have had opportunity to see—on a daily basis for more than twenty years—the range of his interests and commitments, as well as the way in which he has brought them together. He is a person who brings together people, practices, and ideas: an integrator who both creates and lends integrity.

He is a man from Murray, Kentucky, who is at home in Oxford, England, and Bologna, Italy. He is a seminary professor, equally comfortable as a scholar at the Eastman School of Music and as a minister at Beechwood Baptist Church in Louisville. These are examples not of fragmentation, but of broad vision that sees both the Church and the world—indeed, the Church in the world—and the essential connections between scholarship and discipleship.

He is a person of objective distance and subjective involvement. His customary place in faculty meetings was a bit beyond the common circle, where he could observe, ponder, and develop perspective. In the inevitable politics of institution and denomination, he found gentle ways to express firmly-held convictions. During his term as president of the Southern Baptist Church Music Conference, he faced the threat of division with a strategy of inclusion. To these varied venues he brought a healthy balance of dignity and dry humor.

As a professor, Hugh was a demanding encourager, who stretched minds and challenged work habits while practicing pastoral concern. Teaching "Formation for Christian Ministry," he was beloved by students from all ministerial disciplines, some of whom were surprised that this musicologist could help them see more clearly their roles as pastors, social workers, educators, and missionaries. Supervising doctoral dissertations, he was tenacious in requiring pursuit of sustainable fact and defensible thought.

To his work as a teacher and supervisor, Hugh brought immense and interconnected knowledge. He knows the larger historical and theological contexts, as well as the musical developments. He also brought, as everyone who ever wrote for him will recall, a penchant for detail—*correct* detail! (We also thought he was something of a magician, as well, with that briefcase that must have had a false bottom, from which he could produce an entire shelf of books in support of the chilling query: "Mr. Richardson, what can you tell us about this tome?")

He knows those books—every one of them. The development of the superb musicological and hymnological collection at the Boyce Centennial Library has been the work of many hands, but no one did more to shape it than Hugh. What is more, he studied those volumes more than any of his protégés. He remains a perpetual student, whose unquenchable curiosity makes him a reliable guide, cognizant of the latest scholarship and of the traditions on which it rests.

All of these traits reflect a passion for his work, a passion that would not let him separate duty, discipline, and devotion. These intertwining themes are perhaps most evident in the hymn services Hugh conducted in seminary chapels, in his own congregation, and in scores of other venues. Those services, like his classes, were rich in information, insight, and genuine piety.

His passion for his work and his penchant for detail made many of us better thinkers, writers, and teachers. If we might be permitted a single regret about Hugh's career, it is that these traits, which made him such a fine supervisor and editor, combined with heavy teaching loads to limit his own output as a writer.

Many of Hugh's characteristics are evident in his best-known hymn, "We praise You with our minds, O Lord" (see pages 24–25). This text is an engaged and engaging meditation on Mark 12:30, Jesus' response to the scribe's question as to the greatest commandment. The hymn's final phrase, "mind, body, heart, and soul" reiterates the model of comprehensive commitment articulated by Jesus.

This hymn simultaneously acknowledges God as the giver of our multifaceted existence and the object of our responsible stewardship of these gifts in praise. Within this context it locates thinking, teaching, learning, and wisdom. Though it emphasizes this facet of our being and self-giving, it does so alongside consecration of body, heart, and soul.

In its craft, this text pays homage to the two persons whose work established the foundation of English hymnody. Following the pattern of Isaac Watts, it begins with a striking opening line and moves through a carefully-wrought structure to a summary climax of active response. In the manner of Charles Wesley, its language is formed of a biblical mosaic that employs seventeen (by its author's own accounting) allusions to Scripture.

This text does not merely echo the Scriptures or emulate the work of earlier writers; it states what its author has sought to do. This hymn forms Hugh's link in the chain from the Hebrew *Shema´* to the teaching of Jesus, to Hugh's own vocation, to what he hoped for those who have been with him in the studio, the classroom, and the congregation.

The text, as it is now known, is a revision of its first published form. As the language of worship changed, Hugh rewrote his own hymn to enable it to speak convincingly to a new day. In its content and evolution, "We praise You with our minds, O Lord" reflects his thoughtfully progressive approach to life and ministry.

A well-written hymn can give us words better than our own to express our convictions, confessions, and reflections. Hugh's hymn has offered this opportunity to millions. Fred Kaan, the author of numerous texts that have spoken for the Church in our time, has written "A Hymn of Grateful Recall and Renewed Commitment." Its first three stanzas are particularly apt in describing the influence of Hugh's ministry to generations of students, colleagues, and friends:

For all who have enriched our lives,
whom we have loved and known,
for saints alive among us still
by whom the faith is honed,
we thank you, God, who came and comes
through women, children, men,
to share the highs and lows of life;
God-for-us, now as then.

For all who with disarming love
have led us to explore
the risk of reasoning and doubt,
new realms not known before,
we thank you, God, who came and comes
to free us from our past,
from ghettos of a rigid mind,
from truths unfit to last.

For all whose laughter has unnerved
  tradition gone awry,
who with incisive gentleness
  pursue each human "why?"
    we thank you, God, who came and comes
      to those who probe and ask,
    who seek to know the mind of Christ,
      and take the church to task.

I am honored to have been granted this opportunity to express what many have observed and experienced. We join in gratitude to God for the teaching, writing, and living by which Hugh T. McElrath has helped shape us to be better scholars, ministers, and persons.

Hugh T. McElrath

WILLIAM JEFFREY JONES

Hugh Thomas McElrath, affectionately known to colleagues and students as "Dr. Mac," holds a unique place in Southern Baptist church music.[1] As an educator and a practicing church musician, Professor McElrath embodies both the academic and practical approaches of the discipline. His diverse interests, love of teaching, care for his students, and thirst for knowledge have combined to make him the "quintessential seminary professor" and what some colleagues acknowledge as the most interdisciplinary member of the faculty at The Southern Baptist Theological Seminary.

Born into an educated family in Murray, Kentucky, on November 13, 1921, Hugh McElrath developed an eclectic interest in a wide range of subjects at an early age. His home life nurtured his thirst for knowledge and his personal commitment to Christ and the Church. The eldest of four children, he was reared in a family that encouraged, even expected, high levels of achievement. His parents, both educated professionals, were active in Murray's First Baptist Church, where they supported mission work and served the faith community in a variety of roles. They also encouraged their children to pursue a wide range of interests. Led by their example, young Hugh developed a passion for education, the Church, and missions—passions that have remained constant throughout his life.

The McElrath home was always open to visitors. Missionaries, denominational leaders (including church musician B. B. McKinney), college professors, and visiting scholars were welcome. Hugh later recalled sitting for hours as a young boy and listening to his father engage these frequent visitors in conversations on a variety of religious, political, and social topics. Somewhat shy and reserved, young McElrath was more concerned with listening than speaking. This earned him the nickname, "Long Ears."

His brother William has said that Hugh never said much when questioned at home or at school, but what he did say was usually right! Hugh made good grades throughout his academic career and managed to participate in a wide range of extracurricular activities. In high school he was a member of the dramatics club, the Latin club, the camera club, and the debate team. He also served as assistant editor for the class yearbook, participated on the tennis team, sang in various ensembles, played trombone in the high school band, was named a member of the National Honor Society, and graduated as the class valedictorian in 1939.

Although an English major in college, McElrath found time to study and minor in several disciplines. He continued to develop his instrumental, vocal, and acting abilities in college, playing trombone in both the college band and the college orchestra, singing in several choral organizations, and venturing into musical theater. He even gave a solo voice recital during his senior year. His college years were also filled with a wide range of nonmusical activities. McElrath wrote for the college newspaper, held office in various campus organizations, and participated for four years in a club whose focus was international relations. He served as president of both *Kappa Delta Pi*, a national educational society, and the honorary French fraternity, *Beta Pi Theta*. He was a member of the English club, the German club, and the executive council of the Baptist Student Union. In 1942–1943, McElrath earned mention in *Who's Who in American Colleges and Universities.* When he graduated from Murray State University in May 1943, he was awarded the bachelor of arts degree with a major in English and no fewer than four minors—in history, French, education, and music.

The Church also held a place of importance during McElrath's college years. He sang in the church choir (First Baptist Church, Murray, Kentucky), assisted with youth and children's activities, and participated in the Baptist Student Union. He spent summers during his college years working at the Ridgecrest Baptist Assembly in the mountains of North Carolina near Asheville. It was at Ridgecrest in the summer of 1941 that McElrath befriended a young woman from Argentina, Ruth Garcia, whom he later married.

His original career path was to be an English teacher, a career he seriously considered until one summer at Ridgecrest, where Pastor H. W. Baucom, Jr., convinced him to accept a position as music/education director at Western Avenue Baptist Church, Statesville, North Carolina. After serving one year in the local church, Hugh decided he would need more education and training. That year of working in a dual ministry also helped McElrath clarify his interests—music was where he wanted to focus. Though he considered several options, Dr. Ellis A. Fuller, president of The Southern Baptist Theological Seminary, convinced him to enter the fledgling church music program in Louisville, Kentucky. In the fall of 1944, McElrath enrolled in the very first class of church music students at Southern Seminary. He graduated with the bachelor of sacred music and master of sacred music degrees, respectively, in 1947 and 1948.

Two opportunities for service were presented to McElrath upon graduation—one on the mission field, the other at Southern Seminary. Professor of Missions W. O. Carver had recommended Hugh McElrath—without the latter's knowledge—for a foreign teaching position, and upon Dr. Carver's recommendation, Hugh had already been elected to the faculty of the University of Shanghai, China. In the meantime, he was approached about teaching at Southern Seminary and "buttonholed" by the seminary's president, Dr. Ellis A. Fuller. McElrath recalls the president saying to him, "Young man, if you go to China, you are just one missionary teacher in China. If you stay here, you can train others and you can multiply yourself a hundred fold by those who may go to China or somewhere else." McElrath chose to join the faculty of The Southern Baptist Theological Seminary, where he devoted his life's work to the education of church musicians. Over the course of his career at Southern Seminary, he taught virtually every student enrolled in the School of Church Music between 1949 and 1992.[2]

Professor McElrath's career at Southern Seminary spanned five decades. Initially hired as a voice instructor, McElrath maintained a large private studio (sometimes with as many as twenty-four students per term) in addition to his expanding responsibilities in the classroom teaching hymnology, musicology, conducting, and related courses. In the early days of his career, McElrath had the opportunity to teach every music course which was not keyboard related! His work took him beyond the classroom and studio as well. Though not exhaustive, the following highlights nevertheless provide some insight into McElrath's lengthy tenure and broad spectrum of work and influence.

During his early years of teaching, the seminary saw considerable change in leadership and philosophical direction. Caught in the middle of these events, McElrath tenaciously held on to his teaching position without compromising his ideals. Many faculty members chose to leave during these times of discord, but McElrath, though often at odds with the administration, remained and was promoted to assistant professor in 1955.

His career at Southern was marked by a series of firsts. He had been in the first class of church music students at Southern Seminary and was also among the first to graduate with both a bachelor's and master's degree. In 1959, he became the first music professor to sign the seminary's original statement of faith—the *Abstract of Principles*—and to offer an inaugural address to mark the occasion of its signing.

During the 1960s, Hugh dedicated a great deal of time to completing his Ph.D. in musicology from the Eastman School of Music, a program that he had begun in the summer of 1950. He accepted leadership roles in the Southern

Baptist Church Music Conference and joined the editorial board of the seminary's theological journal, *The Review and Expositor.* In addition, he served as president of the Greater Louisville Music Teacher's Association (1968–1970) and, in 1968, chartered the Louisville chapter of The Hymn Society.

By the 1970s, McElrath was established as a scholar and respected as a teacher. Refining much of what he was using in the classroom and dedicating large portions of his sabbatical research efforts, McElrath, who had been publishing articles in professional journals since the mid-1960s, now worked in collaboration with Harry Eskew on what would become their *magnum opus*, the hymnology textbook entitled *Sing with Understanding.*

The later years of his teaching career witnessed an increased focus upon mission work and further involvement at the denominational level first as vice president (1982–1986) and then as president (1987–1989) of the Southern Baptist Church Music Conference. In addition, he served on the Theology/Doctrine Committee for *The Baptist Hymnal* (1991) and as an editor for the *Handbook to* The Baptist Hymnal (1992).

McElrath was elected president of the Southern Baptist Church Music Conference at a particularly difficult time in the life of the Southern Baptist Convention. Southern Seminary Professor Donald P. Hustad later observed that, given the nature of the struggle within the denomination concerning worship styles, McElrath "was as effective as anyone could be" in his role as president.[3] Mark Edwards, who succeeded McElrath as president of the Conference, said that President McElrath "was able to stabilize the organization under [the threat of splitting] and set up a process for communications with the dissenters."[4]

Involvement in the local church went hand-in-hand with McElrath's career as an educator. Far from being adjunct, or treating his church employment as an afterthought, McElrath was deliberate and steadfast in his ministry and commitment to the local congregations in the Louisville area which he served over the years. Dr. McElrath's practical church music experience was so eclectic that there were times during his career when one could find him cantoring on Friday evening at the Jewish temple, singing Gregorian chant on Saturdays in a traditional Latin Mass, serving a local Disciples of Christ Church on Sunday morning as a paid soloist, and, finally, working with youth choirs and directing the worship at Beechwood Baptist Church on Sunday evening! He also encouraged his students to assist him and thereby gain practical experience while pursuing their degrees in church music.

Professor McElrath served as the minister of music at Victory Memorial Baptist Church from 1947 to 1949 and at Hazelwood Baptist Church from 1949 to 1953. Perhaps his most significant work in the local church was accomplished during his twenty-two years of ministry with Beechwood Baptist Church, where Hugh and Ruth worked together as co-ministers of music. Ruth, a fine musician in her own right, bore a significant portion of the work load. This allowed Hugh to travel and participate in other church settings as necessary.

Active in so many arenas, it was nevertheless in his role as a seminary professor that McElrath exerted his greatest influence. He constantly demonstrated an openness to learning while at the same time teaching and challenging students to achieve their highest potential. To many students and colleagues, McElrath was both mentor and friend. Indeed, the comments of students throughout his career indicate that McElrath was deeply respected, indeed revered, as a teacher. Students were frequently impressed by the fact that this scholar with whom they studied was himself a perpetual student. McElrath could frequently be found in the music library poring over a stack of books preparing for the next day's lectures. His physical presence, too, exerted an impact upon the lives of his students: prematurely silver gray, with a commanding voice and a demeanor that tended to be a bit too professorial at times, students often found McElrath somewhat intimidating. Those who had the opportunity to work with him one-on-one, however, were quickly put at ease by the caring and compassionate way in which he took a personal interest in their lives.

The Preface to one of Dr. McElrath's doctoral students' dissertations testifies to the inspiration he fostered in his students: "My passion for thoroughness in research was forged in classes and seminars with Dr. McElrath, whose love of music, especially hymnody, was contagious to all his students."[5]

An anecdote from another former student illustrates further the supreme respect that Professor McElrath engendered:

> He taught music history classes in a room in the basement of the library—always at 8 A.M. His lectures tended to go right up to the 9 o'clock hour and some students complained that they couldn't get across campus to the music school without being late for their 9 A.M. classes. Of course, NOBODY would get up and walk out of McElrath's class before he dismissed everyone. He took the complaint seriously but said he would start right on time in order to finish earlier. He was serious—right on the stroke of 8 he would begin lecturing. Students started coming a little earlier to get settled and pens and notebooks out. Hugh would look around the room and as soon as everyone was present he'd start, so students came earlier yet. By the end of that semester, we were starting class about 7:50 A.M.![6]

Though many have commented on the development of knowledge and expertise gained under McElrath's guidance, the long-lasting influence of his teaching seems to have been exerted even more through his character than through course content. In his role as mentor, Professor McElrath made a particularly profound mark in his students' lives. Jerry L. Warren, professor of music and former dean of the School of Church Music at Belmont University, was a doctoral student at Southern Seminary from 1963 to 1967. Warren said of McElrath: "I look to him in the role of my dissertation chair as the model mentor who gave generously of his time and energy to a graduate student."[7] Warren went on to say:

> Of particular interest is that the period of my writing coincided with Dr. McElrath's completion of his dissertation. Our topics were closely related—composers who were employed at San Petronio chapel in Bologna, Italy, in the 17th century. I remember vividly the day that Dr. Mac pointed out to me the citations of my "unpublished dissertation" in his own work. . . . The day that he had me . . . leaf through his dissertation and look at each page which had a reference to my dissertation remains a high point in my academic life. The fact that he had quoted my work was important, but that he took the time to point them out to me was of even greater significance. Both elements are strong indicators to me of the kind of person that he is.[8]

Professor McElrath's years of faithful service have not gone unnoticed. He has been recognized with numerous awards for his dedicated and unselfish service, as well as for his many and significant contributions to teaching, scholarship, and church life. In July 1991, McElrath had the high honor of being named a fellow of The Hymn Society at a meeting held at St. Olaf College in Northfield, Minnesota. At that time he was only the third Baptist ever to receive that distinction. The Hymn Society also established the McElrath-Eskew Research Fund. During his final year of full-time teaching (1992), Southern Seminary honored Professor McElrath with the Findley B. and Louvenia Edge Award for Teaching Excellence. He was the first School of Church Music professor to receive this award, the seminary's highest distinction for excellence in teaching. Recipients of this award are chosen by a committee composed of faculty, students, and alumni. The award, which includes a twenty-five-hundred-dollar cash prize, "is presented on the basis of effective teaching, personal care for students, and demonstrated concern for students' spiritual needs."

Professor McElrath received an additional honor upon retirement in 1992 when a group of colleagues, former students, and friends created and endowed a lectureship bearing his name. The Hugh T. McElrath Lectureship in Church Music seeks to promote church music and hymnology by bringing in scholars "with established reputations" who reflect the diversity and broad interests which McElrath exemplified throughout his career. McElrath's longtime friend, colleague, and co-author of *Sing with Understanding*, Harry Eskew, was the first to lecture in this series.

Professor McElrath officially retired from The Southern Baptist Theological Seminary in 1992 and was presented with the Hines Sims Award by the Southern Baptist Church Music Conference that same year. Recognition came again in 1995 with the presentation of the Hallelujah Award by the Center for Church Music of Carson-Newman College, Jefferson City, Tennessee. McElrath was the first person ever to receive this distinction. Professor McElrath continued teaching hymnology classes until 1998, fifty years after his life-changing conversation as a young man with Southern Seminary President Ellis A. Fuller.

Hugh McElrath's multi-faceted career as an educator of church musicians capitalized upon virtually every possible venue as yet another opportunity to teach. Students who came in contact with him at the seminary were challenged by his demanding scholarly standards in the classroom and enamored by his own example of continual study. Furthermore, throughout his career as an educator, Dr. McElrath's parallel ministry as a church musician serving the local church provided his students with a living example and inspiration even as he educated those congregations in worship and music. Simultaneously, Dr. McElrath worked at the denominational level for decades, holding key leadership positions within the Southern Baptist Church Music Conference and contributing essays for its publications. In his ultimate role as the conference's president at a pivotal time in the history of the Southern Baptist Convention, he sought to educate, encourage, and reconcile a music conference on the verge of splitting. His commitment to sharing the Gospel around the world—his brother has written in detail about this—can be seen through his dedicated service, and in the time and energy he devoted to mission work during his sabbaticals.

Throughout his career, Hugh McElrath taught by both precept and example. Students, influenced by his model, have been inspired and challenged to reach new heights in music leadership and scholarship in their careers all across the United States as well as overseas. Choristers reared under his music program at Beechwood Baptist Church inherited a life-long love for hymnody and church music. Through his numerous articles and books, he assisted the denomination in the ongoing work of music ministry and provided missionaries with resources for worship and hymnology to aid them in their own ministries. Clearly here is a man who dedicated his entire life to educating others in the broad ministry of church music. Over the course of his lengthy career, Dr. McElrath taught thousands of students and perhaps instructed more students in hymnology than anyone else in history. His students—now scattered around the globe in churches, teaching positions, and mission work—provide ample evidence that President Fuller's prophecy has been fulfilled several times over.

In this collection of essays, we are once again recognizing Professor McElrath as a devoted Southern Baptist, respected scholar, practical church musician, educator, and supporter of missions. We, like others before us, honor Dr. McElrath as one who has encouraged the Church to sing. His many contributions have left an indelible mark not only upon us, his students, but also upon church music—especially in the Southern Baptist tradition. Through his leadership Dr. McElrath has not only helped the Church to "sing with understanding," he has reminded the Church to sing with its "mind, body, heart, and soul."[9]

NOTES

1. The limited biographical sketch provided here offers but a glimpse into the life and work of Hugh T. McElrath. For a more detailed biography, see William Jeffrey Jones, "Hugh T. McElrath: Church Music Educator and Hymnologist" (D.M.A. diss., The Southern Baptist Theological Seminary, 2001).

2. Though eventually he would be promoted to the rank of full professor, Hugh McElrath began his teaching career at Southern Seminary as an instructor in the fall of 1948 at the encouragement of President Fuller, who also found the means to provide his salary that first year. His official appointment began in the autumn of 1949. From 1949–1992, he taught hymnology as a required course in the church music curriculum. His first official retirement came in 1992. After that his teaching responsibilities lessened.

3. Donald P. Hustad, e-mail to the author, July 27, 2000.

4. Mark Edwards, e-mail to the author, August 17, 2000.

5. Roger William Walworth, "The Life and Hymnological Contributions of Robert Lowry (1826–1899)" (D.M.A. diss., The Southern Baptist Theological Seminary, 1994), xv.

6. Deborah Loftis Schoenfeld, letter to the author, August 4, 2000.

7. Jerry L. Warren, e-mail to the author, June 19, 2000.

8. Ibid.

9. The latter phrase is taken from stanza 3 of Hugh T. McElrath's great hymn, "We praise You with our minds, O Lord" (see pp. 24–25).

II.

Hymn Texts and Tunes Composed in Honor of Hugh T. McElrath's Eightieth Birthday on November 13, 2001

Introduction to SOUTHERN SEMINARY

Milburn Price

During the twelve years I served as dean of the School of Church Music at The Southern Baptist Theological Seminary in Louisville, Kentucky (1981–1993), I had the privilege of getting to know and appreciate Hugh McElrath as effective teacher, dedicated church musician, distinguished hymnologist, and personal friend. Therefore, I am both pleased and honored to have been invited to write a new tune for his hymn text, "We praise You with our minds, O Lord," which has been sung widely in Baptist circles and beyond.

Because of Hugh's concern for the practical nature of congregational song, I have tried to make the tune singable in both range and melodic contour. There are intentional melodic and rhythmic allusions to (or "echoes" of) CLONMEL, the tune to which this text has most often been sung. I offer this new tune as a tribute to, and expression of appreciation for Hugh McElrath, whose multi-faceted contributions to church music and church music education have enriched the lives of countless numbers of students and church members and, in doing so, have contributed significantly to God's Kingdom.

We Praise You with Our Minds, O Lord

WORDS: Hugh T. McElrath
MUSIC: Milburn Price

SOUTHERN SEMINARY
8.6.8.6.D. (C.M.D.)

In all our learn - ing may we seek
We give our - selves, a sac - ri - fice,
Al - though a - dor - ing hearts will bow
that wis - dom from a - bove
to live our lives for You;
as age on a - ges roll,
which comes to all: the brave, the meek,
for You a - lone have paid the price
we praise You in our be - ings now,
who ask in faith and love.
to bring sal - va - tion true.
mind, bod - y, heart, and soul.

Introduction to "Because his life was threatened"

Carl P. Daw, Jr.

There was a time when metrical paraphrases and other scripture-based hymns served the singers as reminders of passages they already knew, but that sort of familiarity with the Bible can no longer be assumed for most congregations. This lack of familiarity with biblical content and idiom not only weakens an appreciation of the scriptural allusions in the texts of classic hymn writers such as Isaac Watts and Charles Wesley, but also diminishes their effectiveness as models of practical theology. Recognizing this change in what might be called biblical literacy also has consequences for present-day hymn text writers, because it underscores the need for hymns that both summarize and interpret scriptural passages rather than simply allude to them.

The text presented here is, among other things, an attempt to provide a means of appreciating the power of the concluding petition, "speak through the earthquake, wind, and fire," in John Greenleaf Whittier's widely-used hymn, "Dear Lord and Father of mankind" (which is cited six times in McElrath and Eskew's *Sing with Understanding*). A congregation that knows how those events figure in the story of Elijah in 1 Kings 19 will be able to sing that phrase with much more meaning and depth than one that does not.

Another purpose of this hymn is to model a way of understanding how the narratives of Hebrew scripture can be the vessels of significant truths for Christian readers. Rather than regarding such material as simply a rehearsal or preparation for the revelation of God in Jesus Christ, we find that these passages provide invaluable insights into the recurring patterns of God's care for and guiding of human beings. Learning that Elijah's story is also our story helps us to be attentive to ways that God may be speaking to us today.

Because His Life Was Threatened
(A Meditation on 1 Kings 19)

1. Because his life was threatened,
   Elijah ran away;
   into the sun-scorched desert
   he traveled for a day,
   till by a broom tree pausing,
   prayed God his life to take,
   then fell into deep slumber
   and never hoped to wake.

2. But suddenly an angel
   was telling him to rise
   and eat the food provided
   before his doubting eyes.
   Twice nourished by this wonder,
   he journeyed night and day
   until he found at Horeb
   a cave where he could stay.

3. Then from the cave God called him:
   "Come forth, Elijah, stand
   before me on this mountain
   for I am near at hand."
   Rock-splitting wind came rushing;
   an earthquake shook the ground;
   a raging fire swept after
   with burst of light and sound.

4. Yet in no mighty portent
   could God be found or heard;
   but from the pregnant stillness
   came forth the holy word:
   "Why are you here, Elijah,
   a prophet on the run?
   Return and bear my message;
   your work is not yet done."

5. So God still guides and guards us,
   still nourishes, still prods,
   till when we least expect it,
   we hear, against all odds,
   a voiceless, piercing summons
   that bids us risk and dare
   to claim what once we ran from
   and find that God is there.

WORDS: Carl P. Daw, Jr.
MUSIC: Sing to tunes in 7.6.7.6.D. meter.

Introduction to AUSTIPOL

Austin C. Lovelace

AUSTIPOL is a new tune setting of Ted Wilde's text, "Christ, engage us in your mission," which was composed in 1984 and included in the *Moravian Book of Worship* (1995). The hymn's author was executive director of the Board of World Mission for the Moravian Church, which makes his text doubly appropriate for the theme of missions.

The hymn's first stanza challenges us, "Christ-like going," to make the world our mission, our parish. Ted Wilde explains that this concept, "Christ-like going," is borrowed from the Japanese theologian, Kosuke Koyama.[1] The Great Commission (Matt. 28:19–20) charges us not merely to go, but to "go therefore and make disciples of all nations." In other words, we are to "go on the basis of the life and ministry of Jesus Christ, his love, his self-denial, his hope, his death, his resurrection. Only so are we to make disciples of all nations." Koyama explains further, "'Christ-like going' is not 'one-way traffic.' It is intensely two ways." Whereas in our world today non-believers all too often are characterized as living in darkness and believers as living in the light, providing a deceptively comfortable theology for the latter, Koyama points out that Christ's command in the Great Commission demands what Christ himself set forth by his own example—service in self-denial. "The Son of Man came not to be served but to serve, and to give His life as a ransom for many" (Matt. 20:28). Thus the hymn reflects the emphases upon humble Christian service and the worldwide growth of missions that also marked the great love of Hugh McElrath's teaching and ministry.

NOTE

1. Kosuke Koyama, *Three Mile an Hour God: Biblical Reflections* (Maryknoll, N.Y.: Orbis Books, 1980; rep. ed., 1982), 52–53, cited by Ted Wilde in his letter to the composer, October 22, 2001.

Christ, Engage Us in Your Mission

1. Christ, en - gage us in your mis - sion; world - wide let our par - ish be. We take up this great com - mis - sion, trav - eling first to Cal - va - ry, there ab - sorb - ing Christ - like go - ing, taught by your hu - mil - i - ty.
2. Long be - fore our pro - cla - ma - tion you an - nounced God's li - ber - ty, seed - ing hope in ev - ery na - tion of un - end - ing ju - bi - lee. Thus the King - dom spreads its bran - ches, grows in all hu - man - i - ty.
3. O - pen then our hearts and sen - ses to your Spi - rit's var - ied ways. O - ver - come our self - de - fen - ses so we hear the prayer and praise which the folk of count - less cul - tures in new words and rhy - thms raise.

WORDS: Theodore (Ted) Wilde
MUSIC: Austin C. Lovelace

AUSTIPOL
8.7.8.7.8.7.

Introduction to "When all the world is wounded"

Rae E. Whitney

"When all the world is wounded" was the first text I wrote after receiving the invitation to contribute to this Festschrift in honor of Professor McElrath. At first I wondered whether the text was appropriate, since it sprang directly from the horrendous events of September 11, 2001. However, Michael Raley, one of the editors for this volume, assured me that indeed it was, since Dr. McElrath had in fact already suggested such a theme for a new text.

Normally I would not have released the text until its publication in the Festschrift, but seeing its usefulness was immediate, I shared it with some friends. Since then, I have discovered that the hymn has been used not only in the United States, but also in New Zealand, Kosovo, Bulgaria, Canada, and the United Kingdom. It was first sung (to AURELIA) on October 17, 2001, at the Baptist World Aid Headquarters, McLean, Virginia, during regular morning worship. Several other tunes also work well. For example, John Thornburg has suggested singing the first two stanzas to PASSION CHORALE and then, after an organ interlude, switching to AURELIA for the final two stanzas.

The text expresses an experience which we have all shared and, therefore, to which we can all immediately relate. The horror and pain of September 11, 2001, are reflected in the text, but so, too, are our faith in God and our steadfast belief in the coming of God's Kingdom—hence the echo of the Lord's Prayer in the final phrase. Thus, although stemming from a specific event, the hymn is general enough to be sung in response to any global crisis.

In honor of Dr. Hugh T. McElrath

When All the World Is Wounded

1. When all the world is wounded,
   with nations primed for war,
when horrors of destruction
   loom larger than before,
when we, confused, encounter
   those who delight to kill,
O Prince of Peace, draw nearer,
   and help us know your will!

2. When all the world is watching
   cruel actions of a few,
it stands, bereft, bewildered,
   uncertain what to do;
revenge is not the answer,
   nor is an empty peace;
Lord, may respect for justice
   throughout the earth increase!

3. When all the world is fragile,
   aware it might explode,
we count on you, Creator,
   our spirits to uphold;
though hearts are sick and grieving,
   and nothing seems secure,
relying on your goodness,
   by faith we will endure.

4. When all the world is ready
   to live in harmony,
when goods of every nation
   are shared out lovingly,
when your commands are followed,
   true peace will bless each home;
then, Lord, we'll know your kingdom
   on earth has surely come!

WORDS: Rae E. Whitney, 2001 (stanza 2 revised 2002)
MUSIC: Sing to tunes in 7.6.7.6.D. meter such as AURELIA, MUNICH, EWING, or PASSION CHORALE

Introduction to McElrath

Hal H. Hopson

One day after the tragedy of September 11, 2001, I received an e-mail from the Festschrift committee asking me to submit a hymn tune to honor Dr. Hugh T. McElrath. Fred Kaan's text, "For the healing of the nations," immediately came to mind, particularly the lines:

All that kills abundant living,
  let it from the earth be banned:
Pride of status, race, or schooling,
  dogmas that obscure your plan.
In our common quest for justice
  may we hallow life's brief span.

The writing of the hymn tune McElrath has several influences: the poignant text by Fred Kaan within the context of September 11, 2001, and certainly my deep appreciation for Hugh T. McElrath, for his gentle spirit, his passion for congregational hymn singing, and his knowledge and ability to teach others.

For the Healing of the Nations

1. For the heal - ing of the na - tions, Lord, we
2. Lead us for - ward in - to free - dom, from de -
3. All that kills a - bun - dant liv - ing, let it
4. You, Cre - a - tor God, have writ - ten your great
pray with one ac - cord, for a just and e - qual
spair your world re - lease, that, re - deemed from war and
from the earth be banned: pride of sta - tus, race, or
name on hu - man - kind; for our grow - ing in your
shar - ing of the things that earth af - fords. To a
ha - tred, all may come and go in peace. Show us
school - ing, dog-mas that ob - scure your plan. In our
like - ness bring the life of Christ to mind; that by
life of love in ac - tion help us rise and pledge our word.
how through care and good-ness fear will die and hope in - crease.
com - mon quest for jus - tice may we hal-low life's brief span.
our re - sponse and ser - vice earth its des - ti - ny may find.

WORDS: Fred Kaan
MUSIC: Hal H. Hopson

McELRATH
8.7.8.7.8.7.

Organ Interlude and Coda (Play after stanzas 1, 2, and 4)

* * * * * * * *

Suggestions for introducing "For the Healing of the Nations" as an anthem:

Voice Assignments:

Stanza 1: SA (unison voices)
Stanza 2: TB (unison voices)
Stanza 3: Solo (or ensemble)
Stanza 4: SATB (unison voices)

Introduction to LEXINGTON ROAD

A. L. Butler

I am glad Dr. McElrath recommended several texts of Fanny Crosby for our consideration. In the gospel song, "How wonderful the story," the spirit and optimism of her life come through beautifully. The text holds together well with the first stanza serving as an introduction and the second and third stanzas focusing upon the life and ministry of Christ. The refrain serves as a fine capsule of praise and adoration.

In this musical setting the flavor of the gospel song is evident throughout, especially in the melodic and rhythmic content of the stanzas. Though the rhythmic pattern continues in the refrain, the melody utilizes more text painting and drama.

The harmony of the hymn tune is traditional, but it leaves the late nineteenth-century gospel song style occasionally with altered and substitute chords. The E-major chord in measure 20 is strategic to the idea of providing some fresh chords to complement the more basic ones.

In this tune I have sought to capture the spirit of Fanny Crosby's writings. The music is straightforward, blending basic composition techniques with a feeling of optimism.

How Wonderful the Story

1. How won - der - ful the sto - ry, whose words of truth un -
2. How won - der - ful the sto - ry from an - gel tongues that
3. For us He toiled and la - bored through long and wear - y
fold. A love sur - pass - ing know - ledge, whose
rang, when "glo - ry in the high - est" o'er
years; He trod the path of sor - row, and
depth can ne'er be told; the love of God, the
Ju - dah's plains they sang. How won - der - ful the
bore our griefs and fears. He gave His life our
Fa - ther to sin - ful men be - low, His
sto - ry that woke the dew - y morn, when,
ran som; the world He o - ver - came, that

WORDS: Fanny J. Crosby
MUSIC: A. L. Butler

LEXINGTON ROAD
7.6.7.6.D. with Refrain

in - fin - ite com - pas - sion too great for us to
cra - dled in a man - ger, the Prince of Peace was
we, through His a - tone - ment, might con - quer in His
Refrain
know.
born. We bow our heads with rev - erence, His
name.
good - ness we a - dore, and praise Him for the
mer - cy that saves for - ev - er - more.

Introduction to "Good news!"

Brian Wren

In his book, *God the Spirit* (Minneapolis: Fortress Press, 1994), Michael Welker points out that the crowd's bewilderment at Pentecost arises not because the Spirit's action is hard to grasp, but because of its extreme and startling clarity: People are amazed to hear the mighty works of God in their own native tongue.

Welker's insight is the starting point for my hymn, whose opening line provides the pattern for succeeding stanzas. The exclamation ("Good news!") is followed, in every stanza except the last, by parallel comparison: too clear, too hopeful, too strange, and too good. The second and third stanzas summarize the heart of the Christian gospel—Christ's acceptance of Isaiah's Suffering Servant role and the centrality of cross and resurrection to the outpouring of the Spirit. Stanza 4 counters our culture's individualism with the affirmation that this good news calls us into a community, as we leave the payroll of "sovereign self-hood" and join Christ's other friends in worship, service, and witness. In the opening stanza the phrase "delighted drunkards" is poetic license: though not intoxicated, the disciples were bowled over by the Spirit. The main scripture references are: stanza 1—Acts 2:1–13; stanza 2: Isaiah 41:1–4; stanza 3: Acts 2: 23–24 and 32–33.

For Hugh McElrath, with affectionate appreciation

Good News!

1. Good news! – Too clear to be ignored:
delighted drunkards fill the street,
and yell, in every mother-tongue,
"The Spirit comes! To you! To all!"

2. Good news! – Too hopeful to refuse:
"A servant filled with Spirit-breath,
shall break the sword with gentle speech
and humbly rule a peaceful earth."

3. Good news! – Too strange to be untrue:
"Though executed by the State,
the servant reigns, alive in God,
and sends the Spirit on us all."

4. Good news! – Too good to hear alone:
and so, reclaimed by wondrous love,
from sov'reign selfhood we resign,
and to the friends of Christ belong.

5. Good news! – In Christ, the Spirit's breath,
awaking gifts we never knew,
shall make us one to give the world
goodwill, good witness, and good news.

This hymn was completed on February 22, 2002, and also appears (with music by Dan Damon) in Brian Wren, Christ Our Hope: 33 New Hymns and 6 Reissues *(Carol Stream, Illinois: Hope Publishing Company, 2004).*

WORDS: Brian Wren
MUSIC: Sing to suitable tunes in Long Meter (8.8.8.8.).

Introduction to MARY CHARLOTTE

Louis Ball

A few years ago, Carson-Newman College commissioned a hymn text to help celebrate the 150th anniversary of its founding. Although I was on the committee, I decided to attempt to write a tune for the anniversary. However, I was stuck in the middle of the melody with no solution for the last two lines.

When I looked at the possible hymn texts which Dr. McElrath deemed worthy of setting, I realized that at least the beginning two lines reflected the Fanny Crosby text, "For the joys of full salvation." Within a few minutes, the melody came easily to complete the setting, with phrases in the chorus rising to the final praise.

The tune is named for my wife, who was blessed with a name from each grandmother.

To Dr. Hugh T. McElrath

For the Joys of Full Salvation

Introduction for first stanza only
All voices in unison
1. For the joys of full sal - va - tion and the peace those joys af - ford, let our souls, and all with - in us,
2. We were lost till Je - sus found us, till His blood our ran - som paid; now the gate of life is o - pen,
3. Sound a - loud the gos - pel trum - pets, shout a - loud the sweet re - frain; bless - ed be the Lord for - ev - er,

WORDS: Fanny J. Crosby
MUSIC: Louis Ball

MARY CHARLOTTE
8.7.8.7. with Refrain

mag - ni - fy and praise the Lord.
full a - tone-ment He has made.
bless - ed be His ho - ly name.
Refrain
Praise Him all ye floods of o - cean;
praise Him all ye stars a - bove.
Praise Him, ev-'ry liv-ing
crea - ture;
praise and sing His won-drous love!

Introduction to OCTOGENARIAN

Carlton R. Young

My setting of Carl Daw's text, apropos a graceful, musical, creative, and caring Deity, expresses Hugh McElrath's understated humor, unassuming scholarship and a pedagogy always assuring, supportive, and pastoral.

For my friend and colleague, Hugh T. McElrath

God of Grace and God of Laughter

*See fourth page for optional flute part.

**Suggested sequence: stanza 1, solo with flute; stanza 2, choir; stanza 3, choir and congregation with flute.

WORDS: Carl P. Daw, Jr. (Job 38:7; Isaiah 35:10)
MUSIC: Carlton R. Young

OCTOGENARIAN
8.7.8.7.D.

stars and all there - af - ter joined in
seems dis - cor - dant mad - ness, help us
souls and voic - es ring - ing; tune our
(Em) (C/E) (D) (Bm/D)
Fm Db/F Eb Cm/Eb
cos - mic har - mo - ny: give us songs of joy and
find a mea-sured calm. Stea - dy us with mu - sic's
hearts in true ac - cord, till we form a might - y
(C) (G/B) (Bm) (Em) (G)
Db Ab/C Cm Fm Ab
+Fl.
won - der, mu - sic mak - ing hearts re - joice; let our
an - chor when the storms of life in - crease; in the
cho - rus join - ing an - gel choirs a - bove, with all
(D) (G) (C) (C/A) (D) (D/F#)
Eb Ab Db Db/Bb Eb Eb/G

prais - es swell like thun - der, e - cho -
midst of hurt and ran - cor, make us
those who went be - fore us, in e -
(G) (G/C) (D) (G)
A♭ A♭/D♭ E♭ A♭
-Fl.
1., 2.
3.
ing our Mak - er's voice.
in - stru-ments of peace.
ter - nal hymns of love.
(Am) (Em/B) (Bm) (Em) (Em)
B♭m Fm/C Cm Fm Fm
+Fl.
+Fl.
rit.
(E) (C) (Am) (E)
E♭ D♭ B♭m F
rit.

God of Grace and God of Laughter

Flute Part

MUSIC: Carlton R. Young

Introduction to "O God, in Your Word You instruct us to sing"

FOSTER HALL III

Donald Eugene Winters

I am pleased to contribute to this Festschrift which honors Dr. Hugh T. McElrath on the occasion of his eightieth birthday. Dr. McElrath is a lifelong friend of my family. He was a student of (and later a teaching colleague with) my parents, Donald and Frances Winters, at The Southern Baptist Theological Seminary in the early days of the School of Church Music and Worship. I have known him since I was a very small child.

Throughout his career, Dr. McElrath's work and interests have focused upon evangelism through church music. This became my point of departure for writing the hymn, "O God, in Your Word You instruct us to sing." In Matthew 22:37–40, Jesus clearly states our *raison d'être*, i.e., love God with all your heart and mind and soul and strength, *and* love your fellow human being. If the body of Christ is not worshiping and having an intimate, Abba Father relationship with God through Jesus Christ, we really have nothing to share. Indeed, our very act of worship *is* a witness to our faith. Through the worship of God we are both *inspired* and *edified*—personally and corporately. So our music becomes an offering of worship, a vehicle for teaching, *and* a means of outreach, viz., evangelism.

The scriptural basis for this hymn is Psalm 33:1–8. In addition, I've alluded to that famous statement by Martin Luther which says: "Music is a fair and lovely gift of God . . . . Next after *theology* I give to *music* the highest place and the greatest honor."[1]

The tune FOSTER HALL III garners its name from my first remembrance of Dr. and Mrs. McElrath, when I was no more than four or five years old. Both of our families lived in Foster Hall on the seminary campus for awhile. My folks helped them move into their third-floor apartment, and I remember the McElraths' graciousness to my parents then and over the years. I am especially thankful to them for participating in the memorial services for both my father and my mother upon the occasions of their deaths.

It is my hope that this hymn embodies the spirit of Dr. McElrath's teaching and honors that ministry.

NOTE

1. Cited and trans. in Roland H. Bainton, *Here I Stand: A Life of Martin Luther* (New York: Mentor/Penguin, 1955; rep. ed., 1977), 266–67, emphasis added.

O God, in Your Word You Instruct Us to Sing

1. O God, in Your Word You in - struct us to sing, to
2. We glad - ly ac - know - ledge that, next to Your Word, our
3. The world needs to hear all the songs that we sing; to
lift up our voi - ces in praise; to
hearts are most stirred and in - spired by
view how we faith - ful - ly live in
of - fer be - fore You a new song, O King, to
mu - sic - al strains which can up - lift, or gird, or
ho - nor of Je - sus, our Lord and our King; to
wor - ship You all of our days. O
com - fort us when life gets mired. O
grasp the sal - va - tion You give. O

WORDS: Gene Winters (Ps. 33:1-8)
MUSIC: Gene Winters

FOSTER HALL III
11.8.11.8.D.

God, in Your Word You in - struct us to play with
help us to fash - ion our mu - sic with care: to
God, in Your Word You in - struct us to sing and
skill on our in - stru-ments, too; for
of - fer our wor - ship to You; to
love You and oth - ers as well; O
tone can en - hance what mere words can't con - vey, the
build up Your church; to have cour - age to share, to
grant that our songs might re - sound - ing - ly bring You
depths of our deep love for You!
wit - ness in all that we do.
glo - ry, and Your gos - pel tell.

III.

Essays Written in Honor of Hugh T. McElrath

Purpose and Use of Carol Manuscripts

PAULETTE MOORE CATHERWOOD

Previous studies of the English carol have examined its form as a musical and literary genre having a prehistory in dance and monophonic song.[1] Arguments for and against a role in liturgical celebrations have also been advanced and debated at great length.[2] However, neither a study of the earliest origins of the carol nor of its purpose and use in former centuries adequately explains the origin, purpose, and use of the fifteenth-century vernacular polyphonic carol. Moreover, the history of the literary carol is not necessarily the same as that of the polyphonic carol, even during a given period of time. In short, the current tenets about the carol (ring-dance origin, popular, monophonic unwritten history, Franciscan propagation) tell us nothing conclusive about the origin, purpose, and use of the poems, music or actual manuscripts at hand. Each point is merely a theoretical reconstruction based on individual links which may or may not belong to a common chain. Even if one discovered the factors which caused people to write carol-form poems in any given period, this might not define the carol's function at that or any other time.

Before any conclusions can be advanced concerning the purpose and use of the carol, the evidence of the manuscripts in which the music and verbal texts of carols are found must be taken into account. Such a study promises to provide a more certain foundation by formulating a theory about the purpose and use of the carol manuscripts themselves.[3] Such a theory will then allow one to consider (with caution) the purpose and use of the carols which appear in them.[4] This study proposes to follow this methodology in seeking to address the question of whether the manuscript evidence confirms or rejects the long-held view advanced by musicologist Richard J. Greene and amplified by Manfred Bukofzer of the carol as a burden-stanza *forme fixe* (i.e., one of several forms of late medieval poetry characterized by a fixed rhyme scheme with refrain) that is popular by destination, but not by origin.[5]

Types of carol manuscripts

There are more than one hundred extant manuscripts which contain carols. Most of these are housed in British libraries.[6] Of these, fourteen manuscripts have polyphonic and seven have monophonic carol settings (with partial settings in two further manuscripts). The remainder (and vast majority) have only the poetic texts with the infrequent reference to the name of a tune.

Monophonic carol settings appear in primarily literary manuscripts intended for private use (or for the use of a small group of individuals), and may have been copied by amateur or professional scribes coming from a variety of professional backgrounds. Monophonic settings do not necessarily presuppose a popular origin or destination.[7] For the most part, these literary manuscripts reflect the tastes of the literate, educated classes. One possible exception is the sermon of a Franciscan friar found in two extant manuscripts.[8] In each case, a carol appears within the sermon text as an illustration. This one carol, copied by or for clergy, may have reached an audience extending beyond the educated classes (see, however, note 13).

Manuscripts with polyphonic settings of carols seldom contain any monophonic music and are generally copied by or for professionals who are presumably in the employ of (or seeking the employ of) royalty, nobility, or clergy. Polyphonic carol manuscripts are usually intended for occasional public performance by a small group of professionals serving an upper-class audience. By definition, this is a limited context. The main opportunity for the common populace to hear polyphony would be in the context of the open church services (e.g., Lady masses) in establishments (such as abbeys and monasteries) which had choirs that performed polyphony. Some parish churches had polyphonic manuscripts, but this was rare until the later fifteenth century.[9] During the first half of the fifteenth century, polyphony was infrequent within the liturgy and the liturgical year.

None of the manuscripts containing polyphonic carols has been associated conclusively with a religious order or house. One contains some carols by a Devonshire rector and may be connected with Exeter Cathedral (secular) or a local household chapel or foundation.[10] Most polyphonic carol manuscripts are associated with collegiate foundations, or with royalty or nobility and their households. The polyphony which was sung in private chapels or private services and offices would not have been heard by any persons other than those in the ranks of the elite and their servants. If carols were not used as part of church or chapel services (excluding sermon recitations) and only as household after-dinner entertainment in royal and noble establishments,[11] this further would have limited the possibility of the polyphonic carol gaining popularity among the masses. Granted, household servants who were present in the hall would hear the entertainment, but there is no evidence to suggest that a popular tradition of carol singing was nurtured by this means. Those polyphonic manuscripts which were used primarily as exemplars or as reference or portfolio copies contain pieces whose ultimate destination was the same.

This points to the main distinction between the use of literary and polyphonic musical carol manuscripts: semi-private versus semi-public use. While polyphonic manuscripts were used by the educated elite within a restricted context, literary manuscripts may have had a wider-ranging social audience. However, further research is necessary to determine whether literary and polyphonic carol manuscripts were used by the same types of people (e.g., the educated elite) or by a wider variety of people.

Table 1 categorizes carol manuscripts according to their primary contents. The number of manuscripts which contain monophonic carols appears in regular typeface and the number of manuscripts which contain polyphonic carols appears in boldface print in parentheses following the number for that category. All the rest are literary manuscripts or manuscripts containing only non-carol music.

Table 1
Categories of Carol Manuscripts

Key: s. = *siècle*, or century; thus, s. xiii = thirteenth century

Date	Poetry anthologies	Prose anthologies	Po/Pr anthols.	Single works	Sermon	Common-place books	Polyphonic mss.
s. xiii	0	0	2	0	0	0	0
s. xiv	0	0	1	1	1	1	0
s. xv$^{1/2}$	4	3	6 (1)	1	1	3 (2/**2**)	5 (1/**4**)
s. xv	0	0	0	1	0	0	0
s. xv$^{2/2}$	5 (3)	9 (1/**1**)	13	0	0	8	1 (**1**)
s. xvi	3 (1)	2	1	2	0	8	4 (**4**)
Printed	2	1	0	0	0	0	1 (1)
s. xviii	1	0	0	0	0	0	0
Totals	15 (4)	15 (1/**1**)	23 (1)	5	2	20 (2/**2**)	11 (2/**9**)

This analysis shows that the type of manuscript into which carols were copied changed during the course of carol history. In the beginning, carol texts (or stanzas from which later carol texts were derived) were copied into a variety of carol manuscripts. However, by the fifteenth century, carols with monophonic and polyphonic music appear. Polyphonic carols appear both in manuscripts with other polyphonic music and in "commonplace books" (books in which the owner records memoranda for future reference). The two commonplace books which contain polyphonic carols are both too small for use by more than one person (or two having excellent eyesight).[12] Monophonic carols are usually found in mixed anthologies and commonplace books. Carol texts without music occur mostly in anthologies of poetry and/or prose. During the next half-century, commonplace books have become more prevalent and are growing in importance as sources of carol texts. Anthologies remain the most significant source group for carol texts. By the sixteenth century, the commonplace book is the primary type of manuscript in which carol texts are found, although some are copied in anthologies. Polyphonic carols from now on appear only in manuscripts of polyphonic music. Following this period, carol-related texts (without the burden) appear only in poetry anthologies.

The evidence of manuscripts tells us only what literary or musical items were considered important or interesting by those people who could afford manuscripts and/or the time to write or read them. The works of Chaucer, Gower, Lydgate, Hoccleve, Mandeville, and Rolle frequently appear in manuscripts throughout the period of the literary carol. However, this indicates nothing more than a fashionable taste or popularity among a very restricted, educated, bourgeois, and often upper-class audience. Nor does it necessarily tell us what poems, songs, rhymes, or stories were in general circulation among all the people, literate and illiterate, rich and poor. The inclusion of a carol in a Franciscan sermon may appear to hint at the wider circulation of the carol, although the proof of this is by no means conclusive.[13] At the same time, it may reflect a useful snatch of vernacular (or translated) poetry known among the clergy and deemed handy for the occasion. How and by whom it was received and whether it was further used by the listeners is not known. In sum, then, the idea that polyphonic carols were not popular by origin but were popular by destination has little grounding in the manuscript evidence studied so far.

Franciscan connections reconsidered

Greene's and Bukofzer's theory of popular destination is based largely on the known musical activities of Franciscans on the continent and on the poems and instructions of *The Red Book of Ossory*. This collection of Latin *cantilenas*, often in carol form, contains Latin *contrafacta* of popular secular songs (i.e., songs whose secular texts have been replaced by new, sacred texts in Latin) and was intended for Franciscan clergy based in Kilkenny in Ireland. It claims to have been written in order that clerics would not "pollute their throats by popular, immoral, and secular songs."[14] While this does seem to indicate that the carol form was in use during major holidays and celebrations and enjoyed some degree of popularity in vernacular, secular situations, it does not identify the extent of its popularity or the people among whom it was popular (other than the Franciscan clergy). It does seem likely, however, that the original lewd and secular songs came from an English community (whether secular or religious) rather than the Irish people of Kilkenny, since these Franciscans came from England to Kilkenny, a primary center of English power in Ireland in addition to Dublin.[15] So the statement to clergy in Kilkenny does not necessarily relate to songs which they learned or heard in Ireland, but more likely to an unidentified English context.[16] Nothing, however, is known about the actual context or lyrics of the songs which the *contrafacta* were intended to neutralize, not even if they were all vernacular.[17] Neither is it known how (or in what context) the Franciscans used the Latin songs found in the manuscript.

The one conjecture of Greene and Bukofzer (i.e., popular destination) has led to a series of further supporting theories (of widespread Franciscan carol singing and its extensive impact among the common populace) and to conclusions rooted in the original conjecture (e.g., that *The Red Book of Ossory* proves the widespread practice of vernacular carol singing among the common populace and the use of *contrafacta* carols by Franciscans to evangelize the immoral people). Even if it were possible to prove a strong Franciscan connection with the literary carol, however, this would not explain the origin or presence of polyphonic carol manuscripts.

One further assumption underlies most statements about Franciscans and the carol: the Franciscans are seen as moving primarily or exclusively among the common populace. Certainly this was their original remit, but was it their exclusive practice in fourteenth- and fifteenth-century England? Without this assurance, one must adopt a skeptical view concerning the statements about Franciscans and their use of the carol.

By the fourteenth century, most Franciscans had moved from an itinerant mendicant lifestyle to a conventual style of existence. Franciscans were no longer necessarily confined to ministry among the poor or to a life of poverty. Some were involved in primarily academic pursuits. Several continental friars are known to have been under the patronage of wealthy nobles; others had fancy living quarters and servants.[18] Robert Grosseteste, bishop of Lincoln, had a friar acting as a confessor in his household. John Pecham, a friar, became archbishop of Canterbury. The large number of bequests made to friaries in the wills of the wealthy would indicate more than a passing acquaintance between the two groups. These factors argue against an exclusively "popular" view of Franciscan ministry in the late middle ages and counsel one to look carefully at each situation to determine if the Franciscan in question was conventual, mendicant, peripatetic, or living under patronage; an academic, preacher, confessor, or collector. There was a revival of traditional Franciscan observance in the late fifteenth century, but only among a minority of English friars.

If the carol was used regularly by Franciscan preachers, one would expect more manuscript evidence from the collections containing their sermons. The Franciscan, James Ryman, produced what is today the largest extant collection of carols by one author.[19] However, the purpose and use of his collection is not specified. It may have been for his own amusement and edification, or it may have contained carols which he used in sermons. He received a license to hold a parish in 1499, after the carols had been entered into the collection.[20] Whether he was specifically associated with Franciscans while he was compiling the collection is not readily apparent, though certainly this would have been possible. Many of the poems are less than catchy or inspiring from a literary point of view, and the lack of concordances (i.e., multiple manuscript sources) for all but two of these carols makes it doubtful that they enjoyed a wide circulation.[21] Thus Ryman's carol collection provides us with a single collection showing that the carol was known to some Franciscans, but does not in itself provide strong support for the theory that Franciscans were among the chief propagators of the religious carol.[22]

The manuscript context

The heavy reliance on a theory of Franciscan dissemination of the carol has obscured the need for a wide-ranging study of the relationship of manuscript sources and the carol. A recent work by a Cambridge church historian, however, reopens the discussion of "popular religion" in light of manuscript and iconographical evidence.

Eamon Duffy, in his major work, *The Stripping of the Altars*, includes an examination of late medieval manuscripts and their relationship to the work of the Church and to the private devotional lives of laity and clergy alike.[23] He argues effectively against the use of the term "popular religion" and says that there may not have been a great gulf between social classes in their religious observances. Instead, he advocates the use of "traditional religion," which includes all classes, rather than "popular religion," which usually refers to the lower and middle classes who were largely uneducated or illiterate (at least in Latin). Duffy points to the remarkable spread of literacy and the ownership of books among fourteenth- and fifteenth-century mercantile and artisan classes.

An increasing number of devotional and edifying materials circulated among the laity for use at home and in church. Primers were the most popular and available of vernacular religious books and were essentially liturgical in content. They included the elements of the Little Office or Hours of the Blessed Virgin Mary (BVM) as well as liturgical calendars, saints' lives, and other materials. However, the reaction to Lollardy (i.e., the followers of John Wyclif) in the early fifteenth century led to the suppression of English-language primers until the 1530s. Latin primers, meanwhile, were encouraged only among the elite.

Laity of varying social backgrounds as well as ecclesiastics began to collect their own devotional materials, medical recipes, English poems, charms, and proverbs, sometimes including these in primers or in commonplace books. The collection of the sixteenth-century London grocer, Richard Hill, is the most celebrated of these.[24] His manuscript includes the type of material found in primers as well as a large collection of carol-form poems. Interestingly, this vernacular collection comes from the same period in which printers began to produce primers in Latin and English bilingual editions.

The most popular devotions of the late medieval period were directed towards the Passion of Christ (especially the Five Wounds), the Five Sorrows of Mary, and the Fifteen Woes of Bridget. The Five Joys of Mary were familiar to all and central to the *Corpus Christi* plays. Marian piety lent itself naturally to vernacular elaboration for devotional purposes. The topics and forms of Latin poems were widely imitated in English.[25] The primers reflect these devotional emphases. Even the liturgy itself was in flux during this period, responsive to pressure from the laity, "a mirror of the devotional changes and even fashions of the age."[26] Besides new votive masses (those for a special intention, not part of the prescribed liturgy) and feasts, there was the multiplication within the Sarum, or Salisbury,[27] rite (a variant within England of the Roman rite) of hymns and sequences using the meter of the medieval sequences, *Stabat Mater* and *Dies Irae*. This penchant for elaboration and the emphasis on the Virgin Mary and the saints are both characteristic of late medieval culture.

Duffy's analysis provides a useful framework for examining the manuscripts in which carol-form poems are found. Of the hundred or so carol manuscripts, six may have been intended primarily for lay, and ten for ecclesiastical, devotional use.[28] The remainder are literary anthologies, commonplace books, directions to parish priests, sermon collections, single longer works (e.g., travel, literature, law, history) with carols added at a later time, and collections of polyphonic repertoire. Thus about 16 percent of carol manuscripts fall within the category of devotional interest. The only later carol manuscript collection to include mainly primer material is Balliol 354. By this time, vernacular primers were becoming a much more common possession of bourgeois and elite alike. Without marks of ownership, in fact, it is very difficult to distinguish which manuscripts were once owned by the bourgeoisie and which by the nobles. Some historians have attempted to categorize the literature preferred by peasant, bourgeois, and noble, but this is based on a small number of identifiable manuscripts and a great deal of conjecture.[29]

Since vernacular primers were discouraged during the first half of the fifteenth-century in particular, and Latin primers were encouraged only among the elite, does this then say anything about the role or development of the carol (as first strictly vernacular, then macaronic [e.g., lines in both Latin and English], then all Latin as well)? The carol began to appear in large quantities during the very time that the popular vernacular primer was taken out of circulation. Are these two circumstances in any way related? Did the vernacular carol act as a devotional substitute for elements of the vernacular primer? Was it used as a Catholic response to proto-Protestantism? Was it both a lay and a clerical devotional form?

If the carol did act as a devotional substitute, one would expect to find a similar range of topics in the carols as we see in the primers. It has long been observed that many carols exhibit Marian piety. Marian carols frequently give praise to her attributes, particularly her Motherhood, and also refer to the Five Joys. However, they do not refer to the Five Sorrows, a staple of the primer and of late medieval devotion. Nor do more than ten carols address the Passion. Rather, the main focus of the carol corpus is on the Nativity and Marian devotion with secondary emphasis on other saints, moral uprightness, and festive occasions. Carols often show the influence of hymns, prayers, and Latin liturgical elements, but not specifically that of primers.

Nonetheless, it is still interesting to note that the rise of the vernacular carol parallels the suppression of the vernacular primer, even though the subject matter differs in its focus. The theology of the carols reflects traditional Catholic religion and piety. It could very well be that, in the fifteenth century, the carol was one means among many of combating proto-Protestant forces within England. This, along with the natural rise of other forms, could help to explain the decline of the carol following the reign of Henry VIII. The carol lost favor along with the other *formes fixes*.

Despite the difference in subject matter, some carol manuscripts and primers do have another point in common. Duffy notes that primers frequently used rubric print and the sign of the cross to establish their sacred character. Rubrics reminded one of the appearance of the books used at altars and in the liturgy. Certain carol manuscripts also use rubrics or the sign of the cross.[30] Was this a means of establishing the sacred character of the contents and/or the manuscripts? This could explain the use of a cross on the first pages of both Passions in the manuscript known as British Library (BL) Egerton 3307 (see next page). Were those rubrics found in ecclesiastical manuscripts simply the result of habit, or were they used to convey the sacred character of the material within? It is interesting to muse upon this point; however, crosses appear so frequently in medieval manuscripts of this period that one must not attach too much special meaning, either religious or heraldic, to their presence.

As we have seen, the essential core of primers was liturgical. However, carols were seldom copied into collections of primarily liturgical material. They do appear as a much later addition in a Benedictine breviary containing medical recipes and antiphons, and in polyphonic manuscripts of masses and other liturgical music.[31] However, carols are most frequently associated with non-liturgical materials. They occur mainly in literary manuscripts which have some vernacular material and especially in those manuscripts which give medical recipes, calendars, or other everyday items in addition to the main contents.

These commonplace books and miscellanies had varying purposes.[32] Some included a sample of the literary items of the day. Others stressed useful, helpful material, such as calendars and recipes. The fact that an item appears in a commonplace book or anthology may not necessarily provide us with an index of its popularity or the extent of its usage. However, one must give attention to those manuscripts which have large numbers of carols or other poems. Were their compilers merely collectors, unconcerned with the usefulness of the material? Were the collections used for choosing sermon examples or songs for corporate use or private devotional use? Did collectors gather together carol poems because of some fashionable trend, personal taste, or devotional piety? Table 2 lists the major carol collections (having seven or more carols) by period and type. Note that large collections were often amassed by one person or were collated for choral use.

Literary vernacular carol collections from the second quarter of the fifteenth century: purpose and use

The first major carol collections, whether literary or musical (polyphonic), appeared between 1420 and 1450. The highest percentage of polyphonic and

Table 2
Major Carol Collections

Manuscripts s. xv 1/2	Type	Number of polyphonic carols	Number of literary carols	Hand	Purpose of manuscript
CTCC O.3.58	polyphonic	13	0	primary	Portfolio?
Selden B.26	polyphonic	31	0	11 hands	Performance copy
Egerton 3307	polyphonic	33	0	primary	Exemplar/ fine copy
Bodley 88*	polyphonic	7	0	primary	Not enough information, manuscript incomplete
Sloane 2593	literary	0	57	primary	Poetry anthology
Douce 302	literary	0	26	primary	Devotional collection—Audelay
CGCC 383	literary	0	9	primary	Student commonplace book
CSJC S.54	literary	0	20	3 primary hands	Pocketbook anthology of carols
8 manuscripts	4 polyphonic; 4 literary	84 carols; 43%	112 carols; 57%		various

Manuscripts s. xv 2/2	Type	Number of polyphonic carols	Number of literary carols	Hand	Purpose of manuscript
BL Addit. 5665	polyphonic	45	0	primary	Performance copy
Oxf. Eng. Poet. E.1	literary	0	67	3 hands	Poetry anthology
CUL Ee.1.12	literary	0	120	3 hands	Poetry anthology—Ryman
3 manuscripts	1 polyphonic; 2 literary	45 carols; 19%	187 carols; 81%		Choral/poetry anthologies

Manuscripts s. xvi	Type	Number of polyphonic carols	Number of literary carols	Hand	Purpose of manuscript
BL Addit. 5465	polyphonic	8	0	primary	Choral anthology fine copy
BL Addit. 31922	polyphonic	12	0	2 hands	Choral anthology fine copy
Oxf. Balliol 354	literary	0	78	primary	Devotional anthology Hill
3 manuscripts	2 polyphonic; 1 literary	20 carols; 20%	78 carols; 80%		Choral/poetry anthologies

literary carols are found in this period, as is the largest number of major carol collections of any type. Although the significant literary collections of the following periods are larger, they are fewer in number. All literary manuscripts but one appear to have been poetry anthologies, yet these collections may have had different uses. The following discussion summarizes the contents and possible use of each major carol collection during the second quarter of the fifteenth century.

CGCC 383 is a student commonplace book from Oxford containing a wide range of materials, mostly practical. Some of the carols differ in nature from the rest of the material. Five carols have amorous themes; one is convivial; two are about St. Thomas Becket (and show no signs of damage from frequent use or erasure); one is for the BVM; and one is a Nativity carol. The carols are located in three separate quires and are not grouped according to theme. The remaining material in the book consists of Latin grammar exercises, French letters, accounts and deeds, one French *carole*, and a gloss on certain liturgical offices. The languages used, the nature of the materials, and the fact that the writer was apparently at one time a university student show that this manuscript once belonged to a member of the elite. Why he collected the material or how he used it is less certain. Besides the carols and the gloss on liturgical offices, all the contents are of a useful, practical nature, perhaps materials the collector wished to have on hand for reference during his student days and later in the course of business. Some of the carols and the liturgical gloss show a concern for things religious, common enough at the time. But why would amorous or convivial carols be included? This commonplace book represents the variety of materials which touched upon the life of a university-trained gentleman. Convivial, amorous, and devotional carols may all have had their place in either the college life (entertainment or private devotion) or the home life of the elite. The reference to two tune names, and the inclusion of a monophonic melody for one further carol, reinforce the conclusion that these carols were performed within the community in which the student (or graduate) resided.

CSJC S.54 is a small paper pocketbook of carols with a membrane cover, much worn and easily transportable, possibly carried around from place to place. The mix of fine and poor hands may indicate compilation by various persons, some of whom were unaccustomed to regular writing. The number of carols for or about women points to use among women or in mixed company. Women were becoming increasingly literate at this time and were known to have collected various materials for primers and anthologies. This collection uses East Anglian dialect. It shows signs of extensive use, but to what purpose? Most carols are suited to Christmastide, Lent, Marian celebrations, or festive occasions. Several hands copied the carols over a relatively short period. The pocketbook may have traveled with members of a household or with a succession of individuals who read and collected such carols for private thought, perusal, and entertainment.

BL Sloane 2593 has several features in common with CSJC S.54: East Anglian dialect, similar small size, paper support, primarily a carol anthology, two common concordances, and similar spread of themes, with primary emphasis on Christmastide. Both manuscripts include carols on the following ten themes: Nativity, various saints, Epiphany, lullaby, the Passion, the Five Joys of Mary, Doomsday and/or mortality, satirical matter, women, and amorous matter. CJSC S.54 also has carols on the holly and the ivy, Christ's pleading, Christ, and the boar's head. BL Sloane 2593 includes carols for Advent, the Annunciation, the Eucharist, religious and moral counsel, repentance, marriage, and convivial topics. Forty percent of the CSJC S.54 carols are for Christmastide, with the remainder spread fairly evenly among the various topics, especially lullaby carols and songs about love and women. BL Sloane 2593 has 35 percent Nativity carols, but also emphasizes carols for the BVM, carols of counsel, and satirical carols. The two concordances are a carol for Epiphany and a lullaby carol.

CJSC S.54 also has five carols (25 percent of the collection) with concordances in other manuscripts: one on Epiphany, one on the Five Joys, and three lullaby carols. Four manuscripts are earlier or contemporary, two are from the latter part of the fifteenth century, one is from the sixteenth century (and three are Victorian or later).[33] BL Sloane 2593 is primarily a carol collection, and has nineteen carols (33 percent of the collection) with concordances: one on Advent, three on the Nativity, one to St. Thomas, four on the Epiphany, two lullaby carols, one passion carol, three to the BVM, one on the Annunciation, two carols of moral counsel, and one on women. Nine manuscripts are earlier or contemporary, three are from the latter part of the fifteenth century, and three are from the sixteenth century.[34]

This represents a wide spread of concordances and indicates that CJSC S.54 and BL Sloane 2593 may contain some of the main early carol repertoire then in circulation. Early CJSC S.54 concordances are found in manuscripts from East Anglia (two manuscripts) and Somerset; later concordances are from Yorkshire and London (the more recent of these are from Birmingham, York, Dudley, and London). The earlier BL Sloane 2593 concordances come from East Anglia (three manuscripts), the Midlands (including Oxford), and Dorset. Later concordances are from Lincoln, Yorkshire, the West Midlands, Somerset, and London. Both collections lend themselves to private ownership and use in devotional and leisure pursuits.[35]

Oxford, Douce 302 comes from Haughmond Abbey in Shropshire and has fewer concordances, five carols (20 percent), on the following topics: Advent, New Year, Epiphany, the BVM, and the Five Joys. Concordances are found in three manuscripts from the same period and in one later manuscript.[36] Earlier concordances come from East Anglia (two manuscripts) and the West Midlands; later ones from London. Douce 302 is more didactic in character and may have been useful for personal or corporate edification at the Augustinian abbey.

Polyphonic vernacular carol collections from the second quarter of the fifteenth century: purpose and use

Three major music collections of carols from this period seem to have had different purposes and uses. TCC O.3.58 is a bare-bones repertoire or portfolio representing the Christmas festival. Selden B.26 is a growing collection of primarily Marian pieces used by singers who needed some help with polyphony. BL Egerton 3307 is a fair copy, possibly circulating as an exemplar, used as a status symbol, but not necessarily by royalty (whose books often were finer). It would be useful in performance by experienced singers of polyphony. Bodley 88* appears to be a fair copy, but too little remains to make a guess as to use or total repertoire.

Some literary manuscripts label a variety of poetic forms as "carols." Polyphonically-set carol-related poems are found among carol-form poems (as in Selden B.26 and BL Egerton 3307) with no rubrics to distinguish one from the other. Both types of poem are found among antiphons, hymns, motets, and songs (Selden B.26, BL Egerton 3307, and Ritson 5665). Trinity O.3.58 and what remains of Bodley 88* are unique in that they contain only polyphonic settings of carol-form poems. Selden B.26 shows no sign of organization by form or by use. Antiphons and carols are interspersed, with drinking songs at the end. BL Ritson 5665 segregates carols and songs from antiphons and Mass music, but labels pieces according to their appropriate liturgical season.[37] This might indicate that distinction of form (or *forme fixe*) was not as important as recording those pieces of music which were useful for a particular community.

BL Egerton 3307, with its highly organized contents, may shed some light on this issue. Carols, carol-related poems, and motets are contained in the third booklet, apart from the explicitly liturgically appropriate pieces. This booklet may have circulated separately and may have been used in a different context than that of the processional music, passions, and Mass. Certainly it was used during a different part of the liturgical year.

This evidence provides no reason to affirm that each community in which the polyphonic carol had a role used this musical genre for the same purpose(s) at any or all times. We are limited in what we can know about the use of the literary and polyphonic carol by the nature of the manuscript evidence. That it had widespread popularity among the educated elite in some regions seems certain. However, it would be ill-advised to suggest that the carol enjoyed the same reception among the vast majority of the populace. This leads to the conclusion that the long-held view of the carol as popular by destination but not by origin is not supportable. Indeed, many manuscripts available for study today are both elite by origin and by destination. Their contents may have had a wider circulation, but there is no firm evidence for this.

Carol collections: summary

Carol collections with known provenance were compiled by or for fifteenth-century monastics, friars, students, and nobles, and sixteenth-century royalty, nobles, and businessmen. Did these people collect items which they had heard (either read or sung) in public gatherings (large or small) or which they had read privately? Did they compile literary anthologies primarily for devotional purposes or for private entertainment?

Carol manuscripts and poems come mostly from those regions of the country in which there were strong networks of lay and ecclesiastical magnates with household or collegiate chapels. Household and collegiate chapels are a likely milieu for spreading a new trend or form.[38] Some singers moved from one establishment to another over time and might have taken a new form with them. Nobles and their families stayed in one another's households and were exposed to a variety of musical resources and repertoire. It is not at all surprising to find a proliferation of carols (literary or polyphonic) in places of economic prosperity, in a period in which there was a demonstrable propensity for collecting (anthologies, commonplace books, primers), when there was a rise in the number and importance of household chapels, a new emphasis on polyphonic singing, and a decided surge in personal devotion and a search for new means of fulfilling devotional desires and liturgical requirements.

If there were once large numbers of Northern carol manuscripts, they did not survive. Nor did they exercise great influence on the extant written carol tradition. Indeed, there are few Northernisms in the remaining poems. Northern scribes with posts in the Midlands, Southern, or Kentish regions may be responsible for those which can be found. Nor are there many references to life in the North of England. It may therefore be that the polyphonic and the literary carol were not such strong phenomena in the North.

The carol was not a difficult form to set polyphonically, requiring normal (but learned) resources of composition and performance, sometimes allowing for improvisation using faburden techniques (in which two other parts were improvised, respectively, the one a 4th above, and the other in 3rds and 5ths below, the melody in the middle voice). The form and musical style of the first half of the fifteenth-century polyphonic carol were textually inspired, easy to follow, and adaptable to serve practically any subject. The carol would provide an ideal polyphonic vehicle for small groups of singers, such as those in collegiate chapels or in the household chapels of aristocrats and ecclesiastics who wished to display their resources or to offer entertainment of a devotional or more celebratory or festive nature. This form was also an excellent means (a) of training individuals and groups to sing solo or choral polyphony or (b) of rehearsing their skills during leisure time. As the music grew more elaborate, the polyphonic carol moved more exclusively into royal circles where the choirs had greater abilities and flexibility.

From this study of carol manuscripts, it would seem that both literary and polyphonic vernacular carol manuscripts were the property of the literate upper classes and, sometimes, of the bourgeoisie. There is no evidence in the manuscripts of a wide popular audience or a monophonic pre-history. Rather, the carol seems to have spread in regions where there was a fair degree of economic prosperity and where the household chapels of ecclesiastics and nobles were concentrated. Furthermore, most carol manuscripts whose provenance is known are associated with urban areas rather than with rural or isolated areas. Why there is no manuscript evidence of a strong carol tradition in the North is not immediately apparent. However, the documents at hand are only part of the original corpus and reveal only part of the story of the vernacular carol, polyphonic or literary. What is apparent is that, in the medieval carol, we have what David Fallows calls "that most distinctive and vital of English musical genres" and "probably the finest and most exciting Christmas music outside Bach."[39]

SIGLA

Manuscripts are referred to in abbreviated form (*sigla*) throughout the text. Following is a list of manuscripts and their *sigla*:

Ashmole 189: Oxford, Bodleian Library, Ms. Ashmole 189
Ashmole 1393: Oxford, Bodleian Library, Ms. Ashmole 1393
Balliol 354: Oxford, Balliol College, Ms. 354
Bodley 88*: Oxford, Bodleian Library, Ms. Bodley 88*
BL Addit. 5465: London, British Library, Additional Ms. 5465
BL Addit. 5665: London, British Library, Additional Ms. 5665
BL Addit. 5666: London, British Library, Additional Ms. 5666
BL Addit. 31042: London, British Library, Additional Ms. 31042
BL Addit. 31922: London, British Library, Additional Ms. 31922
BL Cotton Titus A. XXVI: London, British Library, Ms. Cotton Titus A. XXVI
BL Cotton Vitellius D.XII: London, British Library, Ms. Cotton Vitellius D.XII
BL Egerton 3307: London, British Library, Ms. Egerton 3307
BL Harley 275: London, British Library, Ms. Harley 275
BL Harley 2253: London, British Library, Ms. Harley 2253
BL Harley 2380: London, British Library, Ms. Harley 2380
BL Harley 7358: London, British Library, Ms. Harley 7358
BL Royal 20.A.1: London, British Library, Ms. Royal 20.A.1
BL Sloane 2593: London, British Library, Ms. Sloane 2593
CGCC 383: Cambridge, Gonville and Caius College, Ms. 383
CSJC S.54: Cambridge, St. John's College, Ms. S.54
CUL Ee.1.12: Cambridge, University Library, Ms. Ee.1.12
Dublin TC 432: Dublin, Trinity College, Ms. 432
Eng. Poet. E.1: Oxford, Bodleian Library, Ms. English Poetical E.1
Manchester, JRL Lat. 395: Manchester, John Rylands Library, Ms. Lat. 395
NLS Adv. 18.7.21: Edinburgh, National Library of Scotland, Ms. Advocates 18.7.21
NLS, Adv. 19.3.1, Edinburgh, National Library of Scotland, Ms. Advocates 19.3.1
Oxford, Bodley 26: Oxford, Bodleian Library, Ms. Bodley 26
Oxf. Douce 137: Oxford, Bodlein Library, Ms. Bodley 137
Oxf. Douce 302: Oxford, Bodleian Library, Ms. Douce 302
Oxf. Laud Misc. 601: Oxford, Bodleian Library, Ms. Laud Miscellaneous 601
Oxf. Laud Misc. 683: Oxford, Bodleian Library, Ms. Laud Miscellaneous 683
Porkington 10: Brogynton, Oswestry: Lord Harlech, Ms. Porkington 10 (Microfilm in Aberystwyth, National Library of Wales)
Selden B.26: Oxford, Bodleian Library, Ms. Arch. Selden B.26
TCC O.7.31: Cambridge, Trinity College, Ms. O.7.31
TCC O.9.38: Cambridge, Trinity College, Ms. O.9.38
ULL 657, London, University Library London, Ms. ULL 657

NOTES

This article is a revision of the concluding chapter of C. P. Catherwood, "English Polyphonic Carol Manuscripts, ca. 1420–1450," 2 vols. (D.Phil. thesis, University of Oxford, 1997).

1. Richard L. Greene, *Early English Carols*, rev. ed. (Oxford: Clarendon Press, 1977); *The New Grove Dictionary of Music and Musicians* (London: Macmillan, 1980), s.v., "Carol," by John Stevens, 3:802–813; *The New Oxford History of Music* [hereafter NOHM], eds. A. Hughes and G. E. Abraham (Oxford: Oxford University Press, 1964), s.v., "Popular and Secular Music in England (to ca. 1470)," by Manfred Bukofzer, 3:117–125.

2. Greene, *Early English Carols*; Stevens, "Carol"; Bukofzer, "Popular and Secular Music in England"; M. Sahlin, "Étude sur la carole médiévale" (Ph.D. diss., University of Uppsala, 1940); R. H. Robbins, "Processional," *Studies in Philology* 66 (1959): 559–582; Roger Bowers, "Trinity College, MS O.3.58," in *Cambridge Music Manuscripts: 900–1700,* ed. Iain Fenlon (Cambridge: University of Cambridge Press, 1982), 88–90; idem, ed. *Music in Medieval and Early Modern Europe: Patronage, Sources, and Texts* (Cambridge: Cambridge University Press, 1981), 1–19; and John Caldwell, "Relations between Liturgical and Vernacular Music in Medieval England," *Music in the Mediaeval English Liturgy: Plainsong and Mediaeval Music Society Centennial Essays*, eds. S. Rankin and D. Hiley (Oxford: Clarendon Press, 1993), 285–93.

3. R. H. Robbins has categorized the manuscripts in which secular lyrics of the fourteenth and fifteenth centuries appear in *Secular Lyrics of the XIVth and XVth centuries,* 2nd ed. (Oxford: Clarendon Press, 1961). Many of these include carols.

4. Scholars have studied individual manuscripts or groups of manuscripts in this manner, but have not compiled an overview of the entire body of carol manuscripts. See especially Greene, *Early English Carols*, cxviii.

5. Ibid. According to Greene, the phrase "popular by destination" refers to texts which are "designed to appeal to an audience including people of scant formal education and social refinement."

6. For a complete list, see P. Catherwood, "Carol," in *Die Musik in Gegenwart und Geschichte: allgemeine Enzyklopädie der Musik*, 2nd ed., gen. ed. Ludwig Finscher (Kassel: Bärenreiter, 1994–), Tome 1, Bd. 2, 460–62.

7. It has been argued that the unison sections within a few polyphonic carols point to a monophonic origin for these polyphonic carol tunes (Stevens, "Carol"). However, this may only show that the performers were accustomed to, and perhaps more comfortable with, monophonic singing in general and that polyphony of any sort was the exception. It does not argue conclusively for or against a monophonic predecessor for the polyphonic carol.

8. Oxford, Bodley 26 (s. xiv) and ULL 657 (s. xv$^{med.}$) contain the same poem, but the latter has no burden.

9. See Andrew Wathey, *Music in the Royal and Noble Households in Late Medieval England: Studies of Sources and Patronage* (New York: Garland, 1989) for a discussion of polyphonic manuscripts in the possession of parish churches.

10. BL Addit. 5665.

11. Bowers, "Trinity College, MS O.3.58," 88.

12. Ashmole 1393 is neatly copied by a professional clerical hand, while BL Addit. 5666 is copied somewhat haphazardly by an amateur collector. Of course, books may have been used by one singer at a time to learn the part or by a musician teaching others, rather than by multiple singers in actual group sight-reading or performance.

13 It must be noted carefully that this is only one carol, found in a single Franciscan sermon extant in two manuscripts (see n. 8 above), out of a total of more than five hundred carols. No theory of the widespread popular usage of the carol can be based on this evidence.

14. Bukofzer, "Popular and Secular Music in England"; see also Richard L. Greene, ed., *The Lyrics of the Red Book of Ossory*, Medium Aevum Monographs, New Series, 5 (Oxford: Blackwell for the Society for the Study of Medieval Languages and Literature, 1974), iii–iv: "the Bishop of Ossory has made these songs for the vicars of the cathedral church, for the priests, and for his clerks to be sung on the important holidays and at celebrations in order that their throats and mouths, consecrated to God, may not be polluted by songs which are lewd, secular, and associated with revelry and since they are trained singers, let them provide themselves with suitable tunes according to what these sets of words require." This is to be paralleled on the continent.

15. E. B. Fitzmaurice and A. G. Little, eds., *Materials for the History of the Franciscan Province of Ireland, A.D. 1230–1450* (Manchester: The University of Manchester Press, 1920), xxiv, xxvi.

16. Greene, *Ossory,* suggests that the concordance for "Maid in the Moor Lay" comes from Coggeshall, Essex.

17. The English and French lines which precede some lyrics may indicate the name of a tune.

18. John Moorman, *A History of the Franciscan Order from Its Origins to the Year 1517* (London: A. and C. Black, 1976), 364.

19. CUL Ee.1.12 (ca. 1492). Eventually the Canterbury community of which Ryman was a member became Observant in 1498 (*after* the 1492 colophon in the manuscript).

20. *Calendar of Entries in the Papal Registers Relating to Great Britain and Ireland: Papal Letters*, xvii, part 1, ed. Anne Fuller (Dublin: Irish Manuscripts Commission, 1994), 82, entry 136.

21. Kele copied one of the carols; another, earlier carol, not by Ryman, appears in four other manuscripts. For an alternative viewpoint, see David Jeffrey, "James Ryman and the Fifteenth-century Carol," in *Fifteenth-Century Studies: Recent Essays*, ed. R. F. Younger (Hamden, Conn.: Yale University Press, 1984), 303–320.

22. Two fourteenth-century Franciscan collections illustrate the use of the carol in sermons, Bodley 26 (one carol) and NLS Advocates 18.7.21 (four carols).

23. Eamon Duffy, *The Stripping of the Altars: Traditional Religion in England, ca. 1400–1580* (New Haven, Conn.: Yale University Press, 1992), 11–205 (work of the Church), and 209–298 (devotional lives of laity).

24. Balliol 354.

25. Duffy, *The Stripping of the Altars*, 259.

26. Ibid., 45.

27. Sarum is an (inaccurate) abbreviation of the Latin *Sarisburiensis*, or Salisbury. The Sarum Rite is particularly associated with Salisbury Cathedral, but was then widely used throughout England.

28. Lay devotional use: xiv$^{1/2}$: BL, Harley 2253; xv$^{\text{med.}}$: BL, Cotton Titus A. XXVI and Cotton Vitellus D. XII; xv$^{2/2}$: Oxf. Laud. Misc. 601, Porkington 10, Edinburgh, Adv. 19.3.1. Ecclesiastical devotional use: xiii–xiv$^{\text{med.}}$: Oxf., Bodley 26; xiv$^{\text{ex.}}$–xv$^{\text{in.}}$: BL Harley 7358, BL Harley 2380; xv$^{1/4}$: ULL 657; xv$^{2/4}$: Oxf. Douce 302; xv$^{\text{med.}}$: BL Harley 275, TCC O.9.38; xv: TCC O.7.31 (carols, xvi); xv$^{2/2}$: Oxf. Eng. Poet. E.1; xv$^{4/4}$: Manchester, JRL Lat. 395.

29. E.g., Charles Ross, *The Wars of the Roses: A Concise History* (London: Thames and Hudson, 1976), 175: "This was an age of steadily advancing vernacular culture, expressing itself in the ballads, lyrics, carols and play cycles popular with the ordinary people, in the histories, chronicles, and didactic treatises favoured by the merchants, and in the chivalric romances now increasingly being translated into English from their original French and Burgundian versions, enjoyed by the court and the nobility."

30. Duffy, *The Stripping of the Altars*, 214. Rubrics appear in: Oxf. Douce 302, Oxf. Laud Misc. 683, Dublin TC 432, and BL Addit. 5665. Crosses appear in: NLS Adv. 18.7.21, CGCC 383, BL Egerton 3307 (not with carol booklet), and BL Cotton Titus A XXVI (indicates the reversal of stanzas).

31. TCC O.7.31.

32. See Robbins, *Secular Lyrics*, xxviii–xxx.

33. Epiphany: BL Sloane 2593 (xv$^{1/2}$), Oxf., Eng. Poet. E.1 (1492), BL Harley 541 (s. xv; no burden); Lullaby: Oxf., Douce 137 (1822), *The Good Christmas Box* (1847), *Popular Carols* (1908), BL Sloane 2593 (xv$^{1/2}$), NLS Adv. 18.7.21. (1372), BL Harley 2380 (xv$^{1/2}$), CUL 5943 (xv$^{\text{in.}}$); Five Joys: Oxf., Eng. Poet.E.1 (1492), Balliol 354 (xv$^{1/2}$).

34. Advent: Douce 302 (xv$^{1/2}$); Nativity: Eng. Poet e.1 (1492; 2 carols), BL Royal 20.A.1 (xv$^{1/2}$), Balliol 354 (xvi), Ashmole 189 (xvi); St. Thomas: CGCC 383 (xv$^{1/2}$); Epiphany: Douce 302, Balliol 354 (2 carols), Porkington 10 (xv$^{2/2}$), CSJC S.54 (xv$^{1/2}$), Eng. Poet. E.1; Lullaby: CSJC S.54, Eng. Poet. E.1; Passion: NLS 18.7.21 (xiv), BL 31042 (xv$^{2/2}$), Eng. Poet. E.1, Kele (xvi); BVM: Selden B.26 (xv$^{1/2}$), Eng. Poet. E.1, Balliol 354; Annunciation: TCC O.3.58 (xv$^{1/2}$), Selden B.26, Balliol 354; Moral counsel: Eng. Poet.E.1; Balliol 354; Women: BL Harley 7358.

35. Devotional activities were one form of leisure pursuit at the time. Today's division of the two activities should not be projected anachronistically onto the fifteenth century.

36. Advent: BL Sloane 2593; New Year: TCC O.3.58 (xv$^{1/2}$), Selden B.26 (xv$^{1/2}$); Epiphany: BL Sloane 2593, Balliol 354 (xvi); BVM: Balliol 354; Five Joys: Balliol 354.

37. Eamon Duffy shows that most of the medieval world viewed life in terms of the liturgical cycle.

38. Cambridge students often stayed on within East Anglia during their working lives. If they were among those who heard or performed polyphonic carols in college gatherings, they may have helped to continue the fashion in the region.

39. David Fallows, "Radio News," *Early Music News*, February 1993, 16.

John Newton

Beyond "Amazing Grace"

MEL R. WILHOIT

The Gospel Music Hall of Fame is really more of a concept than a tangible entity. Unlike the Baseball Hall of Fame in Cooperstown, New York, or the Rock and Roll Hall of Fame in Cleveland, Ohio, where a visitor can actually see the memorabilia of the honorees, the Gospel Music Hall of Fame is more of an honor and recognition by members of the Gospel Music Association. Inductees are included by virtue of having made significant contributions to the world of gospel music. Names of inductees include Virgil Stamps, Bill and Gloria Gaither, Mahalia Jackson, and Anglican preacher and hymnist John Newton![1]

Although this eighteenth-century cleric and hymn writer appears to be a strange bedfellow among other Gospel Music Hall of Fame notables such as Mosie Lister and J. D. Sumner, there is an obvious reason for Newton's inclusion: his universally-known autobiographical hymn, "Amazing Grace," which will undoubtedly remain forever bound to the hymn tune NEW BRITAIN.[2]

The song achieved pop music status in 1970 via Judy Collins with her folk-style rendition from the album *Whales and Nightingales*.[3] A year later, a most unusual bagpipe version of the tune performed by the Royal Scots Dragoon Guards also scored high on the charts. Then, in 1972, Aretha Franklin and James Cleveland recorded the song in a soul-styled version that would become closely associated with this hymn on an album appropriately titled *Amazing Grace.* (As Newton's collaborator and friend, William Cowper, has reminded us: "God moves in a mysterious way, His wonders to perform!")

While American revivalist groups had been singing the hymn for generations, by the 1970s it had caught on with the public at large and achieved such status that even the more staid liturgical and high-church folks could hardly issue a new hymnal without its inclusion. The intervening years saw little decrease in the song's fame. In 1994, journalist Bill Moyers hosted a PBS documentary entitled *Amazing Grace* featuring the hymn's manifold incarnations and celebrating the wide degree of its popularity. Over the last few decades it has also become associated with funerals; thus, after the World Trade Center bombing in 2001 and the massive loss of life that accompanied it, "Amazing Grace" was constantly broadcast on the airwaves in tandem with almost every funeral or memorial service.[4] One could make a strong case that this hymn is so well known as to be an unofficial national song (perhaps much as "Guide me, O Thou great Jehovah" was at one time in Wales). And on that hymn alone rests Newton's fame—at least in the popular sphere.

It is interesting to observe that, contrary to accepted opinion, Newton's congregation would never have sung "Amazing Grace" to the tune NEW BRITAIN, for the tune was an American folk melody that was not coupled with Newton's hymn until William Walker facilitated the happy marriage in his *Southern Harmony* of 1835.[5] It is also interesting to note that hymnologists writing before the middle of the twentieth century neither admired Newton's hymn nor recognized it as important.[6]

Of course, students of hymnology realize that Newton has provided a host of once-respected and well-loved hymns that have rightly elevated him to the rank of a major hymn writer. These include "Glorious things of Thee are spoken," "How sweet the name of Jesus sounds," "May the grace of Christ our Savior," and "Safely through another week." Newton also penned a stirring account of his life in 1764, *An Authentic Narrative of Some Remarkable and Interesting Particulars in the Life of* ***,[7] *Communicated in a Series of Letters to the Rev. T. Haweis,* that has kept his fame and work alive, long after most other contemporary hymnwriters have all but been forgotten. A Newton well beyond "Amazing Grace" and the *Narratives*, however, may be found in the labor of love that he designed for his first congregation at Olney in England, a work entitled *Olney Hymns, in Three Books*, one of the most important hymn collections of all time.[8]

Olney Hymns has been widely studied and much admired, so this investigation will not focus primarily upon analyzing the collection nor attempting to shed new light on it. Rather, it will reflect and share this hymn lover's delight after having discovered the humble pastor and poet in his daily rounds.

Newton went to the village of Olney in Buckinghamshire in 1764 as a lowly curate. Erik Routley succinctly described the position as "a now defunct order in the Church of England which in effect meant the burden of parish work without the usual sources of clerical emolument."[9] Newton's lowly ministerial estate resulted in part from his lacking credentials from Oxford or Cambridge and from his suspected sympathies with nonconformists and Wesleyan "enthusiasm." At Olney, John Pollock related in *Amazing Grace: John Newton's Story*:

> Newton quickly won his parishioners' love. Unlike many rural clergy of the day he visited them frequently in their sickness and their health and regarded himself as their servant. He was no coldly distant scholar or idle sprig of gentry but a jolly sea captain turned parson; deeply serious in teaching and aims, something of the quarter-deck about him, but larding his sermons with anecdotes and nautical allusions, and his conversations with quaint sayings and touches of fun. He seldom wore clerical dress on weekdays, preferring to visit the sick in his old sea jacket . . . .[10]

Although lacking in pulpit eloquence, Newton's folksy preaching and personal concern for his spiritual flock filled the small church to overflowing, and a balcony was soon built. In addition to regular Sunday services, Newton conducted weekly preaching and prayer services as well as children's meetings that were eventually held in the great room of the Great House, a previously abandoned mansion on a nearby estate. For these meetings, the popular pastor often produced a hymn that both taught and personified the spiritual aim of his sermon. Yet, as Madeleine Forell Marshall and Janet Todd observed in *English Congregational Hymns in the Eighteenth Century*, these hymns were not arid, didactic polemics, for they reflected Newton's very concept of God's cosmos and Newton's place in it.

> The impulse that led Newton to see himself as God's illustration of his grace for the benefit of all people also inclined Newton to magnify all experience to mythic proportions. He projected on a large screen, as it were, the imposing oversize figures of Satan, Olney, Britain, and the preacher. Personal redemption, daily life at Olney, and current international events are all on the same scale, all signs of divine purpose and essentially no different from the experience recorded in the Old and New Testaments.[11]

In 1779 Newton published *Olney Hymns*, a collection of 348 hymns resulting from the combined efforts of Newton and his friend William Cowper, whose best-known contributions to this volume were "Oh, for a closer walk with God" and "God moves in a mysterious way." Unfortunately, during much of the compiling of the volume Cowper was ill, so Newton provided 282 hymns, the majority of the collection's contents. Although *Olney Hymns* contains the contributions upon which Newton's reputation rests, it also contains numerous hymns that now seem inappropriate for congregational singing because of either their highly personal or topical nature. Yet such hymns provide a fascinating insight into the mind and heart of a gifted hymn writer and beloved pastor whose storied life would undoubtedly make an epic movie if faithfully depicted on screen.

The hymnal is organized in three sections, or books. Book I contains hymns suggested by specific passages in the Scriptures and is arranged in the order of the books from the Old and New Testaments. "Amazing Grace" appears as hymn XLI under the heading of 1 Chronicles with the citation, "Faith's Review and Expectation. Chap. xvii. 16, 17." "How sweet the name of Jesus sounds" appears as hymn LVII in correspondence with Song of Solomon 1:3. Many of these poems are sermon-hymns wherein Newton sets forth a Scriptural passage in verse and then makes a spiritual application for his flock.

The second book contains occasional hymns suited to particular seasons or suggested by unusual events. Entitled "On occasional Subjects," Book II is organized into four sections: "Seasons," "Ordinances," "Providences," and "Creation." It is from this section that a number of fascinating hymns are found. The first selection under "Providences," for instance, is subtitled "On the commencement of hostilities in America." It begins:

1. The gath'ring clouds, with aspect dark,
  A rising storm presage;
Oh! to be hid within the ark,
  And shelter'd from its rage!

2. See the commission'd angel frown![12]
  That vial in his hand,
Fill'd with fierce wrath, is pouring down
  Upon our guilty land!

Two items seem of immediate interest. One is that a lowly curate in a backwater village should have much knowledge of, or interest in, the empire's distant politics. Second is the ominous tone of the initial stanzas alluding to the angel of Revelation who seemed poised to judge England for some unspecified guilt.[13] Newton continues:

3. Ye saints, unite in wrestling pray'r,
  If yet there may be hope;
Who knows but Mercy yet may spare,
  And bid the angel stop?[14]

4. Already is the plague begun,[15]
  And fir'd with hostile rage;
Brethren, by blood and int'rest one,
  With brethren now engage.

Certainly these are odd sounding expressions to be coming from the pen of a loyal Englishman and a minister of the Anglican state church. Yet he continues:

> 5. Peace spreads her wings, prepar'd for flight,
> And war, with flaming sword,
> And hasty strides draws nigh, to fight
> The battles of the LORD.

From both the poetry and the organization of this hymn within the collection, it becomes clear that Newton perceived the conflict with the colonies as more than just a political squabble with some recalcitrant members of the British Empire. It clearly possessed spiritual dimensions. The coming war was, to Newton, a sign or warning of God's judgment concerning sinful Britain, a picture he painted in the hymn's eighth stanza:

> 8. May we, at least, with one consent,
> Fall low before the throne;
> With tears the nation's sins lament,
> The churches [*sic*], and our own.

One of the nation's sins that had been increasingly troubling Newton while at Olney was that of the slave trade. It was a business he knew all too well, having made his living at it before, and for sometime after, his conversion. But by the time of the "hostilities in America," Newton was fast becoming convinced of the slave trade's evil nature. He had begun to doubt its moral lawfulness as early as 1764 with the publication of his memoirs concerning his life as a slaver, but he did not yet attack it publicly. By 1776 Newton had read John Wesley's attack on the slave trade, and by the time Newton removed to his London parish, he was becoming quite vocal in his opposition. "My heart shudders that I was ever engaged in it."[16]

Then, in 1785, he met secretly with the young William Wilberforce, member of Parliament, who had requested to see Newton for spiritual counsel. The two became close friends, with Newton taking every advantage to convince Wilberforce of the need to abolish the slave trade. Although Newton's pleas did not bear fruit for another two decades, he was among the strongest voices in demanding an end to what he viewed as one of the nation's sins.[17]

Within a year of penning "On the Commencement of Hostilities in America," Newton wrote to a friend:

> I have lately read Robertson's History of Charles V., which, like most other histories, I consider as a comment upon those passages of Scripture which teach us the depravity of man, the deceitfulness of the heart, the ruinous effects of sin, and the powerful, though secret rule of divine providence, moving, directing, controlling the designs and actions of men . . . to the accomplishment of His own purposes, both of mercy and judgment.
>
> What an empty phantom do the great men of the world pursue, while they wage war with the peace of mankind, and butcher . . . perhaps hundreds of thousands, to maintain the shadow of authority over distant nations, whom they can reach with no other influence than that of oppression and devastation. But when we consider those who are sacrificed to their ambition, as justly suffering for their sins, then heroes and conquerors appear in their proper light, and worthy to be classed with *earthquakes and pestilences* [emphasis mine] as instruments of divine judgment.
>
> We are fallen into a state of gross idolatry, and self is the idol we worship.[18]

These opinions seem quite astounding to say the least. It seems probable from Newton's comments that he was not so concerned with the plight of the colonists as he was in perceiving this or any conflict as a judgment of God on the people. One cannot help but wonder what conversations Newton might have had on the subject with his friend and benefactor, the Earl of Dartmouth, who was one of the few Evangelicals in a high position of government, acting as King George III's secretary of state for the colonies at the war's commencement.[19]

Continuing in Book II under the subheading of "Providences," a group of seven hymns is listed as "Fast-Day Hymns." Two of these are of special interest. The first is entitled "On the earthquake." The date given is September 8, 1775.

> 1. Altho' on massy pillars built,
> The earth has lately shook;
> It trembled under Britain's guilt
> Before its Maker's look.

One will remember from Newton's letter quoted earlier that such phenomena were interpreted much differently than such occurrences would be today, for Newton saw such "natural occurrences" as God warning sinners in His great mercy:

> 3. But mercy spar'd us while it warn'd,
> The shock is felt no more;
> And mercy, now, alas! is scorn'd
> By sinners, as before.

Or meting out judgment:

4. But if these warnings prove in vain,
   Say, sinner, canst thou tell,
 How soon the earth may quake again,
   And open wide to hell?

5. Repent before the Judge draws nigh;
   Or else when he comes down,
 Thou wilt in vain for earthquakes cry,
   To hide thee from his frown.

The last three stanzas contrast the earlier picture of a quaking earth with the sure foundation for the believer who trusts in an all-controlling God. The final stanza concludes:

8. JESUS, your Shepherd, LORD, and Chief
   Shall shelter you from ill,
 And not a worm or shaking leaf
   Can move, but at his will.

One wonders how Newton's poetic expression of his theology conformed to his scientific understanding of the world around him. He was undoubtedly familiar with the work of another Newton (this one being Isaac) who had helped to change not only the way man thought about his world but also the way man thought about God. Slowly but certainly the concept of God, among even the most pious, was changing from a view of One who arbitrarily ruled a perplexing world (of thunder, earthquakes, or plagues) to One who was the designer of an orderly and discernable world. This in no way meant that God could not or did not use war or natural disasters as warnings or chastisements, but it did eventually mean that, as the natural laws behind certain events became more fully understood, a supernatural explanation of those same events became minimized in sermon and song. (By the nineteenth century, even highly pietistic gospel songs such as "All the way my Savior leads me" or "God Will Take Care of You" were more likely to stress God's provision and care during perilous times rather than see such events as God's warning or judgment. Although accident or disaster came to be seen as simply a normal part of the natural world in which a believer lived, the Christian could still rely on supernatural support or care from the One who still controlled—in some naturalistic way—all things.) As for John Newton, the world he inhabited was clearly a cosmic canvas on which God revealed his works and will, with Newton as one of His most vivid interpreters.[20]

The second hymn of interest in this section is entitled "On the fire at Olney" and is dated September 22, 1777.

1. Wearied by day with toils and cares,
 How welcome is the peaceful night!
Sweet sleep our wasted strength repairs,
 And fits us for returning light.

3. 'Tis of the Lord that we can sleep
 A single night without alarms;
His eye alone our lives can keep
 Secure, amidst a thousand harms.

4. For months and years of safety past,
 Ungrateful, we, alas! have been;
Tho' patient long, he spoke at last,
 And bid the fire rebuke our sin.

Although Newton was much loved for his kindness and respected for his integrity of character, he had not managed to turn Olney from its sin into a paradise on earth. It still reflected much of the England that the artist Hogarth vividly depicted in his scathing paintings, "Gin Lane" and "The Rake's Progress." In addition, Newton also had his opponents when it came to reforming social practices such as traditional holiday feasting wherein public drunkenness and its attendant results were common. And as Newton later remarked, he had labored long enough at Olney "to bury the old crop, on which any dependence could be placed."[21]

Thus it was still a parish with plenty of sin to rebuke. Newton's poetic description of the fire itself resulted from either his vivid imagination or firsthand accounts by those present since he and Polly, his wife, had been "providentially called to London a few days before the fire."

5. The shout of fire! a dreadful cry,
 Imprest each heart with deep dismay,
While the fierce blaze and red'ning sky
 Made midnight wear the face of day.

6. The throng and terror who can speak?
 The various sounds that fill'd the air!
The infant's wail, the mother's shriek,
 The voice of blasphemy and pray'r!

A few days later, Newton described the details of the fire in a letter to a friend:

> The fire devoured twelve houses; and it was a mercy, and almost a miracle, that the whole town was not destroyed; which must, humanly speaking have been the case, had not the night been calm, as two-thirds of the buildings were thatched. No lives were lost, no person considerably hurt; and I believe the contributions of the benevolent will prevent the loss from being greatly felt. It was at the distance of a quarter of a mile from my house.[22]

These particulars found their way as well into his hymn's seventh stanza:

> 7. But pray'r prevail'd, and sav'd the town;
> The few, who lov'd the Saviour's name
> Were hear'd [*sic*], and mercy hasted down
> To change the wind, and stop the flame.

And just as Martin Luther could see God's hand and a spiritual lesson or truth behind nearly every event, so too could Newton summarize:

> 8. Oh, may that night be ne'er forgot!
> LORD, still encrease [*sic*] thy praying few!
> Were OLNEY left without a Lot,
> Ruin, like Sodoms' [*sic*], would ensue.

Although Newton clearly discerned God's hand at work in the fire, it is less clear how he interpreted subsequent events since he has left behind no hymn explaining a rather awkward postscript. After the fire, Newton suggested to the town's celebration committee that the annual "customary riotous, drunken bonfire orgy" that accompanied national Guy Fawkes Day be forgone for obvious safety reasons in a town full of thatched cottages. The committee agreed and requested Newton to serve notice at church.

Deprived of its annual release from restraint, a drunken mob blamed the messenger—Newton—and began marching towards the rectory, breaking windows and demanding money along the way. A horrified parishioner quickly rushed to inform the ex-sea captain who had certainly withstood more formidable foes in his adventurous past. But while Newton was determined to confront the lot, wife Polly appeared terrified as a reported forty to fifty men "full of fury and liquor" approached the house. Both her terror and implorations caused John to reconsider, and he was "forced to send an embassy and beg peace. A soft message, and a shilling to the captain of the mob, secured his protection" and all slept that night in safety.[23]

The fourth division of Book II is entitled "Creation" and contains numerous fascinating insights into the mind of the preacher and poet. A few examples will suffice to demonstrate both Newton's sense of poetic metaphor and keen spiritual insight.

Thunder.

1. When a black overspreading cloud
Has darkned [*sic*] all the air;
And peals of thunder roaring loud
Proclaim the tempest near.

2. Then guilt and fear, the fruits of sin,
The sinner oft pursue;
A louder storm is heard within,
And conscience thunders too.

8. Believers, you may well rejoice!
The thunders [*sic*] loudest strains
S[h]ould be to you a welcome voice,
That tells you, "JESUS REIGNS!"

Lightning in the night.

2. So light'ning in the gloom of night,
Affords a momentary day;
Disclosing objects full in sight,
Which soon as seen, are snatch'd away.

6. Just so, we by a glimpse discern
The glorious things within the vail;
That when in darkness, we may learn
To live by faith, till light prevail.

On the eclipse of the moon. July 30, 1776.

6. How punctually eclipses move,
Obedient to thy will!
Thus shall thy faithfulness and love,
Thy promises fulfill.

8. But lo! the hour draws near apace,
   When changes shall be o'er;
 Then I shall see thee face to face,
   And be eclips'd no more.

And finally, an amazingly penetrating description:

On dreaming.

1. When slumber seals our weary eyes,
   The busy fancy wakeful keeps;
 The scenes which then before us rise,
   Prove, something in us never sleeps.

2. As in another world we seem,
   A new creation of our own;
 All appears real, tho' a dream,
   And all familiar, tho' unknown.

4. What schemes we form, what pains we take!
   We fight, we run, we fly, we fall;
 But all is ended when we wake,
   We scarcely then a trace recall.

7. One thing, at least, and 'tis enough,
   We learn from this surprising fact;
 Our dreams afford sufficient proof,
 The soul, without the flesh, can act.

8. This life, which mortals so esteem,
   That many choose it for their all,
 They will confess, was but a dream,
   When 'waken'd by death's awful call.

There is a wonderful story about the young Isaac Watts, whose childhood conversation was "so annoyingly metrical that after various prohibitions against rhyming, his father started to whip him, whereupon the rhymester cried out through his tears:

O father, do some pity take,
And I will no more verses make."[24]

What further action Isaac's father took is not recorded, but perhaps he may have realized that his son's versifying was close to an involuntary reflex over which he had little control. Perhaps it was that way with Newton, who simply saw the most mundane things around him as natural opportunities to wax poetic or form another practical tool for the teaching and exhortation of his flock. Such was certainly the case when a tamed lion was brought to the Cherry Fair at Olney. As Newton recounted in a letter to a friend:

> The lion was wonderfully tame . . . obedient as a spaniel; yet the man told me he had his surly fits, when he durst not touch him. . . . I know and love my Keeper and sometimes watch His looks that I may learn His will. But oh! I have my surly fits too . . . as though I had forgotten all. I got a hymn out of this lion . . . .[25]

That hymn was number XCIII, "The Tamed Lion," under the "Creation" section of Book II.

By the time that *Olney Hymns* appeared in print in 1779, Newton had left the Olney congregation for St. Mary's, Woolnoth, in central London.[26] Unfortunately, there seems to be little record concerning congregational song at either Olney or St. Mary's during Newton's tenure. Newton's hymns are all the more interesting, however, because he wrote them for his congregation at a time when only metrical psalms were considered acceptable in the official worship services in the Church of England. Isaac Watts had produced grand hymns and psalm paraphrases earlier, but Watts was a Congregationalist or Independent and therefore hardly an immediate influence on the hegemonic state church. The Anglican Wesley brothers were also generating hymns for practically every occasion, but were widely dismissed within the established Church as "enthusiasts" operating on the religious fringe. Olney, on the other hand, was a small, rural parish not only with limited resources, but also undoubtedly with conservative ideas about music in worship. Such conservatism generally translated into a preference for the traditional practices of psalmody typical of the English parish church. This usually meant the absence of an organ since the psalms were typically sung *a cappella*. If any instruments were admitted, they were probably the popular barrel organ or the wind and string instruments of players who attempted to accompany the psalms from the gallery.

Exactly which psalms and/or tunes were sung in official worship at Olney is uncertain. During the 1700s, there developed a movement within the Anglican Church to assign certain psalms to specific days and services, but more often than not the psalms to which the members of the congregation raised their collective voices in worship were the personal choices of the clerk.[27] It was even theoretically possible to sing most of the psalms to a small handful of tunes that even the most untutored congregation could navigate week in and week out. But that raises the question of Newton's hymns and how he might have taught them to his parishioners.

First, Newton must have been acutely aware of the popular new models of hymnody so widespread among the nonconformists and the Methodists. In fact, Newton was often criticized for being too much at ease with those outside the official Church—visiting, entertaining, and supporting to various degrees their ministries. Congregationalists had long been singing Watts's hymns, and both John and Charles Wesley had apparently perfected the method of teaching new hymns on a regular basis to "class meetings" (informal preaching and teaching services much like Newton conducted in the Great House at Olney) and to large congregations meeting in homes, private chapels, or the open air.

Second, Newton—without knowing it—was in the midst of a paradigm shift in congregational worship practice that slowly but surely replaced the revered psalms of the "Old Version" (by Sternhold and Hopkins) and the "New Version" (by Tate and Brady) with "hymns of human composure" popularized by Watts, Wesley, Newton, and a host of Evangelical hymnwriters.[28] Perhaps without ever intending to do so, Newton hastened this shift within official Anglican worship by the publication of his *Olney Hymns.* As Louis Benson has observed:

> *Olney Hymns* is best understood as a revival hymn book. In its day it had the same welcome and popularity that *Gospel Hymns* of the Moody and Sankey revival had in ours. . . . It was the Evangelical theology put into rhyme for singing, but even more for reading and remembering. It became an Evangelical handbook, printed over and over in England and America, and it exerted an immense influence.[29]

Whether or not, and if so how, Newton may have employed the newly published *Olney Hymns* at his recent appointment to St. Mary's, Woolnoth, in the heart of London is unclear. The converted old slave trader must certainly have experienced significant culture shock as he proceeded from the penurious backwater of Olney to the sophistication of St. Mary's, especially as it related to public worship, for at St. Mary's there was already an established musical tradition boasting current trends. Some of these trends reflected Restoration ideas about music as they had trickled down from the lavish court of Charles II who, a century earlier, had supported extravagant and highly-public celebrations of music based upon continental models—all being a far cry from the more modest and private practices of music under the Puritan Commonwealth. Perhaps because the lord mayor of London attended St. Mary's—the lord mayor's official residence, Mansion House, could be found in that parish—the church had the resources and a reputation for better music than most. In 1700, it was one of only eighteen churches in the old City of London possessing an organ (dating from 1681),[30] though its role was generally limited to accompanying the metrical psalms and playing voluntaries for morning and evening prayer. However, in some of these churches enterprising organists had begun to ornament psalm tunes with turns, shakes, and interludes, eventually eclipsing the congregation's contribution altogether.

This may have been the case with one John Reading [Jr.] (ca. 1685–1764), a composer and organist educated under John Blow at the Chapel Royal. In 1700, he accepted positions as the organist at Dulwich College and as master of the choristers and singing teacher at Lincoln Cathedral. He later completed a nearly twenty-year tenure as organist at St. John's, Hackney, in Central London, where he composed numerous church compositions including anthems in the Italian style. His stay there was not without controversy, however. Parish records document "irregularities relating to the execution of his Office," specifically citing his "playing the Voluntary too long, and using persistently too light, Airy and Jyggy Tunes." In 1727, he was given three months' notice and forbidden any longer to play the parish instrument. Subsequently he moved to St. Mary's, Woolnoth, continuing as organist there until his death in 1764.[31] One can at least surmise from Reading's tenure, which predated Newton's by some fifteen years, that the music at St. Mary's was of a fairly progressive and sophisticated variety.

Reading was replaced by John Selby, who held the position until late 1771 when he immigrated to the colonies. It is unclear who then presided at the organ during Newton's early years in London, but in 1798 Thomas Busby took up the position. Busby was an extremely active composer, especially as it related to the theater. His most significant composition was music for Thomas Holcroft's *A Tale of Mystery*, purported to be the first English melodrama that enjoyed popularity both at home and abroad. Perhaps somewhat ironic and even troublesome to John Newton was Busby's *The Prophecy* of 1799, billed as the only oratorio composed in England during the last thirty years.[32]

Although Newton apparently approved of lavish music, including that for the theater, he clearly disapproved of Scripture being made into musical entertainment, as he believed Handel had done with *Messiah*. This is clear from a series of sermons he preached at St. Mary's beginning in 1783, a result of the widespread attention to the upcoming Handel Commemoration to be held at Westminster Abbey. For a series of fifty sermons, Newton selected and preached on the same Scripture texts that furnished the libretto for Handel's work. It is clear, however, from the fourth sermon in the series that Newton believed that employing Scripture in a theatrical setting trivialized God's Word to the extent that its hearers took no notion of its spiritual truth. Newton summarized his feelings about the unregenerate who ignorantly sang of God's warnings set to pretty tunes: "though I might admire the musical taste of these people, I should commiserate their insensibility."[33] One can only speculate what the outspoken Newton thought of his own organist, Busby, who not only composed religious oratorios but also sang tenor at the Handel Commemoration![34]

Whatever the musical situation may have been at St. Mary's, it is highly doubtful that Newton ever resurrected the majority of his topical hymns included in the *Olney* collection.[35] In fact, most of those hymns would have been quickly forgotten soon after their initial introduction, as the passage of time would have muted the relevance of any topical event as congregational song. Yet Newton must have believed them to be more than ephemeral, for he included them in a permanent collection that was intended as much for reading and meditation as it was for singing. And therein lies a vital key to comprehending the role of many topical or autobiographical hymns: while their value as corporate congregational song would have been highly limited apart from the specific events that inspired them, they retained great worth as hymns for reading and contemplation—a practice fairly common to the pious of that age.[36]

Today, nearly two hundred years after Newton, reading poetry is hardly in style, and the practice of contemplation has been lost in the rush to cram more productive activities into our schedules. In addition, the very definition of a hymn has often implicitly or explicitly required it to be sung. While Augustine of Hippo long ago defined a hymn as "praises to God with singing," The Hymn Society in the United States and Canada also currently seems to emphasize the sung nature of devotional poetry as it defines a hymn as "congregational song."[37]

However, if one experiences the autobiographical and topical hymns that Newton produced from a contemplative standpoint, they take on a completely different cast, providing occasion to consider the wonder of God's creation through Newton's spiritual eyes of faith. In fact, that was how I came to be amazed by their vibrancy of language and uniqueness of perspective. They have certainly provided me with an entirely new appreciation of both Newton and the God he was continually amazed to serve. Perhaps his epitaph, inscribed on a plaque at St. Mary's and on his tombstone at Olney, provides his most powerful hymn:

John Newton
Clerk
Once an Infidel and Libertine
A Servant of Slaves in Africa
Was
By the rich Mercy of Our Lord and Saviour
Jesus Christ
Preserved, Restored, Pardoned,
And Appointed to Preach the Faith
He had long labored to destroy.
S.D.G.

NOTES

1. Newton was inducted in 1982, sharing honors with the likes of B. B. McKinney, Lowell Mason, and Thomas A. Dorsey. Inductees for 2001 included the Rambos, Keith Green, and Elvis Presley! This particular Gospel Music Hall of Fame is run by the Gospel Music Association (http://www.gospelmusic.org). There is apparently a highly similar, albeit more recent (1995), rival, the International Gospel Music Hall of Fame and Museum (http://www.igmhf.org) in Detroit, which inducts a dozen or more worthies annually. As of this writing, Newton seems to have been temporarily overlooked by this group.

2. The tune has also been known as ST. MARY'S, GALLAHER, HARMONY GROVE, SYMPHONY, SOLON, REDEMPTION, and AMAZING GRACE. Jere V. Adams, ed., *Handbook to* The Baptist Hymnal (Nashville: Convention Press, 1992), 92.

3. Collins describes her relationship to this song in the Foreword of Steve Turner's *Amazing Grace: The Story of America's Most Beloved Hymn* (New York: Ecco [Harper Collins], 2002), a recent Newton biography.

4. The bagpipe version heard at many funerals, particularly for firefighters and police officers, has been credited to the plaintive version popularized by the Royal Scotts Dragoon Guards recording of 1971.

5. Harry Eskew and Hugh T. McElrath, *Sing with Understanding*, 2nd ed. (Nashville: Church Street Press, 1995), 184. The tune had been published as early as 1829, but with another text.

6. Louis F. Benson, *The English Hymn: Its Development and Use in Worship* (New York: George H. Dorna, 1915; rep. ed., Richmond, Va.: John Knox Press, 1962), 339, lists three of Newton's hymns as having lasting value; "Amazing Grace" is not among them. The same opinions are expressed in Maurice Frost, ed., *Historical Companion to* Hymns Ancient and Modern (London: William Clowes and Sons, 1962), 106, and Albert Edward Bailey, *The Gospel in Hymns: Backgrounds and Interpretations* (New York: Charles Scribner's Sons, 1950), 127–130.

7. First published anonymously.

8. *Olney Hymns, in Three Books: Book I. On select Texts of Scripture. Book II. On occasional Subjects. Book III. On the Progress and Changes of the Spiritual Life* (London: W. Oliver, 1779). Although both Newton and his friend William Cowper contributed to the collection, for all practical purposes, Newton was the editor/compiler.

9. Erik Routley, *A Panorama of Christian Hymnody* (Chicago: GIA Publications, 1979), 38.

10. John Pollock, *Amazing Grace: John Newton's Story* (San Francisco: Harper and Row, 1981), 154.

11. Madeleine Forell Marshall and Janet Todd, *English Congregational Hymns in the Eighteenth Century* (Lexington, Ky.: University of Kentucky Press, 1982), 102.

12. Newton's footnote reference: Revelation 16:1.

13. It is also interesting that Newton calls the colonies "America" in his heading to the hymn.

14. Newton's reference: 1 Samuel 24:16.

15. Newton's reference: Numbers 16:46.

16. John Newton, "Thoughts Upon the African Slave Trade" (London: printed for J. Buckland and J. Johnson, 1788).

17. Pollock, *Amazing Grace*, 173–75.

18. John Newton, *The Utterance of the Heart* (Grand Rapids: Baker Book House, 1979), 105, 107; a reprint of Morgan and Scott's edition of 1780, originally titled *Cardiphonia.*

19. Pollock, *Amazing Grace*, 149–50.

20. The great Lisbon earthquake of 1755 could not have been far from Newton's consciousness as he penned this theological explanation of the local tremor. The Lisbon quake has often been called the first modern disaster and elicited no end of disputations, both scholarly and popular, concerning its meaning and relevance. Of particular interest are the arguments supporting a naturalistic versus a supernatural perspective, reflecting the growing influence of Enlightenment thinkers such as Voltaire and the tensions created for those espousing a theological cosmogony.

21. John Newton, *The Life of the Rev. John Newton, Rector of St. Mary Woolnoth, London* (London: Religious Tract Society, n.d.), 111.

22. Newton, *The Utterance of the Heart*, 260.

23. Pollock, *Amazing Grace*, 167–68.

24. Bailey, *The Gospel in Hymns*, 46.

25. Pollock, *Amazing Grace*, 171.

26. The Olney parishioners certainly sang most of these hymns that grew out of Newton's Olney experiences. But they likely did so from loose-leaf copies or broadsides. Exactly how Newton was able to print and distribute new hymns as he produced them is unclear, especially considering the generally poor economic conditions of the parish.

27. Frost, *Historical Companion*, 103–104.

28. For a detailed account of this tectonic shift in congregational practices, see Frost's *Historical Companion*, especially chapters XIV–XVIII; one can also trace this development in Bailey's *The Gospel in Hymns* and in the definitive treatment by Benson in *The English Hymn.*

29. Louis F. Benson, *Studies of Familiar Hymns*, 2nd ser. (Philadelphia: Westminster Press, 1923), 134–35.

30. Nicholas Temperley, "London: Religious Institutions—Parish Churches," http://www.grovemusic.com (accessed August 1, 2002).

31. Susi Jeans and H. Diack Johnstone, "John Reading (ii)," http://www.grovemusic.com (accessed August 1, 2002).

32. Jamie C. Kassler and Linda Troost, "Thomas Busby," http://www.grovemusic.com (accessed August 1, 2002).

33. Newton, *The Life of the Rev. John Newton*, 122–24.

34. Kassler and Troost, "Thomas Busby."

35. Exceptions might have included popular topics such as the Lisbon earthquake. Newton apparently did not write a hymn on the Lisbon quake, but he did employ earth tremors at Olney as opportunities to press spiritual truths as he interpreted them and may well have resurrected earlier topical hymns as they became relevant to current events.

36. It was common to meditate upon both the Bible and a prayerbook (often bound together) or later, a hymnal.

37. Eskew and McElrath, *Sing with Understanding*, x.

Isaac Watts and the Shape-Note Tradition

HARRY ESKEW

Isaac Watts is widely acknowledged as the "Father of English Hymnody." It was he who developed a philosophy of congregational song that went beyond traditional metrical psalmody. Furthermore, he was the first to write a large body of hymns to become widely used in worship, both in Great Britain and in the American colonies. Anyone who has spent much time with the early singing-school tune books will find the hymns of Isaac Watts by far to be the most frequently used. When did Watts's psalms and hymns become widely used in singing-school tune books, and what factors led to their becoming a part of the shape-note tradition? This study will seek to provide at least some partial answers to these questions and directions for further inquiry.

Watts's Publications

Isaac Watts's first book of verse, his *Horae Lyricae* (1706), has been described as "a laboratory notebook of his early experiments with Christianized psalms and hymns" and as "the seed-plot of his mature work."[1] In 1709, a second edition of *Horae Lyricae* appeared. This and all subsequent editions omitted several Christianized psalms that had been included in the first edition. However, the second edition was nearly twice the size of the first.

Watts's two major collections for congregational singing are well known. In 1707, he published his hymnal, entitled *Hymns and Spiritual Songs*, dividing his hymns into three books, as indicated on the title page:

I. Collected from the Scriptures.
II. Compos'd on Divine Subjects.
III. Prepared for the Lord's Supper.

His first edition included a "Short Essay Toward the Improvement of Psalmody," which was not included in later editions. This essay constituted Watts's call for the reform of metrical psalmody.[2] Watts had published Christianized psalms as early as the first edition of his *Horae Lyricae* in 1706, but his crowning work in psalmody, which Watts seemed to regard as his *magnum opus* of congregational song, was his *Psalms of David Imitated in the Language of the New Testament*, published in 1719, some thirteen years after his *Horae Lyricae.*

It did not take long for the psalms and hymns of Watts to be reprinted in the American colonies. Watts's hymns were reprinted in Boston around 1720–1723. Even earlier, in 1715, a selection of twenty-two hymns by Watts had been published in Boston under the title, *Honey Out of the Rock.*[3] None other than Benjamin Franklin published the first American reprint of the *Psalms* from his Philadelphia press in 1729. As observed by hymnologist Louis Benson, this reprint "represents his admiration for Watts rather than any actual demand, since Franklin two years afterwards complained of its remaining unsold upon his shelves."[4] Benson lists twenty-nine American reprints of the *Psalms*, fourteen reprints of the *Hymns*, and four American reprints of the *Psalms* and *Hymns* together.[5] After the American declaration of independence from England in 1776, Watts's *Psalms* appeared in several American revisions, such as those of Mycall, Barlow, and Dwight. In a recent dissertation, Rochelle A. Stackhouse made a detailed study of these American revisions and included a list of numerous later editions published between 1781 and 1835.[6]

In her monumental study of the publishing history of Watts's *Hymns and Spiritual Songs*, Selma L. Bishop listed a growing number of editions published each decade or so in both Britain and America. She described this rapid increase, giving publication figures showing the annual average growth in these editions. Whereas the average ratio of publication rose from 0.50 to 6.46 yearly, the American annual rate alone leaped from 0.09 to 4.32. Such advances taken widely, Bishop noted, "indicate growing interest in Watts wherever he was known." Editions of *Hymns and Spiritual Songs*, printed in London, experienced instant reprinting in Boston, and vice versa. Bishop surmised, "[The] Cause of the rising rate in publication of the *Hymns and Spiritual Songs* was that all churches sang Watts; that all homes and most schools owned Watts's hymnals. New England children learned to read from Watts's hymnbooks."[7]

Watts's psalms and hymns were so popular that the introduction of new hymns took place by publishing them as supplements to Watts's *Psalms* and *Hymns*, bound in one volume. One of the best-known of these supplements was that of the London Baptist pastor, John Rippon, popularly known as "Rippon's Selection."[8] Published in London in 1787, it was reprinted in New York as early as 1792.[9] Another of the supplements to Watts's collections, compiled by James M. Winchell, pastor of the First Baptist Church of Boston, was known as "Winchell's Watts." In the same volume, after the psalms and hymns of Watts, Winchell attached *A Selection of More than Three Hundred Hymns, from the Most Approved Authors*

(1818).[10] As described by Benson, "'Winchell's Watts' attained, and for many years held, in New England a use so wide that it has been described as 'universal.'"[11]

Watts's Texts Enter Singing-School Tune Books

Not only were these collections of Watts's psalms and hymns popular in early America, his psalm and hymn texts also found their way into numerous singing-school tune books. This widespread acceptance of Watts's texts by the compilers of tune books was underscored in a recent communication which I received from the American musicologist, Karl Kroeger:

> . . . in the various editing projects I've undertaken, I've been aware of the popularity of Watts with American psalmodists from the very beginning. Billings's *New England Psalm-Singer* uses a number of Watts's hymns, and he continues to be the most important source of tune texts for Billings, Read, Holden, French, Holyoke, etc., on into the 19th century. Every other text source is very secondary to the popularity of Watts. (Tate and Brady's *New Version of the Psalms* is a distant second.) You'll find an enormous number of Watts's texts in all American tune books.[12]

I also asked Nym Cooke, another specialist in early American psalmody, which tune book was the first to include a significant number of texts by Watts. He responded:

> Certainly Read's *American Singing Book* of 1785, with 41 of its 48 metrical texts coming from Watts, is an early example of "Watts's domination." Is 28 of 61 metrical texts in Billings's *Singing Master's Assistant* "significant?" The runners-up here are Messrs. Tate and Brady with 11 texts, then Billings himself with 10.[13]

No New England composer-compiler paid a greater tribute to Watts than Samuel Holyoke of Massachusetts. Holyoke's tune book, *The Columbian Repository of Sacred Harmony*, was published in the first decade of the nineteenth century.[14] Benson described this book "as a colossal monument of the ascendency of Watts over the congregational praise of New England."[15] Holyoke's tune book of 496 pages includes a complete reprint of Watts's *Psalms of David Imitated* and his *Hymns and Spiritual Songs*, each set to music in four parts. Benson commented, "As an offering to New England choirs, unable to read at sight or to use so great a variety of music, it was ineffective from the first; but as a New England tribute to Dr. Watts its testimony remains unimpaired."[16]

Another source providing evidence of the pervasive presence of Watts's texts in early American tune books is Richard Crawford's monumental anthology,

The Core Repertory of Early American Psalmody.[17] In this volume Crawford includes 101 of the pieces of sacred music most often printed in America between 1698 and 1810. Of the 101 pieces included, 68 are settings of texts by Watts. These 68 include 45 of his psalms, 22 of his hymns, and one text from his *Horae Lyricae.* It is truly remarkable that 68 of the 101 most-often published pieces of sacred music in our country between 1698 and 1810 were settings of Watts's texts. Clearly Watts dominated early American psalmody long before the (nineteenth-century) advent of the shape-note tradition.

Watts Texts Enter the Shape-Note Tradition

The first system of shape notes to gain general acceptance was that found in *The Easy Instructor* of William Little and William Smith, published in 1801. As settlers moved toward the South and Middle West, shape-note tune books appeared in cities along the routes of travel. To the New England repertory of psalm and hymn tunes, fuging tunes, and anthems was added an additional category—hymns based upon oral tradition that we now call folk tunes. The first shape-note tune book to contain a significant number of folk hymns that were reprinted in subsequent collections was John Wyeth's *Repository of Sacred Music, Part Second*, published in Harrisburg, Pennsylvania, in 1813.[18] After 1813, shape-note tune books were published primarily in three geographical areas. The first was the Middle West, from Cincinnati to St. Louis. The second was from Philadelphia through the Shenandoah Valley of Virginia. And the third was further south, including Tennessee, South Carolina, and Georgia.

The tune books of the Shenandoah Valley are illustrative of the dominance of Watts in the early shape-note tradition. Ananias Davisson's *Kentucky Harmony* of 1816, published in Harrisonburg in the heart of the Shenandoah Valley, was the first Southern shape-note tune book. Of 137 texts for which authors have been identified in its various editions, 124 were either from Watts or Rippon. In Davisson's *Supplement to the Kentucky Harmony* (1820), 28 of the 88 texts with known authors are by Watts. Although Davisson's *Supplement* was designed for use by Methodists, only two texts were found to be by Wesley, as compared with 28 by Watts. The one Shenandoah Valley tune book which continues in use today is *Genuine Church Music*, compiled by the Mennonite Joseph Funk. Funk, unlike most of his fellow compilers, was careful to indicate the sources of his texts. In the first edition of 1832, he noted 48 texts from Watts's *Psalms* and 47 from Watts's *Hymns*, for a total of 95 texts by Watts. Clearly Watts was number one among the authors of texts found in early shape-note collections of the Shenandoah Valley.[19]

Watts's texts also dominated the shape-note tune books of other areas, such as the Middle South and the Middle West. The earliest Tennessee shape-note tune book was Alexander Johnson's *Tennessee Harmony*, published in 1818, and a later representative Tennessee tune book is William Caldwell's *Union Harmony* of 1837. In the *Tennessee Harmony*, 83 of 214 texts, or 39 percent, are by Watts; and in the *Union Harmony*, 59 out of 153 texts, again 39 percent, were penned by Watts. The leading shape-note tune book of the Middle West was Allen Carden's *Missouri Harmony*, first published in 1820 and subsequently appearing in nine editions plus numerous reprints through at least 1857.[20] In the ninth edition (1846), some 83 of 214 texts, or approximately 39 percent, are once again by Watts.

Watts's Texts in The Southern Harmony *and* The Sacred Harp

In the Deep South during the period prior to the Civil War, probably the most popular shape-note tune book was *The Southern Harmony* by William Walker of Spartanburg, South Carolina. First published in 1835, it went through five editions, the last issued in 1854. Walker indicated in 1866 that it had sold about six hundred thousand copies.[21] *Southern Harmony* has been used in an annual singing in Benton, Kentucky, for well over a century. The 1854 edition was reprinted several times in the twentieth century.[22]

Another Deep South tune book of this period is *The Sacred Harp*, compiled by Benjamin Franklin White and Elisha J. King in western Georgia. First published in 1844, it appeared in two further editions before the Civil War, one in 1850 and the other in 1859. King died shortly before *The Sacred Harp* was published, but White lived until 1879, fostering the spread of his tune book through singing conventions and serving on revision committees. Today *The Sacred Harp* is the most widely used of the early shape-note tune books, not only in the South, but in singings from coast to coast. The most recent revisions of *The Sacred Harp* were published in 1991 and 1992.[23]

A survey of the texts by Isaac Watts in the three early editions of *The Sacred Harp* and the first five editions of *The Southern Harmony* shows that Watts is well represented, especially in the three editions of *The Sacred Harp*, in which the totals of Watts's texts increased over the course of these editions from 47 to 68 and then to 72. Although somewhat lower, the totals in *The Southern Harmony* nevertheless grew from 35 in the first edition to 61 in the fifth (1854) edition.

In the case of *The Southern Harmony*, Walker gave on his title page the names of the hymnals for whose texts he sought to provide music. In addition to Watts's *Psalms* and *Hymns*, he listed an unidentified "Methodist Hymn Book" plus several words-only Baptist hymnals then in use in the South. These included: *Mercer's Cluster* (3rd ed., 1817) by the Georgia Baptist pastor, Jesse Mercer[24]; *The Choice* (3rd ed., 1830) by the Virginia Baptist pastor, William Dossey; *Dover Selection* (1828), compiled for the Dover Baptist Association in Virginia by Andrew Broaddus; and *Baptist Harmony* (1834) by the South Carolina Baptist pastor, Staunton Burdett. Each of these Baptist hymn compilations of the South contains a significant number of texts authored by Watts. To point out just one example, Dossey's *The Choice* includes 79 texts by Watts. Certainly Walker must have recognized the widespread acceptance of Watts's texts when he chose them for *The Southern Harmony*.

Conclusions

What conclusions can we draw from this overview of the transmission of Watts's texts in early American tune books and the later shape-note tradition? First, the popularity and general acceptance of Watts's psalms and hymns were such that it was only natural that tune book compilers should select his texts for their publications. Furthermore, the tune book tradition was nondenominational, so publishers sought texts with appeal beyond a single denomination. As observed by Nicholas Temperley in his *Hymn Tune Index*,

> Publishers were not disposed to reduce their market by including controversial or narrowly denominational texts, but the "sacred" character of the book was maintained for the sake of custom and decorum. The widely known psalms and hymns of Watts or Tate and Brady suited the purpose well, and supplied the texts for a majority of tunes in these books.[25]

Another conclusion is that Watts continued to be widely accepted even though new hymns were introduced. When supplements to Watts were published by Rippon, Winchell, and others, they printed both Watts's *Psalms* and *Hymns*, known as the "Watts Entire," along with their selection of new hymn texts, all bound together in one volume. One of the greatest indicators of the acceptance of Watts's texts in early American tune books is the fact that the most frequently printed tunes were often settings of Watts's texts—as evidenced by the 68 out of 101 pieces included by Richard Crawford in his *Core Repertory of Early American Psalmody*. Clearly the dominance of Watts's psalms and hymns continued in the shape-note tradition of the early nineteenth century, as the tune books of the Shenandoah Valley compiled by Ananias Davisson and Joseph Funk, as well as those of Tennessee and Missouri, attest. Furthermore, Watts's texts continued to occupy a leading place in Deep South tune books during the decades before the Civil War. Illustrative of this are the five editions of *The Southern Harmony* and the three editions of *The Sacred Harp* published prior to 1860. Although recent editions of *The Sacred Harp* have not been included in this study, the 1991 revision has a far greater number of Watts' texts—144—than the earlier editions. Quite probably *Sacred Harp* singers are performing even more hymns by Watts today than their predecessors did in earlier times.

There is a great need for more research on Isaac Watts and his impact upon the singing school tradition and upon congregational singing in general. There is no published index to the complete hymns of Watts, including those published in *Horae Lyricae, Hymns and Spiritual Songs, Divine Songs, Psalms of David Imitated*, and his volumes of sermons.[26] A complete index to Watts's hymns would certainly facilitate serious research in this field. There is also a need to study further the impact of Watts upon early American psalmody, including the shape-note tradition.

One final observation: although singers performing from *The Southern Harmony* and *The Sacred Harp* and other shape-note tune books sing texts from a variety of hymn writers, without Watts they would have far less to sing. In terms of texts set to music in the early American shape-note tradition, Isaac Watts reigns supreme!

NOTES

1. Harry Escott, *Isaac Watts, Hymnographer: A Study of the Beginnings, Development, and Philosophy of the English Hymn* (London: Independent Press, 1962), 5.
2. Ibid., 175.
3. David W. Music, "Isaac Watts in America Before 1729," *The Hymn* 50 (January 1999), 32.
4. Louis F. Benson, *The English Hymn: Its Development and Use in Worship*, rep. ed. (Richmond: John Knox Press, 1962), 162. An alternate interpretation is that Franklin may have thought the psalter would sell well only to find out otherwise over time.
5. Ibid., 163.
6. Stackhouse's dissertation has been published as *The Language of Psalms in Worship: American Revisions of Watts' Psalter*, Drew Studies in Liturgy, 4 (Lanham, Md., and London: The Scarecrow Press, 1997). See esp. pp. 133–139.
7. Selma L. Bishop, *Isaac Watts's Hymns and Spiritual Songs (1707): A Publishing History and a Bibliography* (Ann Arbor, Mich.: The Pierian Press, 1974), ix–x.
8. Its full title is *A Selection of Hymns from the Best Authors, Intended to be an Appendix to Dr. Watts' Psalms and Hymns* (London: Thomas Wilkins, 1787).
9. Benson, *The English Hymn*, 144–45 and 163.
10. James M. Winchell, *An Arrangement of the Psalms, Hymns and Spiritual Songs of the Rev. Isaac Watts, to which is added a supplement, being a selection of more than three hundred hymns from the most approved authors, including all the hymns of Dr. Watts,*

adapted to public and private worship, not published in the common editions (Boston: James Loring, 1818).

11. Rollin H. Neale, *An Address Delivered on the Two Hundredth Anniversary of the Organization of the First Baptist Church, Boston, June 7, 1865* (Boston: Gould and Lincoln, 1865), 38, cited in Benson, *The English Hymn*, 204.

12. E-mail letter from Karl Kroeger to Harry Eskew, October 5, 2000.

13. E-mail letter from Nym Cooke to Harry Eskew, October 6, 2000.

14. Samuel Holyoke, *The Columbian Repository of Sacred Harmony* (Exeter, N.H.: n.d.).

15. Benson, *The English Hymn*, 172.

16. Ibid.

17. Richard Crawford, *The Core Repertory of Early American Psalmody*, 2 vols., Recent Researches in American Music, 11 and 12 (Madison, Wis.: A–R Editions, 1984).

18. This tune book has been reprinted with a new introduction by Irving Lowens (New York: Da Capo Press, 1964).

19. Harry Lee Eskew, "Shape-Note Hymnody in the Shenandoah Valley, 1816–1860" (Ph.D. dissertation, Tulane University, 1966), 31, 46, and 92.

20. Shirley Bean, Introduction to the reprint edition of Allen Carden's *Missouri Harmony*, 9th ed. [1846] (Lincoln: University of Nebraska Press, 1994), x–xiii.

21. William Walker, *The Christian Harmony* (Philadelphia: E. W. Miller and William Walker, 1867), iii.

22. The most recent reprint of the 1854 edition was published together with a musical anthology by the Benton singers on compact disc by the University of Kentucky Press in 1987.

23. These are: *The Sacred Harp* ([Bremen, Ga.]: Sacred Harp Publishing Co., 1991); and *The B. F. White Sacred Harp,* ed. W. M. Cooper (Samson, Ala.: Sacred Harp Book Company, 1992).

24. A recent study by Kay Norton focuses on the 1810 edition: *Baptist Offspring, Southern Midwife—Jesse Mercer's* Cluster of Spiritual Songs *(1810): A Study in American Hymnody*, Detroit Monographs in Musicology/Studies in Music, 34 (Warren, Mich.: Harmonie Park Press, 2002).

25. Nicolas Temperley, *The Hymn Tune Index*, 4 vols. (Oxford: Clarendon Press, 1998), 1:25.

26. Marcus Merrin of Arcadia University in Nova Scotia has compiled a database which seeks to include the first lines of every stanza of Watts's hymn texts. He reported to this writer in late 2002 that he lacks only a few obscure sources to complete his Watts hymn text database. He can be contacted at marcus.merrin@emptyair.com.

George Cook Sedwick and
A Selection of Hymns and Spiritual Songs *(1815)*

PAUL A. RICHARDSON

Only three copies survive of *A Selection of Hymns and Spiritual Songs*, published in 1815, in Fredericksburg, Virginia, by the firm of Green & Cady. The book's compiler is identified on the title page as "George C. Sedwick. Pastor of the Baptist church at Rock-Hill, Stafford Co., Virginia."[1] Both the compiler and the collection are engaging subjects.

The Compiler

George Cook Sedwick was born on November 3, 1785, in Calvert County, Maryland, to Joshua Sedwick [III] and Joshan Manning Sedwick.[2] In 1791, the family, consisting of the parents and five surviving children, moved to a farm in Frederick County, Maryland.[3] Joshua Sedwick died soon thereafter, and his widow married John Montgomery in 1792. George Sedwick's parents and step-father were members of the Protestant Episcopal Church.[4]

In 1802, George was indentured as a tailor to one Richard Griffith.[5] The date on which this obligation was completed is no longer apparent, and it is not known when he became a Baptist. According to Joseph Watts, George and his younger brother William were converted by Baptists from Virginia and were associated with the historic Nanjemoy Baptist Church, located about fifty miles down the Potomac from Washington.[6] Other accounts of George's life report that he studied theology with William Staughton,[7] the prominent British-born pastor and teacher who taught theological students in his home in Philadelphia, but there are no extant records to substantiate Sedwick's participation.

The next certain date in Sedwick's life is that of his marriage to Sarah Elizabeth (Sally) Hall on August 15, 1806, in Westmoreland County, Virginia.[8] In this same year, he was received by letter into the membership of Hartwood Baptist Church, Stafford County, Virginia.[9] George and Sally Sedwick became the parents of four children: Robert Hall, Elizabeth, Adoniram Judson, and Frances Virginia.[10]

Sedwick's involvement in various congregations in Northern Virginia can be traced through church and associational records. In August 1811, he was listed among the messengers to the Ketockton Association as a licensed preacher from Hartwood.[11] On October 12 of that same year, he was ordained by that congregation and dismissed to serve Grove Baptist Church, a newly constituted body formed by members out of Hartwood.[12] The "Perpetual Roll" of Grove Baptist Church lists him as pastor from 1812 to 1816.[13] From 1813 through 1816, he is listed as a messenger from Rock Hill Baptist Church to the Ketocton [*sic*] Association.[14] In 1815, he changed his residence to Dumfries, but continued to serve Grove Baptist Church until January 1817.[15]

Perhaps in anticipation of his departure, the November 1816 minutes of the Grove congregation record their consideration of a new pastor.[16] This relocation was to Winchester, where he became pastor of Winchester Baptist Church and, according to Ryland, also "conducted a Female Seminary."[17] The 1817 minutes of the Ketoctan [*sic*] Association list him as member and pastor of Winchester Baptist Church.[18]

In 1820, Sedwick moved to Zanesville, Ohio, where a year later he founded the First Baptist Church and subsequently became a leader in the Baptist life of that area.[19] He helped to establish the Meigs' Creek Association in 1825 and the Ohio Baptist Convention in 1826. In that same year, he founded *The Western Religious Magazine*, the first Baptist periodical in Ohio. This editing venture was followed in 1829 by his founding of *The Western Miscellany*, which subsequently became *The Regular Baptist Miscellany*. Sedwick figured prominently in the 1831 founding of the Granville Literary and Theological Institution, which became Granville College, the forerunner of Denison University.[20] Denison historian Francis Shepardson, reporting Sedwick's delivery of the school's inaugural address, "The Importance of a Well-Directed Course of Education," on December 13, 1831, characterized him as "the leading spirit in the organization of the Ohio Baptist Educational Society, which, in turn, founded the college."[21]

Following the death of his first wife, Sedwick married Eliza H. Dare in Zanesville on June 29, 1826.[22] Seven children were born of this union: Jane Patterson, Harriet Ann, George Cook, Jr., Jeremiah D., William S., Joseph Holden, and Howard Malcolm.[23] Sedwick was in Wheeling, [West] Virginia, in late 1836 and early 1837, serving a congregation that had been unable, until his arrival, to secure a pastor. He was one of nine ministers in the western part of the state at that time whose work was supported by the Baptist General Association of Virginia.[24] His service in Wheeling was brief, for within months, he became pastor in Frankfort, Kentucky.[25]

In 1830, while still living in Ohio, Sedwick had preached in Frankfort at a meeting of the Franklin Association that had been called to address the controversy arising from the views of Alexander Campbell.[26] His words in opposition to the Campbellite position no doubt raised his visibility among the Regular Baptists in that area. Shortly after his move to Kentucky, he was among those at the October 20, 1837, meeting in Louisville in which the General Association of Baptists in Kentucky was constituted.[27] At about this same time, Sedwick also became pastor of the church in the nearby town of Paris.[28] In 1842, he accepted the call as pastor of the Baptist church in Georgetown, Kentucky.[29] According to his obituary, he was also "principal of the Female Seminary" at Georgetown.[30]

In 1844, Sedwick returned to Virginia, this time as pastor of the Baptist church in Parkersburg.[31] He apparently found both the surroundings and the focus on pastoral duties gratifying, for in a letter to the *Religious Herald*, he commented: "My health, though generally good for the last twenty years, has rather improved, since I have left the recitation room, and exchanged the hall of science, for the romantic scenery of Western Virginia."[32]

Following a five-year stay in Parkersburg, Sedwick returned to Ohio in 1849.[33] The 1850 census records his residence in Duncan Falls and identifies him as a minister.[34] Denominational records for 1851 list him as the pastor of five congregations in three adjoining associations: Duncan Falls (Meigs' Creek), Salt Creek (Wills Creek), Stillwater (Zoar), Ebenezer (Zoar), and Morristown (Zoar).[35] By 1860, Sedwick, then seventy-five, had moved back to Zanesville and had, apparently, retired from the pastorate, though the census still lists him as a Baptist minister.[36] He died on August 25, 1864, at the Dare homestead, the ancestral home of his second wife, situated near Zanesville.[37] He is buried in that town's Greenwood Cemetery.

The Collection

Sedwick's *Selection* begins with a two-page Preface, which sets forth the compiler's aims under four headings: "Occasions of this Selection," "Materials," "Order of this Volume," and "Conclusion."[38] The principal objectives identified are to provide reliable versions of texts in place of those that are "corrupted" and to make available solid theological expressions rather than those considered "unsound."[39] As any hymnal editor knows, these principles are sometimes in conflict! Therefore, notwithstanding his first aim, Sedwick acknowledged later in the Preface that he had "altered those which in my humble opinion needed correction in language or doctrine."[40] As to the audience and purpose for which he hoped, he wrote, "This selection is respectfully dedicated to the Baptist Church, yet I wish it not confined there"[41]; and that it was "intended more for the private christian [*sic*] than for the public character."[42]

The collection is arranged alphabetically, though the alphabetization does not consistently go beyond the first letter. (One text beginning with "I" follows those starting with "J," but the intermingling of those initials was not unusual in this period.) A *nota bene* at the end of the Preface advises, "The number of each hymn and song agrees with the page on which it stands, which is advantageous to the finding of the hymn or song, as a single glance of the eye will discover the number of the page."[43] The 124 hymns are numbered in the index with Arabic numerals and on the page with Roman numerals. Though the index lists "Come, happy souls, approach your God," as number 23, that text is numbered XXII on the page, and there is no hymn XXIII. However, there are two hymns numbered 46, both in the index and on the pages: "Dear Lord, and hast thy pard'ning love" and "Earth has engross'd my love too long."

Two other points in the Preface show Sedwick's approach to analysis and organization of the hymns. First, he wrote, "I have noticed the different metres, and in some instances the tunes suitable, or those which are generally sung to the hymn or song." Further, "The texts of scripture explained or alluded to in this selection, are all set in a table at the end of this volume."[44] The content of each hymn page reflects this plan and provides additional information as well. Typically, there are two lines above each text. The first has a Roman numeral, an indication of poetic meter, and a citation of source. The next line, in italic type, is a heading that usually includes a topical description, which is sometimes followed by a Scripture reference. Running headers at the tops of the pages pick up the themes of the hymns, often duplicating or condensing the heading immediately above the text itself.

Sources

Sedwick selected his texts from a wide range of sources: well-known, little-known, and unknown. The Preface says as much:

> As this book is a supplement to those in use among us, I have selected a few hymns from each of them, as well as from authors more remote. Though I do not claim poetic talents, yet on different occasions I have thrown my thoughts into verse, and present them to my brethren and friends, distinguished in this book by the letters G. C. S. I have selected from all the books and MSS. that fell under my notice, without any objections to sect or denomination.[45]

The compiler was not consistent in the way in which he identified sources. For example, the most cited work, William Parkinson's *A Selection of*

Hymns and Spiritual Songs (1809),[46] to which he turned twenty times, is variously listed as "selec.," "Selec.," "sel.," and "Collection."

Sedwick chose six texts from John Rippon's *Selection*,[47] four from Samuel Jones's and Burgis Allison's *Selection*[48] (which is named in varying ways), and four from Jesse Mercer's *Cluster*,[49] cited by Sedwick as "Mercer's collec." Two each were taken from "Toplady's collec.,"[50] a "Boston Collection,"[51] a "Baltimore Collection,"[52] and "Mead's Selection."[53]

One variation in title offers an important bibliographic clue. Two texts are identified with "Broaddus's Collection," while three are credited to "Broaddus's Selection." The former would appear to be the *Collection of Sacred Ballads*[54] by Richard Broaddus and Andrew Broaddus, published in Richmond in 1790. Both texts linked by Sedwick with the "Collection" are contained in the 1790 book, but this is true of only one of those said to be from the "Selection." The other two, "Arise my dear love, my undefil'd dove" (9) and "Rise, my soul, and stretch thy wings" (98) are not found in the *Collection*. This argues for the existence of *A Selection of Hymns and Spiritual Songs*, a 1798 compilation by Andrew Broaddus, which is not known to be extant and had been thought, perhaps, to be a bibliographic ghost.[55]

The sources cited are, presumably, those from which Sedwick took the texts, since several hymns can be attributed to authors whom he does not identify. For example, "Come, guilty souls, and flee away," (32) by Joseph Humphreys, is listed as from "Toplady's collec." Similarly, John Fawcett's "How precious is the book divine" (65) is simply said to be from "Rippon's Selection." One unusual attribution is that of "Eternity, unequal thought" (47), to "P———." This is the only acknowledgment in the book in this enigmatic style, and the text in question is reliably credited to William Parkinson. This form of attribution is made even more curious by the numerous citations of Parkinson's *Selection*.

Most of the hymns in Sedwick's *Selection* would not be known by worshipers today. The small number that might qualify as common repertory includes: "Alas! and did my Saviour bleed"; "Blest be the tie that binds" (so listed in the index, though the first line on the page reads: "Blest be the ties that bind"); "Come, we that love the Lord"; "Come, Holy Spirit, heav'nly dove"; and "How firm a foundation." The few others that appear in contemporary hymnals, but are less well-known, are "Come, ye sinners, poor and wretched" (now usually altered to "needy"); "Jerusalem, my happy home"; "O for a closer walk with God"; and "On Jordan's stormy banks I stand." Taken together, these total less than ten percent of the content of Sedwick's book.

As one would expect, Isaac Watts is the author whose works appear most frequently. [See the essay by Harry Eskew in this collection, entitled "Isaac Watts and the Shape-Note Tradition."—Editor] Fifteen texts are attributed to him, and three others are identifiable as his. Ten texts are credited to John Newton, including one, "To keep the lamp alive" (110), which is, in fact, the work of his collaborator William Cowper. Three additional texts, not so identified, are Newton's. Cowper is named but once, for "O for a closer walk with God" (89).

Authors with two or more texts in the *Selection* are: Watts (eighteen identifiable inclusions/fifteen attributions), Newton (thirteen/ten), Joseph Hart (six/two), John Fawcett (four/three), John Leland (three/three),[56] Philip Doddridge (three/two), Joshua Marsham [*sic*; Marshman] (two/two), Thomas Baldwin (two/one), Cowper (two/one), Richard Burnham (two/zero), _________ Campbell (two/zero), Thomas Gibbons (two/zero), John A. Granade (two/zero), and Charles Wesley (two/zero).

Sedwick's Texts

There are six of Sedwick's own texts, marked, as stated in the Preface, by "G.C.S." The absence of all of these from the first line index of *The Dictionary of American Hymnology* Project (DAHP)[57] suggests that none was reprinted beyond this *Selection*.

"Come doubting soul, says Christ" (34) is a five-stanza hymn in Short Meter with the heading, "I am the way.—John xvi. 6" [*sic;* the correct reference is John 14:6]. The first stanza quotes the biblical phrase, while each of the others develops an aspect of "the way."

"Distress'd with sin I cri'd to God" (43) consists of five stanzas in Common Meter beneath the heading, "An answer to Prayer.—Psalms XL. 1, 2, 3, 4." In the manner of Watts, it Christianizes the idea drawn from the psalter and twice uses the phrase, "sov'reign grace," in urging trust in God.

"Poor careless sinners that stand by" (94) is "a warning address to the audience at the water side," in two stanzas of Common Meter Double. In making a confrontational appeal to those witnessing baptism, it uses two obvious structural devices. The opening lines are parallel in their address, while the other long lines of both stanzas display an interesting, if rough, inner rhyme.

> Poor careless sinners that stand by,
>   You need a Saviour too;
> Christ is the one; then to him come,
>   No other name will do.
> O could I know, which of you'd go,
>   I'd take you by the hand,
> And lead you on, the way Christ's gone,
>   Toward the heavenly land.

Poor careless sinners, how will you,
  At that great day appear?
When at God's bar, Christ will declare,
  His word you would not hear.
The saints will go to Christ, I know,
  Along with Jesus dwell;
There they shall range the heavenly plains,
  Poor sinners all farewell.

Form is the most prominent aspect of "Say when, dear Jesus, shall I stand" (99). On a line between the usual item number, meter, and attribution and the heading, "Heavenly-mindedness," Sedwick put in parentheses: "(Acrostick [*sic*] for Elder S. Templeman.)." Its four stanzas of Long Meter have, of course, sixteen beginning letters. The opening line is built on the initial of his first name, while the first letters of lines seven through fifteen spell the surname. The text is about the desire for heaven.

"While young in years the Lord began" (116) is headed: "Miss Simms' Experience." A narrative of personal testimony is traced through its ten Long Meter stanzas. Along the way we hear of wickedness, fear, grief at the death of her mother, discovery of faith through the biblical story of Abraham, repentance, profession of faith, and prayer for perseverance. It appears that Miss Simms was a member of the congregation of which Sedwick was pastor at the time the *Selection* was published. The seventh and eighth stanzas, respectively, refer to the good parson and Rock Hill Baptist Church:

At length I got a chance to tell
  A preacher what I knew and felt;
My situation he knew well,
  And my poor feeble hopes he help'd.

'Twas thus encourag'd forth I came,
  To Rock Hill Church, and try'd to tell
How Christ, the Lord, had borne my shame,
  And sav'd my precious soul from hell.

"Why shoulds't thou let thy fair one's [*sic*] die" (117) honors another acquaintance of the author, as stated in the heading: "Lines on the death of J. Fant, Deacon of Hartwood Church." While nothing more is known about Fant, this congregation was the one by which Sedwick was ordained. Seven stanzas in Common Meter present a typical perspective on the death of a believer and the assurance of eternal life in Christ. The hymn opens with four rhetorical questions of two lines each. Both this text and that for Elder Templeman speak of participation in the "song" that is part of life in heaven.

Other Notable Texts

The *Selection* contains a large proportion of distinctive material. In addition to the compiler's own hymns, there are twelve others said to be from manuscript. Though authors can be determined for as many as five of these, those of the other seven remain unidentified. Two of these have interesting qualifiers in their attributions. "O, ye Americans, be thankful to God" (90) is marked "altered," while "When man was first created, in Eden he was plac'd" (113) has above it, "Ancient M. S." Neither of these is found in the DAHP records.

"O, ye Americans," headed "The American Song," is as rough as it is vigorous. The meter and accent pattern are irregular, and the first stanza lacks a verb in its third line. (The spelling below is that found in the hymnal.)

O ye Americans, be thankful to God,
For the thousands of blessings upon you bestow'd;
While some other nations in bondage severe,
The gospel of Jesus still sounds in your ear.

Salvation, through Jesus, is spreading abroad,
And many Americans believe on the Lord;
The gospel of Jesus is not at a stand,
The harden'd opposers are yet in the land.

You've been faithfully warned by night and by day;
When to judgement you're coming, what think you to say?
What amazement of horror will seize on your heart.
To hear the dread sentence, ye cursed depart!

O sinners, take warning, be intreated by me,
To seek the Redeemer that dy'd on the tree;
There he pray'd, groan'd and suffer'd, and shed all his blood,
To bring rebels home to the kingdom of God.

My heart's now in trouble, poor sinners, for you,
But when up to glory my spirit shall go,
My warnings and sorrow will be at an end,
And I'll sing salvation to Jesus my friend.

Hymn 16, said by Sedwick to be from a manuscript, has the heading: "The Virginia Baptist Song." Typical of the period, its fervor for Christian conversion of the world far outweighs any sense of respect for other religions.

Blest be my God that I was born
  To hear the gospel sound;
That I was born to be baptiz'd,
  And dwell on Christian ground:
That I was born where God appears,
  In tokens of his grace;
The lines are fallen unto me
  In a most pleasant place.

I might have been a pagan born,
  Or else a blinded Jew,
Or cheated with the Alcoran,
  Which Turks in blindness view.
Dumb pictures might have been my hope,
  Dark language my devotion;
And thus I might with blinded eyes
  Have drunk a deadly potion.

Thus in a dungeon dark as night,
  I might have spent my days,
But God has sent me gospel light,
  To his eternal praise.
The Sun that rose up in the east,
  And drove the shades away,
With healing beams has reach'd the west,
  And turn'd the night to day.

Virginia once an Egypt was,
  Involv'd in nature's night;
But now a Canaan 'tis become,
  And I enjoy the light.
Blest be my God that he has driven
  That dismal night away,
Kept me in Providence's womb,
  To a more joyful day.

Blest be my God for what I see,
  My God for what I hear,
I hear such joyful news from heav'n,
  I death nor danger fear.
I hear the Lord for me was born,
  The Lord for me did die,
The Lord for me arose again.
  And did ascend on high.

On high he reigns and pleads my cause;
  Whence he'll return again,
And take me to his glorious throne,
  Where I with him shall reign.
All glory to the Father be,
  All glory to the Son,
All glory to the Holy Ghost,
  Glory to God in one.

The text at number 112 tells of a specific event: "On the burning of the Theatre in the city of Richmond, December 26th, 1811." There is no entry for this text in the DAHP files. Its author is identified by Sedwick as "J. Grigg." This is certainly not the British Presbyterian pastor and hymn writer Joseph Grigg (ca. 1720–1768). The poet displays skills in imagery and structure even as he articulates a horrific divine determinism.

Wearied by day with business, toils, and cares,
  How welcome is the peaceful night;
Sweet sleep our spirit and our strength repairs,
  And fits us for returning light.

Yet, when our heavy eyes in sleep are clos'd,
  Our rest may break e'er well begun;
To dangers every hour we stand expos'd,
  That we cannot foresee nor shun.

'Tis of the Lord, that we can ever sleep,
  A single night without alarms;
His eyes alone our lives in safety keep,
  Secure amidst a thousand harms.

For months and years of peace and safety past,
  Ungrateful we, alas! have been;
The voice of God our city rous'd at last,
  And bade the fire rebuke our sin.

The shout of fire, a dismal, doleful cry,
  Impress'd each heart with deep dismay;
The furious blaze ascends the red'ning sky,
  'Till midnight wears the face of day.

The bells with jingling sounds and awful tolls,
  Declare the horrors of that night;
Alas! alas! how many precious souls,
  Departed e'er the morning light!

The throng, the terror, who can ever speak,
  The various sounds that fill'd the air?
The children's cry, the tender parents' shriek,
  The voice of blasphemy and prayer.

But prayer prevail'd, and many souls were spar'd,
  And pluck'd as firebrands from the flame;
In time of need the Saviour's arm was bar'd,
  And prov'd his grace was still the same.

The house of joy becomes the house of death,
  All in a moment wrap'ed in fire;
The sons of mirth in thee resign'd their breath,
  Thy flames extinguished their desire.

O! may that night be never more forgot,
  Lord, still increase the praying few;
Were Richmond left without a righteous Lot,
  Ruin like Sodom's would ensue.

Believe, my friends, there is a righteous God,
  Nor can religion e'er be in vain;
Though infidels may boast aloud,
  Impiety must end in pain.

While we lament our dear departed friends,
  Let us adore his love and power;
Who to the wretched his salvation sends,
  And saves at the eleventh hour.

One measure of the distinctive content of the *Selection* is the number of texts not found in the records of the DAHP. In addition to the six hymns by Sedwick and two cited above, "O, ye Americans" and "Wearied by business," there are a dozen others: "All those who love a throne of grace" (4, by Oliver Holden, better known for his tune, CORONATION); "And cans't thou then believe, my soul" (7, from the "Boston collection"); "Come all you dear believers" (33, by Jeremiah Moore); "Farewell, beloved friends, once more farewell" (56, from the India Mission); "Jesus, Saviour, thine forever" (74, "Elder Pitman's *Experience*"); "Join all ye saints with me in joyful lays" (75, by Jael West); "My God, my Saviour, thee I love" (80, from Parkinson's *Selection*); "O God of matchless love" (84, by "Mr. Marsham in India"); "Smile, Lord, on each divine attempt" (101, by Ward); "The wond'rous love of Jesus" (104, from a manuscript); "Thou God, who sit'st enthroned above" (109, by H. Brooks);

and "When man was first created, in Eden he was plac'd" (113, from an "Ancient" manuscript). Thus, 20 of the 124 texts in Sedwick's *Selection* have not been recorded by the most comprehensive index of hymns in North America.

Topics

While Sedwick's choices range widely, there are recurring emphases. Fifteen of the texts—more than a tenth of the contents—begin with the word "come." Some of these invite the conversion of the unsaved; others, celebration by the saved; while one invokes the presence of the Holy Spirit.

One prominent theme is missions. The headers across the tops of pages mark six texts as "Missionary" or "Missionaries." "Farewell, beloved friends, one more farewell" (56) is attributed to "India Mission" and bears the heading, "The affectionate advice to parting Missionaries to India." "From realms where the day first her dawning extends," number 58, is by "Ezra Darby, a Member of Congress—addressed to Rev. E. Holmes, Indian Missionary."[58] From Rippon's *Selection* come "Great God, the nations of the earth," headed "Prayer for Missionaries" (60, Thomas Gibbons), and "Grace, 'tis a charming sound" (63, Doddridge), with its heading "Salvation by grace from first to last. Ephe[sians]. ii. 5." Credited to "Mr. Marsham (In India)" are "Hail precious book divine" (64), headed "On finishing the translation of the New Testament in Bengalee," and "O God of matchless grace," (84), with the heading, "On the first Hindoo loosing [*sic*] all for Christ's sake."

"Mr. Marsham" appears to be Joshua Marshman (1768–1837), a British Baptist linguist and missionary colleague of William Carey in India. Marshman is identified by Burrage as the author of "Hail, precious book divine" and as the translator of "O, thou my soul, forget no more" by the Indian Baptist, Krisha Pal.[59] "Smile, Lord, on each divine attempt" (101) is credited to "Ward" and headed "Prayers for Missionaries on the sea." This author is William Ward (1769–1823), who worked as a printer in India alongside Carey and Marshman.[60]

One other text has a clear link to the mission endeavor, though it lacks the designation in the page header. "The glorious light of Zion is spreading far and wide" (105), said to be from a manuscript, has the heading "The spread of the Gospel." The DAHP records give the author's surname only, Campbell. There is one additional connection to missions, though it is authorial, rather than topical. Hymn 111, "Warm was his heart, his faith was strong," is the work of Samuel Pearce (1766–1799), a strong advocate of the efforts of his friend, Carey.[61]

Prayer is another frequent topic. This has already been seen in two of the mission hymns, 60 and 101. Other headings display this same emphasis: "Prayer for a Minister and People" ("Dearest Saviour, help thy servant," 40, by Toplady);

"For a Prayer Meeting" ("Dearest Lord, thou has commanded," 41, by Burnham, from Parkinson's *Selection*); "An answer to Prayer.—Psalms XL, 1, 2, 3, 4" ("Distress'd with sin I cri'd to God," 43, by Sedwick); "Prayer answered by cross" ("I ask'd the Lord that I might grow," 70, by Newton, from the "Baltimore Selection"); "The Backslider's Prayer" ("Jesus, let thy pitying eye," 76, Wesley, from Rippon's *Selection*); and "Blind Bartimeus, or a prayer for spiritual light. Mark x. 46, 50" ("Thou God, who sit'st enthroned above," 109, attributed to "H. Brooks").

It is not surprising that in a book such as this, there should also be several hymns of "Experience." Sedwick applied this one-word heading to "Come brethren and sisters that love my dear Lord" (31, author unknown, from Broaddus's *Selection*); "Come old, come young, and hear me relate" (35, by Leland); "Come all you who ever have mercy obtained" (36, author unknown, taken by Sedwick from a manuscript); and "I am a stranger here below" (69, author unknown, from Parkinson's *Selection*). Two other headings identify the experience of a particular person: "Jesus, Saviour, thine forever" (74, "Elder Pitman's *Experience*"); and Sedwick's aforementioned "While young in years the Lord began" (116).

Meter, Music, and Scriptures

Sedwick did, indeed, "notice" the meters, which vary widely. There are some 38 different patterns, if one distinguishes "doubles," among the 124 texts. Most frequent are Common Meter (34, plus 4 doubled, for a total of 38), Long Meter (22 + 2 = 24), 11.11.11.11. (9, with several of these being somewhat irregular), Short Meter (6 + 1 = 7), 7.7.7.7. (5), 7.6.7.6. (4, all doubled), and 6.6.6.6.8.8. (4). The last form, sometimes analyzed as 6.6.6.6.4.4.4.4. and called "Hallelujah Meter," is marked by Sedwick as "P.M."—that is, "Particular Meter"—a designation he also used once each for 5.5.11.5.5.11., 8.8.8.8.8.8., and 8.8.8.8.6.6. Several texts, particularly those with long lines, are irregular, suggesting a ballad-like style with the grouping of accents, rather than a consistent number of syllables, to the stresses of a tune.

Tunes are indicated for nine texts. LENOX (6.6.6.6.8.8.), a fuging tune by Lewis Edson, is suggested for three of the four hymns in its meter. SUFFIELD (C.M.), a minor mode tune by Oliver King, and SOPHRONIA (10.8.10.8.), by A. King, are designated twice each. STAFFORD (S.M.), a fuging tune by Daniel Read, and COLE HILL (C.M.) are each listed once. Two of the tune citations accompany Sedwick's own texts: SUFFIELD for "Distress'd with sin I cri'd to God" (43) and COLE HILL for "Why shoulds't thou let thy fair one's [*sic*] die" (117). COLE HILL is, in all likelihood, COLESHILL, an anonymous minor tune first published in London in 1644. Surveying its publication in early American collections, Richard Crawford observed that the texts with which it commonly appeared are "all doleful in mood."[62] That is certainly true of Sedwick's hymn. COLESHILL, LENOX, STAFFORD, and SUFFIELD are included in Crawford's *The Core Repertory of Early American Psalmody*.[63] With the exception of STAFFORD, all of the tunes named by Sedwick appear in Freeman Lewis's *Beauties of Harmony*,[64] a tune book published in Pittsburgh in 1814, suggesting that this collection may have been known to Sedwick.

Scriptural citations are found in the headings of thirty-seven hymns. Though the Preface says that all are listed in the table of scriptures, only thirty are included there (there does not seem to be a pattern to the omissions). The references are almost evenly divided between the Old and New Testaments. Of the eighteen to the first Testament, six are to the Psalms and five are to Isaiah. Eleven of the nineteen New Testament references are to the Gospels.

The final item in the book is a note from the compiler: "Notwithstanding my care, and the good attention of the printers, I have found upon examination a few errors in this work; the following ERRATA is [*sic*] intended to correct them."[65] Five omissions or corrections are noted.

Conclusion

In memorializing George Cook Sedwick, the Ohio Baptist Convention observed: "Father Sedwick was a man of fine mind, scholarly erudition, deep earnestness and fervent piety. He wielded a wide and powerful influence."[66] He was, undeniably, a man of activity, imagination, and energy. While the motivation for his many moves is seldom evident from the surviving information, it is apparent that in each new setting he quickly became a leader, not only in his own congregation, but also in many kinds of cooperative undertakings. His organizational, promotional, and educational interests helped establish ventures, such as the Ohio Baptist Convention and Denison University, that have enduring value.

A Selection of Hymns and Spiritual Songs was more ephemeral. It shows the same inclinations toward organization and education, but there is no indication that it influenced other compilers or even that Sedwick relied on it to support congregational life in the many places he served after 1815. One wonders why he never undertook such an endeavor again. The book stands on its own, as evidence of the interests of the period, with its fervor for missions, prayer, and personal experience. It contains distinctive material, some from the compiler's own pen, that reflects the creativity of the era. In its own way, it still discloses to the careful reader—as a collection of hymns uniquely can—the character of the compiler. The traits recalled by those Ohio brethren who had seen his ministry across more than forty years are evident in the hymnal compiled when he was but a young minister of thirty in Virginia: a "fine mind, scholarly erudition, deep earnestness and fervent piety."[67]

NOTES

This article demonstrates the dependence of writers on those willing to contribute to the success of historical and documentary research. In addition to those persons named in the notes below who provided helpful information, I wish to acknowledge with gratitude the multifaceted assistance of Elizabeth Wells, Special Collection librarian in the G. Harwell Davis Library, Samford University, who invested considerable time and effort in helping locate, examine, and interpret various sources.

1. George C. Sedwick, *A Selection of Hymns and Spiritual Songs: Designed to engage the Children of God, in their private circles and public assemblies, "to speak to each other in Psalms, Hymns, and Spiritual Songs* [*sic*; there is no close to the quotation]. *As a supplement to those selections now in use* (Fredericksburg: printed by Green & Cady for the author, 1815). One copy is at the Virginia Baptist Historical Society, Richmond, Virginia. It is missing two leaves entirely, and parts of several other pages are torn away. Another is held by Duke University, Durham, North Carolina. The third, at the American Antiquarian Society in Worcester, Massachusetts, is included as item 25892 in the second series of *Early American Imprints*.

2. Much information about George Cook Sedwick and other members of this family can be found at sedgwick.org, a Web site devoted to genealogy. Note that the surname is spelled both with and without the "g." This variation in spelling is found even in reference to individual members of the family, including George Cook Sedwick. Dennis Sedgwick, the manager of the Web site, suggests that the ancestral name may be "Siggeswick." Sedgwick.org contains a number of family documents, as well as excerpts from and links to historical records, interpretive materials, and deductions (some of which are necessarily speculative). Four persons who have made substantial contributions to the Web site have also been particularly helpful in responding to my inquiries about the family: Dennis Gilmore Sedgwick, Una A. Swanson Bowman, Elizabeth Ann (Liz) Klukas, and Nola Miles Rogers. My first connections with the genealogical records of this family came through a descendant, Thelma H. Miller. I am grateful to each of these individuals for assistance.

3. Letter from William Sedwick to T. R—T—by, Esq. [*sic*], November 20, 1868. This letter, the latter portion of which has been lost, is an autobiographical sketch, written in Adamsville, Ohio. It has been transcribed by Una A. Bowman and posted at sedgwick.org. William Sedwick was born February 5, 1790, in Calvert County, Maryland. He also became a Baptist minister and served churches in Virginia, the District of Columbia, and Ohio. Cathcart lists him as "A.M." (Master of Arts), though the autobiographical sketch mentions no formal degree but that he studied theology with Burgiss Allison, congressional chaplain. (Allison and Samuel Jones were co-compilers of the "Philadelphia Collection," from which George Sedwick borrowed several texts. See

note 48 below.) William Sedwick died November 30, 1871, in Zanesville, Ohio. His son, George Cyrus Sedwick (1824–1903), was also a Baptist pastor, serving most notably in Martin's Ferry, Ohio.

4. William Sedwick letter.

5. Margaret E. Myers, "Frederick County Indentures," *Western Maryland Genealogy* 5, no. 3 (July 1989), 131. Transcribed by Una A. Bowman and posted on sedgwick.org.

6. Joseph T. Watts, *The Rise and Progress of Maryland Baptists* ([Baltimore]: The State Mission Board of the Maryland Union Association, [1953]), 17.

7. William Cathcart, *The Baptist Encyclopedia; A Dictionary of the Doctrines, Ordinances, Usages, Confessions of Faith, Sufferings, Labors, and Successes, and of the General History of the Baptist Denomination in All Lands. With Numerous Biographical Sketches of Distinguished American and Foreign Baptists*, 2 vols. (Philadelphia: L. H. Everts, 1881), 1039, s.v., "Sedgwick" [*sic*]. Study with Staughton is also cited in Sedwick's obituary in *Minutes of the Thirty-Ninth Anniversary of the Ohio Baptist Convention* (Mansfield, Ohio: L. D. Myers & Bros., *Herald* Book and Job Office, 1865), 17. I am grateful to Stuart Campbell, Director and Archivist of the American Baptist Historical Society, Rochester, New York, for locating this obituary and for tracing several of the citations of Sedwick in Baptist historical records, as noted below. William Staughton was also a hymn writer. See Henry S. Burrage, *Baptist Hymn Writers and Their Hymns* (Portland, Maine: Brown Thurston & Company, 1888), 242–45.

8. "Marriages—Virginia before 1824," *Early Virginia Marriages, Westmoreland County*, 114, August 15, 1806, at ancestry.com linked to sedgwick.org.

9. Hartwood Baptist Church Roll. The records of this extinct congregation are at the Virginia Baptist Historical Society. For his painstaking search of these and other records of Virginia Baptist churches and associations, I am indebted to Fred Anderson, executive director of the Virginia Baptist Historical Society.

10. Robert Hall Sedwick was born May 2, 1808, in Westmoreland County, Virginia, and died January 19, 1883, in Zanesville, Ohio. He was a Baptist minister in Ohio and Virginia before a throat problem forced him to give up public speaking, after which he became a dentist and relocated to his childhood home of Zanesville.

11. Minutes, Ketockton Baptist Association, per Anderson.

12. Minutes, Grove Baptist Church, per Anderson.

13. Perpetual Roll, Grove Baptist Church, per Anderson.

14. Minutes, Ketokton [*sic*] Baptist Association, per Anderson.

15. Minutes, Grove Baptist Church, per Anderson.

16. Ibid.

17. Garnett Ryland, *The Baptists of Virginia, 1699–1926* (Richmond: Baptist Board of Missions and Education, 1955), 171, n. 24. Ryland identifies Sedwick as pastor of both Rock Hill and Chappawomsick Baptist Churches in Stafford County.

18. Minutes, Ketoctan [*sic*] Baptist Association, per Anderson.

19. Cathcart, *The Baptist Encyclopedia*, 1039.

20. The role of Sedwick in the history of this educational institution and in related organizations is treated in some detail in two histories of Denison University: Francis W. Shepardson, *Denison University, 1831–1931: A Centennial History* (Granville: The Board of Trustees, Denison University, 1931), 1–29, passim; and G. Wallace Chessman,

Denison: The Story of an Ohio College (Granville, Ohio: Denison University, 1957), 1–31, passim. Page six of the Shepardson history contains an image of Sedwick. Its source and present location are not known, according to retired Denison University archivist Florence W. Hoffman. Letter to the author, January 2, 2002. A different likeness can be found on the Sedgwick Web site.

21. Shepardson, 20–21. On page three, Shepardson incorrectly identifies George Cook Sedwick as George Cyrus Sedwick, apparently conflating the subject of this study with his nephew. See note 2.

22. Muskingum County, Ohio, Marriage Records, Book 2, 1828, per Liz Klukas.

23. William S. Sedwick, born May 24, 1836, in Zanesville, Ohio, became a leader in the Sunday school movement, first in Zanesville, later in New York City, and, finally, as a worker for the General Association of Kentucky Baptists. He died in Bardstown, Kentucky, on September 29, 1866. J. H. Spencer called him, "probably the most active and useful Sunday school worker that has ever labored among the Baptists in Kentucky." J. H. Spencer, *A History of Kentucky Baptists from 1769 to 1885, Including More than 800 Biographical Sketches,* manuscript revised and corrected by Mrs. Burilla B. Spencer, 2 vols. (Printed for the author, 1866; reprint, Lafayette, Tenn.: Church History Research & Archives, 1976), 719.

24. *Religious Herald* (Virginia), January 13, 1837, 2 (col. 5). An earlier letter to this paper by Sedwick, published in the December 23, 1836 issue, 2, reported that he and his family had arrived in Wheeling on September 25, 1836.

25. Frank N. Masters, *A History of Baptists in Kentucky* (Louisville: Kentucky Baptist Historical Society, 1953), 115.

26. Ibid., 217.

27. Sedwick was one of eleven individuals appointed to the Board of Managers. Ibid., 268.

28. Ibid., 119. In the description of the church at Paris, Masters gave the dates of Sedwick's pastorate as 1837–1838. However, in recounting the report of the Board of Managers for 1840, he located Sedwick at Paris, which was named as one of only nine Kentucky Baptist churches with "full-time" preaching. Spencer placed Sedwick in Paris from 1840 until 1843 in his *History of Kentucky Baptists*, 26–27.

29. Ibid., 105. Sedwick was pastor of this congregation when it dedicated a new building on June 23, 1842. The 1843 Minutes of the Elkhorn Association record his presence as a messenger from Georgetown Baptist Church, per Campbell.

30. *Minutes of the Thirty-Ninth Anniversary of the Ohio Baptist Convention*, 17. Both Spencer and Masters gave 1845 as the founding date of the Georgetown Female Seminary. Given that Sedwick had by this time left Georgetown, the teaching cited in the obituary and in Sedwick's letter to the *Religious Herald* (see the next paragraph) must have been in another institution.

31. *Religious Herald*, February 22, 1844, 2 (col. 4).

32. Letter from Sedwick, *Religious Herald*, December 19, 1844, 2 (col. 5).

33. The Minutes of the May 1849 and October 1849 meetings of the Ohio Baptist Convention list Sedwick as pastor in Duncan Falls, per Campbell.

34. Sedwick is listed in the 1850 census as an "NSB Minister," residing in district 114, town of Duncan Falls, Wayne Township, Muskingum County, Ohio, age sixty-four, as of

September 11, 1850. Also living in this household were Eliza, age forty-five; William S., age fourteen; Joseph, age eleven; and Malcolm, age seven. These census records may be accessed through Sedgwick.org.

35. J. Lansing Burrows, ed., *American Baptist Register for 1852* (Philadelphia: American Baptist Publication Society, 1853), 282, 288, 291. The information for Ohio carries the heading: "Returns for 1851." In addition to these entries for George Cook Sedwick, there are listings for William Sedwick (brother, living in Adamsville and serving as pastor of Salem Township Baptist Church) and R. H. Sedwick (son, living in Zanesville and serving as pastor of New Concord Baptist Church).

36. Sedwick is listed as a "Baptist Minister" residing in house no. 838 in Zanesville at the time of the 1860 census on July 24, 1860. The value of his personal estate is given as one hundred dollars. The residence seems to have been the dwelling of James and Jane Warner and their five children. George and son Malcolm are among seven others at this address (George's second wife, Eliza, had died in 1855). These census records may be accessed through Sedgwick.org.

37. History of the Lafayette Lodge at its one hundredth anniversary, per Bowman.

38. Sedwick, *A Selection*, [iii]–iv.

39. Ibid., [iii].

40. Ibid., iv.

41. Ibid., [iii].

42. Ibid., iv.

43. Ibid.

44. Ibid.

45. Ibid., [iii].

46. William Parkinson, *A Selection of Hymns and Spiritual Songs, Designed (especially the former part) for the Use of Congregations as an Appendix to Dr. Watts's Psalms and Hymns* (New York: D. and G. Bruce, 1809).

47. John Rippon, *A Selection of Hymns from the Best Authors, Intended to Be an Appendix to Dr. Watts's Psalms and Hymns* (London: Thomas Wilkins, 1787). This collection, which had a strong influence on the content of subsequent hymnals in both England and the United States, was reprinted in New York City and Elizabeth-Town, New Jersey, as early as 1792.

48. Samuel Jones and Burgis [*sic*] Allison, *Selection of Psalms and Hymns, Done under appointment of the Philadelphian Association* (Philadelphia: R. Aitken, 1790).

49. Jesse Mercer, *The Cluster of Spiritual Songs, Divine Hymns, and Sacred Poems; Being Chiefly a Collection*, 3d ed. (Augusta, Ga.: Hobby & Bunce, 1810). Earlier editions are not known to be extant. Counted among these four is Hymn 96, "Quite weary, near to faint," which carries the citation, "Merce's Selec." I have not identified any anthology of hymns whose compiler's name is "Merce," and this text does appear in *The Cluster*. This argues in favor of a typographical error. On the other hand, Sedwick used the term "collection" (or an abbreviation for this word), rather than "selection," in the other attributions to *The Cluster*; and he provided only three of the five stanzas included by Mercer.

50. Augustus Montague Toplady, *Psalms and Hymns for Public and Private Worship* (London: E. and C. Dilly, 1776).

51. It is presumed that this is *The Boston Collection of Sacred and Devotional Hymns: Intended to Accommodate Christians on Special and State Occasions* (Boston: Manning and Loring, 1808).

52. In all probability, this is *Hymns and Spiritual Songs for the Use of Christians* (Baltimore: Warner & Hanna, 1801). The WorldCat entry notes that the book's alternate title is "Baltimore Collection."

53. Stith Mead, *A General Selection of the Newest and Most Admired Hymns and Spiritual Songs, Now in Use* (Richmond: Seaton Grantland, 1807).

54. Richard Broaddus and Andrew Broaddus, *Collection of Sacred Ballads* ([n.p.], 1790).

55. See Paul A. Richardson, "Andrew Broaddus and Hymnody," in *Singing Baptists: Studies in Baptist Hymnody in America*, eds. Harry Eskew, David W. Music, and Paul A. Richardson (Nashville: Church Street Press, 1994), 51–63.

56. "Farewell, my brethren in the Lord" (54), attributed to Leland, is the work of Justus Hall; while "The day is past and gone" (103), Leland's most-published text, is not identified with him by Sedwick. The versions of "Brethren, I am come again" (18) and "Come old, come young, and hear me relate" (35) in Sedwick's *A Selection* differ at points from those in John Leland, *The Writings of the Late Elder John Leland, Including Some Events in His Life, Written by Himself, with Additional Sketches &c. by Miss L. F. Greene, Lanesboro, Mass.* (New York: G. W. Wood, 1845; rep. ed., New York: Arno Press, 1969), 317–318, 326–327.

57. Leonard Webster Ellinwood, ed., *The Dictionary of American Hymnology: First-Line Index* (New York: University Music Editions, 1984). This content of this on-going project, hereafter DAHP, is in the process of being made available on CD-ROM. Thanks to Paul R. Powell, who is directing this conversion for The Hymn Society in the United States and Canada, I had access to a trial version of this resource for my research.

58. Ezra Darby (1768–1808) represented New Jersey in the United States House from 1805 until his death.

59. Burrage, *Baptist Hymn Writers*, 120–122.

60. Ibid., 124–26. The first stanza of this hymn is the last of number 60. Hymn 55, "Father, is not thy promise pledg'd," comes from the same lengthy original that forms the torso of number 60. Burrage describes the connection between the work of Ward and Thomas Gibbons on page 126.

61. Ibid., 116–119.

62. Richard Crawford, ed., *The Core Repertory of Early American Psalmody*, vols. XI and XII of *Recent Researches in American Music* (Madison, Wis.: A–R Editions, 1984), xxxii.

63. Ibid.; for COLESHILL, see xxxii and 38; for LENOX, xli and 79–80; for STAFFORD, lix–lx and 144–45; for SUFFIELD, lx–lxi and 147–48.

64. Freeman Lewis, *The Beauties of Harmony* (Pittsburgh: Cramer, Spear & Eichbaum and Freeman Lewis, 1814).

65. Sedwick, *A Selection*, [128].

66. *Minutes of the Thirty-Ninth Anniversary of the Ohio Baptist Convention*, 17.

67. Ibid.

The Christian Lyre *and Its Influence on American Hymnody*

Paul Hammond

American evangelical Christianity in 1830 was undergoing a radical transformation. From 1800–1835, the Second Great Awakening reshaped much of America's religious life. The work of the New Haven theologians, including Joseph Bellamy (1719–1790), Jonathan Edwards, Jr. (1754–1801), Samuel Hopkins (1721–1803), Yale President Timothy Dwight (1752–1817), and Nathaniel W. Taylor (1786–1856) tempered the strict Calvinism that heretofore had dominated American theology. The emotional revival preaching of Charles G. Finney (1792–1875) further tempered the Calvinist doctrine of election. Moreover, Finney transported the evangelical fervor of the frontier camp meetings to urban America and thereby helped create the theology and practice of what we consider modern revivalism.

Music was also an important issue during the Second Great Awakening. Metrical psalmody, which had prevailed throughout the previous century, began to be challenged by the improved psalms and hymns of Isaac Watts (1674–1748) and other English authors. As English hymns were making an inroad into American churches, the battle between indigenous American and European musical styles was taking shape. Lowell Mason (1792–1872), Thomas Hastings (1784–1872), and their followers espoused a European model for "correct" church music, while Joshua Leavitt (1794–1873) and others championed popular, folk, and camp-meeting styles to express the increased fervor of revivalism. Compilers distinguished their collections of congregational song for revivals, prayer meetings, inquiry meetings, and other gatherings outside the regular Sunday worship service by labeling them for use in "social worship." The incorporation of this lighter style of hymnody into the regular worship of the Church was accomplished by the time the gospel song achieved widespread popularity in the latter part of the century. Leavitt's compilation, *The Christian Lyre*, became an important source of hymns and tunes from both camps, and its contents exerted a lasting impact on future generations.

In response to the enthusiasm generated by revivals, Congregational minister Joshua Leavitt began in 1830 to publish the *Evangelist*, a pro-Finney periodical. The first monthly installments of *The Christian Lyre* began appearing in the November 1830 issue. Volume one was completed in April 1831, and volume two followed that same October.[1] With this new hymnbook for social worship in circulation, Leavitt immediately wrote Charles G. Finney in an attempt to persuade him to adopt the *Lyre* for his revival meetings. Finney, whose beliefs about music in a revival were diametrically opposed to Leavitt's and who had already aligned himself with another musician, never responded to Leavitt's petition.

Finney's full-time evangelistic career had begun in Oneida County, New York, in 1826 following a brief legal career. His Rochester, New York, revival in 1830–1831 marked the beginning of his urban revivals. Finney became pastor of Second Free Presbyterian Church in New York City in 1832, later organized New York's Broadway Tabernacle, and in 1835 became president of Oberlin College. In his *Lectures on Revivals of Religion*, he defined a revival as the "purely philosophical result of the right use of the constituted means."[2] Even though he retained Calvinistic beliefs about the serious nature of his revival meetings and about the steps to salvation of awakening, conviction, conversion, and rejoicing, Finney's revival *practices* began to challenge the doctrine of election. For him, each individual had the power to accept or reject salvation. He believed that the revivalist's function was "to utilize the laws of mind in order to engineer individuals and crowds into making a choice which was *ostensibly based upon free will*" (italics mine).[3] Finney employed several controversial "new measures" during protracted meetings lasting three to four weeks. These new practices included emotional, dramatic preaching; "anxious seats" (front pews reserved for souls under conviction); "enquiry meetings," for conversations with those under conviction; praying for sinners by name; and public prayer by women (a novelty in a day of strict adherence to the Pauline proscription against women speaking in church). Manipulative tactics thus began to replace the Calvinistic belief that revivals came at the divine initiative of a sovereign God.

Joshua Leavitt mistook Finney's dramatic, extemporaneous preaching as a signal that the evangelist would welcome music of the same kind. Finney himself was a competent musician who played the cello, and he was known to promote good choral singing in his revivals. His Calvinistic beliefs, however, left him suspicious of the potential harm that music might inflict on a revival meeting.

> A *great deal of singing* often injures a prayer meeting. The *agonizing spirit of prayer* does not lead people to sing. . . . Singing is the natural expression of feelings that are joyful and cheerful. The spirit of prayer is not a spirit of joy. It is a spirit of travail, and agony of soul, supplicating and pleading with God with strong cryings and groanings that cannot be uttered.[4]

Furthermore, Finney claimed that "singing dissipated the deep feeling that was necessary for conversion. . . . It is no time for [young converts] to let feeling flow away in joyful singing, while so many sinners around them, and their own former companions are going down to hell."[5] Evoking warm childhood memories of home and feelings of security were to be the practice of later evangelists such as Dwight L. Moody and Ira D. Sankey.

During a revival in Utica, New York, in 1825–26, Finney developed an association with Thomas Hastings, who had recently become editor of the *Western Recorder.*[6] Together with Lowell Mason, Hastings led a reform of American church music toward a European-based repertoire and also provided hymnody for revivals in their joint collection, *Spiritual Songs for Social Worship* (1832). Hastings said of the *Lyre*: "We are truly sorry that any minister of the gospel . . . should have associated his name with such a wretched publication as this."[7] Leavitt in turn accused Hastings and Mason of imitation, and a running feud ensued between the *Evangelist* and the *Western Recorder.* In their Preface to *Spiritual Songs for Social Worship*, the two musical reformers espoused their own views of revival music:

> In the larger and more dignified assemblies, psalmody will continue to hold its appropriate place; but for social and private uses, something is needed which is more familiar, more melodious, and more easy of execution. . . . The consequence [of a lack of good tunes for revivals] is, that a multitude of insipid, frivolous, vulgar, and profane melodies, have been forced into general circulation, to the great disparagement of the art, as well as to the detriment of musical reform.[8]

In spite of opposition by these three evangelical giants, *The Christian Lyre* made several lasting contributions to hymnody in America. Among the innovations of Leavitt's collection were its format, its introduction of several important new hymns and tunes, its parodies of secular tunes and texts, and its inclusion of the rural shape-note repertoire which Mason and Hastings so firmly rejected.

The manner in which the hymns were arranged differed from predecessors such as *The Hartford Selection* (1799), compiled by Congregationalist pastors Nathan Strong, Abel Flint, and Joseph Steward, and *Village Hymns for Social Worship* (1824), collected by Calvinistic evangelist Asahel Nettleton. *The Hartford Selection* was intended as a supplement to the regular hymnal during times of awakening. By incorporating hymns from John Newton's and William Cowper's *Olney Hymns* and hymns written by other evangelicals such as Philip Doddridge and John Rippon, this collection moved away from the dominance of Isaac Watts's psalms and hymns. *Village Hymns for Social Worship*, too, was intended to supplement Watts's psalms, hymns, and spiritual songs. Moreover, hymnologist John Julian credits Nettleton with championing the work of older American hymn writers such as William B. Tappan, Abby B. Hyde, Lydia Huntley Sigourney, Phoebe Brown, Nathan Strong, and Joseph Steward.[9] The inclusion of a section of missionary hymns represents another innovation on Nettleton's part. The hymn texts contained within *The Hartford Selection* and *Village Hymns for Social Worship* were each supplemented by separate companion tune books. *Harmonia Coelestis* (1799), by Jonathan Benjamin, accompanied *The Hartford Selection* while *Zion's Harp* (1824), by Nathaniel and Simeon S. Jocelyn, provided the music for *Village Hymns. The Christian Lyre*, however, brought hymns and tunes together in one volume.

In his one-page Preface, Leavitt acknowledged the work of Nettleton and the Jocelyns in providing "hymns and music of a different character from those ordinarily heard in the church." They were deficient, however, in that they excluded "many pieces, which have proved of great use in revivals." The purpose of the *Lyre* was to provide tunes for "evening meetings and social worship, and chiefly such as are not found in our common collections of sacred music."[10] His sole criterion for selecting the contents of the *Lyre* was "the known popularity and good influence of what is selected. And it is intended to embrace the music that is most current among different denominations of christians [*sic*]."[11] Leavitt's book, like several before it, was a privately printed volume for prayer and conference meetings, family worship, and revival services. Such social hymn books, according to Louis Benson, "differing in purpose and quality as they did, . . . may be said to have modified and then succeeded the Camp Meeting Song Book type."[12] Leavitt's kinship with the shape-note books certainly reinforces Benson's claim. In 1831, Leavitt added a supplement of the "best and most common psalm tunes" to serve as a companion volume for churches and as a less expensive alternative for singing schools. Sixty-six of his psalm tunes were taken from Nettleton's *Village Hymns*.

Leavitt's book contains 330 hymn texts, 203 tunes, and 108 psalm tunes and texts. Hymns and tunes appear on facing pages, often with as many as three texts assigned to one tune. The supplementary psalm tunes contain one tune per page and only one stanza of interlined text. Most are syllabic, but there are a few in the more florid style of earlier revival tune books. The compiler arranged the tunes alphabetically under metrical headings. Leavitt believed that more than two voice parts distracted the worshipper and that "the *religious* effect of a hymn is heightened by having all sing the air only."[13] Leavitt's instruction calls to mind the Calvinistic practice of unison singing, and his collection presents each hymn tune in only a soprano and bass part.

Leavitt caught the spirit of the new revivalism and in so doing enriched the Church's song for future generations. His book reflected the era's theological change by arranging the texts of the first two volumes in a random order. Whereas the organizational structure of many earlier collections organized hymns by the Calvinistic steps of conversion (awakening, conviction, conversion, and rejoicing), Leavitt's break with that pattern acknowledged the growing evangelical emphasis on free will as opposed to the doctrine of predestination. His eclectic choice of material included the compositions of a wide variety of evangelical hymn writers, parodies of secular tunes and texts, and revival hymns with choruses, as well as a number of tunes that found widespread acceptance among shape-note singers.

Leavitt's use of secular tunes was not a new practice in Christian hymnody. Since at least the fourth century, when St. Ambrose borrowed popular tunes for texts advocating his beliefs, Christians have often appropriated well-known secular music for Christian texts. Musicologists employ the terms parody and *contrafactum* to describe the reworking of a tune or text from the original source. Both terms usually refer to the quotation of preexisting music within a later work or to the substitution of one text for another. In hymnody, the new text is usually sacred, and the tune is more often than not a familiar secular melody. Thus *contrafactum* describes the process of providing a new text for a preexisting tune, often a sacred text to a secular tune. Two American musicologists have compiled seven types of parody related particularly to nineteenth-century hymnody. Ellen Jane Lorenz Porter identified three parody types: (1) folk tunes adapted to sacred texts; (2) popular songs transformed into hymns with sacred texts; and (3) instrumental or opera classics used with sacred texts. Esther Rothenbusch Crookshank added four additional categories: (4) "answer songs," which respond to the sentiment of the original by elaboration, continuation, or opposition; (5) song imitation, which often incorporates the same opening line of the original as a "hook"; (6) tune parody, in which the new tune is modeled on an existing one; and (7) phrase parody, which borrows only a phrase from the well-known hymn that becomes the "hook" for the new one.[14]

If we look closely at *The Christian Lyre*, we will discover a number of pieces which illustrate these categories of parody and also recognize practices in Christian music that are centuries old. The most notable parody in *The Christian Lyre* is James Waddell Alexander's translation of "O sacred Head, now wounded," which appeared here for the first time in any American hymnal. The tune is identical to PASSION CHORALE, composed by Hans Leo Hassler and first published as a secular song in 1601.[15] Leavitt explains his choice of the tune name HOFWYL in a note that precedes the hymn: "Furnished for the Lyre, by Mr. Kammerer, of New-York, formerly Professor of Music at Hofwyl." He includes eight stanzas with a heading: "Translated from Gerhard[t]'s favorite, German Hymn, 'O Haupt voll blut und wunden.'"[16] Subsequent to its publication in the *Lyre*, this Pietistic expression moved into both mainstream and folk traditions, as evidenced by George Pullen Jackson's inclusion of it among the 152 folk hymns in *Down-East Spirituals*.[17]

Another tune in classical style was first printed in the *Lyre* and found acceptance in both the shape-note and urban repertoires. The hymn, "Jesus, I my cross have taken," had been written by Henry F. Lyte and first published in his *Sacred Poetry* (1824). Seven years later, the text appeared in the *Lyre* with a tune commonly known as ELLESDIE, but it was identified as DISCIPLE by Leavitt and later tune-book compilers. Leavitt was the first compiler to print this anonymous tune in America. William Walker acknowledged the tune's source as the *Lyre* in the 1854 edition of *The Southern Harmony*; it does not appear in the original *Southern Harmony* of 1835.[18] The tune has often erroneously been attributed to Mozart, but it is likely derived from an unknown person with the initials L. S. D.[19] The text and tune continue to the present day to appear together in such collections as *The Baptist Hymnal* (1991) and *The Celebration Hymnal* (1997).

Other tunes from European sources have also found staying power in American hymnody. Haydn's AUSTRIAN HYMN, entitled HAYDN'S by Leavitt, is the setting for "Come, thou long-expected Jesus." LEONI appears with "The God of Abraham praise" in twelve stanzas divided into three sections. "Awake, my soul, in joyful lays," by Samuel Medley, was first published in London in 1782. The oft-used tune LOVING KINDNESS appeared in William Caldwell's *Union Harmony* (1837), as well as in several subsequent tune books, with the identification "Western Melody."[20] Leavitt's pairing of this tune with "Awake, my soul, in joyful lays" predated *Union Harmony* by six years and may be the source from which Caldwell borrowed. VESPER HYMN, sung in later years to "Now on land and sea descending," appears as a setting for two texts: "Lord, with glowing heart I'd praise thee" and "Far from mortal cares retreating." The tune was written by Sir John Stevenson and first published in London in 1818.[21] COME YE DISCONSOLATE, by Samuel Webbe, was first published in London in 1792 and also appeared in Mason's and Hastings's *Spiritual Songs for Social Worship* (1831).[22] Leavitt's version is a setting for soloist and three-part chorus. Hugh Stowell had recently published "From every stormy wind that blows" in London in 1828; Leavitt included all six stanzas of the original with an acknowledgment of Stowell's authorship.[23]

One of the most popular songs of the day, "Home, sweet, home," appears with a hymn text by British Baptist pastor David Denham (1791–1848), author of more than a thousand hymns. The text's first publication in England was in Denham's large compilation of original hymns, *The Saints' Melody* (1837), under the title "The Saints' Sweet Home."[24] According to *The Dictionary of American Hymnology*, the first American printing of Denham's parody occurred in 1829, just six years after the song's premiere, in *Hymns of Zion; being a Selection of Hymns for Social Worship, compiled chiefly for the use of Baptist churches*.[25] Joshua Leavitt included Denham's original in *The Christian Lyre* with an additional text on the facing page, "An alien from God, and a stranger to grace."

'Mid scenes of confusion and creature complaints,
  How sweet to my soul is communion with saints;
To find at the banquet of mercy there's room,
  And feel in the presence of Jesus at home.

Chorus

Home, home, sweet, sweet home,
  Prepare me, dear savior, for glory, my home.

Compilers also included SWEET HOME in such notable collections as *The Sacred Harp* (1844), *The Christian Minstrel* (1846), and *The Social Harp* (1855). As late as 1928, *The New Cokesbury Hymnal* contained stanzas 1, 2, 4, and 5 of "'Mid scenes of confusion and creature complaints."[26]

Leavitt even incorporates *La Marseillaise* as a hymn tune to a text "written, by request, expressly for the Christian Lyre, L. H. S."[27] The tune name and heading are MARSEILLES [*sic*]—*The Restoration of Man* (I, 70–72).

The host of heaven that throne surrounding
  Where everlasting splendors glow,
'Mid lyres with ceaseless praise resounding,
   Beheld the earth involved in woe.

It concludes with the birth of Christ:

The star o'er Bethlehem gleam'd,
  And angels tuned their harps of joy,
To hail a world redeem'd.

This text appeared in only three other hymnals, all of which were published in Louisville, Kentucky between 1850 and 1854.[28]

Another parody was set to the tune GRATEFUL MEMORY, or "Auld Lang Syne," with a text written for the *Lyre* by "W. M." (II, 32–33).[29]

1. Jesus! Thy love shall we forget;
And never bring to mind
The grace that paid our hopeless debt,
And bade us pardon find?

Chorus

Our sorrows and our sins were laid
On thee—alone on thee;
Thy precious blood our ransom paid—
Thine all the glory be.

2. Shall we thy life of grief forget,
Thy fasting and thy prayer;
Thy locks with mountain vapors wet,
To save us from despair?

3. Gethsemane, can we forget;
Thy struggling agony—
When night lay dark on Olivet,
And none to watch with thee?

4. Can we thy platted crown forget,
The buffeting and shame;
When hell thy sinking soul beset,
And earth reviled thy name?

5. The nails—the spear—can we forget;
The agonizing cry—
"My God! My Father! wilt thou let
Thy Son forsaken die?"

6. Life's brightest joys we may forget—
Our kindred cease to love;
But He, who paid our hopeless debt,
Our constancy shall prove.

This tune moved into the shape-note tradition as PLENARY and appeared as one of George Pullen Jackson's eighty most popular tunes in *White Spirituals of the Southern Uplands* (1933). "Jesus! thy love shall we forget" was not, however, a popular text with shape-note singers. Jackson listed the most commonly used texts as "Hark, from the tombs a doleful sound" and "There is a land of pure delight where saints in glory reign." PLENARY also was included in *The Southern Harmony*, *The Sacred Harp*, *The Social Harp*, and *The Western Psalmodist.*[30]

Leavitt's affinity with the rural shape-note tradition provides further evidence of his support for the emotional style of Charles G. Finney, but it may also explain Finney's rejection of the compiler's overture. *The Christian Lyre* stands at the crossroads of the urban-rural intersection in American music. While his book influenced subsequent compilers in both camps, the predominant influence on urban revivalism was the work of Lowell Mason and Thomas Hastings.

Eighteen tunes from the Southern folk tradition, catalogued as well by George Pullen Jackson, appear in *The Christian Lyre*. Three have already been mentioned: HOFWYL, GRATEFUL MEMORY, and HOME. The Appendix provides each tune's name, its location in the *Lyre*, the Jackson source in which it is named, his numbering of the tunes, and the page number.

The era of the Second Great Awakening represents a period of upheaval in American Christianity not unlike the late twentieth- and early twenty-first centuries. While the movement in the early 1800s was away from strict Calvinism, the early twenty-first century is witnessing a resurgence of five-point Calvinism among fundamentalists. In times of religious awakening, the Church's song has always undergone significant alteration, and Leavitt published several new texts and tunes that became standards for well over 150 years. As the format of hymnals evolved during the first half of the nineteenth century, *The Christian Lyre* stood out as a model for printing both words and music in the same volume. Our own era is grappling with a fundamental change in the delivery of hymn texts and tunes by electronic means. Inroads made by popular and folk music during the Second Great Awakening began a process that helped create the gospel song and the contemporary Christian styles of our own day. *The Christian Lyre* reflects many of the innovations in evangelical worship and theology after 1800 and certainly deserves greater recognition than it has heretofore received.

APPENDIX

Hymn Tune Title	*The Christian Lyre*	Jackson Source—Hymn no. (page)
HEAVENLY HOME	1:18	DES 120 (p. 135)
MISSIONARY HYMN	1:24	WS 75 (p. 148)
CONFIDENCE	1:30	DES 142 (p.152); WNS 2 (p.146)
PILGRIM'S FAREWELL	1:37	WS 78 (p. 149)
EXPOSTULATION	1:40	DES 87 (p. 107)
SUFFERING SAVIOR	1:42	DES 184 (p. 189)
GARDEN HYMN	1:46	DES 158 (p.166)
HEAVENLY UNION	1:74	DES 9 (p. 24)
GOSPEL POOL	1:82	DES 185 (p. 190)
STAR IN THE EAST	1:104	DES 182 (p.188)
THE RESOLVE	1:118	WNS 47 (p.178
HEAVENLY LOVE [FIDUCIA]	1:122	DES 183 (p. 189)
MELODY [PRIMROSE]	1:128	DES 165 (p. 172); WS 5 (p. 134)
HARVEST HOME	1:134	DES 136 (p. 147)
SOMETIMES A LIGHT SURPRISES	1:136	DES 170 (p. 177)
HOME	1:142	WS 73 (p. 148)
PISGAH	1:150	WNS 27 (p.164); SFS 123 (p.144)
PLEADING SAVIOR	1:156	SFS 100 (p. 126)
HIDING PLACE	1:162	DES 35 (p. 54)
WHO'S LIKE JESUS	1:164	DES 82 (p.102)
DE FLEURY [GREENFIELDS]	1:178	WS 72 (p.148)
HOFWYL [PASSION CHORALE]	1:196	DES 129 (p.142)
SACRAMENT	1:198	DES 137 (p.148)
NIGHT THOUGHT	2:18	DES 65 (p. 89); WNS 108 (p. 222)
CHINA	2:24	DES 112 (p. 129)
GRATEFUL MEMORY [PLENARY]	2:32	WS 32 (p. 140)
OLD GERMAN	2:37	DES 134 (p.146)
WINDHAM	2:96A	DES 103 (p.120)
HAMILTON	2:112	DES 67 (p. 91)
CORYDON	2:156	DES 26 (p. 42)
HARVEST [END OF THE WORLD]	2:210	DES 28 (p. 45)

Key to George Pullen Jackson Sources

DES: *Down-East Spirituals and Others* (New York: J. J. Augustin, 1943).

WNS: *White and Negro Spirituals: Their Life Span and Kinship* (New York: J. J. Augustin, 1943).

SFS: *Spiritual Folk-Songs of Early America* (New York: J. J. Augustin, 1937; rep. ed., New York: Dover Publications, 1964).

WS: *White Spirituals in the Southern Uplands: The Story of the Fasola Folk, Their Songs, Singings, and "Buckwheat Notes"* (Chapel Hill: The University of North Carolina Press, 1933; rep. ed., New York: Dover Publications, 1965).

NOTES

1. Joshua Leavitt, *The Christian Lyre: A Collection of Hymns and Tunes, Adapted for Social Worship, Prayer Meetings, and Revivals of Religion*, 24th ed., rev., 2 vols. in 1 (Andover, Mass.: Gould, Newman and Saxton, 1840), supplement advertisement.

2. Charles G. Finney, *Lecture on Revivals of Religion*, 2nd ed. (New York: Fleming H. Revell, 1868), 12.

3. William G. McLoughlin, *Modern Revivalism: Charles Grandison Finney to Billy Graham* (New York: Ronald Press, 1959), 86.

4. Finney, *Lectures on Revivals of Religion*, 126.

5. Ibid., 127–28.

6. The *Western Recorder*, edited by Thomas Hastings and Ova P. Hoyt, was published in Utica, N.Y., from 1824–1833, and therefore is not to be confused with the *Western Recorder* published by the Kentucky Baptist Convention.

7. Thomas Hastings, *Western Recorder*, December 28, 1830, cited in Robert Samuel Fletcher, *A History of Oberlin College: From Its Foundation through the Civil War*, 2 vols. (Oberlin, Ohio: Oberlin College, 1943), 1:14.

8. Thomas Hastings and Lowell Mason, *Spiritual Songs for Social Worship* (Utica, N.Y.: William Williams, 1833), 3.

9. John Julian, *A Dictionary of Hymnology*, 2 vols. (London: J. Murray, 1907; rep. ed., New York: Dover Publications, 1957), 1:795.

10. Leavitt, *The Christian Lyre*, 3.

11. Ibid.

12. Louis F. Benson, *The English Hymn: Its Development and Use in Worship* (Philadelphia: The Presbyterian Board of Publication, 1915; rep. ed., Richmond: John Knox Press, 1956), 300.

13. Leavitt, *The Christian Lyre*, 3.

14. Ellen Jane Porter, "The Devil's Good Tunes: A Study of the Secular in Protestant Hymnody," *The Diapason* 62 (1972): 18–20; Esther Heidi Rothenbusch, "The Role of *Gospel Hymns: Nos. 1 to 6* (1875–1984) in American Revivalism," (Ph.D. dissertation, University of Michigan, 1991), 292–313.

15. Harry Eskew, "O Sacred Head, Now Wounded," in *Handbook to* The Baptist Hymnal, ed. Jere V. Adams (Nashville: Convention Press, 1992), 208–209.

16. Leavitt, *The Christian Lyre*, 1:196–97.

17. George Pullen Jackson, *Down-East Spirituals* (New York: J. J. Augustin, 1943).

18. William Walker, *The Southern Harmony and Musical Companion . . .* (Philadelphia: E. W. Miller, 1854; rep. ed., Lexington: The University Press of Kentucky, 1987), 123.

19. William J. Reynolds, "Jesus, I My Cross Have Taken," in *Handbook to* The Baptist Hymnal, ed. Jere V. Adams (Nashville: Convention Press, 1992), 170.

20. William J. Reynolds, *Hymns of Our Faith* (Nashville: Broadman Press, 1964), 20.

21. Ibid., 134.

22. Ibid., 36.

23. Ibid., 48.

24. Ernest K. Emurian, *Stories of Songs About Heaven* (Grand Rapids: Baker Book House, 1972), 68–73.

25. Leonard Webster Ellinwood, ed., *The Dictionary of American Hymnology: First Line Index*, 179 microfilm reels (New York: University Music Editions, 1984), 1:142–145.
26. Emurian, *Stories of Songs About Heaven*, 72.
27. There is no internal evidence as to the identity of "L. H. S."
28. William Gunn and Thomas Harrison, *The Christian Melodist* (Louisville: Morton and Griswold, 1850); F. E. Pitts, *Zion's Harp* (Louisville: Morton and Griswold, 1852); Silas W. Leonard and A. D. Fillmore, *The Christian Psalmist* (Louisville: S. W. Leonard, 1854).
29. Again, the identity of "W. M." remains unknown.
30. George Pullen Jackson, *White Spirituals in the Southern Uplands: The Story of the Fasola Folk, Their Songs, Singings, and "Buckwheat Notes"* (Chapel Hill: The University of North Carolina Press, 1933; rep. ed., New York: Dover Publications, 1965), 140.

"The Minister and His Hymn Book"
John A. Broadus as Hymnologist

Esther Rothenbusch Crookshank

Introduction

What was the legacy of John Albert Broadus in the field of hymnological study and teaching, and why is it important? A founding faculty member and the second president of The Southern Baptist Theological Seminary, Broadus was the first professor ever to develop a hymnology course at a Protestant seminary in the United States.

Of the four founding faculty members of the seminary, two were hymnologists who profoundly influenced church music in the South and laid the foundation for the musical worship of Southern Baptists—Broadus as a teacher of hymnology and Basil Manly, Jr., as the leading Southern Baptist hymnal compiler. These men are called by Timothy George and David S. Dockery "two Southern Baptist giants who significantly influenced Baptist thought at the close of the nineteenth century. . . . Broadus was a brilliant linguist, but he made his greatest contribution in the area of pastoral theology, particularly through his preaching textbook."[1] Broadus's book, *A Treatise on the Preparation and Delivery of Sermons* (1870),[2] has for the past century deservedly stood as the foundation for Baptist preaching, according to Thomas McKibbens.[3] It has been revised and translated multiple times, and within thirty years of its appearance passed through twenty-five editions. Basil Manly, Jr., and his father compiled the first American hymnal to include the word Baptist in its title, *The Baptist Psalmody* of 1850.[4] At the end of his life he published the collection entitled *Manly's Choice,* in which he intended to preserve the best standard hymns in the face of the influx of popular gospel hymnody.[5] The impact of the collaboration of these two men in their hymnological endeavors for the churches can hardly be overestimated.

Born in Culpeper County, Virginia, in 1827, Broadus graduated from the University of Virginia at the top of his class, pastored a church in that state, and served as chaplain to his alma mater. Thereafter he was appointed to the committee that planned Southern Seminary, in which he was responsible for developing the curriculum. Ultimately he became a charter faculty member and, in 1889, he was elected president of Southern Seminary. When the seminary was forced to close during the Civil War, Broadus served as a military chaplain under General Lee. When it reopened with a handful of students after the war, Broadus had only one student in the preaching class, and he was blind. His lectures to that student formed the basis of Broadus's legendary textbook.

The substance of his contribution to hymnology is contained in seven documents. Of these, his address at Southern Seminary in the fall of 1884, entitled "English Hymns of the Nineteenth Century," appears to have been lost. The others are found in the seminary archives and were available for the present study: the original edition of his textbook, particularly the chapter entitled "Conduct of Public Worship"; his typescript lecture entitled "The Minister and His Hymn Book," part of the Lyman Beecher Lecture series he delivered at Yale University in January 1889[6]; a printed copy of his *Syllabus as to Hymnology* (1892); and three bound undated copybooks of his handwritten lecture notes with some loose handwritten pages inserted.[7]

The Early Courses in Hymnology

The 1859–1860 academic *Catalogue* shows that Broadus taught a unit on hymns and hymn writers in his homiletics course from the first year of the seminary's existence.[8] By the next year, he had added to the course description "exercises in reading the Scripture and Hymns, with an account of the metrical structure of English Hymns."[9] In 1872, his book was listed as a required textbook for the first time and he had added the sentence, "The class is freely exercised in reading the Scriptures, and reading Hymns, and much stress is laid upon the proper conduct of Public Worship."[10] Hymnology as a discipline is first mentioned in the *Catalogue* of 1879–80: "There is also a series of Lectures on Hymnology."[11]

By 1885 Broadus had divided the material between English hymnody, essential for every preaching student, and the study of foreign-language hymns as an elective course. Thus in the *Catalogue* of 1885–86, the first year in which special studies courses were offered, the course title "Foreign Hymnology" appears in that category, along with Arabic, Aramaic, and Theological German. The course included: "Latin Hymns, some Greek Hymns, and either German or French Hymns. Lectures are given on the history of hymns in the several languages. Besides oral translations, the class make [*sic*] some written translations, in prose and in verse."[12] By 1887–88, Broadus had increased the workload still more: "Readings . . . in Latin and Greek hymns, German and French hymns."[13] In the *Catalogue* of 1891–92 the phrase appears, "Books furnished."[14]

Beginning in 1892, E. C. Dargan had begun to assist Broadus in teaching homiletics and, for the next two years, was listed as co-professor of the class.[15] Broadus died on March 16, 1895, and Dargan completed the academic year as teacher of the course. Dargan used Broadus's hymnology syllabus as one of the textbooks for homiletics from 1895 through 1901.[16] He also taught foreign hymnology for four years after Broadus's death, after which the course was discontinued.

Syllabus as to Hymnology

Henry S. Burrage, the great pioneer biographer of Baptist hymn writers, acknowledged Broadus's hymnological expertise in a letter to him in 1886, thanking Broadus for a copy of his *Syllabus* and indicating that it would be "exceedingly helpful" to him in its suggestions.[17] He gratefully acknowledged the latter's help to him throughout the writing of his famous book, noting that Broadus had sent to him, "from the library of the Seminary, twenty-one hymn books, many of them rare; and in other ways from the beginning of my work he has aided me in its prosecution."[18] Burrage also praised the progressive nature and apparent uniqueness among Baptists of Broadus's hymnology course: "I am glad to know that in one of our Seminaries work of this kind is done."[19]

No copies of the first edition of Broadus's *Syllabus*, dated 1883, appear to be extant.[20] The copy of Broadus's *Syllabus* preserved in The Southern Baptist Theological Seminary Archives is a booklet of twenty-three pages, 5.5 inches wide by 8 inches long, labeled "*Syllabus as to Hymnology* by John A. Broadus. Printed for the use of the class in Homiletics. Second ed. January, 1892." It was privately published and is the only one of Broadus's hymnological writings, apart from the chapter on worship in his textbook, to have appeared in print. It presents the course material in an extended outline, often in incomplete sentences and in paragraph form. Broadus's main subject headings, numbered according to his unique system of outline form and italicization, are reproduced in Table 1.

His approach to his subject from the outset was two-fold: scholarly and applied. As his first order of business, Broadus established the legitimacy of art in worship from historical and biblical perspectives, beginning from the question, "What place may Art have in Worship?" On the topic of art, Broadus's vast literary background, evident from his writings, should be mentioned. He was at home not only in the poets of his own century—Longfellow, Wordsworth, and Tennyson—but also in Shakespeare, Dryden, Milton, Spencer, Doddridge, and others. His knowledge of choral music was equally impressive, but did not keep him from being conversant with the new genres of Sunday school songs and gospel hymns, the popular styles of his time. As one examines Broadus's views on art, it is apparent that he was thoroughly versed in what musicologist H. Wiley Hitchcock has called both the "cultivated" and "vernacular" traditions of music and poetry flourishing in the United States in the nineteenth century.[21]

Table 1. Overall Outline of Broadus's Hymnology *Syllabus*

PART I.
DIDACTIC HYMNOLOGY.

Chapter I.	FUNDAMENTAL INQUIRIES.
Chapter II.	AIM OF HYMNOLOGY.
Chapter III.	DEFINITION OF HYMNS [see page 138].
Chapter IV.	THE MATERIAL OF HYMNS.
Chapter V.	THE FORM OF HYMNS.

PART II.
HISTORICAL HYMNOLOGY.

LITERATURE, *General works.*
Chapter I. SCRIPTURE HYMNS.
Chapter II. HYMNS MENTIONED IN THE 2ND AND 3RD CENTURIES.
Chapter III. HYMNS REMAINING FROM 4TH AND FOLLOWING CENTURIES TO CLOSE OF THE MIDDLE AGES.
- I. *Syriac* Hymns.
- II. *Greek* Hymns.
- III. *Latin* Hymns. LITERATURE.

Hints as to Reading the Latin Hymns.

Chapter IV. GERMAN HYMNS.
- I. Before the Reformation.
- II. Luther's Hymns.
- III. Since Luther.

Chapter V. FRENCH HYMNS.
Chapter VI. ENGLISH HYMNS. (The *numbers* refer to *The Baptist Hymnal* [1883].)
- I. First Period. Only psalms sung in worship, in very literal metrical versions.
- II. Second Period. Hymns begin to be used with the Psalter.
- III. Third Period. Psalms themselves are converted into hymns by free metrical translation. Isaac Watts.
- IV. Fourth Period. Hymns of the Wesley and Whitfield movement.
- V. Fifth Period. Hymns of the Evangelical movement in the Church of England.
- VI. Hymns of the Oxford Movement (Puseyite), beginning about 1830.
- VII. Hymns of the Unitarian movement.
- VIII. We now reach several groups which proceed on a different principle.
  - 1) Hymns of the Missionary movement.
  - 2) Hymns of the Sunday School movement.
  - 3) Hymns of the Y. M. C. A. and lay preaching movement.

Chapter VII. General remarks on the history of Christian hymns.
Chapter VIII. BAPTIST HYMNS WRITERS AND BAPTIST HYMN BOOKS.
A. *Leading Baptist Hymn Writers.*
BAPTIST HYMN BOOKS.

To address the role of art in worship, Broadus began by grouping the elements of worship into three general categories: "a) Architecture, sculpture, painting, flowers; b) Music, studied eloquence, poetry; and c) cushions, carpets, etc."[22] Then he summarized the treatment of these elements in a variety of historic worship traditions. The Quakers, he observed, "have endeavored to exclude art altogether" in their rejection of singing, church ornamentation, and "prepared discourses," the "Roman Catholics have long represented the opposite extreme," and "English and American Baptists were long averse to the artistic in worship." In his summary of Baptist worship practices, his tone of disapproval was unmistakable: "Change [in worship practices among Baptists] not made upon any definite principle, but [upon] (a) growing general taste for art, (b) demands of the young, (c) rivalry with other denominations, (d) reaction, uncertain and sometimes violent."[23] Broadus was too passionate about the spiritual maturity of the churches not to denounce what he viewed as a serious failing of theirs—a lack of principle in their conduct of worship which made them susceptible to passing fashions, to the demands of the spiritually immature, and to drastic, thoughtless reactionism.

Broadus then settled emphatically the question of art for Baptists by his declaration: "Now we can not wholly exclude art from worship." For one, he argued, the Bible itself contains much poetry; secondly, he asserted, "the Bible enjoins *singing*, which necessarily becomes artistic. Art then must be employed in worship," he argued, adding in an Augustinian tone: "But it is apt to become hurtful, as in Roman Catholic worship. What principles will guide?"[24]

Broadus's four "guiding principles" offered a carefully-qualified license for the use of art in worship. First, art is permissible only as subservient to religion, so long as it is not pursued "for the sake of mere aesthetic gratification," and second, so long as its "character and extent . . . be determined by the more spiritual and at the same time more intelligent of the church, with careful consideration of what is best for all classes."[25] Here Broadus addressed from a pastoral standpoint the issue of class relations in the local church. Equally thought provoking was his third tenet: "The extent to which . . . [art] may be employed without injury and with benefit will vary somewhat according to the art culture of the worshipers, but not in direct proportion thereto." Broadus seemed to assert by this that a congregation need not—indeed must not—sink aesthetically to the level of the surrounding culture merely to conform or to please its members; conversely, even a congregation enthusiastically devoted to the arts ought not to have a worship service consisting entirely of "high art" music. His instincts thus tended toward a "blended" worship style a century before such a concept was known. His fourth principle was foundational to all the rest: "The pastor must constantly strive . . . to make all the congregation employ the externals as mere helps to spirituality, and to exclude or repress what would distract."[26]

Broadus defined hymns as "lyrical poems, adapted to worship. Poetry is imaginative thought or sentiment, expressed in highly rhythmical language . . . anything that awakens a similar sentiment may be called poetical. . . . Lyrical poetry is that which is designed to be sung. . . . *Christian* hymns are lyrical poems adapted to Christian worship." He evaluated all types of hymns, whether subjective, objective, or a combination of the two, by the criteria: "(1) Thoroughly true; a) the doctrine Scriptural, (b) the sentiments genuine. (2) Devotional in tone, and edifying. (3) Suited to *public* worship."[27]

Broadus on Hymnological Sources

The nineteenth century saw the rise of Western hymnology as a discipline, and the publication of seminal works in English, German, and French hymnology. It was the era of the rediscovery of Greek and Latin hymns in the Oxford Movement in England, and of the great translations of these texts into English by John Mason Neale, Edward Caswell, and others. Notable collections in Latin were Hermann Daniel's *Thesaurus Hymnologicus* (Leipzig, 1841–56)[28] and Francis March's *Latin Hymns, with English Notes* (1874).[29] Philipp Wackernagel had published his monumental five-volume historical and bibliographic study of German chorale texts by 1877.[30]

Broadus's bibliographic annotations show his close familiarity with these sources and with the full spectrum of works in the field in his day.[31] Sources in English include Josiah Miller's *Singers and Songs of the Church* (1869),[32] whose second edition Broadus called "Best work in existence for the general student," and Burrage's groundbreaking *Baptist Hymn Writers and Their Hymns* of 1888[33] ("Very thorough and satisfactory, giving much that was not previously known").[34] But Broadus also treated popular devotional works for a general readership, such as Hezekiah Butterworth's compilation of biographical sketches, *Story of the Hymns* (1875)[35] ("a pleasant volume"), *Evenings with the Sacred Poets* by Frederick Saunders (1869)[36] ("Pleasant for family reading—with *specimens* as well as history"), and John Prescott's *Christian Hymns and Hymns Writers* (1883)[37] ("Four popular lectures, pleasant and sensible").

Broadus's annotations tell us of the cultural role of hymnody at his time and the broad devotional interest in hymns and hymn study for personal edification and diversion. Hymn reading and meditation were a normal part of the private devotions of Christians; hymn memorization was a spiritual exercise taught not only to children at school and church from an early age, it was a lifelong pursuit for many, cultivated especially by ministers. This era brought not only a flood of hymns by lay women in the churches, but a lively interest in hymn study among women generally. Broadus described one popular collection, *The Seven Great Hymns of the Mediaeval Church*, with the remarks: "Originals and translations, with explanatory material. Very pleasant. Ladies enjoy it."[38]

As his textbook Broadus chose *The Baptist Hymnal* of 1883, to which he referred throughout the syllabus.[39] Jointly edited by theologian E. H. Johnson of Crozer Seminary and the well-known composer of gospel hymn tunes, William Howard Doane, its publication marked some significant "firsts." This substantial volume of 726 hymns was published in a format progressive for the time, with tunes printed beneath the text, as well as in a words-only version. Broadus praised its historical scope, probably unprecedented in a Baptist collection of American imprint to that time: "The hymns are well chosen, comprising translations from Latin and Greek, French and German." He commended its thoughtful balance between "numerous standard English hymns and some of the best recent 'Gospel Songs,'"[40] and even claimed that "the music far surpasses [that of] any previous book." It also represented the first significant collaboration between Baptists of the North and South since the Civil War.[41] According to Broadus, the book was already "having a very wide circulation" by the time of his writing in 1892.[42]

Hymnological Survey

A comparison between the *Syllabus* and his Yale lecture shows that Broadus attempted to condense in that lecture the essence of his entire course, an endeavor in which he succeeded to a remarkable degree. Broadus started his historical survey with the Psalms and the biblical canticles (which he called "some other beautiful songs scattered throughout the O[ld] T[estament] and N[ew] T[estament]," including the five Lukan canticles[43]) and the "extracts from Christian hymns in the Epistles: 'Who was manifest' [1 Tim. 3:16], 'Awake, thou that sleepest' [Eph. 5:14], &c."[44] Here he anticipated important modern research on the Lukan texts and the Christ-hymn fragments in the New Testament Epistles.[45]

He began his discussion of medieval hymnody with the memorable passage entitled "Hints as to Reading the Latin Hymns," a classic introduction awaiting discovery by the modern student.[46] In it he advised the reader to begin with the hymns of Ambrose, "marked by a rugged and vigorous simplicity that is truly Roman, and very different from the elaborate elegance and sweetness of the Medieval hymns."[47] At every point in both the *Syllabus* and lecture he clearly intended to make his material speak to his audience of young preachers. For example, he emphasized that "the great age of the production of Latin hymns was the 12th and 13th centuries. E.g., Bernard of Clairvaux (St. Bernard), Bernard of Cluny, Adam of St. Victor. . . . Observe that this was the age of the foremost Medieval preachers also, Peter the Hermit, St. Bernard, Antony of Padua, Thomas Aquinas. Concurrence interesting."[48]

He traced the Reformation chorale and the rise of metrical psalmody under Calvin, followed by the freer, Christianized psalm paraphrases of Watts. Broadus naturally devoted special attention to writers within his own confessional tradition. He esteemed the first major Baptist hymn writer, Anne Steele (1716–78), as "one of the leading hymn-writers in English (after Watts and Wesley)," ranking her with John Newton, William Cowper, and James Montgomery. Broadus singled out as noteworthy Robert Robinson (author of "Come Thou Fount of ev'ry blessing"), despite his inclinations to Socinian heresy in later years. He also noted John Rippon, compiler of a famous hymn supplement to Watts's *Psalms of David*,[49] and Samuel Medley's hymns ("some of our best"). The American pioneer preacher John Leland (1754–1851) received praise for his "many good hymns," of which "The day is past and gone" is in *The Baptist Hymnal* (1883). The obscure Khrisna Pal[50] (1764–1882), remembered by Broadus as the "first Baptist convert in Hindoostan" who was baptized in the Ganges in 1799, wrote several Bengali hymns, of which *The Baptist Hymnal* included "O, thou my soul, forget no more." The list of Baptist notables also included John Fawcett (author of "Blest be the tie that binds"), Adoniram Judson ("Come Holy Spirit, Dove divine," a baptism hymn), Lydia Baxter ("Take the name of Jesus with you"), Charles Haddon Spurgeon ("Amidst us our beloved stands," a communion hymn), Robert Lowry ("Shall we gather at the river"), and Basil Manly, Jr. ("Soldiers of Christ in truth arrayed," the official hymn of Southern Seminary). Manly died on January 31, 1892, at the beginning of the semester for which the *Syllabus* was printed.

World missions, one of the great themes of Broadus's century, received a special overview in Broadus's *Syllabus*. He named Anglican Bishop Reginald Heber and Baptist minister Samuel Francis Smith as the two "great writers" of missionary hymns. Students may be inspired by his account of Heber's writing of the missionary classic, "From Greenland's icy mountains." Noting that "Heber wrote this hymn almost impromptu,"[51] Broadus was careful to identify the origin of this hymn's greatness in both skill and devotional fervor: "Mark you," he told his Yale audience, "the author was 36 years old, practiced from childhood in composition of prose and verse, and filled with that enthusiasm for missionary work, which four years later led him to India as a missionary bishop."[52] In the *Syllabus* he added, "Mere genius could not have accomplished this, had he not long felt a deep interest in the mission work, so that mind and heart were full of the subject, and imagination was readily fired." Broadus likewise emphasized to his students that Samuel Francis Smith wrote his great mission hymn, "The morning light is breaking," at the age of twenty-four while a seminary student at Newton [later Andover-Newton] Seminary.[53] Explaining the success of this and Smith's other "great hymn," "My country, 'tis of thee," Broadus noted that each was "married to a thoroughly congenial tune."[54]

In his survey of hymns from various confessional traditions, Broadus showed a remarkable ecumenism untouched by the slightest theological compromise; he had the discernment to appreciate excellence and artistry without embracing doctrinal heterodoxy in the process. He also decisively rebuked a "party" spirit that did not carefully examine all sides of a subject. For example, he concluded his memorable comparison of the hymns of Watts and Wesley with the observation: "Many judge [these two hymn writers] only by their sympathy with Calvinism or Arminianism . . . but a large part of the best hymns of each are acceptable to all parties." Of Frederick W. Faber, one of several Oxford movement clergy who "became a Romanist," Broadus commented: "[He] has written many hymns of great excellence, some of them showing an intensity of devout feeling that is seldom equaled." As an example, he cited Faber's hymn, "Hark! Hark, my soul! angelic songs are swelling."[55]

On the hymns and hymn writers of Unitarianism, Broadus was careful to commend what he found of excellence within that movement's hymnody: "Several of our favorite hymns are from conservative Unitarians, who are often deeply devout. Thus [Hymn] 387 ['Nearer, my God, to Thee'] is from Mrs. [Sarah Flowers] Adams, who was noted for religious earnestness as well as thorough cultivation." He also named in this connection Sir John Bowring, citing Hymn 126, "In the cross of Christ I glory," and Anna Laetitia Barbauld (author of "Praise to God, immortal praise"). "So among American Unitarians," he continued, "the best hymns are rarely from the now powerful radical wing, but from devout conservatives, some of them semi-orthodox, e.g. [Hymn] 110" ("It came upon the midnight clear").[56] He even cited an "interesting volume called 'Hymns of the Liberal Faith,'" containing "good hymns from Bryant and Longfellow."[57] His counsel in this connection is still invaluable today:

> The hymns now given in practical hymn books come from all denominations of Christians. Many of the best are from the Romanists ([e.g.], Mediæval writers, Xavier, Newman, Faber), from High Church Episcopalians ([e.g.], Keble), or from Unitarians ([e.g.], Mrs. Adams, Bowring). Many Christian sentiments are held in common by devout persons who differ widely upon some important points of doctrine.[58] . . . It is proper to use the fit language of devotion, from whatever source it may originally have come. Some care is, however, necessary, lest associated errors be thereby unconsciously received into the mind, such as Mariolatry in Romanist hymns, Sacramentarianism in Keble, Arminianism in Wesley, etc.[59]

In short, John A. Broadus taught his students how to reclaim the glorious hymnic legacy of the Church, to the inestimable enrichment of their own spiritual lives and that of their congregations, while honing their skills of discernment in "proving all things and holding fast that which is good."

In his historical summary Broadus compared the early Christian hymns, "almost exclusively objective, describing the facts of Scripture history, the attributes of God," with the medieval hymns, in which "the subjective element has become more marked; the sacred facts are made the occasion of expressing religious emotions. In modern times," he continued, "the subjective element has become predominant, almost exclusive." He found this trend characteristic of general poetry as well as of hymnody at his time. "But Christianity is a historical religion," he argued. "All its doctrines rest on facts, and the healthiest Christian sentiment is developed by contemplation of the Christian facts. Would it not then be well to select more frequently than is now common those hymns in which the objective elements predominate?"[60] Broadus's words still speak with striking clarity and currency today. They are a clarion call to churches, pastors, worship leaders, songwriters, hymnwriters, and the Christian music industry to return to a disciplined "contemplation of Christian facts" as they are revealed in Scripture.

Broadus on Contemporaneous Hymnody

Broadus reserved his most pointed comments for the songs and hymns of his own time. The Church in his day was being swept by a new musical style, that of the gospel hymn or song, which had grown out of the Sunday school song and had been popularized in the YMCA movement and the urban revivalism pioneered by Dwight L. Moody and Ira D. Sankey. Gospel hymnody had become not only the musical hallmark of evangelistic, prayer, and mission services, it had also taken over Sunday morning worship in several evangelical denominations by century's end.

Broadus began this section by praising the Sunday school movement for the "great and salutary change" it had wrought "beginning some thirty years ago, by introducing livelier religious songs and sprightlier tunes."[61] He saw the benefit in the practice in this repertory of giving to each hymn its own tune, adding, "We now have many beautiful Sunday School songs, chiefly produced in America." But he sharply objected to what he called "several evils [that] have arisen, which greatly need attention."[62]

He first condemned the poor musical quality and secular origins of the "wretched ditties" that "most of the books contain, . . . which ought to be carefully avoided, and to be judiciously discouraged where they are popular." Second, he charged, "Many tunes have been introduced that are unsuitable for religious use." Broadus believed in "a real distinction between sacred and secular music."[63] While some secular tunes were used, he admitted, "by the Psalmists, and . . . in every period of Christian History, . . . others, though very beautiful, are unfit vehicles of religious sentiment, to say nothing of their fixed associations." Third, he complained, "As children have to *learn* the tunes, there is an aggravated tendency to care more for the music than the words." Fourth and last, he lamented that "most Sunday Schools now almost entirely neglect the standard hymns and tunes that are used in the public worship. But there are great advantages in having the children early become familiar with many of these."[64]

Broadus described the "hymns of the Y.M.C.A. and lay preaching movement" [i.e., gospel hymns] as "familiar and justly prized," and found "some of the hymns and tunes," such as those by Philip P. Bliss, Robert Lowry, and Fanny Crosby, "extremely delightful and profitable." "But with these new songs," as with Sunday school hymns, he reiterated, "we must carefully avoid the four evils mentioned above."[65]

Broadus ended the *Syllabus* with a survey of Baptist hymn books, ranging from the early historic collections of Benjamin Keach and Samuel Stennett through the hymnals of his time. Spurgeon's *Our Own Hymn Book* (1866) in Broadus's words "presents a good working combination of solid hymns and lighter S[unday] S[chool] songs, &c."[66] Broadus also listed some smaller collections, including a few of the many popular books "prepared by and for various evangelists." *The Baptist Hymnal* (1883), on the other hand, presented a comprehensive church hymnal, "suited to the wants of all congregations," that set a completely new standard for both music and texts. As a special innovation, this book offered two tunes for many texts, "one of which is familiar and of proved excellence, and the other . . . carefully-chosen from the best earlier and newer sources."[67]

Broadus's assessments of the hymnals and hymnody of his time showed a comprehensive grasp of emerging regional differences in the United States and of the growing complexity of American society and evangelicalism by the late nineteenth century. Being a Southerner, he was familiar with the shape-note singing tradition, acknowledged its cultural importance in congregational life, and spoke highly of some of its proponents while decidedly not embracing it. In reviewing *The Southern Psalmist* by J. R. Graves and J. M. Pendleton, he wrote in his lecture notes: "These shape-notes are very popular in some parts of South, & many intelligent brethren recommend their use. I think it is like learning a little N.T. Greek. Better do 1 [one] thing really, or not at all. But every one to his opinion."[68]

Being a theologian and preacher of national stature and having spent time in New Haven, he judged the voluminous and scholarly *Service of Song*, with its one thousand-plus hymns, two dozen chants, and "music highly classic—much . . . German music" as "best for private reading, & for many congregations in New England, & some elsewhere. Not for popular use."[69] *The Baptist Praise Book*, on the other hand, compiled by E. M. Levy and H. C. Fish, was clearly a favorite with a wide swath of evangelicalism at the time of his lectures. He summed up the book with his characteristic honesty and terseness: "A good many S[unday] S[chool] hymns, Temperance songs, etc. included. Some trashy pieces, but a very rich collection. . . . Much sprightly & pleasing music, both classic & popular. Most *choirs* prefer this book."[70] His remarks speak not only of the state of congregational singing, but apparently also of choral music in many churches of his time.

He had particular praise for Manly's collection *The Choice*, published the previous year, calling it "a small selection of the very best hymns."[71] It was intended as a concise treasury of lasting old and new hymns for personal as well as congregational use.[72] Broadus concluded his course with an observation still true of Baptists, and with a wearied exhortation: "It is evident that Baptists will not universally adopt, nor long adhere to, any one book, yet there are obvious advantages in uniformity, and it should be encouraged where other conditions permit."[73]

Instructions to Preachers from "The Minister and His Hymn Book"

In January 1889, the year in which Broadus was made seminary president, he was invited to give the prestigious Lyman Beecher Lectures on Preaching at Yale University. He entitled his series "Preaching and the Ministerial Life."[74] It is this famous series of which Broadus's biographer and younger colleague, A. T. Robertson, later made the claim: "This course of lectures created high enthusiasm, more, perhaps, than any since the days of

Henry Ward Beecher's."[75] The titles of Broadus's eight lectures suggest the breadth of training and depth of godly discipline that he envisioned for the young minister: "The Young Preacher's Outfit," "Freshness in Preaching," "Sensation Preaching," "Freedom in Preaching," "The Minister's General Reading," "The Minister and His Hymn Book," "The Minister and His Bible," and "The Minister's Private Life." One may note with surprise that only four lectures dealt with sermons; fully half of the series was devoted to the cultivation of the minister's spirit, mind, and private devotional life through the study of Scripture, hymns, and other edifying reading.

In his lecture on the hymn book, after tracing the same historical sweep that he had done in his *Syllabus* but at breakneck speed, Broadus concluded with practical instructions, still priceless for ministers today. Ministers in that day had the responsibility for hymn selection, yet few had any preparation. Broadus listed three characteristics of a good hymn as a guide to selecting hymns for worship. "Any good hymn will be poetical, in imagery, diction, and rhythm, just in its religious thoughts, and sympathetic, warming." These criteria reflect his high standards of literary quality, his insistence on doctrinal integrity, and his conviction that worship involves the emotions and that hymns ought to express the heartfelt prayers of the people. He further noted the proliferation of hymn books, even good ones, at his time, and the fact that "ministers often change places!—& so, frequently change books. The free competition gives us better books . . . ."[76] "Address yourself then," he advised, "to the task of gaining thorough familiarity with one good book, and the change to another will be no severe undertaking. Such familiarity will save you much time in selecting hymns for the various services you direct, as well as help you to make a good selection."[77]

His instruction revealed a sense of the flow of the worship service rather than a formulaic approach to planning worship. One principle ought to be engraved upon every seminarian's heart: "In selecting for a particular occasion or for use in connection with a particular subject, it is far better to take a good warming hymn that has only a general fitness, than one quite specifically adapted in its ideas, but merely didactic and cold."[78] Broadus taught ministers what type of hymn was suited for each place in the service:

> The first hymn for any regular church service ought to be one of worship, in the broad sense; in general harmony with the sermon, but not specifically related thereto. The second hymn may lead up to the sermon; the third may be chosen to kindle such feelings and stir such purposes as the sermon would prompt. In all cases remember the caution above suggested. Keep a list of hymns you employ in public worship, or mark in your hymn book the no. of times any hymn is sung.[79]

His last remark here might help churches today to avoid the pitfall of singing the same hymns or worship songs month after month.

He expounded passionately on the value of hymn study for pastors:

> What practical benefit will come to the working pastor from a study of the general history of hymns[?] I answer, it will cause him to understand hymns more thoughtfully, to select better, to read a hymn (when appropriate), with far more of sympathetic interest and appreciation. He may sometimes add much to the interest with which a hymn will be sung, by telling something of its origin, or its author in general, or of some instance in which it is known to have made a blessed impression.[80]

He qualified this advice in his textbook by noting that the historical background of hymns was most effectively given within a sermon: "The circumstances connected with the original production of a hymn are sometimes very interesting, and while it is seldom desirable to mention them when the hymn is about to be sung, they may sometimes be stated, with good effect, when it is quoted in a sermon."[81] Furthermore, he saw the value of hymn study for a broad understanding of church history: "The history of hymns abounds in general instruction. We have seen that they stand in very close relation, both as product and as cause, to the general growth of Christian sentiment and Christian life.[82] His understanding of a hymn as both cultural product and catalyst of historical process foreshadows many contextual studies on hymnody and popular piety published in recent decades.[83]

Broadus's instruction extended beyond use of the hymn book. He urged ministers to develop their voices with training and excellence, to undertake vocal instruction for their own health as preachers: "It is . . . very desirable that a minister should be able to sing, and to sing by note. Learn now," he commanded, "if never before. And learn to sing without an instrument. If properly managed, this exercise in singing will improve one's voice for speaking."[84]

On this point, one might add today, learn to sing without a sound system. Some of the most moving hymn singing this writer has ever experienced has been at the graveside of a loved one with only a small circle of people. There is so much that takes place during the final hymn before a burial, the closure that occurs is so enormously important, and the Scripture verse that the pastor reads and the hymn the pastor leads are never forgotten by a bereaved family. The same can be said of hospital singing. In that often noisy, jarring environment, there is comfort in the pastor's familiar voice quietly singing hymns. This need not be intimidating and it is not difficult, but it is ministry.

For missions students, the ability to sing and an understanding of the cross-cultural meanings of singing are essential.[85] Whatever the cultural context, people create community when they raise their voices to sing.

Broadus also urged preachers to listen to and learn great sacred music: "There will be a great gain if one should . . . make acquaintance with . . . the growth of sacred music," he advised, naming Ambrose, Gregory, Palestrina, the great Italian composers of oratorios, Luther, Wesley, the recent Church of England revival in hymnwriting, and Americans Lowell Mason and Ira Sankey among those who had produced church music of excellence or power or delight.[86] In effect, Broadus urged ministers to take a vigorous interest in many aspects of church music if they were to set examples for their congregations to do the same.

His instruction revealed not only his vast musical background, but his wise pastoral care. The end goal for Broadus was always the building up of the Church: "There is very great advantage where the pastor can, through some knowledge of music, have the full sympathy of the choir, and mediate, as will sometimes be needful, between the choir and the congregation. Some pastors greatly enjoy frequent meetings with the choir." Here his example was D. L. Moody: "Even a man who cannot sing may sometimes develop in himself, as Mr. Moody has done, a hearty love for singing, and a just appreciation of good singing, whereby he may greatly increase the interest taken by others."[87] Broadus's shepherding heart, his sense of collegiality, his call for open communication and greater understanding between pastors and members of the church music ministry, and the supportive, encouraging spirit he modeled are greatly needed in churches today. A considerable healing of rifts might begin through a pastor's leadership in this manner.

Broadus's Contribution to Hymnology

The great legacy of the second president of The Southern Baptist Theological Seminary in the field of hymnology was that he understood and powerfully taught the discipline in all its dimensions, theological and pastoral. He mastered its primary sources, theological and literary, and the most advanced scholarship of his time in a richly interdisciplinary synthesis through his prodigious grasp of history, philosophy, poetry, and both classical and modern languages. He demanded much the same mastery of his students. He spent decades building the seminary library's hymnology collection with rare and practical materials for their (i.e., the students') use. Above all, he impressed upon a generation of ministers the essence of historic hymnody and its importance and proper use in their own devotional lives, their ministries, and in the lives of the churches. Broadus understood Christian hymnody to be an expression of, as well as instruction and nurture for, the Church of every age. For Broadus, hymns were essential to the development and ministry of the Gospel preacher. And by establishing the role of art in worship on biblical principles from the outset, he avoided the cultural biases and relativistic pragmatism that plagued many church leaders of his own and succeeding generations.

John A. Broadus taught hymnology in one of the great eras of hymn writing, hymnic resurgence, and hymnological research in history. Like the men of the biblical tribe of Issachar, Broadus understood the times and knew what God's people should do.[88] The legacy of hymnological education at Southern Seminary was carried on in the years following Broadus by Professors R. Inman Johnson, Hugh T. McElrath, Donald P. Hustad, and others. The School of Church Music, founded in 1944, came to include the area of worship studies in 1996. Ironically, while new generations of God-called church musicians continue to be trained for ministry at Southern Baptist seminaries, some churches within the convention are turning away from the discipline of church music study that Broadus worked tirelessly to establish. At this critical time, Southern Baptists can hope and pray that increasingly more among their ranks will follow this historic denominational founder in his passion for biblically-shaped worship and in his keen pastoral vision for what the song of the Church can be. Broadus's hymnological writings have been lost to the Church for over a century. They speak again with prophetic wisdom and urgency to Southern Baptists and to all evangelicals today who find themselves at a cultural crossroads strikingly similar to that faced by Baptists in John A. Broadus's time.

How shall pastors, church musicians, students, and congregation members apply the example and teaching of Broadus today? What principles should mobilize each of us in our ministry contexts?

First, it is striking that he who wrote the definitive Baptist book on preaching admonished his students not to regard preaching as the only event of the worship service. (His chapter on the public reading of Scripture, for example, should be read by all who strive for excellence in public worship.) Certainly it must impress the reader that Broadus began his chapter, "Conduct of Public Worship," with the lines:

> A tendency may often be observed in our religious assemblies to neglect the worship, and think only of the preaching. Indeed, we frequently hear good men speak of the *preliminary* exercises. The devout reading of God's Word, sweet hymns of praise, and "prayer and supplication with thanksgiving"—these, we . . . [are given to understand], are of no great importance, only the porch, the threshold [to the worship service]![89]

Broadus saw all the elements of worship—Scripture reading, prayer, preaching, and song—to be vital to true worship and was zealous that all be rendered with care and excellence.

Second, he was aware of certain pitfalls that plagued the worship of his own day and which still characterize ours. He warned on the one hand against the use of secular musical styles inappropriate to the texts, yet he judiciously approved many gospel hymns and tunes of excellence. He was equally on guard against ritual formalism and what he called "the natural tendency of the human heart to make much of externals." One passage well summarizes his philosophy of worship:

> The freedom, spontaneity, simplicity, spirituality, of New Testament worship must be maintained at all costs. Thoroughly simple in form, so as not to encourage the people to rest in externals, but full of interest, animation, devoutness, solemn sweetness, and with a specific but inelaborate adaptation to the occasion,—such should be our worship. . . . Externals, however they may appeal to aesthetic sentiment, can never create devotion; but animated and earnest expression will strengthen devotion, and this may be achieved while carefully avoiding the danger of formalism.[90]

Although he argued for the judicious use of art in worship and never forbade the use of externals, Broadus nevertheless asserted, "Externals can never create devotion." His words might call to mind cutting-edge trends today toward multisensory and symbol-based worship. Broadus's antidote to pendulum swings in Baptist worship was to uphold and guard the "spontaneity, simplicity, and spirituality of true Christian worship."

Third, Broadus understood the value of hymns for meditation from his own devotional life. In response to the question, "Are we losing the hymns today?," the writer of an article once expressed the view that we lose the hymns when we exclude them from our prayer closet and private devotions by leaving them in the hymnal at church all week.[91] This disjunction between private prayer life and public worship has been a downfall of the twentieth-century Church. For centuries, hymns and metrical psalms were a source of spiritual encouragement, growth, and nurture for believers. Broadus and Manly were both zealous to keep hymns in the daily lives of believers. After their era, however, that kind of personal piety declined, for various reasons. Whatever other factors were involved, the loss of the contemplative life among evangelical Protestants after 1900 seems linked to the commodification and mass production of popular hymnody in the late nineteenth century and to the eventual replacement of the pocket hymnal with the pew hymnal.

Worship scholar Robert Webber calls postmodern believers—many of whom have never become rooted in the Church's historic spirituality—to rediscover the Church Fathers and their rich traditions of Scripture meditation and prayer as a path to personal and corporate worship renewal.[92] John Broadus did not need to recover the Church Fathers because he had never lost them. He was a formidable scholar of the Patristic writers, and their great hymns informed his devotional life. For a recovery of Patristic hymnody today one need look no further than the current hymnic resurgence in contemporary evangelicalism, in some ways parallel to that of Broadus's time. The recording group Passion, part of the worship "movement" by the same name led by Louie Giglio, released as its newest recording a collection of entirely historic hymns with new musical settings.[93] Entitled *Hymns Ancient and Modern*, its selections range from Victorian hymnody to the *Phos hilaron,* or "Hail Gladdening Light," one of the oldest Greek hymns of the Church. The album consciously appropriates the title of the bestselling British hymnal of all time, originally released in Broadus's own day.[94]

Another stream of the current hymn renewal within the modern worship movement is the recovery of Puritan and early Baptist hymnody, led by recording groups and worship leader-songwriters such as Indelible Grace, Bob Kauflin, and others. These artists have introduced to a broad evangelical audience this rich spiritual heritage—now it remains for Baptists to reclaim it in their private and public worship. Anne Steele, for example, does not have a single hymn in the current *The Baptist Hymnal* (1991). Baptists and all believers can rejoice, however, that the modern worship movement is embracing historic hymns, producing a stream of new, stylistically diverse musical settings of them, and deepening the personal and corporate worship of the Church theologically in the process.

Fourth, Broadus had clear curricular goals of what ministers ought to be able to do with hymns. He required a minimum competency of vocal skill for pastors to be able to lead singing when needed. They also were expected to have the ability to select hymns that were theologically correct and glorifying to God, and not just follow the fashions of the day. He believed it was absolutely critical that every minister leaving Southern Seminary be given a thorough grounding in the hymns of the Church—the historic hymns the Church has sung, those of the Baptist tradition, and a knowledge of the popular hymn styles of the time. A minister had to understand the doctrinal basis for a hymn and be able to evaluate its theological soundness.

Fifth, pastors must learn more about singing and hymns in order to shepherd their flocks more effectively—to nurture communication between congregation and worship leaders, and encourage cooperation among all involved in worship leadership, including the choir and, one might add for many of today's churches, the worship team and instrumentalists.

Sixth, musicians today must examine theologically the legacy of both hymns and contemporary songs; teach them winsomely, wisely, and faithfully; judiciously select tunes appropriate to the texts and accessible—singable—for the congregations, whether those be old or contemporary tunes; and weed out all that is less than honoring to Christ.

Lastly, the responsibility of being a prophetic voice within the culture is not solely the purview of either scholars or musicians, but of all believers. If Southern Baptists seek to be faithful stewards of Scripture, the hymnic heritage of the Church, and the legacy of their historic founders, they will continue to create a "new song" glorifying to Christ. They will guard the Church's song from language, imagery, and doctrine that conflicts with scriptural truth and with God's character as revealed in Scripture. All believers are called, like the Old Testament prophets, to be "watchmen upon the walls."

John Albert Broadus valued congregational song that glorified God in His holiness, grace, and truth. May the passion and legacy of Dr. Broadus and the example of Southern Seminary's leaders today mobilize and galvanize the Church to follow with excellence and without compromise the call of Christ and the Gospel.

> So be it, Lord! Thy throne shall never—
> Like earth's proud empires—pass away:
> Thy kingdom stands, and grows forever
> Till all thy creatures own thy sway.[95]

NOTES

The author wishes to thank Jason Fowler and the staff of The Southern Baptist Theological Seminary Archives for the collection of historical data; David L. Gregory, seminary music and audio-visual librarian, for his expertise throughout the course of this project; and Garrett fellow J. Christopher Holmes for research assistance.

1. Timothy George and David S. Dockery, *Baptist Theologians* (Nashville: Broadman, 1990), 689.

2. John A. Broadus, *A Treatise on the Preparation and Delivery of Sermons* (Philadelphia: Smith, English; New York: Sheldon, 1870).

3. Thomas R. McKibbens, Jr., "John A. Broadus: Shaper of Preaching" (Nashville: The Historical Commission of the Southern Baptist Convention, 1987), [4].

4. B[asil] Manly and Basil Manly, Jr., eds., *The Baptist Psalmody: A Selection of Hymns for the Worship of God* (Charleston: Southern Baptist Publication Society, 1850).

5. Basil Manly, Jr., *Manly's Choice: A Selection of Approved Hymns for Baptist Churches* (Louisville: Baptist Book Concern, 1891). See Nathan H. Platt, "The Hymnological Contributions of Basil Manly, Jr., to the Congregational Song of Southern Baptists" (D.M.A. dissertation, The Southern Baptist Theological Seminary, 2004), 113–14, 215–16.

6. John A. Broadus, "The Minister and His Hymn Book," from his typescript lecture series entitled "Preaching and the Ministerial Life," 18–25, delivered as the 1889 Lyman Beecher Lectureship on Preaching, Yale Divinity School. Copy in Boyce Centennial Library, Historical Archives. Also see Yale University Library's Lyman Beecher Lectureship Web site: http://www.library.yale.edu/div/beecher.htm.

7. These have been cataloged by the seminary archives as: "Book 17: Latin, Greek, French, & German Hymns," "Book 20: Hymnology," and "Book 29: Homiletics, Illustrations, Public Worship, Prayer, Pronunciation, Expository Preaching, Hymns," respectively.

8. *History of the establishment and organization of The Southern Baptist Theological Seminary, Greenville, South Carolina; to which is appended The First Annual Catalogue, 1859–1860* (Greenville, S. C.: G. E. Elford, 1860), 48–49.

9. *Catalogue of The Southern Baptist Theological Seminary, Greenville, S. C. Second Session. 1860–61* (Greenville, S. C.: Evans and Cogswell, 1861), 16–17.

10. *Catalogue of The Southern Baptist Theological Seminary, Greenville, S.C. Fourteenth Session. 1872–73* (Norfolk, Va.: Published by the Board, 1873), 15–16.

11. *Catalogue of The Southern Baptist Theological Seminary, Louisville, Ky. Twenty-First Session, 1879–80* (Louisville: A. C. Capterton, 1880), 16.

12. *Catalogue of The Southern Baptist Theological Seminary, Louisville, Ky. Twenty-Seventh Session, 1885–6* (Louisville: Chas. T. Dearing, 1886), 23.

13. *Catalogue of The Southern Baptist Theological Seminary, Louisville, Ky. Twenty-Ninth Session, 1887–8* (Louisville: Chas. T. Dearing, 1888), 26.

14. *Catalogue of The Southern Baptist Theological Seminary, Louisville, Ky. Thirty-Third Session, 1891–92* (Louisville: Baptist Book Concern, 1892), 37.

15. *Catalogue of The Southern Baptist Theological Seminary, Louisville, Ky. Thirty-Fourth Session, 1892–93* (Louisville: Baptist Book Concern, 1893), 33.

16. In the *Catalogue* of 1894–95, the year of Broadus's death, the list of textbooks for Homiletics reads: "Broadus' Preparation and Delivery of Sermons, History of Preaching,

and Syllabus of Hymnology; The Homiletics Exercise Book; Russell's Vocal Culture." *Catalogue of The Southern Baptist Theological Seminary, Louisville, Ky. Thirty-Sixth Session, 1894–95* (Louisville: Chas. T. Dearing, 1895), 38.

17. Cited in Archibald Thomas Robertson, *Life and Letters of John Albert Broadus* (Philadelphia: American Baptist Publication Society, 1901), 352.

18. Henry S. Burrage, *Baptist Hymn Writers and Their Hymns* (Portland, Maine: Brown Thurston, 1888), vi.

19. Robertson, *Life and Letters of John Albert Broadus*, 352.

20. Paul Richardson notes that "Broadus prepared his syllabus in 1883 . . . a landmark in the development of this discipline in the classroom." Paul A. Richardson, "Baptist Contributions to Hymnody and Hymnology," *Review and Expositor* 87, no. 1 (Winter 1990): 69.

21. H. Wiley Hitchcock, *Music in the United States: A Historical Introduction* (Englewood Cliffs, N. J.: Prentice-Hall, 1988), 53–54.

22. John A. Broadus, *Syllabus as to Hymnology* (Louisville: n.p., 1892), 1.

23. Ibid.

24. Ibid.

25. Ibid., 2.

26. Ibid., 2.

27. Ibid., 3. Broadus's criteria are closely paralleled by those of leading modern hymn writer and evangelical Anglican bishop Timothy Dudley-Smith in his article, "What Makes a Good Hymn Text?," *The Hymn* 36, no. 1 (January 1985): 14–18.

28. Hermann Adalbert Daniel, *Thesaurus hymnologicus sive hymnorum, canticorum, sequentiarum circa annum MD usitatarum collectio amplissima,* 5 vols. (Halle and Leipzig, 1841–1856; rep. ed., Hildesheim and New York: Olms, 1973).

29. Francis Andrew March, *Latin Hymns, With English Notes. For Use in Schools and Colleges* (New York: Harper and Brothers, 1874).

30. Philipp Wackernagel, *Das deutsche Kirchenlied von der ältesten Zeit bis zu Anfang des 17. Jahrhunderts,* 5 vols. (Leipzig: Teubner, 1864–77).

31. See "General Bibliography" in John A. Broadus, *Syllabus*, pp. 4–5. Other citations are found throughout the *Syllabus* pertaining to each period.

32. Josiah Miller, *Singers and Songs of the Church* (London: Longmans, Green, 1869).

33. Burrage, *Baptist Hymn Writers and Their Hymns.*

34. Broadus found the *Historical Sketches of Hymns* (1859) by Joseph Belcher (a "Baptist writer") to have been "quite superseded by Miller." His marginal note to himself on this page reads: "Get (1) Miller. (2) Robinson. (3) Burrage." Broadus, *Syllabus*, 4.

35. Hezekiah Butterworth, *The Story of the Hymns* (New York: American Tract Society, 1875).

36. Frederick Saunders, *Evenings with the Sacred Poets: A Series of Quiet Talks about the Singers and Their Songs* (New York: Andon D. F. Randolph, 1869).

37. John E. Prescott, *Christian Hymns and Hymn Writers: A Course of Lectures by J. E. Prescott* (Cambridge, United Kingdom: Deighton, Bell, 1883).

38. Broadus, *Syllabus*, 6; Charles C. Nott, *The Seven Great Hymns of the Mediaeval Church*, 7th ed. (New York: A. D. F. Randolph, 1868).

39. W[illiam] Howard Doane and E. H. Johnson, eds., *The Baptist Hymnal, for Use in the Church and Home* (Philadelphia: American Baptist Publication Society, 1883).

40. Broadus, *Syllabus*, 22.

41. Paul A. Richardson, "Basil Manly, Jr.: Southern Baptist Pioneer in Hymnody," in *Singing Baptists: Studies in Baptist Hymnody in America,* eds. Harry Eskew, David W. Music, and Paul A. Richardson (Nashville: Church Street, 1994), 106. Platt, "Hymnological Contributions," 7–8.

42. Broadus, *Syllabus*, 22.

43. He adds Elizabeth's salutation of Mary to the canticles of Zechariah, Mary, Simeon, and the angelic song, *Gloria in excelsis Deo*.

44. Broadus, "Minister and Hymn Book," 1.

45. See Stephen Farris, *The Hymns of Luke's Infancy Narratives: Their Origin, Meaning and Significance, Journal for the Study of the New Testament,* Supplement Series 9 (Sheffield, United Kingdom: JSOT, 1985); Daniel Liderbach, *Christ in the Early Christian Hymns* (New York and Mahwah, N. J.: Paulist, 1998); Paul Beasley-Murray, "Colossians 1:15–20: An Early Christian Hymn Celebrating the Lordship of Christ," in *Pauline Studies*, eds. Donald A. Hagner and Murray J. Harris (Grand Rapids, Mich.: Eerdmans, 1980), 169–83.

46. Broadus, *Syllabus*, 7.

47. Ibid.

48. Broadus, "Minister and Hymn Book," 4.

49. John Rippon, *The Psalms and Hymns of Dr. Watts, Arranged by Dr. Rippon; with Dr. Rippon's Selection* (Philadelphia: Clark and Lippincott, 1835).

50. In *The Baptist Hymnal* his name is spelled Krishnu Pal. Doane and Johnson, *The Baptist Hymnal*, 228.

51. Here he cites John E. Prescott, *Christian Hymns and Hymn Writers*, 159.

52. Broadus, "Minister and Hymn Book," 17. Heber accepted the position of bishop of Calcutta at age forty and died in India scarcely three years later. "Heber, Reginald," *Handbook to* The Baptist Hymnal (Nashville: Convention Press, 1992): 363–64.

53. Broadus, *Syllabus*, 16, and "Minister and Hymn Book," 18.

54. Broadus, *Syllabus*, 16.

55. Ibid., 15. Faber is known among Baptists today for his hymns "Faith of our fathers" and "There's a wideness in God's mercy."

56. An example from the "radical wing" was Oliver Wendell Holmes's "Lord of all being, throned afar."

57. Alfred P. Putnam, ed., *Singers and Songs of the Liberal Faith; Being Selections of Hymns and Other Sacred Poems of the Liberal Church in America, with Biographical Sketches of the Writers, and with Historical and Illustrative Notes* (Boston: Roberts Brothers, 1875). Broadus cites Bryant on p. 121, where are found "The Mother's Hymn" ("Lord, who ordainest for mankind") and "Thou, God, seest me" ("When this song of praise shall cease") by that poet. He also cites p. 126 for Longfellow, on which page no hymns by the latter are found, but the hymnal contains sixteen Longfellow texts, including the ordination hymn "Christ to the young man said, 'If thou wouldst follow me.'"

58. Broadus, "Minister and Hymn Book," 21–22. Also found in Broadus, *Syllabus*, 18.

59. Broadus, *Syllabus*, 18.

60. Ibid., 17–18.
61. Ibid., 16.
62. Ibid., 16–17.
63. Ibid., 16.
64. Ibid., 16–17.
65. Ibid., 17. Broadus does not name the new genre in this passage but later, in discussing the balanced contents of the new Baptist hymnal, he notes that it contains "numerous standard English hymns and some of the best recent 'Gospel Songs.'" Ibid., 22.
66. Ibid., 21. Charles Haddon Spurgeon, *Our Own Hymn-Book. A Collection of Psalms and Hymns for Public, Social, and Private Worship* (London: Passmore and Alabaster, 1866; rep. ed., Pasadena, Texas: Pilgrim Publications, 1975).
67. Ibid., 22. On this point the editors of the hymnal indicated that the alternative "less familiar tune of highest musical worth" was chosen to please "advancing tastes [that] desire richer effects in harmony." Doane and Johnson, *The Baptist Hymnal*, iii.
68. J. R. Graves and J. M. Pendleton, *The Southern Psalmist* (Nashville: South-Western Publishing House; Graves, Marks & Co., 1859). John A. Broadus, "Book 29: Homiletics, Illustrations, Public Worship, Prayer, Pronunciation, Expository Preaching, Hymns," Louisville, Boyce Centennial Library, Historical Archives, n.d., unpaginated.
69. S. L. Caldwell and A. J. Gordon, *The Service of Song for Baptist Churches* (Boston: Gould and Lincoln, 1871). Broadus, "Book 29: Homiletics, . . . Hymns," unpaginated.
70. Richard Fuller, E. M. Levy, S. D. Phelps, H. C. Fish, Thomas Armitage, E. T. Winkler, W. W. Everts, Geo. C. Lorimer, and Basil Manly, Jr., *The Baptist Praise Book: For Congregational Singing* (New York: A. S. Barnes, 1871).
71. Broadus, *Syllabus*, 23.
72. Basil Manly [Jr.], *The Choice: A Selection of Approved Hymns for Baptist Churches with Music* (Louisville: Baptist Book Concern, 1892).
73. Broadus, *Syllabus*, 23.
74. See Yale University Library Web site, http://www.library.yale.edu/div/beecher.htm. Biographical sketches of the lecturers and analysis of the lectures from 1871 to 1951 are found in Edgar Dewitt Jones, *The Royalty of the Pulpit* (New York: Harper, 1951). For a study of the Lyman Beecher Lectures from the perspective of homiletics, see Batsell B. Baxter, *The Heart of the Yale Lectures* (New York: Macmillan, 1947). See also David A. McCants, "The Lost Yale Lectures on Preaching by John A. Broadus," reprint, *Southern Speech Journal* 36 (1970): 56–57.
75. Robertson, *Life and Letters of John Albert Broadus*, 376.
76. The end of this sentence is lost because the entire last line of text on page 22 is missing; the bottom edge of the page has crumbled away. The first line on page 23 begins: "most every book. Address yourself then . . . ." Broadus, "Minister and Hymn Book," 22–23.
77. Ibid., 22–23.
78. Ibid., 23.
79. Ibid., 23.
80. Ibid., 23–24.
81. Broadus, *Preparation and Delivery of Sermons*, 487.

82. Broadus, "Minister and Hymn Book," 23–24.

83. One recent example is Richard J. Mouw and Mark A. Noll, eds., *Wonderful Words of Life: Hymns in American Protestant History and Theology* (Grand Rapids, Mich., and Cambridge, United Kingdom, 2004).

84. Broadus, "Minister and Hymn Book," 24–25.

85. See Chapters 8 and 9, "The Voice" and "The Song," in J. Nathan Corbitt, *The Sound of the Harvest: Music's Mission in Church and Culture* (Grand Rapids, Mich.: Baker Books, 1998), 229–90.

86. Broadus, "Minister and Hymn Book," 24.

87. Ibid., 25.

88. 1 Chron. 12:32.

89. Broadus, *Preparation and Delivery of Sermons*, 476.

90. Ibid., 477.

91. Esther Rothenbusch, "Are We Losing the Hymns?," *The Southern Seminary Magazine* (*The Tie*) 69, no. 1 (Spring 2001): 8–9.

92. One of Webber's points is central: "Evangelical spirituality in a postmodern world needs to begin with the proclamation that *Jesus is our spirituality*. It is his life, death, and resurrection that make us acceptable to God." Robert Webber, *Ancient-Future Faith: Rethinking Evangelicalism for a Postmodern World* (Grand Rapids, Mich.: Baker Books, 1999): 132.

93. Passion, *Hymns Ancient & Modern: Live Songs of Our Faith* (Brentwood, Tenn.: Sparrow Records/Sixstep Records, 2004), SPD 83817R.

94. *Hymns Ancient and Modern*, ed. W. H. Monk (London: Novello for the Proprietors, 1861).

95. John Ellerton, "The day thou gavest, Lord, is ended" (final stanza), in *Hymnbook 1982* (New York: Church Hymnal Corporation), 24.

The Saga of "To God Be the Glory"

DONALD PAUL HUSTAD

If a hymn dies, can it live again? In the case of "To God Be the Glory" the answer is, "Yes, thanks be to God!" Originally written in America sometime before 1875, it was often published and largely ignored in its native land. However, in 1954, it was rediscovered in England and acclaimed as a new favorite. By the end of the twentieth century, it was included in all evangelical hymnals and in most mainline Protestant books, in English or in a translation, the world around. For these and other reasons, some very surprising, I call this hymn story a "saga."[1]

First Publishing

There is disagreement about the song's first publication, which may have contributed to the misunderstanding of its history. In Britain, hymn researchers say it was in 1870, in the book, *Songs of Devotion,* published by Biglow & Main in New York City; that company had taken over the publishing interests of William B. Bradbury (1816–1868), a pioneer music educator and church musician in the United States. The *correct* date is given in American hymnal companions: It was 1875, and the book was *Brightest and Best,* edited by William Howard Doane and Robert Lowry for Biglow & Main. British scholars should have got it right: It is listed correctly in John Julian's monumental *Dictionary of Hymnology*, first published in London in 1892.[2]

The hymn text was written by Fanny Jane Crosby (1820–1915), the sightless woman who became a living legend, writing thousands (nobody really knows how many) of gospel songs during her long life. Crosby had an agreement with Bradbury, and later with Biglow & Main, to write at least three hymns a week for them. Obviously she far exceeded that requirement and received not royalties, but two dollars as outright payment for each poem. Many composers associated with Biglow & Main wrote music for her words, but her favorite collaborator was William Howard Doane—inventor, businessman, and philanthropist in Ohio. The music for "To God Be the Glory" was a product of his strong, amateur musical gifts.[3]

Published in Great Britain

In August of 1875, the same year in which "To God Be the Glory" first appeared in print, the preacher-musician team of Dwight Lyman Moody and Ira David Sankey were completing twenty-six months of evangelistic ministry in Great Britain. The two Americans were laymen—Moody had been a very successful shoe salesman, and Sankey was formerly a civil servant in the Internal Revenue Service. Sankey had joined Moody in Chicago in 1870 to help in his large Sunday school and church, and also in his budding evangelistic ministry. The venture in Britain began as the result of a few personal invitations from ministers and business friends, two of whom died while the evangelists were en route by ship. Moody and Sankey began the meetings in York, England, as unknowns, with fewer than fifty people in a local church's Sunday morning service and some eight hundred in an afternoon interchurch rally. Sankey said that he took with him only his Bible and a "musical scrap-book" which contained songs he had gathered from here and there, some in printed form, and some perhaps in manuscript. Gradually, the audiences increased in size and, when they left more than two years later, they were known throughout the British Isles because of the thousands of people who had attended their meetings in England, Scotland, Ireland, and Wales. Because their missions were reported in the world press, they were also acclaimed throughout the evangelical Christian world.

Early in their first "British year," Sankey arranged to publish a booklet of sixteen pages, containing twenty-three songs that had already become popular in those missions; he called them *Sacred Songs and Solos*. In the years following, Sankey continued to add new songs to the book, including "To God Be the Glory." Eventually, *Sacred Songs and Solos* grew to twelve hundred titles and sold close to one hundred million copies. More than a century after reaching its largest size, it is still in print!

Also in 1875, Biglow & Main released another book from its New York office, *Gospel Hymns and Sacred Songs*, edited by Ira Sankey and P. P. Bliss (a gifted musician and song writer who had been associated with D. L. Moody before Sankey appeared on the scene). Since Sankey had been in England for more than two years, Bliss must have done most of the technical work on that book. No doubt Sankey participated by mail, suggesting many of the songs he had used as a soloist and songleader in Britain. During the next twenty years, five more books appeared in the *Gospel Hymns* series, and Sankey led in editing each one. However, for some unknown reason, "To God Be the Glory" never appeared in that famous series of songbooks, which tended to define the popular church music we call "gospel." Why was it omitted? Was that omission a key to the failure of "To God Be the Glory" to catch hold of the public's fancy in the United States?

Publishing and Use from 1875 to 1954

Of course, it *was* published, as the new *Dictionary of North American Hymnology* shows.[4] Between 1875 and 1954, "To God Be the Glory" appeared in more than fifty books published in the United States, and sold also in Canada. Most of these were Sunday school songbooks, published either by Biglow & Main, the copyright owner, or by denominational groups, including American Baptists, Presbyterians, Lutherans, Seventh-Day Adventists, Methodists, Mennonites, and Pentecostals.[5] In those days, competing non-church publishers did not often share their copyrights with each other; they regarded them as their principal assets in selling hymnals. Denominational publishers were not seen as competitors, and they were allowed a limited number of "permissions," especially in Sunday school books. Gospel songs were not sung in regular worship in those days, so they were not included in the standard denominational hymnals.

We do not know how much the song was used during its first seventy-five-plus years in America or in Britain. It is commonly thought that Sankey made it popular in England by using it in D. L. Moody's meetings. But Sankey does not mention it in his admittedly-sketchy autobiography, *My Life and the Story of the Gospel Hymns*,[6] where he discusses more than two hundred hymns and gospel songs. George C. Stebbins (1846–1945), another distinguished Moody associate, never mentions it in his *Reminiscences and Gospel Hymn Stories*.[7] Hymn "stories" about favorite songs were popular in the early twentieth century, but "To God Be the Glory" is not included in any such British or American book that I have examined. It seems quite possible that in America, all of its printings were largely ignored, or that the song somehow did not appeal to churchgoers of that time.

We do not have a complete record of the song's publishing in Great Britain; the *HymnQuest* database recently produced by Stainer & Bell for the Pratt Green Trust lists only hymnals that are still in use. No doubt the printings between 1875 and 1954 were fewer than those in America, partly because Britain had fewer religious denominations and partly because their interest in this type of music was more limited. For instance, in Britain all American gospel songs are called "Sankey songs"—as if he were responsible for them all!

Because the British book, *Sacred Songs and Solos,* has had such a long life, it was probably most important in making the song known abroad. "To God Be the Glory" was also printed in *Redemption Songs*, a collection of one thousand pieces published by Pickering & Inglis, which appears to have been something of a competitor to *Sacred Songs and Solos*. Julian's *Dictionary*, 1892, also cites its inclusion in "*The Methodist Sunday School Hymnbook*, the Silver Street *Sunday Scholar's Companion*, and other collections for Sunday schools."[8]

Identifying Gospel Songs

What exactly are "gospel songs?" Gospel songs—sometimes called "gospel hymns"—became part of American popular culture in the late nineteenth century. They were successors of the camp meeting "spirituals" at the beginning of the century and the Sunday school songs for children that appeared beginning in the 1840s. Textwise, they centered in the personal gospel message heard in evangelistic meetings, hence "*gospel* songs/hymns." They were usually subjective texts of personal witness to the "born-again" experience and the spiritual pilgrimage of the singer. Musically, they sounded much like the popular secular songs of the time—in particular the Stephen Foster ballads. Also, like both secular and sacred folk songs, they invariably included an extended refrain, which was sung after each stanza. This was mostly "happy music" in the major mode, often with sprightly rhythm. In revivalist churches, like the one in which I grew up, they often comprised the principal—if not the only—musical diet.

In mainline churches, singing gospel songs was common in Sunday school gatherings or in youth groups. Because of their subjective words and popular musical style, which critics called "emotional" or, even worse, "sentimental," they were not allowed in regular worship. To be sure, their popularity brought them under the condemnation of serious musicians, both inside and outside the Church. John Julian, the English clergyman and hymnist mentioned earlier, made the following comments in the closing lines of his article about Fanny Crosby in *A Dictionary of Hymnology*; like all British writers, he used her married name, Van Alstyne, which seldom appears today in an American hymnbook:

> The combined sales of the volumes of songs and hymns mentioned above have amounted in English-speaking countries to millions of copies. Notwithstanding the immense circulation thus given to Mrs. Van Alstyne's hymns, they are, with few exceptions, very weak and poor, their simplicity and earnestness being their redeeming features. Their popularity is largely due to the melodies to which they are wedded.[9]

The first music history textbook I studied sixty-five years ago was written by the American musicologist Waldo Selden Pratt, who had this to say at the beginning of the twentieth century:

> The defenders of this popular hymnody . . . very often very gravely underestimate the capacity of the popular mind to rise above vulgar embodiments of truth and to shake itself free from perverted sentimentality, and they constantly mistake the zest of animal enjoyment in a rub-a-dub rhythm or the shout of childish pleasure in a "catchy" refrain for real religious enthusiasm.[10]

In 1922, control of "To God Be the Glory" passed to Hope Publishing Company in Chicago, when they purchased the assets of Biglow & Main. In that same year, they included the Crosby-Doane song in *Hymns of Praise for the Church and Sunday School* and again, one year later, in *Selected Sunday School Songs*. In 1925, it appeared in Hope's *Hymns of Praise, Number Two* and, in 1926, in *Hymns of Praise Numbers One and Two Combined*. In 1931, its copyright protection ended, and Hope Publishing Company did not use the song again until 1957, after it had been "born again."

A Personal Confession

It is not difficult for me to understand how this gospel hymn could have been published in so many different books over a period of seventy-five years without becoming widely known. In the mid-twentieth century, I became acquainted with, and used, at least four songbooks that contained it: (1) *Choice Hymns of the Faith* (published in 1944 by the Gospel Perpetuating Fund, an adjunct of the Plymouth Brethren Assemblies); (2) *The Voice of Thanksgiving, Number 5* (published in 1946 by Moody Bible Institute of Chicago); (3) *Inspiring Hymns* (published by Singspiration, Inc., in 1951 as an effort to challenge the leadership of the Rodeheaver Company and Hope Publishing Company in the gospel music field); and (4) *Hymns* (released by InterVarsity Christian Fellowship in 1952, which contained a large number of evangelical hymns in common use in England). I knew personally the editors of three of those books, all of whom were active in the evangelical music scene in the United States.[11] None of them, however, made any particular effort to encourage the use of "To God Be the Glory!"

Beginning in 1942, I was employed in the radio studios of Moody Bible Institute in Chicago; part of my responsibility was to arrange, play, and conduct music from all four of those songbooks. The Institute's new hymnal was edited by William M. Runyan, composer of the music for "Great Is Thy Faithfulness," who worked in the same building and at the same time as I. In addition, in 1950 I began to assist in editing hymnals for Hope Publishing Company, whose *Hymns of Praise Numbers One and Two Combined* was still in print. Yet I never heard "To God Be the Glory" or noticed it in any songbook until 1954!

One Evangelistic Songleader Meets Another—in London

In the early summer of 1954, the Billy Graham evangelistic team conducted its first major crusade in England and, for the first time, used "To God Be the Glory." Songleader Cliff Barrows tells about it:

> I first heard the hymn during one of our early visits to England around 1952. Then in compiling our song book for the Harringay Crusade it was suggested by Rev. Frank Colquhoun that it be included in our *Greater London Crusade Song Book*. This was done, and, from the very outset of the meetings in Harringay, it became one of the favorites and was used almost every night during the last month of those meetings. Upon our return to the states, I began looking through some of the old hymn books and saw that it had been included several years ago in those earlier publications but had been omitted in recent hymnals. We began using it right away in our crusades here [in the United States] and found that people loved to sing it, as well as they did in London. I believe the first crusade we used this hymn in America upon our return was in Nashville in 1954. This was the first crusade upon our return from the meetings at Harringay.[12]

However, like many others before him, Barrows was slow to see the hymn's potential, and, in the pressures of kaleidoscopic crusade activity, his memory faltered a bit. Actually, he must have heard the Crosby-Doane song during British meetings in the mid-1940s, because he included it as the final selection (no. 107) in the 1950 booklet, *Billy Graham Campaign Songs: Singing Evangelism*, published by the Rodeheaver/Hall-Mack Company of Winona Lake, Indiana. Billy Graham had come to international attention one year earlier during his 1949 tent crusade in Los Angeles. For many years thereafter, the Rodeheaver company printed all the songbooks used in Graham meetings. It seems probable that "To God Be the Glory" was present in *all those books*, usually on the last page; yet Barrows did not use it until he heard the Harringay congregation sing it with such enthusiasm that it became a virtual theme song!

Recent Printings and Use in the United States

After our saga song was "reborn" in its native land during the 1954 Nashville crusade, it was included in most every evangelical hymnal and songbook published in America, including those of Pentecostal churches, Baptist churches (both black and white), Plymouth Brethren Assemblies, Brethren in Christ, the Christian and Missionary Alliance, the Christian Reformed Church, Churches of God (in both Anderson, Indiana, and Cleveland, Tennessee), the Evangelical Covenant Church, the Free Methodist Church, Mennonite Brethren, Church of the Nazarene, and Orthodox Presbyterians.

One of the first printings was in *Baptist Hymnal* (1956), edited for Southern Baptists by W. Hines Sims. In 1957, it was printed in at least five books, one of which was *Worship and Service Hymnal*, released by Hope Publishing Company, its former owner; I served as principal editor of that book. Other ecumenical and evangelical hymnbooks followed the pattern during the rest of the twentieth century.

Mainline hymnals were slower to join in the celebration because their denominational sponsors and musicians were still leery of the popular music of evangelism. American Baptists included "To God Be the Glory" in their small, contemporary music book *Hymns and Songs of the Spirit* in 1966, but omitted it in *Hymnbook for Christian Worship* (1970) in which they cooperated with Disciples of Christ. Erik Routley used it (without the refrain) in *Rejoice in the Lord* (1985) edited for the Reformed Church in America. United Methodists used it first in their 1989 hymnal, and the Presbyterian Church (U.S.A.) did the same in their 1990 book. Anabaptist denominations (the Church of the Brethren and two Mennonite groups) added it in *Hymnal: A Worship Book*, published in 1992. Both the Moravian Church and Disciples of Christ included it in their hymnals in 1995. Obviously, more American Christians are singing the Crosby-Doane song than ever before; perhaps the only groups that have not welcomed it to their song repertoire are Eastern Orthodox churches, Roman Catholics, Episcopalians, Lutherans, Quakers, and the United Church of Christ.

Recent Publishing and Use in the United Kingdom

Following the Billy Graham crusade in Harringay Stadium in 1954, British interdenominational publishers rushed to ensure that "To God Be the Glory" was included in their hymnals and songbooks. These books included *Christian Hymns* (1977) prepared by the Evangelical Movement of Wales; *Hymns for Today's Church* (1982) whose editors included several leaders in the evangelical wing of the Church of England; and *BBC Songs of Praise* (1997), with a large number of American gospel songs. The only surprising exception was *Christian Praise*, published by InterVarsity Christian Fellowship in 1957.

Once again, although English Methodists had included it in their hymnbook in 1933, other British mainline churches were slow to respond to the public's desire to sing this song.[13] The Baptist Union added it to *The Baptist Hymn Book* in 1962. The Scottish Church published it in *The Church Hymnary* (3rd edition, 1973) to the tune ST. DENIO, with no refrain. Later, Methodist editors included it in *Hymns & Psalms* and musicians of the Assemblies of God did the same in *Making Melody*, both in 1983. In 1991, the Reformed Church (formerly known as Congregational churches) included it in *Rejoice and Sing*.

The Church of England (Anglican) has never adopted an "official hymnal," despite the fact that one of their available books was titled *Anglican Hymn Book* (1965); that volume included "To God Be the Glory," with a more sophisticated harmonization, but no refrain. Earlier, the best-known series of Anglican books (*Hymns Ancient and Modern*, first released in 1849) had included only one song of the Sankey tradition—"Rescue the Perishing," another Crosby-Doane collaboration—possibly because of its emphasis on social ministry. The latest book in that series has a new title, *Common Praise* (to show its relationship to the *Book of Common Prayer*); it was released in the year 2000, and includes "To God Be the Glory" (as well as "Blessed Assurance," another Fanny Crosby text).

The lone, somewhat-surprising holdout in Britain is the refined, if not elitist, *New English Hymnal* (1986), which includes no hymn with a full-length refrain. Yet the first book in that series—published in 1906 and distinguished by the work of Percy Dearmer and Ralph Vaughan Williams—contained P. P. Bliss's gospel song, "Hold the Fort," a much more improbable choice.[14] We can only guess why—perhaps because it was the top favorite among "Sankey songs" and graced the first page of *Sacred Songs and Solos*.

The Hymn and Tune Analyzed

I am convinced that words constitute the strongest factor in determining any hymn's potential. "To God Be the Glory" is an unusual gospel song in that it is a compelling, almost completely objective expression of praise to God for the grace shown in personal redemption. William J. Reynolds wrote the first comments about the hymn to be published in the United States, almost ninety years after Fanny Crosby's text first appeared in print. He stated that the hymn is "an expression of objectivity not usually found in gospel hymnody. Here is a straight-forward voicing of praise to God, not simply personal testimony nor sharing some subjective aspect of Christian experience."[15]

Following is an outline of the three stanzas and refrain, with analysis:

Stanza One:

To God be the glory, great things he hath done,
so loved he the world that he gave us his Son,
who yielded his life an atonement for sin,
and opened the life-gate that all may go in.

The opening stanza makes a bold statement: God alone must receive the glory for his mighty, loving deeds through Jesus Christ for our salvation—a grace which is offered to all persons.

The hymn's first line and title repeats the motto J. S. Bach inscribed on many of his manuscripts—S.D.G., *Soli Deo gloria*, "To God alone be glory."

Refrain:

Praise the Lord, praise the Lord, let the earth hear his voice!
Praise the Lord, praise the Lord, let the people rejoice!
O come to the Father through Jesus the Son,
and give him the glory, great things he hath done.

The refrain issues a call to all the earth to come to God through Christ (in believing faith and in constant worship)—to "praise the Lord" for the great redemptive works he has done.

Stanza Two:

O perfect redemption, the purchase of blood,
to every believer the promise of God;
the vilest offender who truly believes,
that moment from Jesus a pardon receives.

The second strophe continues the story of how redemption is accomplished. Note the biblical-theological words that define human salvation: redemption, blood, believer, promise, offender, believes, receives.

Stanza Three:

Great things he hath taught us, great things he hath done,
and great our rejoicing through Jesus the Son;
but purer, and higher, and greater will be
our wonder, our transport, when Jesus we see.

The final stanza reminds us that God has revealed himself to humankind through Scripture as well as through his redeeming acts in Christ—"Great things he hath taught us." Our joyful response in worship and obedience is only a weak foretaste of what we will experience in God's presence, "forever and ever, unto ages of ages."

Because my emphasis is on the text of this song, I will not analyze its music in detail. However, I agree completely with what Hugh McElrath says about William Howard Doane's collaboration with Fanny Crosby in "To God Be the Glory":

> . . . W. H. Doane . . . was profoundly moved by Fanny Crosby's text of objective praise. It has enjoyed wide acceptance in hymnals of great theological and cultural diversity. Much of its usefulness can be attributed to Doane's tune which aptly fits the text in both meaning and mood.[16]

Biblical Quotations and Allusions

Fanny Crosby may have intended her entire poem to be a response to the best-known "salvation verse" in the Bible—John 3:16. Virtually every phrase contains quotations from and allusions to the King James version of Holy Scripture, which dominated the Church scene at the time the song was written.

1. To God be the glory,	To God, only wise, be glory . . . (Rom. 16:27)
great things he hath done,	The Lord hath done great things for us . . . (Ps. 126:3)
so loved he the world that he gave us his Son,	For God so loved the world, that he gave his only begotten Son . . . (John 3:16)
who yielded his life	. . . I lay down my life for the sheep. (John 10:15)
an atonement for sin,	. . . Christ . . . by whom we have received the atonement. (Rom. 5:11)
and opened the life-gate	. . . straight is the gate, and narrow is the way, which leadeth unto life . . . (Matt. 7:14)
that all may go in.	. . . that whosoever believeth in him should not perish . . . (John 3:16)
Refrain:	
Praise the Lord, praise the Lord,	Praise ye the Lord. (Ps. 149:1)
let the earth hear his voice!	. . . give ear, O earth, for the Lord hath spoken. (Isa. 1:2)
Praise the Lord, praise the Lord,	Praise ye the Lord. (Ps. 149:1)
let the people rejoice!	We will rejoice in thy salvation . . . (Ps. 20:5)
O come to the Father through Jesus the Son,	[Jesus:] . . . No man cometh unto the Father but by me. (John 14:6)
and give him the glory, great things he hath done.	(see lines 1 and 2, stanza 1)

2. O perfect redemption, the purchase of blood,	. . . Ye are not redeemed with corruptible things, as silver or gold, . . . but with the precious blood of Christ. (1 Pet. 1:18–19)
to every believer the promise of God;	. . . by the will of God, according to the promise of life which is in Christ Jesus. (2 Tim. 1:1)
the vilest offender who truly believes, that moment from Jesus a pardon receives.	. . . where sin abounded, grace did much more abound. (Rom. 5:20)
3. Great things he hath taught us, great things he hath done,	Good and upright is the Lord; therefore will he teach sinners in the way. (Ps. 25:8)
and great our rejoicing through Jesus the Son;	We will rejoice in thy salvation . . . (Ps. 20:5)
but purer, and higher, and greater will be our wonder, our transport, when Jesus we see.	[Jesus:] Father, I will that they also, whom thou hast given me, be with me where I am, that they may behold my glory, which thou hast given me . . . (John 17:24)

Text Alterations

"To God Be the Glory" has been free of copyright restrictions since 1931, so hymnbook editors are free to make changes in the text, either to clarify the meaning or to make a theological adjustment.

The one alteration that appears most frequently, both here and overseas, changes the archaic word "hath" to "has" in the first phrase of stanzas 1 and 3, and in the last phrase of the refrain. The American book, *Advent Christian Hymnal* (2001), prints both old and new versions. In the most radical changes, for which no reasons are given or apparent, *The Presbyterian Hymnal* (1990) omits the second stanza, and the English book, *New Redemption Hymnal* (1986), reverses the positions of stanzas 2 and 3. Also, in earlier paragraphs several hymnals are listed in which the song's refrain is omitted.

A few word changes appear occasionally. In *Rejoice in the Lord* (1985) editor Erik Routley changed "opened the life-gate that all may go in" (stanza 1) to "opened heaven's gateway that all might go in." In two other books produced by Calvinistic groups, that last phrase now reads "that we may go in"—apparently to support the Reformed doctrine of election. In stanza 2, "vilest offender" has been changed by some to "every offender," and "a pardon" has appeared as "forgiveness."

The single word "transport" in stanza 3 has generated the greatest number of alternatives. The *Random House Dictionary* says that one of its meanings is "strong emotion; ecstatic joy, bliss, etc.," with the synonyms "rapture, ecstasy, happiness."[17] Some hymnal editors evidently believe that many worshipers will think more readily of some form of transportation! So now the phrases "our wonder, our transport" may be sung "our wonder, the beauty," "the joy and the wonder," "our wonder, our gladness," "our wonder, our rapture," "our wonder, our victory," or "our wonder, our triumph."

It is a bit surprising that only two recent books have eliminated the song's many male pronouns referring to God the Father. In 1996, The Presbyterian Church in Canada published *The Book of Praise*, which contained both the traditional text and a completely new, copyrighted version. The new lyrics were also used in *Common Praise* (1998) released by the Anglican Church of Canada.

Why?

We come finally to the denouement of our saga story. Why did this song catch on first in England and not in the United States? Why was it (like the prodigal son) welcomed home in 1954? Why was it finally accepted in the bastions of hymn respectability—the mainline hymnals—and that more than one hundred years after it was first published?

I dare to suggest that the hymn was not ever used in Moody-Sankey meetings, even in Britain where Sankey published it; certainly it was not used enough to become a favorite, or it would have been mentioned in Sankey's autobiography and included in the *Gospel Hymns* series of books in the United States. The idea that the campaigns of 1873–1875 made it popular is probably linked to the erroneous belief that it was available to Sankey in 1870. The second, larger edition of *Sacred Songs and Solos* had been released on January 1, 1875, and our saga-song was not published in the United States until later that year.

Could "To God Be the Glory" have been learned during the *second* Moody-Sankey tour of Britain in 1882–1884? That, too, is unlikely, even though by that time it had been added to *Sacred Songs and Solos*. There is no evidence that the gospel singer had used the song in the United States during those intervening years. When he returned to England, he would quite surely have relied on material that had been well received in previous meetings.

Sankey customarily introduced new songs by singing them as a solo in his quasi-recitative style, playing his own accompaniment on a little reed organ, and encouraging the audience to join in the refrains. By the time the second tour of Britain began, his untrained baritone voice was already showing signs of wear from his efforts to be heard in large auditoriums in those pre-electronic days. William Howard Doane's tune, with its long phrases and challenging pitch range, would have been very difficult for him to sing effectively.

Even more, I believe that Sankey was well aware that "To God Be the Glory" did not conform to the model of a typical gospel song—with a strongly subjective (and sometimes sentimental) text and tune. Americans of that period had known gospel music for some time; they were looking for songs like "Safe in the Arms of Jesus," "The Ninety and Nine," "Draw Me Nearer," "Hold the Fort," "Near the Cross," and "Where Is My Wandering Boy Tonight"—all of which must have appeared in the Moody-Sankey campaigns.[18] Even the first phrase of "To God Be the Glory," sung to the first five notes, just doesn't sound like the same kind of song. For all these reasons, it seems extremely doubtful that "To God Be the Glory" was ever heard in a Moody-Sankey meeting.

To be sure, the Moody-Sankey campaigns included praise songs and hymns. The reports mention especially the Doxology (of Thomas Ken) as well as the full 100th psalm ("All people that on earth do dwell,") and also "Jesus, Lover of my soul," "All hail the power of Jesus' name," "Guide me, O Thou great Jehovah," and "In the cross of Christ I glory," all sung to their historic hymn tunes. But Sankey understood that his new songs were different, both in style and in purpose. "I wish people would get the distinction," he once said, "that one class of hymns are to teach, and the other, such as 'Praise God from whom all blessings flow' and 'Jesus, Lover of my soul,' are hymns in which the whole congregation can praise God."[19] Beyond a doubt, he knew that his calling, like that of Moody, was to preach and teach the Gospel.

To overseas audiences, gospel songs were brand new and a little shocking when Sankey introduced them, but eventually the British came to love them—especially the unlikely candidate "Hold the Fort," with its imagery from America's Civil War. Sankey understood that those audiences were more attuned than Americans to singing objective words, like those in "To God Be the Glory," even though the stanzas-and-refrain-style may have seemed strange. It seems probable that, for that reason, he included the song in *Sacred Songs and Solos*. The phenomenal and enduring success of that single, expanding volume meant that such a strong song would eventually be discovered and become a lasting favorite of certain groups throughout the British empire. And Cliff Barrows's advisers for the Harringay crusade in 1954 wisely perceived its potential for the meetings of another American evangelist, who was born in 1918, nineteen years after Moody's death.

When American evangelicals rediscovered "To God Be the Glory" in Billy Graham's Nashville crusade in 1954, they had already begun the march uphill to "better church music," especially to more objective hymns in worship. For them at that time, the song was a nice combination of both their historic and their new preoccupations—a solid, gospel-style tune with a refrain and a biblical and emotional text of praise centered in the simple gospel. They didn't even resent the fact that the British had to teach them one of their own songs!

But this was not enough for mainline churchgoers, either in America or in Britain. Carlton R. Young tells about the skirmish that occurred in American Methodist churches when, one year later, in 1955, "How Great Thou Art" appeared in Billy Graham crusades, and it was eventually considered for inclusion in the 1966 edition of *Methodist Hymnal.*

> Upon hearing of the . . . decision to include the hymn, many church musicians and pastors expressed dismay that the church's official hymnal would bring respectability to the theme song of the Billy Graham crusades. Others brought equally uninformed and unfair criticism on the Methodist Publishing House for presumably dictating editorial policy and cheapening the church's official hymnal.[20]

Even though that 1966 book included "How Great Thou Art," "To God Be the Glory" did not receive the same Methodist approval in the United States until 1989! The whole story sounds a little quaint when we consider the protracted worship wars centering in the church music styles of the last twenty-five years!

Somewhere I once wrote that on our evangelical trek uphill to "better" music, we met the competition (including mainline worshipers) coming downhill, strumming guitars and singing Christian folk music. By 1990, American religion had become so pluralistic that highly emotional worship was one popular goal to cherish, partly because charismatic worship practices and musical leadership had become quite thoroughly acceptable. In the world of praise and worship choruses, "To God Be the Glory" sounds like a classic, historic hymn! Perhaps, by the next round of hymnals, Catholics, Lutherans, and Episcopalians—and even the United Church of Christ—will have accepted it.[21]

Earlier I said that, in the first seventy-five years of its existence, "To God Be the Glory" was not mentioned in hymn commentaries. Finally, the song has been vindicated in a new volume, *An Annotated Anthology of Hymns*, edited with commentary by J. R. Watson, emeritus professor of English at the University of Durham, England. Watson believes that the 250 hymns he selected are representative of the important hymnic literature in the British tradition, and both our saga-song and "Hold the Fort" are included. For the first time in my memory, a British hymnic scholar has examined a "Sankey song" without hedging on his approval. He wrote:

> Frances Jane van Alstyne, sometimes known by her maiden name of Fanny Crosby, was a voluminous and prolific writer whose work became very popular in revivalist meetings and evangelical crusades. This hymn ["To God Be the Glory"] was first printed in William Howard Doane's *Songs of Devotion* (1870), and it was popularized by Ira D. Sankey and Dwight L. Moody in their meetings. It appeared in Sankey's *Sacred Songs and Solos*, where its particular rhetoric of repetition is not out of place. It is simple in its ideas, but forceful in their expression, relying on a *fortissimo* emotionalism which is entirely appropriate for certain kinds of religious gatherings.[22]

Even though the handed-down historical errors remain, Watson's choices remind us that each generation, in its use of music, may be expected to pay attention to its own emotional needs. P. P. Bliss's "Hold the Fort" is not untrue to the Gospel, but it doesn't state it clearly; it is not really one of Sankey's "teaching hymns." Rather, it is a rousing musical call to evangelism's battle against sin, which became an important symbol of the victory God was winning in Britain in those days. Today it would rarely be sung except to satisfy someone's curiosity or nostalgia.

Fanny Crosby's "To God Be the Glory" is perhaps her finest statement of personal redemption—the Gospel—for which we praise God. Yet most American church musicians of the late nineteenth century—even Ira Sankey himself—evidently considered it out of step with the culture. Today it is at home not only in a Billy Graham crusade, but also in the worship of many congregations.

NOTES

1. This is a rewrite of the first paragraph of the hymn's story, told by Cliff Barrows in *Crusade Hymn Stories* (Chicago: Hope Publishing Co., 1967), 93–94. I take this unusual liberty because I served as ghost writer for this entire volume, as Barrows explains in the last paragraphs of that book's Foreword. This account contains Barrows's narration of the story to me and is very similar to that contained in the article by William J. Reynolds, cited in note 12 below.

2. John Julian, ed., *A Dictionary of Hymnology* (London: John Murray, Albemarle Street, 1892), 1204.

3. See Donald Hustad, ed., *Fanny Crosby Speaks Again* (Carol Stream, Illinois: Hope Publishing Company, 1977).

4. This computer disc is available from The Hymn Society in the United States and Canada, 745 Commonwealth Avenue, Boston, Massachusetts 02215-1401.

5. Actually, the copyright holders placed the song in at least twenty different books during that period. One of the "outside" publishers, Aimee Semple McPherson, leader of the pentecostal Foursquare Gospel movement in Los Angeles, California, included it in two books (1920 and 1928). To me this indicates her steadfast conviction that her congregations *should* sing it, whether they did or not.

6. New York: Harper & Brothers Publishers, 1906–1907.

7. New York: George H. Doran Company; reprinted from the edition of 1924.

8. Julian, *Dictionary of Hymnology*, 1204.

9. Ibid. Considering the popularity of D. L. Moody's preaching, which contained the same emphases as the songs, I believe this last sentence falls short of the truth.

10. Waldo S. Pratt, *Musical Ministries in the Church* (New York: Revell, 1901), 62.

11. William M. Runyan (1870–1957) edited *The Voice of Thanksgiving Number Five* for the Moody Bible Institute in Chicago; he was a Methodist minister and evangelist who served both the Institute and Hope Publishing Company as an editorial consultant from 1926 until his retirement in 1948. Alfred B. Smith (1916–2001), who prepared *Inspiring Hymns* for publication, was well known as a songleader in Bible conferences and with Youth for Christ, and in later life published a great deal of gospel music. Paul Beckwith (no dates available) edited *Hymns*, was active in evangelistic meetings with Homer Hammontree (1878–1964), and served in North America as a staff member for InterVarsity Christian Fellowship.

12. William J. Reynolds, *Hymns of Our Faith* (Nashville: Broadman Press, 1964), 216–17.

13. See Carlton R. Young, *Companion to* The United Methodist Hymnal (Nashville: Abingdon Press, 1993), 666.

14. The text to "Hold the Fort" reads as follows:

> 1. Ho, my comrades! see the signal waving in the sky;
> reinforcements now appearing, victory is nigh.
>
> Refrain:
>
> "Hold the fort for I am coming," Jesus signals still;
> wave the answer back to heaven, "By thy grace we will."

2. See the mighty host advancing, Satan leading on;
mighty men around us falling, courage almost gone!

3. See the glorious banner waving! Hear the trumpet blow!
In our Leader's name we'll triumph over every foe.

4. Fierce and long the battle rages, but our help is near;
onward comes our great Commander, cheer, my comrades, cheer!

(Philip P. Bliss, 1838–1876)

15. Reynolds, *Hymns of Our Faith*, 217.

16. See Jere V. Adams, ed., *Handbook to* The Baptist Hymnal (Nashville: Convention Press, 1992), 259.

17. *Random House Dictionary of the English Language* (unabridged edition) (New York: Random House, 1966), 1506.

18. I say this because all these songs are mentioned in the Sankey autobiography and in other historical accounts of the Moody-Sankey meetings and are still known today.

19. John Pollock, *Moody without Sankey* (London: Hodder and Stoughton, 1963; rep. ed., Fearn, Scotland: Christian Focus, 1995), 143–144. This volume lists no primary source books or articles, but identifies a long list of primary source locations.

20. Young, *Companion*, 409–11.

21. Perhaps not. The close of stanza 2 does not leave room for the significance of water baptism in the sacramental traditions. My good friend, the English hymnist Christopher Idle, recently told me that someone in his country suggested this version to solve that problem: "The vilest offender who truly believes through grace in the sacraments pardon receives."

In the case of the United Church of Christ and *The New Century Hymnal,* their editors may have objected more to the song's many "sexist" pronouns referring to God the Father. Their next hymnal (or supplement) may use the new version introduced in the 1996 Canadian Presbyterian hymnal, *The Book of Praise*.

22. J. R. Watson, ed. with commentary, *An Annotated Anthology of Hymns* (Oxford, United Kingdom: Oxford University Press, 2002), 376–77.

"Sing unto the Lord a New Song"

Robert H. Coleman's Gospel Song Books and Hymnals (1909–1939) and Their Impact upon Southern Baptist Hymnody

J. Michael Raley

In August 1908, Dallas churchman Robert Henry Coleman (1869–1946) took the first steps towards publishing a new collection of hymns and gospel songs that would target mission-minded, evangelical Christians. His book would include an ample selection of traditional hymns, of course, but Coleman's true passion lay elsewhere. He desired, more than anything, to feature the "very best, both of the old and new gospel songs"—those which, in his view, most effectively set to music the Gospel message. He intended to make his book available at the lowest possible price so that even the poorest churches "would feel disposed to purchase a sufficient number of books to insist that '*All the people sing*.'"[1] Coleman planned to compile the songs and hymns for his collection himself, but knew that he would need the assistance of an experienced publisher to handle its editorial and production details. He also hoped to obtain financial backing for his project from the American Baptist Publication Society (ABPS), which at the time was still providing literature for many Southern (as well as Northern) Baptist churches.[2]

In this labor of love Coleman aspired, above all, to provide a viable alternative for congregations of his own denomination. The (Southern) Baptist Sunday School Board (BSSB) had published *The Baptist Hymn and Praise Book* in 1904, but it had sold only modestly.[3] Instead of using it, most urban Baptist congregations in the South were singing from the collections of northern evangelical publishers—the Biglow and Main Company, John J. Hood Company, John Church Company, and Hope Publishing Company, to cite but a few—while among southern rural congregations the shape-note collections of the Ruebush-Kieffer Company (with ties to the United Brethren in Christ), A. J. Showalter (a Presbyterian elder), and James D. Vaughan (a Nazarene layman) were quite popular. It was for this very reason, in fact—so that they might compete successfully in northern and southern, as well as urban and rural, markets—that Coleman's song book (as well as the others which followed) would be published in both round and shape notes.[4] And successful they would be. In fact, over the course of the next three decades the Robert H. Coleman Publishing Company would publish at least thirty-six gospel song books, hymnals, and quartet collections for men's and women's voices. (See the Appendix for their titles and dates of publication.) The exact number of Coleman's publications depends, of course, upon whether or not one includes abridgements, special editions, and promotional copies, but however one tallies their number, Robert Coleman eventually sold more than 12,500,000 books—more than any other independent church music publisher of his day.[5]

Coleman's tremendous success in the church music publishing industry may be attributed to at least four factors. The first was his thirteen-year association, beginning in 1908, with the established Chicago editor and "custom" hymnal publisher, Edwin O. Excell, Sr. (1851–1921).[6] Initially, Coleman lacked firsthand knowledge of the church music publishing business; he also had yet to purchase his first copyright. In stark contrast, Excell possessed a lifetime of editorial and publishing experience, and he owned the copyrights to thousands of hymns and gospel songs. In return for a contracted fee—either a wholesale price per book that would include production costs, or, more likely, a royalty of a few cents per book above production costs (manufactured, according to a surviving letter, in lots of twenty thousand copies each)—Excell would grant Coleman access to his entire stock of copyrights as well as to his high quality printing plates. Excell also promised to arrange for the manufacturing of any new plates that might be required—whether for a new song or simply because the plate for a popular favorite had worn out with repeated use—and to oversee the printing and binding of the book, tasks to be handled by outside firms.[7]

By employing Excell's "custom" publishing expertise, Coleman thus gained immediate and unlimited access to all of Excell's copyrights; at the same time, he minimized the expense of manufacturing costly printing plates. Moreover, since Excell was in the midst of publishing five other custom collections at a time when his own books were experiencing a "phenomenal sale," Coleman reaped yet another advantage: Excell offered to "carry the financial end" of his venture provided that the ABPS agreed "to publish and promote the book."[8] Excell would be finished with the project and receive full payment from the ABPS once the initial lots of the book had been printed, bound, and delivered. Coleman, too, would be compensated—probably through a royalty fee per printed book—in return for having compiled the collection. This would leave the ABPS with the primary responsibility of marketing the book at retail, although Coleman also likely retained the right to purchase at wholesale copies of the book for retail sale.[9] With such a vast number of churches in its marketing network, however, the ABPS could reasonably expect that a well-compiled and efficiently-produced gospel song book such as Coleman was proposing would sell well enough to yield at least a modest return on the Society's financial investment.

A second factor in Coleman's commercial success was thus his ongoing relationship with the ABPS. Over the course of the next two-and-one-half decades, the ABPS and Judson Press/Griffith and Rowland Press in Philadelphia would "publish" duplicate editions of all of Coleman's major collections: *The Evangel* (1909), *The New Evangel* (1911), *The World Evangel* (1913), *The Herald* (1915), *Treasury of Song* (1917), *The Popular Hymnal* (1918), *The Pilot* (1922), *Harvest Hymns* (1924), *The Modern Hymnal* (1926), *Gospel Melodies* (1928), *Majestic Hymns* (1930), and *The American Hymnal* (1933). *The Evangel*, Coleman's first book and the only one of Coleman's collections to be published solely by the ABPS, eventually sold nearly 375,000 copies.[10] Although separate sales figures for the Philadelphia editions of Coleman's subsequent collections have not come to light, there can be no doubt that the ABPS—through sales to Northern and Southern Baptist churches using ABPS materials—provided important markets for Coleman's collections.

The third and fourth factors in Coleman's success stemmed respectively from his own ministerial abilities and experiences, on the one hand, coupled with his keen business savvy and ability to capitalize upon the networks he built among the Baptist leadership, on the other. As a bi-vocational lay minister, Robert Coleman served the First Baptist Church of Dallas for many years, first as a deacon and then as assistant pastor, congregational song leader, and Sunday school superintendent.[11] In these capacities he developed a clear perception of the spiritual needs and musical preferences of Southern Baptist congregations.

Coleman's years of service at the First Baptist Church corresponded closely to the pastorate of the renowned Dr. George W. Truett, who also served as president of the Southern Baptist Convention (1927–1929) and the Baptist World Alliance (1934–1939). Truett had given major addresses before the Baptist World Alliance (BWA) as early as its Second Congress, which convened in June 1911 at Philadelphia's Grace Baptist Temple. Coleman was serving at the time on the BWA's Committee on Young People's Baptist World's Organization. Truett's extensive contacts within the Baptist world, coupled with those Coleman cultivated on his own, provided Coleman with opportunities to direct the congregational singing before conventions of the Baptist Young People's Union (BYPU) and the Baptist Student Missionary Movement (BSMM), the Baptist General Convention of Texas and other Baptist state conventions, the Northern and Southern Baptist Conventions, and even congresses of the BWA.[12]

Whenever Coleman led the singing at a convention or a revival, the congregation usually sang from his latest song book or hymnal (provided by

Coleman gratuitously or at cost). Still, even though there can be no doubt that such marketing strategies helped to increase sales, they alone cannot explain the immense popularity of his books. Rather, it seems, Coleman's collections were beloved in their day because the songs and hymns contained within their covers truly touched the hearts of Baptist congregations. Indeed, Coleman's song books and hymnals became so popular among the congregations of his denomination that they helped forge a "Southern Baptist" canon of traditional Protestant hymnody and northern gospel songs, infused with the latest compositions of leading Southern Baptist music evangelists. Chief among these music evangelist-composers would be I. E. Reynolds (1879–1949), who after 1915 would direct Southwestern Baptist Theological Seminary's Department of Gospel Music and between 1916 and ca. 1922 would also edit at least three of Coleman's collections, and Reynolds's former student turned colleague, B. B. McKinney (1886–1952), who would edit Coleman's collections from ca. 1922 until 1935.[13] McKinney's subsequent appointment as music editor of the BSSB in 1935 and as secretary of the Board's newly created Church Music Department in 1941, coupled with the sale of Coleman's firm and his copyrights to the Board in 1945, would assure that many of Coleman's contributions and editorial decisions would be incorporated into the mainstream of Southern Baptist hymnody.

The Birth of the Robert H. Coleman Publishing Company

In 1898, ten years before he approached E. O. Excell, Robert Coleman had compiled a small collection of popular gospel songs and hymns for use at the Texas BYPU convention. "Brother Bob," as he was known, had been actively involved in the Texas BYPU since its inception in 1891, and would serve as its president from 1899 until 1902 and again from 1914 until 1922. One of Coleman's colleagues in the BYPU, B. J. Roberts, was a fellow deacon at the First Baptist Church and also the Dallas director of the ABPS, which at the time was supplying the First Baptist Church with its Sunday school literature. Whatever the precise connection here—whether Coleman was approached by Roberts or the reverse occurred, or perhaps, as Baptist historian Leon McBeth has suggested, some Texas Baptists had been sufficiently impressed by Coleman's earlier effort on behalf of the BYPU to encourage him to publish a larger song book—by August 1908 Coleman had decided to compile a more complete collection of hymns and gospel songs, and to solicit the aid of the ABPS in publishing it.[14] He wrote to the Chicago publisher, E. O. Excell, Sr., to inquire if he might be willing to serve as the musical editor and custom publisher for the collection. Excell replied, "In regard to the editing and publishing of a book for the American Baptist Publication Society, I wish to say I see no reason why we may not get together on such a proposition, provided, of course, you can get your Publication Society to publish and promote the book."[15]

A few days later, Excell received a similar request from Wm. Wistar Hamilton (1868–1951), "General Evangelist" for the Home Mission Board of the Southern Baptist Convention and president of the BYPU of the South. The ABPS was already in the process of publishing two books by Dr. Hamilton, *Sane Evangelism* and *How to Grow in the Christian Life*. Since Coleman and Hamilton shared similar evangelistic goals and both were Southern Baptists with close ties to the ABPS, Excell suggested that they compile a joint collection. If the ABPS would underwrite their project, Excell would serve as the collection's musical editor and custom publisher.[16]

Coleman submitted his proposal to Charles M. Roe, the business manager of the ABPS, but the contract negotiations proved more difficult than expected, stretching out more than three months. In late October 1908, Excell wrote Coleman, "I still believe that you and Mr. Roe will get together on a proposition that will be satisfactory to you both. It must be satisfactory to you both before I [will] have anything to do with the book."[17] Excell's prediction apparently came to pass, for in mid-November he informed Coleman, "Within a day or two I am to prepare the contract, which will be forwarded to Mr. Roe for his signature."[18]

The Evangel

Excell initially suggested that Coleman and Hamilton include in their collection about fifty songs from the public domain, one hundred or so of his own copyrights, and sixty-three new or outside copyrights. If they wished to reduce their expense, they might consider including fewer outside copyrights and rely more upon those owned by Excell. The book should also feature a number of children's songs ("which help to sell the book as much as any other one feature") plus at least eight "chorus selections" (i.e., mini-anthems or extended gospel songs covering two pages). Excell advised Coleman to ask the ABPS to pay for securing the outside copyrights and permissions, but Coleman also purchased two copyrights himself, suggesting that he was already thinking beyond this initial endeavor. Above all, Excell repeatedly reminded Hamilton and Coleman, "You must make sure that you have a perfect right to use every thing that goes into the book so as to avoid getting the publisher into trouble."[19]

Securing copyright permissions to include gospel songs owned by others posed a serious obstacle to publishers of that day. Copyright owners quite naturally were concerned about protecting their investments, and thus often refused to negotiate the use of their songs at any price. Publishing companies, in particular, feared that if they were too generous with their copyrights, customers might purchase their competitors' collections rather than their own. Thus permission to include the very latest and most popular songs usually could not be obtained at any price. Permissions for slightly less popular songs or best sellers that were now four or five years old could sometimes be obtained in return for payment of a substantial fee, while the privilege of including a less popular or still older copyright generally could be secured with far less difficulty and at a more affordable price. The dilemma for Coleman, Hamilton, and the ABPS, on the one hand, was whether or not the permission fees demanded for recently-composed "choice" songs by their owners were, in their view, prohibitive, or, on the other hand, whether those songs whose permissions they could most readily secure at a reasonable cost would be of sufficient merit and popularity to contribute to the overall quality and sales of the book. Their goal, then as always, was to include the "best" and most popular songs of their day at the lowest possible cost.

Coleman and Hamilton had difficulty, for instance, negotiating with the Biglow and Main Company, which owned most of Fanny Crosby's hymns, although they finally did succeed in obtaining permission to include one older, but still quite popular Biglow and Main song, Rev. Edward Mote's text, "THE SOLID ROCK," accompanied by the well-known tune of William B. Bradbury.[20] They also obtained permission from the Winona Publishing Company to include Harper G. Smyth's brand new (1908) text-and-tune (i.e., a text and tune, composed by one author-composer, sharing the name of the text and intended only to be sung together), "MAKE ME A CHANNEL OF BLESSING," but they were unable to negotiate successfully for the newest and most popular songs of the John Church Publishing Company, Hope Publishing Company, and other leading northern publishing firms of that day. This explains why engaging Excell's services was so critical to the success of their venture, for without his copyrights, Coleman and Hamilton would have been forced to rely upon established hymns already in the public domain, supplemented solely by untested new songs of dubious value. There was an added benefit here as well: Excell's permission fees were built into his lump-sum wholesale price for the book and thus required no additional outlay of cash. The timing of Coleman's and Hamilton's venture, moreover, could hardly have been better, for Excell had just purchased one hundred "choice" new copyrights, selected from a list of two thousand titles owned and, for the most part, composed by the prolific Charles H. Gabriel.[21]

Excell warned Coleman that the fees being demanded by one of his fiercest rivals, Philadelphia composer and publisher William J. Kirkpatrick, were excessive. "He is holding you up on account of my connection with the book," Excell wrote Coleman. "He belongs to a 'gang' that are against your Uncle Ex, but your Uncle Ex goes right on without ever suspecting that there was anything on the 'track.'"[22] Kirkpatrick's associate, Henry Lake Gilmour, denied all access to his songs. Kirkpatrick, too, withheld his latest songs, but in the end granted Coleman permission to include his established text-and-tune, "LORD, I'M COMING HOME," as well as his tune for "THE COMFORTER HAS COME," by Frank Bottome. Meanwhile, Coleman secured permission for three older songs owned by "John J. Hood," a pseudonym for the Philadelphia partnership between Kirkpatrick and the late John R. Sweney. One of these was Johnson Oatman, Jr.'s "choice" gospel song, "HIGHER GROUND," set to music by Charles H. Gabriel. In addition, Coleman was able to include such favorites as Katherine Hankey's "I love to tell the story" and James Nicholson's "WHITER THAN SNOW," each set to tunes by William G. Fischer; "THE BANNER OF THE CROSS" by El Nathan (a pseudonym for Daniel W. Whittle), set to music by James McGranahan; and Will L. Thompson's text-and-tune, "Jesus is all the world to me."[23]

Excell was especially anxious about the book's title. A good title, after all, succinctly captures the overall theme of the book; the choice of title can also seriously affect a book's sales. Thus a concerned Excell repeatedly asked Coleman, "What's the title of your book to be? That's a very important matter. Hope you will be able to select a good one."[24] In the end, Coleman and Hamilton opted for a title that captured their revival spirit—*The Evangel*. In the words of the editor and compilers, it was to be "A Bearer of the Good News." Thereafter, Coleman not only paid close attention to the titles of his collections, but also selected a particular song or hymn to coordinate closely with each collection's theme. In the Foreword to *The World Evangel* (1913), for example, Coleman expressed his prayer that the Holy Spirit might use the collection to "Evangelize the World" and specifically directed the reader to Samuel W. Beazley's two-page chorus selection of the same title.[25] *Majestic Hymns* (1930) opened with Samuel Stennett's stately hymn, "Majestic sweetness sits enthroned," set to Thomas Hastings's tune, ORTONVILLE, while the first song of *Precious Hymns* (1938) was Alfred H. Ackley's "PRECIOUS TO ME."[26] Another popular collection, *Harvest Hymns* (1924), commenced with Rev. W. C. Poole's gospel song, "TO THE HARVEST FIELD," whose tune Coleman had commissioned from George C. Stebbins, a well-established songwriter who earlier had worked with D. L. Moody and Ira Sankey. Coleman not only cited Revelation 14:15 (" . . . the time is come for thee to reap, for the harvest of the earth is ripe") to encapsulate the collection's harvest theme, but in a word play, labeled the seventy-eight-year-old Stebbins as "that princely song writer of ripe experience."[27]

To those who criticized his inclusion of the latest gospel songs, Coleman pointed out that "congregations love 'To sing unto the Lord a New Song,' provided that 'New Song' has a meaningful message and melodious music."[28] Throughout his career, Coleman would continue to defend his inclusion of new gospel songs, repeatedly insisting that their popularity stemmed not so much from current musical trends as from the fact that "they give such beautiful and faithful expression to the Gospel Story."[29] At the same time, he took care to point out that a new song required a proper introduction by the song leader and needed to be sung several times by the congregation before one might adequately assess its merit.[30]

At the end of January 1909, Excell wrote to Coleman, informing him, "The book is ready for the printers [*sic*] hands except the index, title and Preface, which I hope to have ready by the time I hear from you."[31] Coleman, meanwhile, had written Excell to inquire about the possibility of including the first thirty-two pages of the book in the program for use at an upcoming BYPU convention. Excell advised strongly against it. Problems might arise with the copyright holders; moreover, Excell's experience had taught him that this was not an effective means of advertising a new collection. Instead, he advocated making arrangements with the APBS to give away copies of the entire book in return for a nominal convention "enrollment" fee, as he himself was planning to do with one of his own collections at an upcoming convention: "There is no advertising that will equal the use of the book itself." Coleman apparently went ahead with his plan to print a few select songs for use at the BYPU convention anyway, but in subsequent years he followed Excell's advice. As a result, Coleman's song books were featured perennially as the convention hymnals of both the Northern and Southern Baptist Conventions.[32] Coleman also published a special convention hymnal for the Baptist Student Missionary Movement (BSMM) in 1916; the following year, those attending the BSMM Convention sang from Coleman's *Treasury of Song*.[33] Meanwhile, he prepared "revival" editions for larger local congregations, and, in 1918, he published *The Temple Hymnal* for the Grace Baptist Church of Philadelphia in honor of the seventy-fifth birthday of its illustrious pastor, Temple College [today Temple University] founder and president, Russell H. Conwell.[34]

Coleman's Creation of a Canon of "Southern Baptist" Gospel Hymnody

As illustrated by the example of *The Evangel*, Coleman typically compiled the hymns and gospel songs of his collections himself, but relied upon others to oversee the technical details of the music editing and publishing processes. Excell almost certainly supervised the production of his early collections, when Coleman still lacked both experience in the church music publishing industry and sufficient numbers of his own copyrights. *The New*

Evangel, *The World Evangel*, *The Herald*, *Treasury of Song*, and even *The Popular Hymnal* all contained large numbers of Excell copyrights (see Table 1 on page 186), tangible evidence of Excell's direct involvement in their publication.[35]

Beyond Excell's copyrights, we have seen, Coleman secured permissions from outside publishers and copyright owners to include what he considered to be "choice" hymns or gospel songs. Most of these gospel songs had appeared first in northern publications (also marketed heavily in the South), but Coleman's repeated inclusion of these established favorites in his best-selling collections—several of which sold more than 600,000 copies each, with *The Popular Hymnal* selling more than 800,000 and sales from *The Modern Hymnal* exceeding one million copies[36]—especially endeared them to Southern Baptist congregations. Indeed, it would be difficult today to imagine a Southern Baptist hymnal without them. A few examples include:

George Bennard's text-and-tune, "THE OLD RUGGED CROSS";

Philip P. Bliss's text-and-tune, "WONDERFUL WORDS OF LIFE"; and tune VILLE DU HAVRE for Horatio G. Spafford's text, "IT IS WELL WITH MY SOUL";

William Howard Doane's tunes PRECIOUS NAME, for Lydia Baxter's text, "Take the name of Jesus with you"; I AM THINE, for Fanny J. Crosby's text, "I am Thine, O Lord"; RESCUE for Crosby's "Rescue the perishing"; and NEAR THE CROSS, for Crosby's "Jesus, keep me near the cross";

Charles H. Gabriel's texts-and-tunes, "SEND THE LIGHT" and "I stand amazed in the presence"; and tunes GABRIEL for William C. Poole's text, "JUST WHEN I NEED HIM MOST"; HIGHER GROUND for Johnson Oatman, Jr.'s text, "HIGHER GROUND"; and MCDANIEL for Rufus H. McDaniel's text, "SINCE JESUS CAME INTO MY HEART";

Elisha A. Hoffman's text-and-tune, "I must tell Jesus"; and his text, "LEANING ON THE EVERLASTING ARMS," set to Anthony J. Showalter's tune, SHOWALTER;

William J. Kirkpatrick's text-and-tune, "LORD, I'M COMING HOME"; and his tune, JESUS SAVES, for Priscilla J. Owens's text, "JESUS SAVES!";

James McGranahan's tune, SHOWERS OF BLESSING, for Daniel W. Whittle's text, "There shall be showers of blessing";

C. Austin Miles's text-and-tune, "IN THE GARDEN";

Leila Naylor Morris's text-and-tune, "LET JESUS COME INTO YOUR HEART."

Even as Coleman was obtaining permission to publish popular gospel songs owned, for the most part, by northern publishers, he also continued purchasing copyrights to promising new songs by such well-known northern composers as Charles H. Gabriel; Bentley D. Ackley, who was associated with Homer A. Rodeheaver; Samuel W. Beazley, who edited collections for the Ruebush-Kieffer Company in Virginia, but resided in Chicago; Harry Dixon Loes, who studied and later taught at the Moody Bible Institute in Chicago; Scott Lawrence, a popular New York composer associated with the Tullar-Meredith Company; and the prominent composer-publisher, Haldor Lillenas.[37] Over time, Coleman would gradually acquire copyrights to more than eight hundred gospel songs. Naturally the majority of these, like those purchased by rival publishers, were short lived, but a number of Coleman's purchases evolved, with widespread and repeated use, into classic gospel songs. Among these are Albert C. Fisher's text-and-tune, "LOVE IS THE THEME"; Luther B. Bridgers's text-and-tune, "HE KEEPS ME SINGING" ("There's within my heart a melody"); James Rowe's text, "LOVE LIFTED ME," set to Howard E. Smith's tune, SAFETY; and a number of B. B. McKinney's songs (more below).

Early in his publishing career, Coleman also began collaborating with a group of talented gospel song composers employed by the Southern Baptist Convention's Home Mission Board (HMB) as full-time music evangelists. These young men included Jack P. Scholfield, E. L. Wolslagel (sometimes spelled as Woleslagel), Isham E. (usually referred to as "I. E.," or "Ike") Reynolds, Daniel R. Wade, and M. J. Babbitt. These evangelists quite literally were Southern Baptist celebrities in their own right, featured as they were in churches, conventions, and revival meetings all across the South. Sometimes they led the music individually, but more often they performed together in various combinations as the "Home Mission Board Quartet."[38] In publishing their songs, Robert Coleman not only capitalized upon the HMB Quartet's popularity across the South; he also promoted a new body of gospel hymnody that stemmed directly from the pens of Southern Baptist composers.[39] However ephemeral many of these songs may have been, they thus served an important function in their day. Moreover, a few of these songs, too, have survived the test of time.

Reynolds's text-and-tune, "JESUS IS THE FRIEND YOU NEED," for example, first appeared in Coleman's *The Popular Hymnal* (1918), while his tune VENTING, which accompanied Alfred Barratt's gospel song, "WONDERFUL PEACE OF MY SAVIOR," was first published in Coleman's *Harvest Hymns* (1924).[40] Both were included in a number of Coleman's collections as well as in the *Baptist Hymnal* (1956); "WONDERFUL PEACE OF MY SAVIOR" also may be found in *The Broadman Hymnal* (1940). Another Reynolds song, "WILL YOU

COME?" ("Jesus waits to welcome you"), appeared in Coleman's *Baptist Student Missionary Movement Hymnal* (1916). Afterwards, the song fell into disuse; it only experienced a revival after its proof sheet was rediscovered in 1949 following Reynolds's death. Subsequently it was published in *Assembly Songbook* (1959), *Crusade Hymns* (1968), and *Baptist Hymnal* (1975).[41]

Jack Scholfield's "I've found a friend who is all to me," otherwise known as "SAVED, SAVED!" quite deservedly has enjoyed a long life. Scholfield composed both text and tune in 1911 during a revival led by evangelist Mordecai F. Ham at which Scholfield was singing and leading the music. Scholfield's song made its debut in *The New Evangel* (1911), which the composer's brother, music evangelist J. Fred Scholfield, helped Coleman compile and edit. Coleman later purchased the rights to "SAVED, SAVED!" and included it in most of his subsequent publications. The song also may be found in Tabernacle Publishing Company's *Sing Joyfully* (1989), as well as in *The Baptist Hymnal* (1991).[42]

Coleman's methodical purchasing of new songs, along with the gradual diminishing of the number of Excell copyrights included in his collections, can be seen in Table 1. Table 2 illustrates his systematic acquisition of gospel songs by Southern Baptist music evangelists.

Select Gospel Songs (1916) and *Kingdom Songs* (1921) reflected cooperative efforts between Coleman and the BSSB. Thus these two collections were, in some ways, anomalies among Coleman's publications. As Table 2 clearly shows, they contained a disproportionately large number of songs composed by Southern Baptist evangelists. Co-edited by Home Mission Board music evangelists Jack P. Scholfield and E. L. Wolslagel, with I. E. Reynolds as musical editor, *Select Gospel Songs* was a small collection of 148 songs, one third of which were compositions of Southern Baptist music evangelists—27 songs by Scholfield, 5 by Wolslagel, 16 by Reynolds, and 1 by M. J. Babbitt. Copyrighted and initially published by Coleman in Dallas, it was reiussed in 1918 by the BSSB as a pocket edition of fifty thousand copies for soldiers fighting overseas. The collection also included a northern copyright recently acquired by Coleman that would grow dear to Southern Baptists, "LOVE LIFTED ME." Significantly, however, the song book contained no copyrights owned by Excell.[43]

Kingdom Songs was co-edited by Ike Reynolds and Robert Coleman. Copyrighted and published by the BSSB with Coleman's permission to include an unlimited number of his copyrights, it too contained an unusually high number of songs (forty-seven) by Southern Baptist music evangelists.[44] A unique copy of this song book that once belonged to Hope Publishing Company's library survives today in the Wheaton College Library Hymnal Collection. Inside its front cover one finds the following words penciled in

TABLE 1
Excell versus Coleman Copyrights in Coleman Song Books and Hymnals

	E	NE	WE	H	SGS	TS	PH	KS	HH	MH
Total Songs	236	326	371	246	148	384	373	333	264	484
Excell Copyrights	126	102	80	59	0	109	59	29	14	24
Coleman Copyrights	2	16	33	27	45	43	30	77	66	70
% Excell Copyrights	53%	31%	22%	24%	0%	28%	16%	9%	5%	5%
% Coleman Copyrights	.8%	5%	9%	11%	30%	11%	8%	23%	25%	14%

TABLE 2
Gospel Songs by Southern Baptist Music Evangelists Published in Coleman's Collections

	E	NE	WE	H	SGS	TS	PH	KS	HH	MH
Jack P. Scholfield	0	2	2	3	27	8	19	11	7	5
E. L. Wolslagel	0	0	0	0	5	1	0	1	0	0
I. E. Reynolds	0	0	0	5	16	12	3	25	2	2
Daniel R. Wade	0	0	0	4	0	1	0	1	0	0
M. J. Babbitt	0	0	0	4	1	4	1	2	1	1
B. B. McKinney	0	0	0	0	0	0	0	7	13	22
TOTAL	**0**	**2**	**2**	**16**	**49**	**26**	**23**	**47**	**23**	**30**

Key

E = *The Evangel* (1909)
NE = *The New Evangel* (1911)
WE = *The World Evangel* (1913)
H = *The Herald* (1915)
SGS = *Select Gospel Songs* (1916)
TS = *Treasury of Song* (1917)
PH = *The Popular Hymnal* (1918)
KS = *Kingdom Songs* (1921)
HH = *Harvest Hymns* (1924)
MH = *The Modern Hymnal* (1926)

large script: "All Plates marked E. are Excell Property." Throughout the song book, various pages are so marked; all told, it appears that 192 hymns and gospel songs out of the total of 333 in the collection were printed with plates owned by E. O. Excell. Although Hope Publishing Company purchased the Excell Company in 1931 and thus might have come into possession of this unusual book at that time, it seems more likely that Hope Publishing Company, which for many years served as the custom song book publisher of the BSSB, produced *Kingdom Songs* with plates on loan from an aged and ill Excell, who had edited collections for Hope Publishing Company in the past and by now also had a long association with Robert Coleman.[45]

If we exclude these two exceptional collections and focus instead upon Coleman's own publications, we witness a gradual increase in the number of gospel songs by Southern Baptist music evangelists included in Coleman's collections from just two songs in *The New Evangel* to thirty songs in *The Modern Hymnal.* Near the end of this period, the emphasis shifted from the songs of HMB evangelists to those of B. B. McKinney. Meanwhile, the percentage of Coleman copyrights in his collections increased overall from just 0.8 percent in *The Evangel* to 11 percent in *Treasury of Song* and 25 percent in *Harvest Hymns.* With *The Modern Hymnal*, the number of Coleman copyrights included increased still further even though the percentage dropped back to 14 percent as a result of the hymnal's much larger size. Meanwhile, the percentage of Excell copyrights in Coleman's collections decreased overall from 53 percent in *The Evangel* to 24 percent in *The Herald*, 16 percent in *The Popular Hymnal*, and just 5 percent each in *Harvest Hymns* and *The Modern Hymnal.* Slowly but surely, Coleman had weaned himself from dependency upon Excell, so that by the time that Excell departed from this world in June 1921, Coleman was fully prepared to move ahead on his own.

Coleman's Role as a Publisher in the Composition Process

The internal operations of Coleman's publishing company have long posed difficulties for historians, primarily due to the paucity of surviving letters and other records from the firm's files. By a stroke of good fortune, however, I. E. Reynolds's diary from 1912–1916, which survives in the archives of Roberts Library at Southwestern Baptist Theological Seminary (SWBTS) and was graciously made available to the author as a photocopy, provides a unique opportunity to examine at least one aspect of Coleman's business during the first decade of the firm's existence. It reveals, in particular, Coleman's direct involvement in the composition process with one of the composers whose gospel songs he was contemplating purchasing.

Although few specifics about their early connections are known, Ike Reynolds was no stranger to Coleman when their association blossomed in 1915. Reynolds, of course, was a well-known music evangelist while Coleman was the prominent congregational song leader of the First Baptist Church of Dallas. Reynolds had performed at the Southern Baptist Convention each year between 1912 and 1915 as a member of the HMB Quartet. Coleman, meanwhile, had provided the song books for these conventions and had led the congregational singing on occasion. Reynolds had been in contact with Coleman even before these conventions, however. His diary records that, in March 1912, he telephoned "Mr. R. H. Coleman" long distance from Bonham, Texas, where for three weeks he was to direct the music in a local revival. Reynolds asked Coleman to "send [some gospel song] books"—almost certainly copies of *The New Evangel*—for use in the revival. Thirteen months later, in April 1913, Ike and Lura Reynolds visited the First Baptist Church of Dallas; in August of that same year, they called upon Bob Coleman at the *Baptist Standard* office, where he was employed as the business manager.[46]

Thus Ike Reynolds and Robert Coleman had known each other for some years when their relationship deepened in 1915. Ike and Lura Reynolds were in Dallas for ten days in February of that year, during which Ike stopped by Coleman's *Baptist Standard* office several times to go over his latest songs with Coleman and his close friend, gospel pianist Robert Jolly. On occasion, the trio met at First Baptist Church organist Will A. Watkin's music store instead.[47] The Reynoldses were back in Dallas briefly in early March, and again from late March through the end of April for a city-wide revival involving twenty-eight area churches. It was an incredibly busy time, with at least two services daily, along with preparatory and publicity meetings, visitation of prospective members, and rehearsals. The HMB Quartet and a ladies quartet including some of the male quartet members' wives performed at the city's "Get-together Meeting" held at the First Baptist Church on Sunday afternoon, April 4. Later that same day, and again on the following two Sunday afternoons, the HMB Quartet sang at men's meetings which convened at the Dallas city hall auditorium. The HMB Quartet was also featured in the joint services conducted weekday mornings at the First Baptist Church; each evening the quartet members dispersed individually to local congregations. The vocal duets of Ike and Lura Reynolds were in particular demand not only in the evening services, but also during the Sunday school hour and Sunday morning worship services of Central Baptist Church (today Cliff Temple Baptist Church) in nearby Oak Cliff. Still, whenever he could find the time, Ike's diary records, he worked on his music and sought feedback from Bob Coleman, Bob Jolly, and Will Watkin at Coleman's *Baptist Standard* office or at Watkin's music store. On at least one occasion, Ike noted in his diary, Lura Reynolds "played over [his] songs for J. P. S. [Jack P. Scholfield] and Coleman."[48]

Just three weeks later, in mid-May, Ike and Lura Reynolds were in Houston to sing before the Southern Baptist Convention. At memorial services conducted during the Convention on Sunday afternoon, May 16, the 1915 Convention *Annual* records, "The song service was conducted by Robert H. Coleman, Texas, assisted by I. E. Reynolds and wife and the Home [Mission] Board quartette." It was following Ike Reynolds's impressive vocal performances at this Convention that SWBTS President Lee R. Scarborough invited him to visit the seminary campus in Fort Worth, where he sang in chapel on May 19. President Scarborough subsequently asked Reynolds to organize and oversee Southwestern Seminary's Department of Gospel Music (after 1921, School of Gospel Music). On May 21, Ike noted for the first time in his diary, he "sold three songs to R. H. Coleman."[49]

Robert Coleman was clearly going far beyond purchasing and publishing new songs. Indeed, he and his circle of musician friends—Robert Jolly, Will Watkin, Ike and Lura Reynolds, Jack Scholfield, and no doubt others—were engaging almost daily in dialogue as a community to produce these songs which, once "perfected," Coleman would promote in his collections. Something else is quite evident here: composing did not come as easily for Ike Reynolds as it did for many gospel music composers. This begs the question of whether or not Coleman's involvement in the composition process extended beyond his contacts with Reynolds. In the absence of more evidence no sure conclusions can be drawn, except to say that the surviving correspondence of other composers who sent him their songs from a distance at times suggests that Coleman may have provided feedback and also encouragement in his letters whenever he rejected one of their songs.[50]

In Ike Reynolds's case, at least, perseverance repeatedly paid off. His diary entry for June 29, 1915, records that he sold Coleman four more songs on that day. Similarly, the entry of Saturday, January 22, 1916, notes that he "went to 1st Bap't. Ch. at 11 A.M. to see R. H. Coleman and Rob't Jolly about songs in manuscript." Later that same afternoon, he met Coleman again at the *Baptist Standard* office, where he "sold him some songs."[51] Among the many songs purchased by Coleman from Reynolds and published just in 1915–1916 alone were Reynolds's tunes for J. O. Barnhart's text, "Knocking, knocking, who is there?," and James Rowe's text, "SWEETER AND DEARER," as well as his texts-and-tunes, "ALL SO FREE," "JOY IN SERVING JESUS," "I am safe from ev'ry storm," "SOME SWEET DAY," "HE LOVES YOU SO," and "WILL YOU COME?"[52]

In 1916, of course, Ike Reynolds also edited *Select Gospel Songs* for Robert Coleman. Coleman would turn to Reynolds again just a few years later, during Excell's final illness, to edit *Kingdom Songs* and *Coleman's Male Quartets*, which together would contain eighteen compositions by the highly-gifted B. B. McKinney. This would mark the first time that McKinney's songs had been purchased and presented to the public by an established music publisher. However McKinney's songs may have first come to Coleman's attention—McKinney had previously published a few of his songs privately which may have sparked Coleman's interest, or Coleman may perchance have heard McKinney singing his own songs at a revival or camp meeting—still, Ike Reynolds, as the musical editor for *Kingdom Songs* and *Coleman's Male Quartets*, must have played a central role in getting these early songs published. Indeed, it is quite conceivable that it may have been Reynolds who first introduced McKinney to Coleman, or perhaps showed Coleman some of McKinney's songs and convinced him to publish them.

Coleman's Working Relationship with B. B. McKinney

Young B. B. McKinney clearly gained an enormous advantage when Coleman, a well-established publisher, began purchasing his songs. McKinney had studied with Professor Reynolds at the seminary from 1915–1918. Later, after serving briefly in the United States Army during World War I, he taught for several years alongside his former professor. Recognizing the first-rate quality of the young professor's compositions, Coleman began publishing them on an unprecedented scale. Indeed, between their first appearances in *Kingdom Songs* and *Coleman's Male Quartets* in 1921 and McKinney's hiring by the BSSB in 1935, Coleman would publish two hundred and thirty of McKinney's gospel songs, hymns, and arrangements.[53] Even today a number of McKinney's songs first published in Coleman's collections may be found in *The Baptist Hymnal* (1991). They include:

"Have faith in God when your pathway is lonely" and tune MUSKOGEE, first appearance in *Pilot Hymns* (1934);
"I am satisfied with Jesus" and tune ROUTH, first appearance in *The Modern Hymnal* (1926);
"LET OTHERS SEE JESUS IN YOU," first appearance of the complete text-and-tune in *Harvest Hymns* (1924; the refrain had appeared two years earlier in *The Pilot*);

"LORD, SEND A REVIVAL" and tune MATTHEWS, first published in *Evangel Bells* (1927), in which it appeared as the theme song (no. 1);

"Serve the Lord with gladness" and tune LEE, first appearance in *Service Songs* (1931), was intended as a potential theme song for a Sunday school Intermediate Department; concerning the drafting of this song, McKinney later wrote, "In my vision I could see great multitudes of happy Intermediates singing a 'new song' unto the Lord"[54];

"Speak to my heart, Lord Jesus" and tune HOLCOMB, first appearance in *Evangel Bells* (1927);

"THE NAIL-SCARRED HAND" and tune LUBBOCK, first appearance in *Harvest Hymns* (1924).

McKinney possessed other talents than just composing, however. Indeed, it would not be long before McKinney would supplant Reynolds not only as Coleman's favorite composer, but also as his musical editor. As a seminary professor, Reynolds would increasingly argue in favor of promoting higher standards of church music while McKinney shared an evangelistic philosophy closer to Coleman's, coupled with a down-to-earth personality that charmed Southern Baptists everywhere he went. Although Coleman would only credit McKinney on the title pages of three collections—*Coleman's New Quartet Book* (1925), *Coleman's Male Choir* (1928), and *Coleman's Songs for Men* (1932)—McKinney would in fact serve as the ghost musical editor for most, if not all, of Coleman's collections published between ca. 1922 and McKinney's relocation to Nashville in 1935.[55] Coleman's continued success in the 1920s and 1930s would be due in large part to the high quality of McKinney's gospel songs, his skills as a music editor, and his promotion of Coleman's collections whenever he led the music at Baptist conventions, music camps, urban crusades, and local church revivals. As William J. Reynolds later noted, "The relationship enjoyed by these two men was mutually beneficial in promoting the sales of Coleman's books and giving exposure to McKinney's songs."[56]

A rare surviving letter from Coleman to McKinney written in November 1925 sheds more light upon the precise nature of their working relationship.[57] At the time, McKinney was in the midst of checking proofs, probably for *The Modern Hymnal* (1926). McKinney, it seems, was about to send the corrected proofs back to the Anderson Brothers, Coleman's music typographers, in Hammond, Indiana (situated just a few miles southeast of Chicago). Here, too, was located Coleman's printer, the W. B. Conkey Company, which boasted that it could turn out forty thousand books per day on its presses.[58] In his letter to McKinney, Coleman noted that he would instruct the Anderson Brothers to turn over the plates to the Conkey Company for printing once they had received McKinney's corrected proofs. Coleman went on to explain that, although he and McKinney had "no financial understanding," he was nevertheless sending McKinney one hundred dollars—a substantial sum in those days—in return for his services rendered in "proof reading and other assistance." "I presume you would not charge so much," Coleman wrote, "but I am glad to pay it and wish it were more." Clearly, then, McKinney was not a regular employee of Coleman's publishing company at this time, but was serving as Coleman's editor on a contractual basis. Coleman noted that he still owed McKinney for his own songs that were to be included in the hymnal, but promised, "the first time I see you and we can go over the matter, I will give you a check for that." In closing, Coleman praised "Mack" in glowing terms, writing, "I love you as a brother, I appreciate you as a friend, and I esteem you as a gifted and capable musician."

Coleman's collaboration with McKinney, coupled with his own experience as the Sunday school superintendent of the First Baptist Church of Dallas, perhaps shone through most noticeably with the publication of *Service Songs* (1931), which was designed to address the specific needs of Sunday schools in a day when worship orders still played an important role in their opening assemblies. Aside from more than three hundred hymns and gospel songs (many by McKinney), *Service Songs* included: (1) four "Opening Programs for Young People's or Adult Department" based, respectively, upon the themes of evangelism, Christian devotion, missions, and stewardship; (2) a suggested "Order of Service for an Intermediate Department"; (3) four Sunday school worship programs based upon the themes of Christian service, missions, stewardship, and salvation; (4) sixteen responsive readings taken from the Scriptures; and (5) a song sermon composed by McKinney, entitled "The Wonderful Savior."[59] Above all, *Service Songs* demonstrates that, even if Coleman and McKinney placed the greatest emphasis upon evangelism, they also strove to nurture new believers in their faith and to equip believers to do the work of the Lord. It also shows that Coleman recognized a tremendous market: in the years to come, the BSSB, selling materials to Baptist Sunday schools all across the South, would become the largest outlet for his books.[60]

The Broadman Hymnal

Throughout his long career, Robert Coleman continued publishing smaller gospel song books (which nevertheless served as the principal "hymnal" for many rural and smaller urban churches). He also published three larger, all-purpose congregational hymnals—*The Popular Hymnal* (1918, with 373 hymns and gospel songs), *The Modern Hymnal* (1926, with 484 hymns and gospel songs), and *The American Hymnal* (1933, with 531 hymns and gospel songs). A denominational music survey conducted in 1938—to which 1,381 Southern Baptist churches responded—indicated that more than 75 percent of all rural Southern Baptist churches were using song books or hymnals published either by Robert Coleman or by the BSSB, while the percentage among urban Southern Baptist churches was even higher—nearly 90 percent. Most urban congregations, the survey revealed, were singing from Coleman's *Modern Hymnal*, which had sold more than one million copies by 1935, or from *Songs of Faith*, a song book published by the BSSB (but printed by Hope Publishing Company) in 1933.[61] Many others were singing from Coleman's smaller collections, several of which had sold hundreds of thousands of copies each during the late 1920s and 1930s.[62] The BSSB, meanwhile, had published the *New Baptist Hymnal* jointly with the ABPS in 1926, but whereas Coleman's *Modern Hymnal*, published in the same year, had quickly become a best seller in the South, the *New Baptist Hymnal* had proved far more popular among Northern Baptist churches.[63]

It was specifically to remedy this lack of a successful denominational hymnal that B. B. McKinney, now in the employ of the BSSB, began work in 1939 on *The Broadman Hymnal*. In this ambitious undertaking, McKinney faced several formidable obstacles. First, Coleman still owned the copyrights to virtually all of his pre-1935 compositions and arrangements, while the BSSB possessed only a handful of copyrights, nearly all of them to songs that McKinney himself had composed since coming to the Board. Second, McKinney's project brought him into direct conflict with the independent publishers whose permissions he would need if he wished to include the most popular gospel songs of that day in his new hymnal.

A major concern of independent church music publishers, we have seen, had long been how best to protect their copyrights and thereby ensure the continued popularity and sales of their books. In 1925, ten of these publishers had met at the instigation of Frank Kingsbury, then president of Hope Publishing Company, specifically to address the critical problems of copyright access and protection. Present at this initial meeting were representatives of the Hall-Mack Company, Lorenz Publishing Company, Tullar-Meredith Company, Rodeheaver Company, E. O. Excell Company, Robert H. Coleman Publishing Company, Hope Publishing Company, Tabernacle Publishing Company, Glad Tidings Publishing Company, and the Adam Geibel Music Company. Together they had organized the Church and Sunday School

Music Publishers' Association (CSSMPA) and agreed henceforth to meet annually to discuss and collectively resolve the difficult issues and problems confronting them.[64]

When McKinney decided in 1939–1940 to compile and publish *The Broadman Hymnal*, it was the CSSMPA members who most objected. McKinney knew that securing copyright permissions from them would be critical if *The Broadman Hymnal* were to have any chance of success. Otherwise, the hymnal would be limited to new songs and hymns already in the public domain. At the same time, the independent church music publishers of the CSSMPA—who had long resented denominational hymnals, not only because of the copyright issue, but also because denominations enjoyed a tax exempt status that the independent publishers perceived as an unfair advantage—were quick to recognize the very real threat posed by *The Broadman Hymnal*. Hope Publishing Company's Herbert Shorney informed Coleman, "We, too, have enjoyed a good sale of our book 'The Service Hymnal' through the south, which will be materially affected—unfavorably—by the Baptist hymnal 'The Broadman Hymnal.'" Torn between a desire to cooperate with McKinney's requests and a fear that granting too many copyright permissions to the BSSB might diminish the sales of their own books in the South, Shorney continued:

> While we want to be fair and cooperate we are nevertheless not short-sighted enough to want to make it possible for them to bring out a strong enough book which will materially put the possibility of the sale of other Association books in the south—not only in the Baptist field but others as well—out of the picture.[65]

Fearing the competition that such a book, published under McKinney's capable leadership and bearing the Board's Broadman Press imprint, might present among Southern Baptist churches, Robert Coleman faced a particularly serious dilemma. As he explained to Hope Publishing Company President Gordon D. Shorney, he now found himself in the "embarrassing situation" of feeling obligated to comply with McKinney's request for copyright permissions even though he feared that the book might "prove [to be] a very serious competitor" for his own hymnals.[66] McKinney's songs, after all, had graced the pages of Coleman's collections for years, contributing significantly to their popularity, while the BSSB was his largest customer.

Meanwhile, at their annual meeting in March 1939, the CSSMPA members had approved a new set of guidelines regulating the granting of copyright permissions to nonmembers. For books of 225 or more pages, permissions of copyrights were to be limited to a total of four per publisher, with a limit of two coming from the most popular "Class A" category of songs. Thus the publishers decided to grant the BSSB permission to include a maximum of two of each publisher's "Class A" songs for a fee of one hundred dollars apiece, plus two less popular "Class B" or "C" songs for the lesser fees of fifty dollars and twenty-five dollars each, respectively. This decision was in complete accord with the Association's policy at the time towards all non-members. McKinney—desiring to make *The Broadman Hymnal* as strong as possible—nevertheless petitioned Hope Publishing Company for permission to include four of its "Class A" copyrights: "Have Thine own way, Lord," "LOYALTY TO CHRIST," "Take time to be holy," and "TRUST AND OBEY." The Shorneys were reluctant to share four of their most popular songs with such a rival. The Rodeheaver Company broke ranks with the CSSMPA, however, and offered to grant the BSSB permission to publish four of its "Class A" songs in return for a payment of $500 (i.e., $125 per song). Herbert Shorney informed Coleman that he still favored sticking to the CSSMPA's original agreement, but if pressured to grant four "Class A" permissions, both the Hope and Coleman Publishing Companies should demand compensation equal to that rendered to the Rodeheaver Company.[67]

For his part, Coleman ultimately granted McKinney permission to include twelve of his copyrights in *The Broadman Hymnal*. These included such favorites as "SAVED, SAVED!," "LOVE LIFTED ME," and even "HE KEEPS ME SINGING," whose copyright renewal recently had cost him $350.[68] Some Baptist historians later claimed that the other independent publishers had allowed Broadman Press the use of only two copyrights each, but this simply was not the case.[69] *The Broadman Hymnal* contains six copyrighted songs each from Hope Publishing Company (including the original four requests plus "THE BANNER OF THE CROSS" and "SINCE I HAVE BEEN REDEEMED") and the Lillenas Publishing Company (including "I am Resolved" and "THE BEAUTIFUL GARDEN OF PRAYER"), five from the Lorenz Publishing Company (including "NEAR TO THE HEART OF GOD"), and three from the Rodeheaver Company (including the highly popular gospel song, "Living for Jesus"). Given their apprehensions, the CSSMPA publishers, it seems fair to say, were rather generous in the end. Their songs came at a price, of course, but their fees can hardly be deemed unreasonable, given the going rates for popular copyright renewals and the potential sales for the United States' largest Protestant denomination.

Still, much bitterness remained. McKinney and others at the BSSB were striving to produce a high-quality book that would appeal to Southern

Baptists and sell well, but they also faced real budget constraints that apparently precluded purchasing even more CSSMPA-owned copyrights.[70] Perhaps because of their own dilemma they were unable to empathize with the independent publishers, who lacked tax exempt status as well as a denomination's financial backing and local church markets. Ironically, the copyright problem was partly McKinney's own making since, in emphasizing gospel music, he opted not to include more hymns from the public domain. It was for this very reason, in fact, that *The Broadman Hymnal* would receive harsh criticism from McKinney's former teacher, I. E. Reynolds, who, in his unwavering support of denominational publications and promotion of higher standards of church music, had long promoted the *New Baptist Hymnal* over its chief competitor, Robert Coleman's *Modern Hymnal.* If anything, Reynolds desired to see a "New Southern Baptist Hymnal" prepared by "a large and representative committee," not simply a new and improved version of *Songs of Faith* compiled by McKinney alone. Speaking at the Ridgecrest Assembly at which *The Broadman Hymnal* was being introduced in 1940, Professor Reynolds reportedly declared, "What we *need* is a *hymn* book. This is no *hymn* book. This is a *song* book."[71]

Of course, more than eight million copies of that "song book" eventually were sold, with copies still selling today, but McKinney faced a good deal of criticism at the time, theological as well as hymnological. A vicious rumor circulated among McKinney's conservative critics that "POWER IN THE BLOOD" had been omitted from *The Broadman Hymnal* because "McKinney and Southern Baptists no longer believed in the substitutionary atonement of Jesus." Many years later, recalling a 1950 conversation with B. B. McKinney, retired BSSB Executive Secretary-Treasurer James L. Sullivan claimed that the Shorneys at Hope Publishing Company had refused to sell at any price permission to include "POWER IN THE BLOOD" in *The Broadman Hymnal,* then had spread the rumor about McKinney as a cover. Perhaps the Shorneys indeed had regarded this song as too valuable to share with a rival publisher, but they would have gained very little, if anything, by fabricating such a rumor. Oddly, Herbert Shorney's letter to Robert Coleman of September 14, 1939, which lists by name the four (above-mentioned) gospel songs first requested by McKinney from Hope Publishing Company, makes no reference whatsoever to "POWER IN THE BLOOD." If McKinney ever asked the Shorneys for permission to include it, he must have done so later in correspondence now lost, for it was not among his initial requests.[72]

In the end, the independent publishers' worst fears were realized. *The Broadman Hymnal* provided stiff competition to CSSMPA publications in the South and helped drive Coleman, aging and in ill health, out of business.

The BSSB finally purchased his firm in June 1945, bringing more than eight hundred copyrights to the BSSB, but this was not the end of the story. Largely because of the copyright problems with *The Broadman Hymnal*, the BSSB purchased Coleman's former typographer, the Anderson Brothers, in December 1947 for $10,000 and moved its operations from Hammond to Nashville. For years the Anderson Brothers had manufactured plates for Coleman, Hope Publishing Company, and many other hymnal publishing firms. Hope Publishing Company, of course, had long served as the custom song book publisher for the BSSB. In 1935, just prior to the hiring of McKinney and the creation of the Board's Church Music Department, Executive Secretary-Treasurer T. L. Holcomb had tried to negotiate better terms for the BSSB with Hope Publishing Company, but the two sides had been unable to reach an agreement. Then the copyright problems associated with *The Broadman Hymnal* had arisen. Hoping to avoid them thereafter, McKinney encouraged the BSSB to purchase the Anderson Brothers, not only to provide the Board with ownership of "the only fully equipped music typesetting plant of this nature" in the country, thereby granting the BSSB more independence, but also to give the Board greater leverage in negotiating copyright permissions in the future. According to James L. Sullivan, McKinney and the BSSB notified the Shorney brothers that the Board henceforth would typeset and engrave new plates for Hope Publishing Company only if Hope granted Broadman Press greater access to its copyrighted songs.[73] The BSSB minutes from December 1947 appear to support Sullivan's claim:

> We believe 1. That we need such equipment *to protect our future song book publication program* since we do not know where else we could obtain it. 2. That we can operate it economically and *serve other publishers' needs* in such a way as to regain the initial outlay in a period of five to seven years. 3. It would further establish us in the field and *would assist us in various phases of our dealings with all gospel music publishers.*[74]

The Board approved the purchase, but Hope Publishing Company shifted soon afterward to offset lithographic printing and ceased using the old style printing plates altogether.[75]

Robert H. Coleman's Contribution to Southern Baptist Hymnody

B. B. McKinney is often credited as having been the loyal Southern Baptist who most profoundly shaped the future course of his denomination's church music. There certainly can be no denying of McKinney's enormous natural talent as a composer and arranger, his loyalty to the denomination, and the influence that he wielded at the BSSB's Church Music Department. McKinney received his first big breaks in life, however, from Robert H. Coleman, who published his songs and employed him as his music editor, and from I. E. Reynolds, who not only taught McKinney from 1915–1918 and then hired him in 1919 to teach at the seminary, but also co-edited the first Coleman volumes in which McKinney's songs appeared.

It was Reynolds, too, who, beginning in 1926, actively campaigned for the creation of a Church Music Department at the BSSB (even though by this time he had turned from gospel songs toward higher church music). Reynolds would later be critical of McKinney's ideas and policies, not only because their philosophies of church music differed so greatly, but also because McKinney, in Reynolds's words, had long worked for "the keenest competitor of the Sunday School Board." Ironically, however, it would be largely on the basis of McKinney's editorial experience with that "competitor," Robert H. Coleman, and not merely because of his skills as a composer and his natural ability to communicate with people, that Executive Secretary-Treasurer T. L. Holcomb would select McKinney in 1935 as the BSSB's first music editor. Given McKinney's and Reynolds's substantial differences in philosophy, it was yet another irony of history that, in 1941, McKinney would be appointed as the first secretary of the Church Music Department for which I. E. Reynolds had so actively campaigned.[76]

Thus all three of these church musicians—Reynolds, McKinney, and Coleman—made important, albeit very different, contributions to Southern Baptist hymnody. I. E. Reynolds was the HMB music evangelist and gospel song composer turned seminary professor and advocate of higher standards of church music; B. B. McKinney was the gifted gospel song composer, arranger, and music editor, beloved by the people; and Robert H. Coleman, with his years of experience in business and ministry, provided the crucial publishing mechanism and made critical editorial decisions in compiling his collections of gospel songs and hymns.

Above all, throughout his long and successful career as a publisher, Robert H. Coleman never lost touch with the musical, theological, and spiritual needs of Baptist congregations. As a lay minister, he sought theologically-sound, evangelical texts. As a congregational song leader, he strove to match these texts with tunes that congregations would love and be able to sing without difficulty. As a gospel song book and hymnal publisher, he endeavored to produce collections that would meet the evangelistic priorities of revival services, the educational requirements of Sunday schools, and the worship needs of Sunday and Wednesday evening services for children, youth, and adults alike. Though sometimes accused of having been the BSSB's "keenest competitor," Robert H. Coleman was in fact himself a loyal Southern Baptist who offered the churches of his denomination "Southern Baptist" song books and hymnals in a day before the creation of the Church Music Department at the BSSB and, one might even argue, provided the Board's future music editor with valuable firsthand training and experience. For these reasons and more, Robert H. Coleman deserves an equal place of honor in the history of Southern Baptist hymnody alongside I. E. Reynolds, B. B. McKinney, and all those who have followed in their footsteps.

APPENDIX
Coleman's Hymnals, Gospel Songbooks, and Quartet Collections (1909–1939)

*The Evangel** (1909) [published by the ABPS, compiled by Robert H. Coleman and W. W. Hamilton, edited by E. O. Excell]

*The New Evangel**♣ (1911) [J. F. Scholfield, co-editor, also distributed by the Methodist Publishing House (South)]

*The World Evangel**♣ (1913)

*The Herald**Ω♣ (1915)

Select Gospel Songs (1916) [J. P. Scholfield and E. L. Wolslagel, editors; I. E. Reynolds, music editor; reprinted in 1918 by the BSSB for WWI soldiers]

Baptist Student Missionary Movement Hymnal: First Annual Convention of the Baptist Student Missionary Movement, Fort Worth, Texas, March 22–26, 1916

*Treasury of Song** (1917)

*The Popular Hymnal** (1918)

The Temple Hymnal (1918) [compiled for Grace Baptist Church, worshipping at the Baptist Temple, Philadelphia]

Kingdom Songs (1921) [compiled and co-edited with I. E. Reynolds, published by the BSSB]

Coleman's Male Quartets (1921) [I. E. Reynolds, music editor]

*The Pilot** (1922)

Revival Selections (1922) [specimen pages from *The Pilot*, also published (with two fewer selections) by the Publishing House of the Methodist Episcopal Church, South, under the title, *Revival Songs* (1922), not to be confused with Coleman's *Revival Songs* (1929), listed below]

Victorious Praise (1922) [abridgement of *Kingdom Songs*, published by the BSSB, also reprinted in 1926]

Hosannas‡ (© 1923 Samuel W. Beazley) [compiled and ed. by Robert H. Coleman, Samuel W. Beazley, and William J. Ramsay]

*Harvest Hymns** (1924)

The Little Evangel (1925)

Coleman's New Quartet Book (1925) [B. B. McKinney, musical editor, principally scored for male quartet, but also including twelve quartets for women's voices]

*The Modern Hymnal** (1926)

Evangel Bells† (1927)

Coleman's Male Choir (1928) [B. B. McKinney, musical editor]

*Gospel Melodies** (1928)

Revival Songs (1929)

Girls' Quartets (1929) [arr. by Ruth Anita Powell, director of the Bellevue Baptist Church Girls' Quartet, Memphis]

*Majestic Hymns** (1930)

Service Songs (1931)

Coleman's Songs for Men (1932) [for male quartet or choir, B. B. McKinney, musical editor]

Reapers (1932)

*The American Hymnal** (1933)
Pilot Hymns (1934)
Glad Tidings (1935)
Leading Hymns (1936)
Ladies' Quartets (1937) [compiled with the assistance of Ruth Anita Powell, Tift College; Mrs. J. H. Cassidy, First Baptist Church, Dallas; E. O. Sellers, Baptist Bible Institute, New Orleans; and I. E. Reynolds, SWBTS]
Precious Hymns (1938)
World Revival Hymns (1939)
Special Convention Songs (1939) [abridgement of *Precious Hymns*, I. E. Reynolds, music editor, compiled for the Texas Training Union Convention, Austin, Texas, November 30–December 2, 1939]

Key

*	Edition also published by the ABPS/Judson Press/Griffith and Rowland Press, Philadelphia.
Ω	Edition also published by Western Baptist Publishing Company, Kansas City, Missouri.
‡	Edition also published by William J. Ramsay in Chattanooga.
†	Edition also published by the Biola Book Room, Los Angeles.
♣	Edition also published/distributed by the Baptist Book Concern, Louisville, Kentucky.

ABBREVIATIONS

ABPS	American Baptist Publication Society
BHH	*Baptist History and Heritage*
BSMM	Baptist Student Missionary Movement
BSSB	(Southern) Baptist Sunday School Board, Nashville, Tennessee
BWA	Baptist World Alliance
BYPU	Baptist Young People's Union
CSSMPA	Church and Sunday School Music Publishers' Association
ESB	*Encyclopedia of Southern Baptists*
HMB	Home Mission Board of the SBC
SBC	Southern Baptist Convention
SBC Annual	*Annual of the Southern Baptist Convention*
SBHLA	Southern Baptist Historical Library and Archives, Nashville, Tennessee
SWBTS	Southwestern Baptist Theological Seminary, Fort Worth, Texas
SWBTS Archives	Archives and Special Collections, A. Webb Roberts Library, SWBTS, Fort Worth, Texas

NOTES

The author wishes to thank Senior Professor Donald P. Hustad of The Southern Baptist Theological Seminary, formerly editor of Hope Publishing Company and director of the Sacred Music Department at the Moody Bible Institute, and George H. Shorney, retired chairman of Hope Publishing Company, for reading earlier drafts of this article and also for sharing a wealth of information concerning the largely unwritten history of the gospel music publishing industry in the twentieth century.

SWBTS Professor Emeritus Robert O. Coleman graciously provided the author with an unpublished biography of his grandfather, Robert H. Coleman. SWBTS Associate Dean of Libraries Robert Phillips, Interlibrary Loan Librarian Helen Bernard, former Archivist Michael Pullin, Archives Secretary Amy Compton, and Bowld Music Librarian Sundi Rutledge provided photocopies and microfilms of critical documents and other materials in the A. Webb Roberts Library and in the Bowld Music Library. SWBTS Professor R. Allen Lott and Professor Emeritus William J. Reynolds, *Baptist Standard* Editor Marv Knox, Baptist General Convention of Texas Archivist Alan Lefever, Mary Louise Van Dyke of *The Dictionary of American Hymnology* Project, former E. C. Dargan Research Library Archivist Ray Minardi and (current) Librarian Stephen Gateley, Southern Baptist Historical Library and Archives Director Bill Summers, and Vivian Skinner, Oak Cliff, Texas, all assisted with the research for this article.

1. Preface to *The Evangel*, compiled by Robert H. Coleman and W. W. Hamilton, ed. by E. O. Excell (Philadelphia: American Baptist Publication Society, 1909), italics original.

2. The resentment against what many southerners regarded as a northern intrusion into the South had led to calls in the closing decades of the nineteenth century for the development of a distinct Southern Baptist identity centered in its own publishing house, the Baptist Sunday School Board. Southern Baptist publishing, and especially the Board's church music program, however, would require decades to develop. For more on the establishment of a Southern Baptist institutional identity, see Ellen G. Harris, "Incorporating 'Our Baptist Zion': The Southern Baptist Convention 1880–1920," at http://xroads.virginia.edu/~MA02/harris/sbc/entry.html.

3. *The Baptist Hymn and Praise Book* (1904) sold about 90,000 copies in its first seven years in print. In contrast, Robert Coleman's *The World Evangel* (1913) would sell 310,000 copies in its first year alone. *SBC Annual,* 1911, 8; *Baptist Standard* (Texas), May 21, 1914.

4. Even as late as 1939, shape-note editions still accounted for 40 percent of Coleman's sales. LaRue Coleman, "Are We Ready to Discontinue the Shaped Note Books?," *Minutes*, CSSMPA, 1939, 4.

5. Robert H. Coleman to T. L. Holcomb, February 16, 1943, cited in Timothy James Studstill, "The Life of Robert H. Coleman and His Influence on Southern Baptist Hymnody" (D. M. A. dissertation, SWBTS, 1991), 104. According to *American Biography: A New Cyclopedia*, 1st series, vol. 50 (New York: The American Historical Society, 1932), s.v., "Coleman, Robert Henry," 242, Coleman was "the largest individual publisher of song books in the world."

6. For more on Excell, see J. H. Hall, *Biography of Gospel Song and Hymn Writers* (New York: Fleming H. Revell Co., 1914; rep. ed., New York: AMS Press, 1971), s.v., "E. O. Excell," 298–302; and William Jensen Reynolds, *Hymns of Our Faith: A Handbook for the* Baptist Hymnal (Nashville: Broadman Press, 1964), s.v. "Excell, Edwin Othello," 288–289.

7. E. O. Excell to Robert H. Coleman, August 18 and November 14, 1908, and January 2, 1909, Archives and Special Collections, A. Webb Roberts Library, SWBTS (hereafter abbreviated as SWBTS Archives), Robert H. Coleman Collection, Folder 11. George H. Shorney, "The History of Hope Publishing Company and Its Divisions and Affiliates," in *Dictionary-Handbook to* Hymns for the Living Church, by Donald P. Hustad (Carol Stream, Illinois: Hope Publishing Co., 1978), 1–21 at 7–8, attests to the outstanding quality of Excell's plates. Excell's fee is not stated explicitly in the surviving correspondence, other than he would produce the book "for a consideration in lots of 20,000 copies." In later years, custom publishers charged a royalty fee of as much as 7½ cents per published copy. See Gordon D. Shorney to Robert H. Coleman, September 18, 1939, SWBTS Archives, Robert H. Coleman Collection, Folder 4.

"Electro plates" were manufactured as follows: after the type for each song had been set and proofread, a molded impression of the page was made on a sheet of "wax" coated with graphite, to which a coating of copper was affixed by electroplating to create a durable printing surface; a backing of molten metal was added for strength and durability. See Edward S. Pilsworth, *Electrotyping in Its Relation to the Graphic Arts* (New York: Macmillan, 1923). Printing plates were usually good for approximately 250,000 impressions before they began to show wear, often allowing their use in more than one book (e-mail of George H. Shorney to the author, November 4, 2004). Excell agreed to share "duplicate plates from some of the former books" with Coleman. Since a major part of the expense in manufacturing plates lay in setting the original type (from which the plates were then manufactured), and since (as a custom publisher) he was making his plates available to many others, Excell manufactured duplicate plates at the same time as the originals in order to defray the expense of having popular hymns and gospel songs typeset a second time until both the original and the duplicate plates had worn out.

A close examination of the plates of highly popular songs published in Coleman's collections suggests that he followed this practice as well. This would explain why, in his hymnals and song books (many of which sold hundreds of thousands of copies each), the plates of certain popular songs appear virtually identical even in their third or fourth collection, after a million or more copies had been printed and replacement plates must have been used. Pages printed from replacement plates manufactured at the same time and from the same master as the original plates would, of course, appear identical to those printed from the original themselves.

8. E. O. Excell to Robert H. Coleman, August 18 and November 26, 1908, SWBTS Archives, Robert H. Coleman Collection, Folder 11.

9. Although the 1908 contract between Coleman and the ABPS has not come to light, in a later arrangement with the BSSB Coleman negotiated a royalty fee of two cents for each published copy of a book for which he served as compiler. He also retained the right to purchase—at wholesale—copies of the book for retail sale. See n. 44 below.

10. *American Biography: A New Cyclopedia*, 1st ser., 50 (1932): 244: If Coleman received two cents per copy, he earned nearly $7,500 from royalties on *The Evangel*.

11. Robert Coleman served as the First Baptist Church's assistant pastor from 1903 until 1909, when he accepted a position as the business manager of the *Baptist Standard*

(Texas). He returned to his position as assistant pastor in 1915 and served in this capacity until his death in 1946. After 1905, he also led the congregational singing at all services, and, beginning in 1910, he oversaw the church's Sunday school as superintendent. See *ESB,* s.v. "Coleman, Robert Henry," by F. M. Ryburn, 1:297; Reynolds, *Hymns of Our Faith,* s.v. "Coleman, Robert Henry," 270; and Studstill, "The Life of Robert H. Coleman," 1–28.

12. *American Biography: A New Cyclopedia,* 1st ser., 50 (1932): 243; *Record of Proceedings,* The Baptist World Alliance, Second Congress, Philadelphia (1911), xvi, and Third Congress, Stockholm (1923), photo facing p. 1 of BWA Congress Song Leader Robert H. Coleman.

13. Reynolds was the musical editor of *Select Gospel Songs* in 1916, and, in 1921, of *Coleman's Male Quartets* and *Kingdom Songs*, whose abridgement, *Victorious Praise*, appeared the following year. McKinney was first credited on the title page as the musical editor with the appearance of *Coleman's New Quartet Book* in 1925. Whether McKinney or Reynolds, or perhaps both, served as Coleman's ghost editor(s) for *The Pilot* (1922) and *Harvest Hymns* (1924) remains unknown. The answer may perhaps lie in Reynolds's diary from these years, in the archives at SWBTS, but the author was unable to examine this volume. For more on McKinney and his music, see Paul R. Powell, *Wherever He Leads, I'll Go: The Story of B. B. McKinney* (New Orleans: Insight Press, 1974), 26–27; William J. Reynolds, compiler, and Alta C. Faircloth, editor, *The Songs of B. B. McKinney* (Nashville: Broadman Press, 1974); William J. Reynolds, "The Contributions of B. B. McKinney to Southern Baptist Church Music," *BHH* 21 (July 1986): 41–49; and Robert J. Hastings, *Glorious is Thy Name! B. B. McKinney: The Man and His Music* (Nashville: Broadman Press, 1986).

14. See the article in *American Biography: A New Cyclopedia,* 1st ser., 50 (1932): 243–44, whose author observed: "Mr. Coleman *was chosen* to publish the song book 'Evangel,' for the American Baptist Publication Society of Philadelphia" (emphasis added). Leon McBeth, *The First Baptist Church of Dallas: Centennial History (1868–1968)* (Grand Rapids, Mich.: Zondervan, 1968), 236, on the other hand, noted, "Texas Baptists liked his selection, and urged him to edit a new hymnal." On B. J. Roberts and the First Baptist Church's use of ABPS literature in its Sunday school, see McBeth, op. cit., 124–25.

15. E. O. Excell to Robert H. Coleman, August 18, 1908, SWBTS Archives, Robert H. Coleman Collection, Folder 11.

16. E. O. Excell to Robert H. Coleman, August 24, 1908, SWBTS Archives, Robert H. Coleman Collection, Folder 11; Studstill, "The Life of Robert H. Coleman," 33; *SBC Annual,* (1907), 204, 310; ABPS, *Report of the Board of Managers,* (1909), 22.

17. E. O. Excell to Robert H. Coleman, October 26, 1908, SWBTS Archives, Robert H. Coleman Collection, Folder 11.

18. E. O. Excell to Robert H. Coleman, November 17, 1908, SWBTS Archives, Robert H. Coleman Collection, Folder 11.

19. E. O. Excell to Robert H. Coleman, November 5, 11, 14, 17, and 26, 1908, SWBTS Archives, Robert H. Coleman Collection, Folder 11. As actually printed, *The Evangel,* contains 59 songs from the public domain, 126 Excell copyrights, 49 copyrights owned by others, and 2 songs owned by Coleman.

20. EDITOR'S NOTE: Throughout this article, the author has employed the style used by Coleman and the editors of *The Baptist Hymnal* (1991) in the indices of their books in order to distinguish clearly between gospel song titles, first line titles, and tune names. "GOSPEL SONG TITLES" appear in large and small caps placed within quotation marks, "First line titles" in normal font inside of quotation marks, and TUNE NAMES in small caps without quotation marks.

21. E. O. Excell to Robert H. Coleman, August 24, 1908, and November 11 and 14, 1908, SWBTS Archives, Robert H. Coleman Collection, Folder 11.

22. E. O. Excell to Robert H. Coleman, November 11 and 26, 1908, SWBTS Archives, Robert H. Coleman Collection, Folder 11. Cf. the observation by the BSSB noted in the *SBC Annual*, 1921, 493: "There have been in the song book world [to date] two groups. The songs controlled by the one group were not used in the books of the other."

23. *The Evangel,* nos. 107, 87, 69 (plus 86 and 105), 138, 202, 82, and 85, respectively.

24. E. O. Excell to Robert H. Coleman, November 14 and 26, 1908, SWBTS Archives, Robert H. Coleman Collection, Folder 11.

25. Foreword to *The World Evangel* (Dallas: Robert H. Coleman, 1913).

26. *Majestic Hymns* (Dallas: Robert H. Coleman, 1930); and *Precious Hymns* (Dallas: Robert H. Coleman, 1938).

27. Foreword to *Harvest Hymns* (Dallas: Robert H. Coleman, 1924).

28. Foreword to *The Pilot* (Dallas: Robert H. Coleman, 1922).

29. Preface to *The New Evangel,* compiled and edited by Robert H. Coleman and J. F. Scholfield (Dallas: Robert H. Coleman, 1911). *The New Evangel* was published and distributed by the American Baptist Publication Society in Philadelphia and the Baptist Book Concern in Louisville, Kentucky, as well as by Robert H. Coleman in Dallas. An edition was also marketed by the (Southern) Methodist Publishing House. Only the Baptist Book Concern edition and that distributed by the Methodist Publishing House (South) credit J. F. Scholfield, brother of HMB music evangelist and gospel song composer Jack Scholfield (more below) and a music evangelist in his own right, as co-compiler and co-editor with Coleman. For more on J. Fred Scholfield, see Reynolds, *Hymns of Our Faith*, 399–400.

30. See, for example, Coleman's Foreword to *The Pilot*: "A new song should be studied and sung again and again until it has had time and occasion to get hold of you."

31. E. O. Excell to Robert H. Coleman, January 25, 1909, SWBTS Archives, Robert H. Coleman Collection, Folder 11.

32. E. O. Excell to Robert H. Coleman, December 12 and 23, 1908, and January 27, 1909, SWBTS Archives, Robert H. Coleman Collection, Folder 11. A BYPU souvenir program from 1915 advertised that, with 1.7 million copies of his gospel song collections already sold, Coleman had "furnished the song books used in practically all the Baptist Conventions, North and South, for [the past] seven years." Cited in Studstill, "The Life of Robert H. Coleman," 82–83.

33. Robert H. Coleman, ed., *Baptist Student Missionary Movement Hymnal: First Annual Convention of the Baptist Student Missionary Movement, Fort Worth, Texas, March 22–26, 1916* (Dallas: Robert H. Coleman, 1916). The present author owns an autographed copy of the 1917 BSSM special edition of *Treasury of Song* (Dallas: Robert H. Coleman, 1917).

34. McBeth, *The First Baptist Church of Dallas*, 150; Robert H. Coleman, compiler and editor, *The Temple Hymnal: Compiled for the Grace Baptist Church, Located at the Baptist Temple, Philadelphia, in the Diamond Jubilee Year of the Life of Russell H. Conwell* (Dallas: Robert H. Coleman, 1918).

35. Thanks to Coleman's inclusion of them, three of Excell's compositions and arrangements survive in *The Baptist Hymnal* (1991): his tune, BLESSINGS, for Rev. Johnson Oatman, Jr.'s text, "COUNT YOUR BLESSINGS"; his arrangement of the early American folk tune associated today with "Amazing grace! How sweet the sound" (including the anonymous final stanza of text); and his text-and-tune "SINCE I HAVE BEEN REDEEMED." The former first appeared in Coleman collections beginning with *The Evangel* (1909), the second with *The New Evangel* (1911), and the latter with *The World Evangel* (1913). On "Amazing Grace," see William J. Reynolds, *Companion to* Baptist Hymnal (Nashville: Broadman Press, 1976), 35.

36. Studstill, "The Life of Robert H. Coleman," 106 (Appendix G).

37. Coleman copyright contracts and payments, SWBTS Archives, Robert H. Coleman Collection, Folder 6.

38. HMB music evangelist J. L. Blankenship also sang in the quartet, but apparently composed no gospel songs. William L. Haas, Jr., "Musical Evangelism of the Southern Baptist Home Mission Board (1910–1928)" (unpublished M.C.M. thesis, New Orleans Baptist Theological Seminary, 1970), 6–7 and 23–24, lists Wade, Reynolds, Blankenship, and Scholfield as the members of the HMB Quartet between 1912 and 1915, but I. E. Reynolds's diary for the years 1912–1916, in the I. E. Reynolds Collection in the SWBTS Archives, records (e.g., entries of April 25, 1912, November 26, 1914, and May 23, 1915) that Babbitt and Woleslagel also sang as members of the quartet. For more on I. E. Reynolds, see Tommy R. Spigener, "The Contributions of Isham E. Reynolds to Church Music in the Southern Baptist Convention between 1915–1945" (B. M. Thesis, SWBTS, 1962); *ESB,* s.v., "Reynolds, Isham Emmanuel," by Sarah Thompson, 2:1164; Reynolds, *Hymns of Our Faith,* s.v. "Reynolds, Isham Emmanuel," 390–391; idem, "I. E. Reynolds: Southern Baptist Church Music Crusader," *Southwestern Journal of Theology* 25 (Spring 1983): 76–88; and idem, "Isham Emmanuel Reynolds: Church Musician," *BHH* 27 (April 1992): 31–41.

39. The songs of Scholfield and Wade also appeared in at least one Ruebush-Kieffer Company collection, *Crown Him King* (ed. by Samuel W. Beazley, James H. Ruebush, and Will H. Ruebush [Dayton, Va.: Ruebush-Kieffer Co., 1914]). This collection, edited by Beazley, was probably printed in Hammond, Indiana, by Coleman's printer, the W. B. Conkey Company (see n. 58). It used several of Coleman's plates. In addition to four songs by Scholfield and two by Wade, *Crown Him King* included six Coleman copyrights, among them Beazley's "EVANGELIZE THE WORLD," the theme song from Coleman's *The World Evangel.*

40. *The Popular Hymnal* (Dallas: Robert H. Coleman, 1918), no. 213; *Harvest Hymns*, no. 68.

41. E-mail from Mary Louise Van Dyke, *The Dictionary of American Hymnology* Project, Oberlin College Library, November 22, 2004; Reynolds, *Companion to* Baptist Hymnal, 127; *Baptist Student Missionary Movement Hymnal,* no. 29; *Assembly*

Songbook (Nashville: Broadman Press, 1959), no. 70; *Crusade Hymns* (Nashville: Broadman Press, 1968), no. 64; and *Baptist Hymnal* (Nashville: Convention Press, 1975), no. 199.

42. *The New Evangel*, no. 89; Reynolds, *Hymns of Our Faith*, 99 and 399–400; Jack Schrader, ed., *Sing Joyfully* (Carol Stream, Illinois: Tabernacle Publishing Co., 1989), no. 345; also see n. 29 above. William J. Reynolds, *The Cross and the Lyre: The Story of the School of Church Music, Southwestern Baptist Theological Seminary, Fort Worth, Texas* (Fort Worth: School of Church Music, SWBTS, 1994), 30, n. 19, notes that the slightly different version of "SAVED, SAVED!" found in *The Baptist Hymnal* (1991) as no. 540 was harmonized by I. E. Reynolds.

43. *SBC Annual*, 1919, 461–462. *Select Gospel Songs* did contain Excell's arrangement of the tune for "Amazing Grace," but it was not copyrighted.

44. In return for the unlimited use of his copyrights in this collection, Coleman was to receive a royalty from the Board of two cents for every copy published—132,500 copies in the first year alone. Coleman retained as well the right to purchase at wholesale, in lots of five thousand, copies of the book for retail sale, which books were to bear his imprint as publisher. "Memorandum of Agreement" between Robert H. Coleman and the BSSB, February 12, 1920, SWBTS Archives, Robert H. Coleman Collection, Folder 8; *SBC Annual,* 1921, 493, and 1922, 403.

45. Wheaton College, Busnell Library, Hymnal Collection, Call No. SC 15-0534. In an e-mail to the author dated October 12, 2004, George H. Shorney confirmed that Hope Publishing Company long served as the BSSB's custom publisher. For Excell's editorial relationship with Hope Publishing Company, see Shorney, "The History of Hope Publishing Company," 8.

46. Entries of March 24, 1912, April 30 and August 23, 1913, Reynolds Diary 1912–1916, SWBTS Archives. In July 1912, Ike married Lura Mae Hawk of Oklahoma City. Thus Robert Coleman and Ike Reynolds each had wives named Lura. Reynolds, "Isham Emmanuel Reynolds: Church Musician," 32–33. On Coleman's employment at the *Baptist Standard*, see n. 11 above.

47. Entries of February 3–13, 1915, Reynolds Diary; McBeth, *First Baptist Church of Dallas*, 150. For more on Jolly, see *ESB,* s.v., "Jolly, Robert Garland," by Jack D. Harwell, 1:709–710.

48. *Dallas Morning News*, April 4, 1915, Part One, 12; April 11, 1915, Part Four, 4; and April 18, 1915, Part One, 11; Entries of March 3–6 and March 22–April 25, 1915, Reynolds Diary. In 1923, the members of Central Baptist Church, Oakcliff, voted to change their church's name to Cliff Temple Baptist Church. E-mail of Oakcliff historian Vivian Skinner to author, February 28, 2005.

49. Reynolds, *The Cross and The Lyre*, 2–14; entries of May 12–21, 1915, Reynolds Diary; *SBC Annual*, 1915, 70. Reynolds would model the new department after the Music Department at the Moody Bible Institute in Chicago, where he had studied under Daniel B. Towner in 1907–1908.

50. For possible evidence of Coleman's influence upon other composers, see the letter of Scott Lawrence to Coleman, January 28, 1922, SWBTS Archives, Robert H. Coleman Collection, Folder 6, in which Lawrence wrote, "Mrs. Lawrence and I value your letters, whether they be ones of acceptance or rejection of my humble efforts."

Unfortunately the rejection letters which Coleman addressed to Lawrence and other composers apparently have not survived.

51. Entries of June 29, 1915, and January 22, 1916, Reynolds Diary.

52. *The Herald* (1915), nos. 98 and 113; *Select Gospel Songs* (1916), nos. 16, 49, 52, 56, 57; *BSMM Hymnal*, no. 29.

53. Powell, *Wherever He Leads, I'll Go*, 27.

54. Cited in Reynolds, *Hymns of Our Faith*, 175.

55. See n. 13 above.

56. Reynolds, "The Contributions of B. B. McKinney," 42.

57. Robert H. Coleman to B. B. McKinney, Seminary Hill, Texas, November 25, 1925, SBHLA, B. B. McKinney Papers, AR 795-310. Throughout October and early November 1925 Coleman had been making payments to obtain copyright permissions for hymns and gospel songs to be included in *The Modern Hymnal*. Studstill, "The Life of Robert H. Coleman," 111 (Appendix L).

58. See http://www.hammondindiana.com/WBConkey.html. Also see the letter of E. G. Firchau, W. B. Conkey Company, to Robert H. Coleman, September 23, 1942, SWBTS Archives, Robert H. Coleman Collection, Folder 5.

59. *Service Songs* (Dallas: Robert H. Coleman, 1931).

60. See the letter of Robert Coleman to T. L. Holcomb, February 16, 1943, cited in Studstill, "The Life of Robert H. Coleman," 104 (Appendix F); also see the letter of Robert H. Coleman to Gordon Shorney, September 19, 1939, SWBTS Archives, Robert H. Coleman Collection, Folder 4.

61. Floyd H. Patterson, Jr., "The Southern Baptist Sunday School Board's Program of Church Music" (Ph.D. dissertation, George Peabody College, 1957), 139–142 and esp. 163–169, summarizing the "Survey of the Musical Program in Southern Baptist Churches" published in the *Southern Baptist Handbook*, 1939, ed. E. P. Alldredge (Nashville: BSSB, 1939), 9–139.

62. Through December 1934, for example, *Gospel Melodies* (1928) sold more than 369,000 copies, *Revival Songs* (1929) more than 375,000 copies, *Majestic Hymns* (1930) over 270,000 copies, and *Reapers* (1932) nearly 347,000 copies. Studstill, "The Life of Robert H. Coleman," 106 (Appendix G). Many of these no doubt were still in use in 1938.

63. *SBC Annual*, 1927, 341.

64. *Minutes*, Special Meeting of the CSSMPA, November 5, 1925, 1; e-mail from George H. Shorney to author, September 27, 2004.

65. G. Herbert Shorney to Robert H. Coleman, September 14, 1939, SWBTS Archives, Robert H. Coleman Collection, Folder 4.

66. Robert H. Coleman to Gordon Shorney, September 12, 1939, SWBTS Archives, Robert H. Coleman Collection, Folder 4. Gordon D. Shorney and G. Herbert Shorney were brothers. Gordon served as president of Hope Publishing Company from 1926 until his death in 1964. Herbert Shorney was first treasurer, then (following Gordon's death) president of Hope Publishing Company. Later (in 1970), he became chairman of the board, and his son, George H. Shorney, assumed the company's presidency. After serving twenty-two years as president, George Shorney assumed the duties of chairman himself in 1992, retiring in 2001. Shorney, "The History of Hope Publishing Company

and Its Divisions and Affiliates," 13–16; *One Hundred Years of Hope, 1892–1992* (Carol Stream, Illinois: Hope Publishing Company, 1992), 10, 18, and 31; e-mail of George H. Shorney to the author, February 16, 2005.

67. *Minutes*, CSSMPA, 1939, 2–3, "Requirement for Granting Permissions" (cf. ibid., 1937, 5, and 1938, 6); Robert H. Coleman to Gordon Shorney, September 12 and 19, 1939, G. Herbert Shorney to Robert H. Coleman, September 14, 1939, and Gordon D. Shorney to Robert H. Coleman, September 18, 1939, SWBTS Archives, Robert H. Coleman Collection, Folder 4.

68. Robert H. Coleman to John Carter (re: Bridgers's "HE KEEPS ME SINGING"), October 12, 1938, SWBTS Archives, Robert H. Coleman Collection, Folder 5. According to the copyright law of 1909, an original copyright extended twenty-eight years, but could be renewed at the end of its first term for an additional twenty-eight years.

69. Reynolds, *Hymns of Our Faith*, xxx; Powell, *Wherever He Leads, I'll Go*, 36.

70. This, at least, is the inference made by James L. Sullivan in his letter to Robert J. Hastings, May 1, 1984, SBHLA, B. B. McKinney Papers, AR 795-310. Also see Patterson, "The Southern Baptist Sunday School Board's Program of Church Music," 147–48.

71. I. E. Reynolds to B. B. McKinney, April 3, 1939 and September 1, 1940, SWBTS Archives, I. E. Reynolds Collection, Folder 20; interview of George W. Card, cited in Patterson, "The Southern Baptist Sunday School Board's Program of Church Music," 224, emphasis added.

72. James L. Sullivan to Robert J. Hastings, May 1, 1984, SBHLA, B. B. McKinney Papers, AR 795-310; and G. Herbert Shorney to Robert H. Coleman, September 14, 1939, SWBTS Archives, Robert H. Coleman Collection, Folder 4. Cf. Hastings, *Glorious Is Thy Name!*, 70–72.

73. Patterson, "The Southern Baptist Sunday School Board's Program of Church Music," 142 and 208–211; *Annual of the SBC*, 1948, 219, 226 (citation), and 275; James L. Sullivan to Robert J. Hastings, May 1, 1984, SBHLA, B. B. McKinney Papers, AR 795-310. Cf. Hastings, *Glorious Is Thy Name!*, 71–72.

74. Minutes, BSSB, December 11, 1947, 3, emphasis added, James L. Sullivan Executive Office Records, AR 795-354, SBHLA.

75. E-mail of George H. Shorney to author, December 4, 2004.

76. Reynolds, "Isham Emmanuel Reynolds: Church Musician," 37; idem, "I. E. Reynolds: Southern Baptist Church Music Crusader," 79; I. E. Reynolds to B. B. McKinney, September 1, 1940, SWBTS Archives, I. E. Reynolds Collection, Folder 20; Reynolds, "The Contributions of B. B. McKinney," 44; and Powell, *Wherever He Leads, I'll Go*, 34.

A Survey of Missions Hymns by Brazilian Baptists

Janelle Ganey

Early exploration and settlement of Brazil was principally a Portuguese, Roman Catholic endeavor. However, a number of other Europeans participated in expeditions throughout the sixteenth century, among them several known evangelicals.[1] Helio Eobano, who settled in what is now São Paulo State, was the son of a personal friend of Martin Luther, the humanist Helio Eobano Hessen. Ulrico Schmidel, who spent nearly twenty years in the New World beginning in 1534, later suffered religious persecution in Bavaria. Both of these men, as faithful Lutherans, no doubt had sung chorales, at least in moments of private devotion.[2]

However, the first record of evangelical hymn singing on Brazilian soil was written by Hessian adventurer Hans Staden.[3] Victim of a shipwreck off the coast of Brazil, he was later captured by a tribe of Tupinambás who were known cannibals. In his moment of distress, according to his own account, he sang Luther's chorale, "Aus tiefer Noth schrei ich zu dir" ("Out of the depths I cry to you"). Evidently his captors were enchanted by his singing, for they asked him to sing other songs and explain their meaning. Staden credited his singing and prayers with saving his life. He was rescued by a French commercial expedition in 1554.[4]

Three years later a group of Calvinists from Geneva established a colony in Guanabara Bay in Rio de Janeiro, where they held the first recorded evangelical service on Brazilian soil. At this service on March 10, 1557, the colonists sang Clément Marot's metrical paraphrase of Psalm 5, "Aux paroles que je veux dire plaise-toi l'aureille prester, . . . Souverain Sire" ("Give ear to my words, . . . O Lord"), translated into Portuguese, with music by Louis Bourgeois (RICHIER, HPCC 387).[5] During the seventeenth-century Dutch occupation of northeastern Brazil, evangelical churches flourished. However, with the expulsion of the Dutch by the Portuguese, much of that activity ended. It was not until the arrival of English merchants in the early nineteenth century and subsequently of American colonists (mostly from the post–Civil War South) and British and American missionaries that records of evangelical musical activity began to appear.[6]

Baptist Mission Activity and the First Missions Hymns

Baptists from the post-war South established two churches in what is now São Paulo State. After baptizing their first Brazilian convert, a former Catholic priest, the first permanent missionaries[7] set out from these English-speaking churches to organize the first Portuguese-language congregations in Salvador, Bahia (1881), then Rio de Janeiro (1882), and from there throughout the country. Even before the Baptists arrived, several missions hymns had been translated by Congregational missionaries. Among the first of these was Daniel March's "Hark! The voice of Jesus calling" ("Ouve, a voz divina clama," SH 458), translated by Sarah Poulton Kalley in 1875.[8] In the same year Mrs. Kalley wrote an original missions hymn, "Nas tormentas desta vida" (SH 453 inspired by Phillip Bliss's "Let the Lower Lights Be Burning" and set to the LOWER LIGHTS tune). These hymns were certainly sung by early Brazilian Baptists who adopted the Congregational *Salmos e Hinos* as their hymnal and included them in early editions of their own hymnal.

Within ten years of the organization of the first Brazilian Baptist church, the first Baptist hymnal, *Cantor Cristão*, was published. Its compiler, Solomon Louis Ginsburg (1867–1927), translated numerous hymns during his lifetime, also writing many original texts, mostly set to tunes from the vast output of gospel songs produced in the late nineteenth century. The most recent edition of *Cantor Cristão* (1971) contains twelve missions hymns by Ginsburg, nine of which are his translations. All three of the original texts are calls for Brazilians to preach the Gospel to their fellow citizens. The final stanza of "A pátria para Cristo" (CC 440), given here in a free (nonpoetic) translation, reflects Ginsburg's evangelical fervor.

> Our homeland for Christ, Oh! May it thus be, my God,
> That every Brazilian hear the appeal!
> And when we hear thy voice from the beyond,
> May every Brazilian attend and enjoy the bliss.

Ginsburg's missionary[9] colleague, William Edwin Entzminger (1859–1930), also contributed greatly to early Baptist hymnody in Brazil. Two translations and two original texts are included among the missions hymns in the 1971 edition of *Cantor Cristão*. Like Ginsburg's original texts, Entzminger's "Minha pátria para Cristo" ("My homeland for Christ," CC 439) and "Ah! Se eu tivesse mil vozes" ("Ah! If I had a thousand voices," CC 386) are prayers for the salvation of their adopted country. These two hymns continue to be among the best-loved hymns of Brazilian Baptists and the missionaries who work with them,[10] sung regularly during the two annual missions emphases.

Missions Hymns in the First Half of the Twentieth Century

When the Brazilian Baptist Convention was organized in 1907, the Brazilian National and World Mission Boards were established. Like their counterparts in the Southern Baptist Convention, they soon began annual missions promotions. In Brazilian Baptist church life it has been traditional to mark any special events—revival meetings, youth and women's congresses, conventions, and so forth—with a theme, a Scripture passage, and a hymn. In the early days, translated hymns or original hymns such as those by Ginsburg and Entzminger were used. Some new hymns continued to appear although only two from this period have survived in hymnals in current use. "Disse Jesus: ide por todo o mundo" ("Jesus said: Go into all the world," CC 438) by Manuel Avelino de Souza (1886–1962) is a more general missions hymn than many discussed so far; it lacks specific references to Brazil. The emphasis is on obedience to Christ's command to preach the Gospel (Matt. 28: 19–20; Mark 16:15). The first stanza begins with a brief summary of the Great Commission. The other two stanzas and the refrain continue the call with such words as "let us proclaim," "let us carry out the mission," "let us take the message," "let us take the light," "let us tell," and "let us preach." These phrases, coupled with a strong, march-like tune by Horatio Richmond Palmer, make for a stirring call to action. The coupling of such tunes with missions texts has been common. At least twelve hymns in *Cantor Cristão* and five in *Hinário Para o Culto Cristão* have such a coupling.[11]

The second early- to mid-twentieth-century missions hymn still in common use is João Filson Soren's (1908–2002)[12] "Quem irá nos campos trabalhar" ("Who will go to work the fields," HPCC 538), written in 1949. The text is firmly rooted in Scripture. Already in the first line we are reminded of the parable of the sower in Luke 8 and of Christ's call for laborers in Matthew 9:37–38. The image then shifts to the cross and the call to take up one's cross and follow Jesus (Luke 9:23). In the second stanza we are called to remember the comparison Jesus made of the people to sheep without a shepherd (Matt. 9:36) and of the people walking in darkness, without light (Isa. 9:2; Matt. 4:16). The refrain calls us to "Speak, speak, and don't be silent," reminding us that if we "keep quiet, the stones will cry out" (Luke 19:40, NIV). Although Matthew 28:19–20, Mark 16:15, Acts 1:8, and the call of Isaiah in Isaiah 6:8 form the background of all missions hymns, this hymn is striking in its constant references to Scripture.

The strong missions consciousness of Brazilian Baptists and other evangelicals in the first half of the twentieth century is apparent in the large number of missions hymns included in *Cantor Cristão* during this period. It carried over even into a hymnal prepared by Soren during his service as a military chaplain in World War II. Brazilian evangelical historian Henriqueta Rosa Fernandes Braga says that three of the favorite hymns of the troops were "Firme nas promessas" ("Standing on the promises," CC 154), "Um pendão real vos entregou o Rei" ("There's a royal banner given for display," CC 469), and Entzminger's missions hymn, "Minha patria para Cristo" ("My homeland for Christ," CC 439).[13]

The Explosion of Missions Hymns

As we have seen, the first seventy years of Brazilian Baptist life were marked by a strong missions emphasis. However, there has been a veritable explosion of writing missions hymns in the past forty years. The impetus for this came with the launching of the National Evangelization Campaign in 1965. The planning committee wanted a hymn that would rally Brazilian Baptists to the cause. A music committee was formed to commission a hymn and also to put together a collection of hymns for use in the campaign. João Filson Soren agreed to write a text. However, as the 1964 deadline approached, Soren informed the committee that his responsibilities as president of the Baptist World Alliance had made it impossible for him to do this. A call went out to known poets and musicians to submit texts and tunes. According to pioneer Southern Baptist music missionary Bill Ichter (b. 1925), when the texts came in, the one by Mário Barreto França (1909–1983), "Do Amapá ao Rio Grande, de Recife a Cuibá" ("From Amapá to Rio Grande, from Recife to Cuibá"), "jumped out."[14] However, no music was attached. Using the pseudonym, Nelson Mariante, Ichter submitted the tune CAMPANHA, which was adopted. The theme of the campaign and of the hymn was "Christ is the only hope." The same theme was adopted by the Baptist World Alliance in 1965 for the Crusade of the Americas and CAMPANHA became the official tune for the Crusade. It was used for at least fourteen different texts, each one particular to the country using it. Rafael Martins Júnior wrote a new text in Portuguese for the Crusade, which Ichter says is more elegant poetry, but França's more popular-style text has been more lasting.[15] The latter, with Ichter's tune, was used as the theme song for the 1999 National Evangelization Campaign.[16]

From that time forward, the idea of commissioning new hymns for the annual promotions of the two mission boards took root. Between 1966 and 2001 at least thirty[17] missions hymns were produced by Brazilian Baptists, as well as new translations such as Edith Margaret Clarkson's "So send I you" ("Eu vos envoi," 1970, HPCC 545); Beverly Terrell's "Give me your vision" ("Dá-me tua visão," 1970, HPCC 546); "Send me, O Lord, send me" ("Envia-me, ó Deus," 1985) by Ross Coggins and set to a new tune by Ronald Oliveira[18]; and, most recently, "Yd y predicad" ("Ide e pregai," ca. 1994 by Josep la Porta).[19]

Mário Barreto França and Bill Ichter collaborated on two additional hymns, both for the Brazilian Baptist World Mission Board (Junta de Missões Mundiais). They were published in promotional materials and later in a small collection, *Coletânea Missionária,* that Ichter put together in 1985. Both texts are quite simple and direct, with only two short stanzas and a refrain in each. "Para que conheçam teu nome" ("That they might know your name," whose first line is "Amando as almas perdidas"["Loving lost souls"], CM 6) calls us to love the lost, cross borders to show our faith and love, preach our belief in Christ, and carry forth the sweet certainty of being heirs of the King, all of this so that the peoples of the earth might know God's name. In contrast, "Ide por todo o mundo" ("Go into all the world," CM 7) describes the state of the world in its stanzas—the quest for power, prevalence of war, disdain of virtue, and the need of faith. Because of this situation, we are to go, full of grace and love, into all the world preaching the Gospel to all peoples and races. Ichter wrote under the pseudonym Jane Oliveira for "Para que conheçam teu nome," but used his own name for "Ide por todo o mundo."

In the same collection are two texts by Rafael Gióia Martins Júnior (b. 1931), who had earlier written the text for CAMPANHA used in the Crusade of the Americas. "Transformai as nações do planeta" ("Transform the nations of the planet," known under the title "É anunciada a vossa fé," CM 4) is a call to transform, conquer, proclaim, and announce in Jesus' name with vigor, bravery, faith, and virtue, so that the violent world may be transformed. The simple text was set by Ichter under the pseudonym Jeremias Oliveira for the 1981 promotion. Ichter indicated that it is to be sung "Em ritmo marcial" (in martial rhythm), a characteristic of nearly all of his tunes for missions hymns. The 1982 text, "Só Jesus nós dá vida e coragem" ("Only Jesus gives us life and courage," known as "Jesus Cristo é o Senhor" from the final line of the refrain, CM 5) is more deeply biblical than "Transformai as nações do planeta." The main thrust comes from Acts 4:12: "Salvation is found in no one else. . . ." The second stanza begins with a reference to John 14:6, naming Jesus as the truth and the way. Mark 10:16 and 1 John 1:7, 9 are evident in the third stanza—Jesus blessing the children and purifying the nations. In the fourth stanza Jesus is water and light, clear references to John 4:14 and 8:12.

By far the most prolific writer of texts for the new missions hymns in this period was Myrtes Mathias (1933–1996), who served as a missionary and in the home office of the Brazilian National Mission Board (Junta de Missões Nacionais). Over the years she wrote thirteen hymns for the annual emphases of the board (only eight were available to the researcher).[20] Her *magnum opus* is considered to be "Nossa gente quer viver em segurança" ("Our people want to live in security," HPCC 533), written in conjunction with Gladis Seitz (b. 1948) and set to the tune PESO DA NOSSA TERRA by Ivo Augusto Seitz (b. 1947) and Marcílio de Oliveira Filho (b. 1947) for the 1980 promotion. In this text, Mathias encourages the mission effort because Christ will provide the hope that is needed. She reminds us that everyone is responsible for the work of Christ: "There is a place for all of us in the harvest." What we give in service to the Lord—"our prayers, our goods, our very lives"—will bring consolation to the people of Brazil. The refrain underscores the urgency of the task: "the scream of our land, the cry of our people who long for a new world in which there is peace and love."

The themes of a people without peace, of longing for a new world, and of giving life and goods in the cause of Christ reappear in many of Mathias's hymns. In her hymn, "O clamor de um mundo novo" ("The clamor for a new world," HPCC 536), set to the tune MISSÃO JOVEM by Marcos Bernardes Gatz (b. 1960), we hear the cries of "people without peace within their hearts" who are clamoring "for a new world." In this new world, "goods and lives laid down on the altar of the Savior, multiplied by Jesus, will be blessings of love."

In her last published hymn, however, written for the 1995 promotion, Mathias makes a striking departure from this pattern. The theme that year was "Bear Fruit" ("Frutifique"). Although one aspect of the Christian's fruit-bearing is witnessing, the emphasis in "Houve o tempo da semente ir à terra" ("There was a time for the seed to go into the earth," known by the title "Tempo de Frutificar," JMN 14) is upon one's relationship with Christ. The scriptural basis is John 15:1–8, 16. The first stanza speaks of the process of planting and cultivating the seed. In the second stanza, the author speaks of grateful submission to the vine and receiving sustenance so that we may grow and bear even more fruit. The final stanza lists challenges to the believer's firmness—uncontrolled violence, fear as the universal language of the world, corruption, and wrong seen as normal. Only with deep roots in Jesus can these things be overcome so that more fruit may be borne. The refrain is a prayer that Jesus will bind the believer to Him.

Although not a native-born Brazilian, Joan Larie Sutton (b. 1930) spent most of her life in Brazil, first as the daughter of missionary parents, then as a career missionary herself until her retirement in 1993. Her influence in missions hymnody is far-reaching, since she was a teacher at The Baptist Theological Seminary of South Brazil of many of the musicians who have written melodies for the hymns. She was also general coordinator of the committee for *Hinário Para o Culto Cristão* (1990). Her most direct contribution, however, is the hymn, "Eu ouvi as palavras de Cristo" ("I heard the words of Christ," known by the incipit of its refrain, "Eu aceito o desafio" ["I accept the challenge"]), and its tune MACEIÓ (HPCC 543). Written in 1985 for the March 1986 world missions promotion, it was the theme hymn every year through 1992 and then was adopted as the official hymn of the Brazilian Baptist World Mission Board (Junta de Missões Mundiais). Text and tune express well the determination to accept the challenge, to live for Christ, and to reflect his light in words, actions, and attitudes.

Another outstanding hymnist from the beginning of this period of explosion is Werner Kaschel (b.1922), who was a major contributor to *Hinário Para o Culto Cristão* with translations of twenty-one texts and author or co-author of another eight. Of these, two are missions hymns written for the 1980 and 1984 promotions. The theme of "Redentor só um existe" ("There is only one Redeemer," co-written with Moisés de Almeida Lobo and more commonly known by its tune name SÓ JESUS CRISTO SALVA, HPCC 542) is the uniqueness of Christ as Savior and salvation by grace alone. In a society dominated by works-oriented religion, this is a frequent theme in Brazilian Baptist churches. Many even have the phrase "Só Cristo Salva" ("Only Christ Saves") painted on their outside walls or roofs. The second stanza emphasizes forgiveness of sins, while the third is a call to witness in all of Brazil. The tune by Nabor Nunes Filho (b. 1944) has hints of Nunes's roots in the Brazilian northeast with its use of both the natural and flat forms of the sixth and seventh degrees within a Bb major context. The other hymn is "Nos últimos dias vivemos" ("We live in the last days," known by the incipit of the refrain, "Testemunhos somos todos" ["We are all witnesses"], HPCC 532). Its tune, BONS MINISTROS, also has a northeastern flavor with stanzas in G minor and the refrain in major. Minor and modal keys are frequent in the popular music of that region. Kaschel's text has a simple structure with only two textual lines, the last of which is repeated. The same thing happens in the refrain. However, this structure is not reflected in Marcílio de Oliveira Filho's tune; the music is different for every line. The first stanza and refrain are thoroughly biblical, with direct references to Joel 3:28, Acts 1:8, and Matthew 5:13–14. The second stanza calls believers to be faithful in doctrine and love, while the third reminds us of the power we have been given for the task. Kaschel and Oliveira also wrote the text and tune for the 1989 hymn, "Quem é que eu vou enviar" ("Whom shall I send"), based on Isaiah 6:1–8.[21]

Marcílio de Oliveira Filho (b. 1947) is one of Brazilian Baptist musicians' most outstanding leaders, having helped found the Association of Baptist Musicians of Brazil (Associação dos Músicos Batistas do Brasil, AMBB) and having served as its president for its first six years. More recently he has spearheaded a series of national music showcases called Louvação at the First Baptist Church of Curitiba and similar regional events. Whereas the events sponsored by AMBB have a more conservative bent, Louvação leans toward cutting-edge, contemporary music. This is reflected in the many tunes Oliveira has composed. In *Hinário Para o Culto Cristão*, he is composer of eight tunes, including three for missions texts (HPCC 531, 532, 533). Besides these he wrote tunes for three other missions hymns: the one to Kaschel's text mentioned above, POR TODA PARTE, written in 1981 to a Myrtes Mathias text based on Acts 8:4, and one to Gladis Seitz's 1993 text, "Toda a Palavra a todo o Brasil" ("The whole Word for all of Brazil"), based on Acts 20:27. Although Oliveira is a native of southeastern Brazil, his tunes have a northeastern flavor with abundant syncopations, altered notes, and excursions into minor keys.

It is interesting to note that the texts of two of the six missions hymns that Oliveira set concern themselves with the end of time and thus the urgency of the missions task. We have already seen this in Kaschel's text, "Nos últimos dias vivemos." The other text, by Guilherme Kerr Neto (b. 1953), is concerned with the dire state of the world of the end times and the difficult battle that Christians will confront: persons dominated and enslaved by addictions and the sin in their hearts, proud and tense, laughing at God and his people, giving first place to money and material things. In contrast to this, we Christians are the light and children of God, who must shine brilliantly, preaching and living God's Word, our secure guide and the source of our love.

No discussion of missions hymns in Brazil would be complete without mention of Ivo Augusto Seitz (b. 1947) and his wife, Gladis (b. 1948). The two were home missionaries in the state of Rondônia for a number of years. He is a graduate of the School of Sacred Music of The Baptist Theological Seminary of South Brazil and she of the Baptist Institute of Religious Education in Rio de Janeiro. Since 1991 he has been executive secretary of the Brazilian Baptist National Mission Board (Junta de Missões Nacionais).

Long before he assumed this position, the two were active writers of missions hymns. Gladis collaborated with Myrtes Mathias in the texts of three hymns: "Nossa gente quer viver em segurança" ("Our people want to live in security," HPCC 533) from 1980, "Vamos por toda parte" ("Let's go everywhere," CHM 8) of 1981, and "Sozinho não faço nada" ("I can do nothing alone," CHM 15) in 1994. Her 1996 text, "Senhor, é firme a tua direção" ("Lord, your direction is firm," CHM 16), is set to her husband's tune, TODOS PRECISAM SABER. In the first two stanzas she speaks of qualities of the Lord: firm direction, light, protection, the way, the reason for our pilgrimage, the truth, keeper of promises, remaining faithful. The third stanza is a prayer that people might live in the way of certain equality and for the increasing of our faith, love, and work so that we may serve with holiness. In the fourth stanza she pleads for her country and that God's servants throughout Brazil might help others to become God's people. The refrain affirms that Christ is truth, that an imitation of His life alone is worth the living. Gladis also wrote the text for the 1993 hymn, "A Bíblia nos fala de uma só Senhor" ("The Bible speaks of only one Lord"), published as "Toda a Palavra a todo o Brasil" ("The whole Word to all of Brazil") with a tune by Marcílio de Oliveira Filho.[22]

Although he has contributed mostly melodies, Ivo Seitz has also written at least four published texts, three of which are missions hymns. One is a translation of "So send I you" ("Eu vos envio," HPCC 545). In 1995 he collaborated with Mytes Mathias in writing "Houve o tempo da semente ir à terra," which we have already discussed. The third, written in 2000 with the tune A DESCOBERTA DOS SÉCULOS by Antônio Carlos G. Mataruna (b. 1946), is "Canto a esperança onde há descrença" ("I sing hope where there is unbelief").[23] In stanza 1 Seitz states that we serve God by singing hope in Christ in the midst of pain and unbelief. Stanza 2 reminds us that we are God's children, singing hope like a laughing and playing child, secure in God's home. Seitz concludes in stanza 3 that singing hope in Jesus Christ enables us to live without fear. The refrain declares that the singing, in fact, becomes a prayer for Brazil.

The theme, "Jesus: Discovery of the Ages," was adopted by the Brazilian Baptist Convention for the 500th anniversary of the discovery of Brazil by the Portuguese. Three of Ivo's published tunes are for missions hymns. They are PESO DA NOSSA TERRA (HPCC 533), written with Marcílio de Oliveira Filho for "Nossa gente quer viver em segurança" in 1980; TODOS PRECISAM SABER (CHM 16) for his wife's text already mentioned; and ELIENAI (HPCC 600) for "De ti, ó meu Brasil," an adaptation of Samuel Frances Smith's "My country, 'tis of thee" by Entzminger. ELIENAI is in F minor, to be sung in unison. While probably influenced by northeastern Brazilian folk music, it also has a bit of a Hebrew folksong flavor. TODOS PRECISAM SABER likewise is written for unison singing and in a simple, popular style.

This study has striven to introduce English-speaking audiences to the rich body of Brazilian Baptist hymnody. New authors and composers are constantly being enlisted every year, especially by the National Mission Board, a clear signal that Brazilian Baptist missions hymns continue to contribute significantly to global hymnody. Although the quality of the texts and tunes varies, as would be expected, these hymns demonstrate clearly the passion of Brazilian Baptists for the salvation of their country and of the world. They reflect a consciousness of the social context in which many people live, so that their concern is not only for people's souls, but for the whole person. One can truly say that, in the thinking of Brazilian Baptists, lives transformed by the Christian faith will result in transformed societies.

KEY TO HYMNAL ABBREVIATIONS

HPCC *Hinário Para o Culto Cristão.* Edited by Joan Larie Sutton. Rio de Janeiro: Junta de Educação Religiosa e Publicações da Convenção Batista Brasileira, 1990.

SH *Salmos e Hinos.* 2nd ed. Lisbon: Livrara evangelica, 1920; 5th ed. Rio de Janeiro: Igreja Evangélica Fluminense, 1975.

CC *Cantor Cristão.* 9th ed. Edited by Bill Ichter. Rio de Janeiro: JUERP, 1971.

CM *Coletânea Missionária.* Compiled and edited by Bill Ichter. Rio de Janeiro: Junta de Missões Mundiais da CBB, 1985.

CHM *Caderno de Hinos Missionários.* Edited by Sandra Regina Bellonce. Rio de Janeiro: Junta de Missões Nacionais, 1997.

NOTES

1. The term "evangelical" is used in Brazil to designate all non-Catholic Christian groups.

2. Henriqueta Rosa Fernandes Braga, *Música Sacra Evangélica no Brasil* (Rio de Janeiro: Erich Eichner, [n.d.]), 31–32.

3. Hans Staden, *Warhaftige Historia und Beschreibung eyner Landschafft der wilden, nacketen, grimmigen Menschfresser Leuthen* . . . (Marburg: Andres Kolben, 1557), cited in Braga, *Música Sacra Evangélica*, 32.

4. Braga, *Música Sacra Evangélica*, 32–33, 37.

5. Ibid., 40–41.

6. Ibid., chapters 3–5.

7. Thomas Jefferson Bowen, a Southern Baptist Foreign Board missionary, was in Rio de Janeiro for about nine months in 1859–60, but for health reasons was unable to remain. See Betty Atunes, *Centelha em Restolho Seca* (Rio de Janeiro: self-published, [n.d.]).

8. See the same text set to a new tune by current missionary Ralph Manuel in HPCC 537.

9. Ginsburg first went to Brazil as a Congregational missionary, but became a Baptist while preparing a pamphlet meant to criticize the Baptists' baptismal practices! He later

came under the sponsorship of the Southern Baptist Foreign Mission Board (now the International Mission Board). The story of this remarkable life is told in his autobiography, *A Wandering Jew in Brazil* (Nashville: Sunday School Board, 1921). The book appeared in Portuguese as *Um judeu errante no Brasil* (Rio de Janeiro: Casa Publicadora Batista [n.d.]).

10. For example, at the April 1997 funeral of missionary "Boots" Blackwell in Baton Rouge, a group of over forty missionaries, former missionaries, and children of missionaries sang "Minha patria para Cristo" as the casket was taken out of the church.

11. CC 432, 434, 435, 436, 439, 441, 445, 449, 450, 451; HPCC 526, 534, 538, 542, 543.

12. Soren was a classmate of Herschel Hobbs and W. A. Criswell at The Southern Baptist Theological Seminary. He was pastor of the First Baptist Church of Rio de Janeiro for fifty years. In the 1960s, he was president of the Baptist World Alliance.

13. Braga, *Música Sacra Evangelica*, 284.

14. Bill Ichter, telephone interview by author, October 2, 2001.

15. Ibid.

16. Sandra Regina Bellonce, ed., *Caderno de Hinos Missionários* (Rio de Janeiro: Junta de Missões Nacionais, 1997), [n.p.].

17. Not all the hymns were available to the researcher.

18. Pseudonym for Bill Ichter. Ichter, telephone interview by author, October 2, 2001.

19. The English version is "Go in Jesus' Name."

20. Bellonce, *Caderno de Hinos Missionários.*

21. Jeremias Nunes. List of hymns in e-mail sent to author, October 8, 2001.

22. Bellonce, *Caderno de Hinos Missionários.*

23. Ivo Augusto Seitz and Antônio Carlos G. Maturuna, "A Descoberta dos Séculos," *Promotor e Igreja* (2000): 8–10.

"The Lord's Song in a Strange Land"

Hymns and Hymn Stories in Indonesia

William N. McElrath

The Psalmist's plaintive cry that forms the title of this paper[1] has special meaning when applied to Christian hymnody in the Republic of Indonesia. The world's fourth most populous nation has a strangely varied religious background. Successive waves of immigration through the centuries have brought successive overlays of religion. For instance, Borobudur, the world's largest Buddhist monument, and Prambanan, one of the world's tallest Hindu temple towers, stand only a few miles apart in the heartland of what is now the largest Muslim nation in the world.

Christianity has not been left out in this strange mixture of faith communities. Some historians say that Nestorian missionaries brought the Good News about Jesus Christ to the East Indies as early as the 1300s. Certainly Roman Catholic missionaries arrived in the 1500s—most notably, St. Francis Xavier. Protestants were not far behind, as Dutch Reformed Christians began moving to Indonesia in the 1600s.

The title of a popular film starring Mel Gibson and Sigourney Weaver has immortalized the phrase, "The Year of Living Dangerously." That year was 1965, when Indonesia's Communist Party, the world's third largest (after the Soviet Union and Mainland China), made a bold bid to take over Indonesia . . . and failed. During the bloody aftermath, Indonesians by the hundreds of thousands turned to Christ. Current Christian historians indicate that somewhere between 10 and 20 percent of Indonesia's two hundred million people now claim to be followers of our Lord.

That same "year of living dangerously" was the year when Betty and I and our two small boys first arrived in Indonesia. Our major work during thirty years there was not in the field of music. I was assigned to the Indonesian Baptist Publishing House—writing, editing, and translating various types of literature as well as training other writers and editors. After our sons were older, Betty worked with a cultivation-evangelism friendship group for Muslim women and girls. Yet both Betty and I, having had training and experience in vocal and instrumental music, found ourselves serving in churches that usually ran short of trained musicians. Is it any wonder that both of us often found ourselves involved in music ministries as well?

This paper may not fit as part of a Festschrift honoring my older brother. Certainly it makes no great claim to scholarship and includes few endnotes, because most of the primary source material is either in my own memory, scribbled notes, or in Indonesian-language sources not available to others. Yet it is fair to say that the unusual story told here relates closely to my brother's lifelong devotion to Christian hymnody.

Both Hugh and I were strongly influenced by our father, a relatively untrained volunteer song leader who loved good hymns so much that he encouraged us to sing them as a part of daily family worship. When I finished college, my older brother's graduation gift to me was a recently-published standard work in the field of hymnody,[2] and I've been a hymn-story buff ever since.

Here, then, is the story (as I experienced it) of "'The Lord's Song in a Strange Land': Hymns and Hymn Stories in Indonesia," viewed under these three headings:

I. Indonesian Hymnody—Foreign and Homemade
II. Problems in Producing an Indonesian Hymnal
III. What Indonesians Don't Know About Hymnody

Indonesian Hymnody—Foreign and Homemade

Short-term visitors to Indonesia are often delighted to find that they can recognize tunes in worship services, even though they don't understand the words being sung. This may speak positively concerning the universality of our faith, but it also speaks negatively concerning the failure of Christianity to take root in the musical culture of "a strange land."

Entirely too much of present-day hymnody in Indonesia uses Western-style melodies, set to texts translated from languages brought over by missionaries—mainly English, but also Dutch, German, and Chinese. This state of affairs applies not only to old standard hymns and gospel songs: Most of the frequently heard newer selections such as Scripture songs and praise choruses are also the same as those being sung in other lands. Translated Scripture songs, however, come with a Catch-22: The Indonesian Bible, like any good version of the Scriptures, does not follow along word for word with the English Bible. Yet the tunes of Scripture songs, by their very nature, have been arranged around the English text; rarely can they be adapted to fit the cadences of another language. Young Indonesian Christians often belt out a Scripture song without realizing it because the words they are singing no longer match the Bible verse that was the original text!

Sometimes a search for original Indonesian hymns can lead to strange results. Ross C. Coggins, Jr., found that out in 1955 when he heard Indonesian Christians singing a hymn about the Lord's promised return. Discarding the syncopated rhythms of the hymn's refrain, he matched the melody of the stanzas with a new text. Only after Coggins's discovery and creation had gotten into print did anyone find out (in Brazil, of all places) that he had actually recast an Indonesian translation of a Dutch translation of an American gospel song long forgotten in the land of its birth! This is how Elisha A. Hoffman's "The Lord Is Coming" got a new lease on life as "Send Me, O Lord, Send Me."[3]

Even a sincere attempt to foster indigenous tunes and texts may not achieve the desired results. After all, in some parts of Indonesia people have been singing Luther's "Ein' feste Burg" longer than people have been singing it on the North American continent. Is it surprising when Indonesian Christians assume that true Christian music has to have European roots?

More than once Indonesian Baptists have sponsored a hymn-writing competition, complete with modest prizes. Yet most of the entries turned in have sounded vaguely like "Blessed Assurance" warmed over. Missionaries, blessed with wider cross-cultural experience, have sometimes been able to see more clearly than Indonesian Christians themselves that Indonesian hymnody sounds too foreign. Yet when we have tried to encourage acceptance of church music that "sounds Indonesian," some of our Indonesian brothers and sisters in Christ have told us that it doesn't "sound Christian."

There may be deeper reasons why many Indonesian Christians have been slow to utilize their own musical heritage in hymnody. The Javanese are the dominant and most numerous tribe in Indonesia, followed closely by the Sundanese. Indigenous music of these two major tribes is mostly built on five- and seven-tone scales. Javanese and Sundanese families of musical instruments (some made of bamboo, others consisting mainly of metallophones), along with their owners' sense of what makes a melodic line and constitutes proper vocal production—all of these seem far removed from what most of us know as hymnody. Even beyond that, some of these indigenous melodies are so strongly associated in Indonesians' minds with polytheism and mysticism that they seem tainted and unworthy for evangelical use.

In spite of all these obstacles, indigenous hymnody is indeed taking root in Indonesia. Indonesian Christians are singing their own tunes and texts—not as often as they should be, but more often than they used to do.

Some of these songs of Indonesian origin, as indicated above, have Western-style melodies and strophic texts that sound much like the translated hymns making up the bulk of Indonesian hymnody, but a few of them have a different sound.

Two of these "Indonesian-sounding" Indonesian hymns have been included as illustrations. One of them, "Only You, O Lord My God" (please see page 233), has enjoyed a rather wide acceptance; Indonesian Christians across the gamut from Baptists to Roman Catholics are singing it. It has also been published in America (with my own keyboard arrangement and translation into English) in a recent book of resources for worship[4] as well as in a music study course book for boys and girls.[5]

The author and composer of "Only You, O Lord My God," is Javanese, yet he chose to write a Sundanese-style melody. (At least that's what our Indonesian friends tell us; my own expertise does not extend to making a clear distinction between the two styles.) This somber, striking heart-cry in song won first prize in a hymn-writing contest (thanks in part to the persistence of some of us on the jury who felt strongly that it should not be beaten out by yet another new Indonesian hymn sounding suspiciously like "When the Roll Is Called Up Yonder").

"Only You, O Lord My God" was written by a man who was working at the time as a postal clerk; later he became one of my editorial colleagues at the Indonesian Baptist Publishing House. Since then he has been involved with writing or editing every workday; yet—like the creator of at least one other well-received hymn[6]—Andreas Sudarsono has never to my knowledge shown much inclination to try his hand at writing another hymn.

The other Indonesian hymn included here, "Pujilah Allah Bapa kita" ("Come, sound the praise of our Father God!," please see pages 234–35), echoes a different tradition from "Only You, O Lord My God."[7] Indonesians describe it as "sounding like a song from the desert." What they mean is that it sounds like the kind of melodies heard in Islamic tradition, and of course Islam came to Indonesia from the Middle East. With its strong Trinitarian statement, its review of the whole story of redemption in only three stanzas, and its sturdy drum-like rhythm, this fine hymn deserves to be better known.

Note the name of the author-composer; can you imagine a more resoundingly Muslim name than Mohammed Syamsul Islam? Indonesian baptismal candidates often choose new names, usually biblical names. Yet this pastor and hymn writer stuck with his old name. He explained why: "Let it stand as a testimony that the Lord Jesus Christ can not only save but even call into the ministry someone with a name like mine."

Problems in Producing an Indonesian Hymnal

In 1965, Betty and I arrived in Indonesia to find the Baptist churches there using a thin hymnal compiled seven years earlier—thin both in size and in content. When we compared it with hymnals used by other churches, there wasn't much improvement. We were told a committee was at work on a new hymnal, but its progress seemed glacially slow.

In the mid-1970s, the decision was made to transfer responsibility for the projected new hymnal from a large and unwieldy committee to the Indonesian Baptist Publishing House. We formed a new working team of four Indonesians (from three different tribal backgrounds) plus two missionaries. For several years we devoted an afternoon of almost every week to this project. As team secretary I put in many extra hours preparing materials for consideration. When the team had finished its work, several of my colleagues and I continued to work hard for many months in preparing the hymnal to go to press. Here are a few of the problems we had to overcome:

1) Among the minority of Indonesians who can read music, a majority can read only solfege written with numbers, lines, and dots. To see how this works, note the following illustration showing the first two lines of the tune SWEETEST NAME (accompanying the gospel song, "There's within my heart a melody," or "He Keeps Me Singing") as printed in numeric notation and intended to be performed in the key of G:

1=G 4/4

3 3 2̸ 3 4 3 | 3 2 6 . |

7 1 1̸ 2 5 4 | 3 . 4 . |

The numeral "1" is always *do*, in this case G. The melody then starts on "3," or *mi*. The dot above the numeral indicates that this is *mi* in the octave above *do*, not the octave below it. The line above the first two number-notes shows that the beat is divided between them, thus making them eighth notes in 4/4 time. The diagonal line marked across the third note indicates that it is to be sharped. The dot to the right of the "6" at the end of the first line shows that this number-note gets one extra beat. There's much more to the secret code, but one can easily see that a system like this (found in many countries) works passably well for vocal lines, but provides little assistance for the accompanist.

Most Indonesian hymnals (like the thin one published by Baptists in 1958) show only "number notes." This means that the pianist, organist, or guitarist has to look for the melody with harmonization written in standard notation in some other book, usually a hymnal imported from abroad. To end all this scrambling around to find accompaniments, we decided to publish two complete parallel editions of the new hymnal: one with four-part vocal music in number notation, the other with four-part music and accompaniment in standard notation.

2) Through the years, many hymns in English, Dutch, German, and other languages have been rather lamely translated into Indonesian. These translations have been weak both as to fidelity to the original and as to quality and singability of the resultant text. We made a determined and thorough effort to improve, simplify, and beautify the texts of hymns widely sung among Indonesian Christians (especially Baptists).

3) Many of the same hymns have been published in several different Indonesian translations. At the same time our hymnal team was at work, an ecumenical committee was trying to produce standardized texts of hymns most widely sung—if for no other reason than to simplify hymn singing in interdenominational worship services. The ecumenical committee was kind enough to send us rough drafts of their work, and we did the same for them. We soon discovered, however, that any two Indonesians (let alone any two Indonesian committees) find it hard to agree on the best way to put a poetic text into the Indonesian language. We gave up on trying to go along with the standardized translations, and they didn't accept many of our efforts, but at least there was some helpful cross-fertilization between their work and ours.

4) Most Indonesian hymnals have been notoriously lax in listing names of authors and composers, let alone obtaining permission to use their works. Indonesia was one of the last major countries of the world to become a signatory to any international copyright agreement, so almost anything was considered fair game. However, we made a careful and conscientious effort to give full credit where credit was due. Most copyright holders recognized our unusual situation and gave us free permission.

5) Buying power in Indonesia is rather low compared to the economic status of Western countries. Fortunately we received subsidies so that our new hymnal could be offered at prices the churches could afford. We did, however, keep the price of the edition with standard notation rather high; we figured that if a church could afford to purchase a keyboard instrument, then that church should also be able to buy one copy of the accompaniment edition.

The new hymnal, finally published in 1982 (and still very much in print), is entitled *Nyanyian Pujian* (*Songs of Praise*).[8] It includes 363 selections, of which more than twenty have original Indonesian texts, tunes, or both. The hymnal gives pertinent scripture references with each hymn and includes sixty-six responsive readings.

What Indonesians Don't Know About Hymnody

The average Indonesian churchgoer knows even less about hymnody than does the average American churchgoer. All of the standard misconceptions are present in full force, such as:

- Hymns just "happen," or are created by whoever publishes the hymnal.
- Text and tune are always created at the same time by the same person.
- A tune used with a given text "belongs" to that text and seems out of place when used with a different text.
- A text used with a given tune "belongs" to that tune and seems out of place when used with a different tune.

Even the minimal hymnological information provided in American hymnals has usually not been available to Indonesian worshipers; as mentioned above, most Indonesian hymnals have been quite remiss in acknowledging their sources.

Of course if an American worshiper is really interested in knowing "how we got our hymnal," he or she can find dozens of hymn-story books in Christian bookstores.[9] By contrast, when Betty and I first got to Indonesia in 1965, we discovered that there were no hymn-story books available in the Indonesian language.

Recognizing a publishing niche when I saw one, I soon started what turned out to be a long-term project. From as many different denominational backgrounds as possible, I gathered as many different hymnals as I could find. First I listed hymns and gospel songs included in more than half of these—quite a task when you remember that most of the translated texts were worded differently from one hymnbook to another.

Selecting sixty of the most universally accepted hymns, I arranged these into four paperback books of hymn-stories. The first edition used a rather clumsy title (even longer in Indonesian than in English): *Stories of Indonesian Christians' Favorite Hymns.*[10] A revised and expanded edition helped with our publicity campaign by including the title of the new hymnal in the title of the series: *Selected Stories from* Songs of Praise.[11]

This paperback series, like the hymnal, is still in print—and, so far as I know, is still the only hymnological source material available in the Indonesian language. I am glad I could help our Indonesian brothers and sisters in Christ start learning more about our common heritage in song. Having done a bit myself to "push back the darkness" in this field, I have also been happy to see a recent series of articles in an Indonesian Baptist magazine, written by a young university professor who has obviously used his computer to analyze the contents of the hymnal *Songs of Praise* according to origin, meter, key signature, possible use in medleys, and several other variables.[12]

Of course most of the stories included in my series of books are about hymns translated from English into Indonesian—hymns well known to American worshipers. The few indigenous Indonesian hymns that have been written are usually limited to a particular denominational tradition, and so they did not make it into the list of those most widely accepted in all kinds of churches.

There are, however, a few hymn-stories in the series that might be new to American hymnologists. Here are two notable examples from European hymnody that apparently never made it to North America:

1) A beautiful hymn by Gerhard Tersteegen (1697–1769) about the great love of God (seemingly not the same as that translated by John Wesley as "Thou hidden love of God") was written in a humble cottage in Germany by a deeply pious man who made his living by manufacturing ribbons. This text has been wedded to the stately tune, ST. PETERSBURG, which has been attributed to Dmitri Bortniansky (1752–1825). Thus in the providence of God a text from a German cottage and a tune from a Russian palace have been brought together to become one of Indonesian Christians' favorite hymns.[13]

2) "B'rilah hormat," *Nyanyian Pujian*, 61, is based upon a Dutch translation of Luke 2:14 ("Glory to God in the highest") and set to a chorale-like arrangement (EERE ZIJ GOD, 1870) of a secular tune by G. A. Schulz which originally accompanied a song entitled "Het Nachtegaaltje," or "The Nightingale." All through the ages the people of God have set to music the very words of the Scriptures and then sung them. When Indonesian worshipers sing this text, however, they often don't realize that they are singing a Scripture text because the wording as translated no longer matches Luke 2:14 in their Indonesian Bibles. Yet this simple melody, sung *adagio* with deep feeling, is one of the two or three very top favorite Christmas carols among Indonesian Christians of all persuasions.

An unfortunate development in the two decades since the publication of *Songs of Praise* in 1982 has been its elevation by some to near-canonical status. Churches in Indonesia, like churches everywhere, have experienced what some people have called "worship wars." Older pastors, fearing too much influence from charismatic movements, have reacted against the use of praise songs at church. They have said that only the music included in the "red book" (the cover of the standard edition of *Songs of Praise*) is true "Baptist music" (ignoring the fact that this hymnal, like almost any other, includes tunes and texts written by everybody from Roman Catholics to Pentecostals). In reaction, younger people have thrown out the baby with the bath water, insisting that nothing in the "red book" is fit to sing in their celebrations (ignoring the fact that *Songs of Praise* includes Indonesian adaptations of such selections as "Morning has broken," "I've got peace like a river," "Alleluia," "God is so good," "Glory be to God on high" with the MICHAEL tune, and several stirring Indonesian praise songs such as "In the name of Jesus" and "Happy is my heart").

Of course hymnody must grow and change. My colleagues and I never intended to close the canon with the publication of *Songs of Praise* in 1982. Yet I must admit that for the past few years I've been watching from afar with a wry smile on my face: Indonesian Baptists, in seeking to prepare a praise-song supplement to the hymnal, have had to struggle through some of the very same disagreements and delays as we did in preparing the hymnal itself in the first place!

This paper—more anecdotal than scholarly—has attempted to show how the influence and example of my older brother, Dr. Hugh Thomas McElrath, has indirectly affected hymnody in Indonesia. Three positive outcomes have been noted:

1. a significant increase in indigenous hymnody among Indonesian Christians;
2. the preparation and publication of a major Indonesian hymnal; and
3. the preparation and publication of the first hymnological source materials ever made available in the Indonesian language.

NOTES

1. Psalm 137:4, King James Version.

2. Albert Edward Bailey, *The Gospel in Hymns: Backgrounds and Interpretations* (New York: Charles Scribner's Sons, 1952).

3. William J. Reynolds, *Companion to* Baptist Hymnal (Nashville: Broadman Press, 1976), 157–58.

4. "Only You, O Lord My God," in *For the Living of These Days: Resources for Enriching Worship*, ed. C. Michael Hawn (Macon, Ga.: Smyth and Helwys, 1995), 25. Andreas Sudarsono wrote the original text and tune, from which the present author, with permission, made his English translation and arrangement. The song appeared in *Nyanyian Pujian* [*Songs of Praise*] (Bandung, Indonesia: Lembaga Literatur Baptis, 1982), 232, under the title of "Hanya PadaMu, Tuhan."

5. William N. McElrath, *Sing His Song Around the Earth* (Nashville: Convention Press, 1979), 40.

6. Maltbie D. Babcock (1858–1901), author of "This is my Father's world."

7. "Pujilah Allah Bapa kita," by Mohammed Syamsul Islam, in *Nyanyian Pujian*, 6, translated by the present author (with permission) as "Come, sound the praise of our Father God!"

8. See n. 4 above for the bibliographic information.

9. A book reviewer recently found no fewer than 452 "hits" on Amazon.com when he typed in "hymn stories"; see Larry Wolz's review article in *The Hymn* 56, no. 4 (Autumn 2005): 51–53.

10. *Cerita-Cerita dari Lagu-Lagu Rohani Kesayangan Kaum Kristen Indonesia*, 3 vols. (Bandung, Indonesia: Lembaga Literatur Baptis, 1968–1973).

11. *Riwayat Lagu Pilihan dari Nyanyian Pujian*, 4 vols. (Bandung, Indonesia: Lembaga Literatur Baptis, 1983–1989).

12. Paul Nugraha, in numerous bimonthly issues of *Suara Baptis* (*The Baptist Voice*), published in Bandung, Indonesia, by Lembaga Literatur Baptis.

13. The Indonesian title is "Aku bersyukur atas kasihMu," found in *Nyanyian Pujian*, 122. The text from which the present author and his colleagues worked was an archaic Indonesian paraphrase, made from the German original or perhaps from a Dutch adaptation of the original. For information about Tersteegen, see Bailey, *The Gospel in Hymns*, 337–38; and Harry Eskew and Hugh T. McElrath, *Sing with Understanding: An Introduction to Christian Hymnology* (Nashville: Broadman Press, 1980), 97.

Only You, O Lord My God

Unison
1. When storm winds blow and clouds make dark my day,
surge and sweep a - cross my way,
2. Be - cause of You, O Lord, my soul is bright:
me, O Lord, in dark - est night,
1.
I run to You for shel - ter, O Lord; when storm waves
I lean for strength up - on You, O
Your glo - ry shines on each step I take; You com - fort
when sor - row makes my sad heart to
2.
Refrain
Lord.
On - ly You, O Lord my God! I hang my
break.
hopes, my hopes on You. Yes, on - ly You, O Lord my
God! I yield my life, my life to You.

WORDS: Andreas Sudarsono, trans. by William N. McElrath
MUSIC: Andreas Sudarsono, arr. by William N. McElrath

HANYA PADAMU, TUHAN
10.9.10.9. with Refrain

Pujilah Allah Bapa Kita
(Come, Sound the Praise of Our Father God!)

Unison
1. Pu - ji - lah Al - lah Ba - pa ki - ta, Pu - ji pa - da Pu-tra
2. Ma - nu - si - a di - cip - ta - kan - Nya, A - tas pe - ta dan te -
3. Kar - na ber - i - man ke - pa - da - Nya, Tum - buh u - mat-Nya di
1. Come, sound the praise of our Fa - ther God! Come, sound the praise of His
2. In the be - gin - ning our Fa - ther God made in His im - age hu -
3. Christ Je - sus calls from the world His Church, peo - ple of God out of
tung - gal - Nya, B'ri - kan pu - ji Roh Ku - dus pu - la,
la - dan - Nya, Ta - pi I - blis su - dah meng - go - da,
du - ni - a, Yang tak per - nah di - ting - gal - kan - Nya,
on - ly Son! Come, sound the praise of the Ho - ly Ghost!
man - i - ty; then when the temp - ter be - gan to work,
ev - ery race; nor will he ev - er de - sert His own;
Al - lah Tri-tung - gal Yang E - sa Yang men-cip - ta - kan se -
Hing - ga ja - tuh da - lam do - sa; Na - mun te - lah di - te -
Di - p'li - ha - ra o - leh Roh - Nya, Di - ja - ga - Nya dan di -
God in three per - sons, yet but one, God who cre - a - ted the
all fell in - to in - i - qui - ty. But now the glo - ri - ous
Christ's Spi - rit moves in ev - ery place. Com - fort and strength come from

WORDS: Mohammed Syamsul Islam, trans. by William N. McElrath
MUSIC: Mohammed Syamsul Islam, arr. by William N. McElrath

PUJILAH ALLAH BAPA KITA
9.9.9.8.9.9.9.9.

ga - la - nya, A - lam se - mes - ta dan i - si - nya.
bus pu - la O - leh da - rah Ye - sus yang mu - lia.
bim - bing - Nya, Di - hi - bur dan di - ku - at - kan - Nya.
un - i - verse, all that live in it and all their ways.
blood of Christ for all our sin and trans - gres - sion pays.
Him a - lone; Christ guards and guides us through all our days.
Naik - kan - lah pu - ji ke - pa - da - Nya
Naik - kan - lah pu - ji ke - pa - da - Nya
Naik - kan - lah pu - ji ke - pa - da - Nya
Great is the Lord God in all His works!
Great is the Lord God in all His works!
Great is the Lord God in all His works!
O - leh se - bab ke - be - sar - an - Nya!
O - leh se - bab ke - mu - rah - an - Nya!
O - leh se - bab ke - se - tia - an - Nya!
Lift up your voice, come and sound His praise!
Lift up your voice, come and sound His praise!
Lift up your voice, come and sound His praise!

"For Everyone Born, a Place at the Table"

Hospitality and Justice in the Hymns of Shirley Erena Murray

Deborah Carlton Loftis

A new and inspiring voice has come to us from Aotearoa/New Zealand.[1] Shirley Erena Murray's hymns, first introduced to the United States in *The Presbyterian Hymnal* in 1990, have enjoyed a growing presence in the hymnals published in the United States over the last decade.[2] Though Murray's hymn texts cover the spectrum of the Church's life and worship, a major theme in her work is that of unity—persons coming together in peace around Jesus Christ. In moving toward that goal, Murray calls us to welcome each other into the Body of Christ and to focus on the dignity and equality of all persons in the eyes of God. These themes of hospitality and justice—echoed in the hymns of Brian Wren, Rae Whitney, and Carl Daw, Jr., included in this volume—call for a social gospel that would transform not only the Church, but also the entire world.

Background

In an interview conducted in January 2000 with this author, Shirley Murray explained that she began writing hymns because of "positive and negative promptings."[3] First of all, she was irritated with the "unpalatable and unbelievable" things available in the hymnal, comparing these hymns to "a little bit of grit in your teeth." In part, her hymn writing started to fill a personal need: she needed to make what she was singing in worship authentic for herself. In an article written for a New Zealand journal, Murray shared some of the reasons why she writes:

> I write out of controlled desperation with the Church for its inability to deal seriously with new theological insight. I write with an awareness of what we are not yet saying to one another. . . .
>
> I write also to help anyone who asks what the Christian Story is about, but has no access to understanding the Bible. Many of the hymns we have traditionally sung were meant for the Biblically literate and larded with references, incomprehensible without some Bible teaching. . . .
>
> I write hopefully, however, because people will never stop singing about what they believe at Spirit level.[4]

Then secondly, she encountered a "positive prompting" as she realized that her hymn writing might help to fill the huge gaps that existed in the body of hymnody. Her attitude became, "I need to sing about this [a particular topic]. If nobody has written anything, I'll have a go at it."[5] Her own words speak eloquently to this process:

> After years of being married to a lively theologian who is also a Presbyterian minister, I became engaged with the difficulties of constructing a liturgy in which the Word preached had no hymns to support or reflect it. To be theologically adventurous was to be bereft of anything relevant to sing. The hymnbook often dragged us back into the past, rather than providing energy for faith ventures into the future.[6]

Fortunately, Shirley and her husband, John, worshipped in a church in Wellington with a congregation and worship leader who embraced the challenge and journey of singing new texts. Shirley described their process of adding new hymns to their worship: "At first this meant using familiar tunes, marriages of convenience of words and known music, which soon dissolved when compared to the freshness and vitality of new tunes with new texts."[7]

Another positive prompting has been the work of the New Zealand Hymnbook Trust, which began with the dream of John Murray and Colin Gibson (another outstanding hymnist and composer) to introduce new hymns into the worship of congregations in New Zealand. What emerged was *Alleluia Aotearoa*, an all-New Zealand ecumenical hymnbook published in 1993. That was followed in 1996 by *Carol Our Christmas: A Book of New Zealand Carols.* Before these collections were published, however, John Murray and Colin Gibson were working to edit hymns they had gathered. With papers spread all over the floor, Shirley looked over some and said, "I could help that a bit." John and Colin invited her to "come and be a words person!"[8] Thus began not only her close work with the Hymnbook Trust, but also her friendship with Colin Gibson, who often sets Shirley's texts to music. Of her collaboration with Colin, Shirley said:

> Nearly always with a new text I send it to Colin first. He never turns it down and sometimes I don't like his particular approach, but always he has a very good reason for the mode of music he chooses and mostly they're wonderful. He faxes them to me. He nearly always comes back within one day if he's not too busy—two days if he's really busy. We are critical of each other because we're used to being editors on the same editorial group. But it's better if we're in a bigger group—makes you freer to criticize each other's work. Yes, it's not so personal, but it's terribly important that you do [get critiques of your work]. I appreciate being critiqued by someone I respect.[9]

For Colin's part, he wrote an article recently about working with Shirley which opens:

> It's Wednesday morning, September 8, and I check my fax machine. Yes, there's a message there, from Shirley Murray. "Dear Colin," it begins, "Have you a moment to look at something?" I can already guess what the "something" will be: this is going to be a good day. It brings with it a precious gift. The text of a brand-new hymn: a hymn that's hardly been born, let alone had time to breathe yet. The first-sight freshness of a hymn-text by Shirley always amazes and elates me, because by now, after working with her for many years, I know that the words will have the first-class quality of composition by an experienced and immensely talented writer.[10]

Though she has written on a wide variety of topics for the Church, she describes her passion in hymn writing as being rooted in peace and justice issues, human rights, inclusivity, and the integrity of creation. Ten of Murray's texts that appear in United States hymnals and hymnal supplements provide the basis for this discussion of hospitality and justice which follows below. A table at the end of this article will list these texts and their United States hymnal sources.

Hospitality

Hospitality has become a popular topic in current discussions of the Church's life. How do we embody hospitality in our faith community and in our corporate worship? One way to define hospitality is "welcome." In order to make persons welcome, we must notice their presence and make space for them in our midst. This is "inclusion" in the broadest sense. For Murray, making the Church a hospitable place is the first step in our Christian work for justice, human rights, and dignity. She would have us recognize that, in Christ, we all belong to the same family. We say, metaphorically, that one "has a place at the table" to indicate a sense of belonging—having a recognized position within a group. Murray uses this phrase to remind us of our family connections, but also draws on the association of Eucharist—everyone has a place at Christ's table. In the opening stanza of her text, "A Place at the Table," Murray declares that everyone deserves the basic necessities of life: clean water and food, shelter, safety, and a relationship with God:

> For everyone born, a place at the table,
>   for everyone born, clean water and bread,
> a shelter, a space, a safe place for growing,
>   for everyone born, a star overhead,

It is not surprising that the second and third stanzas enumerate the value of including everyone: women and men, young and old. What may be surprising, however, is the idea of the fourth stanza:

> For just and unjust, a place at the table
> abuser, abused, with need to forgive,
> in anger, in hurt, a mindset of mercy,
> for just and unjust, a new way to live.

It is startling, perhaps uncomfortable, to acknowledge that God's table has room for sinners as well as saints. Murray's phrases call to mind the scriptural admonition that God makes the rain fall on the just and the unjust. The final stanza sums up all the others: everyone deserves a place to be and the right to be free.

> For everyone born, a place at the table,
> to live without fear, and simply to be,
> to work, to speak out, to witness and worship,
> for everyone born, the right to be free.

That Murray considers this broad inclusivity a part of the Church's work for justice is underscored in the refrain, "and God will delight when we are creators of justice and joy, compassion and peace."

The issue of belonging is addressed in "Who is my mother, who is my brother?" Everyone can come together around Jesus Christ. The origin for these words came from Murray's attendance at the World Council of Churches Assembly 1991, "where meeting people of many orientations, including the differently abled, evoked the words of Jesus from Mark 3:31."[11] Murray names those who are often invisible in our midst:

> Differently abled,
> differently labeled
> widen the circle
> round Jesus Christ:
> crutches and stigmas,
> cultures' enigmas,
> all come together
> round Jesus Christ.

She declares that love and the presence of Christ are the determining factors which create family. Those factors which normally divide us do not apply here:

Love will relate us—
  color or status
can't segregate us,
  round Jesus Christ:
family failings,
  human derailings—
all are accepted,
  round Jesus Christ.

Shirley Erena Murray ©1992
Hope Publishing Company, Carol Stream, Illinois 60188.

The final stanza asserts that, bound together in our vision and mission through Jesus Christ, we become one family.

Murray picks up the theme of family united through Christ in her powerful text, "O God, we bear the imprint of your face." No matter our appearance, we bear God's image. When we hate each other because of race or class distinctions, we dishonor God's image. Our very survival depends on recognizing our kinship to one another through Christ, our brother.

O God, we bear the imprint of your face:
  the colors of our skin are your design,
and what we have of beauty in our race
  as man or woman, you alone define
who stretched a living fabric on our frame
  and gave to each a language and a name.

Where we are torn and pulled apart by hate
  because our race, our skin is not the same;
while we are judged unequal by the state
  and victims made because we own our name,
humanity reduced to little worth,
  dishonored is your living face on earth.

O God, we share the image of your Son
  whose flesh and blood are ours, whatever skin,
in his humanity we find our own,
  and in his family our proper kin:
Christ is the brother we still crucify,
  his love the language we must learn, or die.

Shirley Erena Murray ©1987
Hope Publishing Company, Carol Stream, Illinois 60188.

Murray also voices for many women the need to find a more complete place within the Church. In her text, "Of women and of women's hopes we sing," she reminds us that women, too, are created in God's image.

We praise the God whose image is our own,
  the mystery within our flesh and bone,
the womanspirit moving through all time
  in prophecy, Magnificat and dream.

She recognizes the work and hope of women within the family of Christ:

We labor for the commonwealth of God,
  and equal as disciples, walk the road,
in work and status, asking what is just,
  for sisters of the family of Christ.

In the final stanza, she states what women are seeking:

a finer justice, and a peace more true,
  the promise of empowering for our day . . . .

Using broader images for God is part of the process of widening the welcome around the table. In "Loving Spirit," the Holy Spirit is likened to both mother and father, using images which recognize and validate the nurturing role of both parents.

Like a mother you enfold me,
  hold my life within your own,
feed me with your very body,
  form me of your flesh and bone.

Like a father you protect me,
  teach me the discerning eye,
hoist me up upon your shoulder,
  let me see the world from high.

For Murray, when we understand that everyone in the Body of Christ belongs to the same family, all created in God's image, and that everyone has a valued place in the community, we will be extending genuine hospitality in our congregations.

Justice

It is not enough, however, to broaden our recognition and welcome for those within the Church. Murray would remind us that the work of the Church involves work for justice and peace for all people. Moving outside the comfort zone of the Body of Christ is the next step in working toward justice. In "Community of Christ," Murray challenges the Church with a series of action verbs: live, risk, look, see, take, cry out, disarm, turn. In stanza 1 she begins with the admonition to "live out your creed and risk your life for God alone." Stanzas 2 and 3 describe how that might be done—the actions necessary to live out our creed:

Community of Christ,
look past the church's door
and see the refugee, the hungry,
and the poor.
Take hands with the oppressed,
the jobless in your street,
take towel and water, that you wash
your neighbor's feet.

Community of Christ,
through whom the word must sound—
cry out for justice and for peace
the whole world round:
disarm the powers that war
and all that can destroy,
turn bombs to bread, and tears of anguish
into joy.

Murray concludes that as we do this work, we are doing God's will and the result will be peace, love, kindliness, and unity.

Too often, however, the Church does not respond to needs in this active way. In her text, "Through all the world, a hungry Christ," Murray reflects the story in the Gospel of Matthew in which Jesus says:

> I was hungry and you gave me no food, thirsty and you gave me nothing to drink, I was a stranger and you did not welcome me, naked and you did not give me clothing, sick and in prison and you did not visit me (Matt. 25:42–43, NRSV).

A hungry Christ scavenges and begs for food while we have our daily bread; a leper Christ reaches out to touch those whom we stigmatize; a prisoner Christ cries out for justice and liberty while we enjoy our freedom. Murray concludes with penitence and a prayer for forgiveness.

Through all the world, a hungry Christ
must scavenge for his daily bread,
must beg the rich for crumb and crust—
  we are the rich, the daily fed.

Beyond the Church, a leper Christ
takes the untouchable by hand,
gives hope to those who have no trust,
  whose stigma is our social brand.

In torture cell, a prisoner Christ
for justice and for truth must cry
to free the innocent oppressed
  while we at liberty pass by.

We do not know you, beggar Christ,
we do not recognize your sores;
we do not see, for we are blind:
  forgive us, touch us, make us yours.

"God weeps" is a poignant reminder of the pain that God suffers because of the injustice and suffering in the world. In short, terse lines, Murray catalogues the hurts around us and challenges us to change the ways in which we as the community of faith relate to those around us. The hymn ends with a hopeful assurance of God's patience with us.

God weeps
    at love withheld,
    at strength misused,
    at children's innocence abused,
and till we change the way we love,
        God weeps.

God bleeds
at anger's fist,
at trust betrayed,
at women battered and afraid,
and till we change the way we win,
God bleeds.

God cries
at hungry mouths,
at running sores,
at creatures dying without cause,
and till we change the way we care,
God cries.

God waits
for stones to melt,
for peace to seed,
for hearts to hold each other's need,
and till we understand the Christ,
God waits.

In her own work for justice, Shirley Murray embodies the call she extends to others. Her involvement with Amnesty International, working on behalf of those displaced or imprisoned by the upheaval of political conflict around the world, began in the 1970s. When asked how she became involved with this work, she offered this response:

> I was drawn to the whole idea of A. I. [Amnesty International] because it seemed such a lively expression of the Christian conscience in action—an immediate connection to Jesus, the prototype prisoner of conscience, and a way for ordinary people to do something positive, however small. With a friend, I started up an inner-city group at our church, for commuters to come to on their way home at night. Later, I became Religious Affairs Co-ordinator for the national scene, putting out worship material for church, and connecting where I could with other faiths. It has always seemed surprising to me that the Christian churches do not take up the Amnesty mandate during Holy Week, when we have the unjust trial, torture and capital punishment themes right there in the Story. But that's only one aspect of human rights, and I guess I'm a natural protestant/protestor.[12]

The following two texts are directly influenced by her work with Amnesty International. "Great God of earth and heaven" echoes the theme of the Church's failing to meet the needs of those around us, focusing specifically on the needs of refugees. The text was written in 1986 as "a protest against apathy and 'the comfortable pew.'" Its first use was on Refugee Sunday in Murray's inner-city parish, St. Andrew's on the Terrace.[13] Murray contrasts our comfortable lives with the difficulties of homeless refugees, those suffering from hunger and injustice and escalating armaments, and ends each stanza with a prayer for God to work in our lives. In juxtaposition to the plight of the refugee and the hopelessness and despair of their lives, Murray asks forgiveness for our comfortable lives, an end to apathy, and a restoration of our passion to work for wholeness. The hymn culminates in a plea for us to have the mind of Christ, filled with mercy and working for peace.

Great God of earth and heaven
whose Spirit is our breath,
at Christmastime born human,
at Easter shared our death:
all-generous, all-loving,
in whom all beauty thrives—
forgive your sons and daughters
the comfort of our lives!

While refugees go homeless
and die before they live,
while children have no future—
our apathy forgive!
Where hope fades to depression,
despair erodes the soul,
restore in us a passion
to make the broken whole.

Where hunger kills your people,
injustice cries aloud,
while weapons grow more lethal
and only power stands proud—
God of our flesh and fiber,
whose mercy does not cease,
implant your mind within us,
create a world for peace!

An early text on justice, "God of freedom, God of justice," was written in 1980. In "Notes on the Hymns" at the end of *In Every Corner, Sing*, Murray says of this text, "One of my first 'gap-fillers.' I wrote it for Amnesty International's Campaign Against Torture when I could find nothing relevant to sing at a service for Prisoners of Conscience." The text asks God to put an end to torture and imprisonment, recognizing that Christ understands this pain, having endured it himself.

God of freedom, God of justice,
you whose love is strong as death,
you who saw the dark of prison,
you who knew the price of faith—
touch our world of sad oppression
with your Spirit's healing breath.
Rid the earth of torture's terror,
you whose hands were nailed to wood;
hear the cries of pain and protest,
you who shed the tears and blood—
move in us the power of pity
restless for the common good.

The importance of human participation in this process of justice is underscored as the third stanza concludes the hymn:

Make in us a captive conscience
quick to hear, to act, to plead;
make us truly sisters, brothers
of whatever race or creed—
teach us to be fully human,
open to each other's needs.

Murray reminds us that the true expression of our own humanity is rooted in our understanding that we are family—sisters and brothers in Christ—and in our openness to the needs of others.

Conclusion

Through these texts, Murray's concept of hospitality shines clearly. The welcome of Christ includes everyone regardless of race, status, gender, or even level of faith. One task of the Church is to widen our concept of acceptance and family so that all within the Body of Christ are recognized and valued. "For everyone born, a place at the table" is Christ's attitude. To make it a reality within the all-too-human Body of Christ will take intentional changing and stretching of our attitudes and actions. At the same time, the Church must work for justice throughout the world and beyond the boundaries of the Christian community. If God values all persons, then our work of hospitality will never be complete until all are treated with justice, dignity, and respect. The same welcome of Christ extends everywhere—we are all family, all made in God's image.

> O God, we share the image of Your Son
>   Whose flesh and blood are ours, whatever skin,
> In His humanity we find our own,
>   And in His family our proper kin:
> Christ is the brother we still crucify,
>   His love the language we must learn, or die.

Shirley Erena Murray © 1987
Hope Publishing Company, Carol Stream, Illinois 60188.

Our love for each other, rooted in Christ, empowers our work for justice. In the end, these two tasks form two sides of the same coin: we are family because all belong to God. As we recognize and value each person around us in the community of faith, we are able to see more clearly the need for acceptance and dignity of all persons, and are empowered to work for justice in the world. When we labor to remove barriers to justice, empower the helpless, or feed the hungry, our understanding of our kinship with others in the Body of Christ is enhanced. Shirley Murray's hymn texts challenge and encourage us to be about this essential work, reminding us that "God will delight when we are creators of justice and joy, compassion and peace."

Appendix: Hymns Cited and Their United States Hymnal Sources

Title	Hymnal
Community of Christ	C NC WR
God of Freedom, God of Justice	C
God Weeps	FWS
Great God of Earth and Heaven	NC
Loving Spirit	C P WR
O God, We Bear the Imprint of Your Face	C NC P
Of Women and of Women's Hopes We Sing	C
Place at the Table, A	WR
Through All the World, a Hungry Christ	NC
Who Is My Mother, Who Is My Brother?	C WR

HYMNAL ABBREVIATIONS

C *Chalice Hymnal.* St. Louis: Chalice Press, 1995.
NC *The New Century Hymnal.* Cleveland: Pilgrim Press, 1995.
P *The Presbyterian Hymnal.* Louisville: Westminster/John Knox, 1990.
WR *Worship & Rejoice.* Carol Stream, Illinois: Hope Publishing Co., 2001.
FWS *The Faith We Sing.* Nashville: Abingdon, 2000. Supplement to the *United Methodist Hymnal.*

NOTES

1. *Aotearoa* is the indigenous name for the island nation we know as New Zealand. Among residents there, using Aotearoa is a part of the effort to show respect for the Maori people and to make their culture more visible in today's society.

2. Five Murray texts appear in *The Presbyterian Hymnal* (1990); *The New Century Hymnal* (1995) contains eleven texts; *Chalice Hymnal* (1995) ten texts; *The Faith We Sing* (2000), a supplement to *The United Methodist Hymnal,* nine texts; and *Worship and Rejoice* (2001) sixteen texts. Most of Murray's hymnic work is published in three volumes. The first was *In Every Corner Sing: The Hymns of Shirley Erena Murray* (Carol Stream, Illinois: Hope Publishing Company, 1992). Murray had previously published privately a small collection by the above name, but the collection published by Hope drew together all her texts to that date with a musical setting for most of them. A second collection, *Every Day in Your Spirit* (1996), includes texts written between 1992 and 1996. Her latest collection, *Faith Makes the Song* (2003), collects texts written between 1997 and 2002. Hope Publishing Company holds the U.S. copyright for all of Murray's texts.

3. Interview with the author, January 19, 2000.

4. Shirley Murray, "Company of Clowns and Cripples: Personal Confession about Writing Hymn Texts," *Music in the Air: Song and Spirituality,* 1 (Summer 1996): 16. This journal is published in New Zealand, ISSN 1173-8669, and may be obtained by contacting John Thornley, Songpoetry, 15 Oriana Place, Palmerston North, Aotearoa/New Zealand.

5. Interview, January 19, 2000.

6. Murray, "Company of Clowns and Cripples," 17.

7. Ibid.

8. Interview, January 19, 2000.

9. Ibid.

10. Colin Gibson, "Shall We Have a Shot at This? Working with Shirley Erena Murray," *Music in the Air: Song and Spirituality* 9 (Summer 2000): 2.

11. Shirley Erena Murray, "Notes on the Hymns," *In Every Corner Sing.*

12. Shirley Erena Murray, e-mail exchange with the author, July 24, 2002.

13. Murray, "Notes on the Hymns."

Analyzing Congregational Song

An Addendum from a Global Perspective

C. Michael Hawn

"How will Christians of the future sing?
As members of the universal Church, or not at all."[1]

For centuries, a conflict has raged—sometimes silent, at other times less so—among church musicians, preachers and theologians, and believers in the pew. On the one side stand those from J. S. Bach to Isaac Watts to Ralph Vaughan Williams who favor a loftier style of congregational singing with stately tunes and rich poetic texts which, they argue, accord well with more liturgical forms of worship and thereby bring greater glory and honor to God Almighty. On the other side lie those from Martin Luther to today's contemporary Christian artists who insist that music sung by the congregation in worship should have an evangelical thrust and, at the same time, a popular style that will both attract the masses and enable individuals, each in his or her own way, to give praise and glory to God. These deep-seated and fundamental differences both transcend and transect denominations. Broadening the discussion has been the introductions into Western hymnody of non-Western musical and textual traditions. Until recently, these were of less interest to Western churches, since they remained the domain of their foreign missionaries, but in these days of rapid globalization the world has become a much smaller place. Token examples of non-Western music now find space in virtually every denominational hymnal, but many questions remain. What is the proper role and/or purpose of congregational singing in worship? What musical styles and texts most glorify God? Do local congregations share a heritage and bond with the universal Church (past and present, global and local), or only with those who are near and dear?

Above all, this raises the question, "How will Christians of the future sing?" When selecting congregational songs, many congregations focus on the cultural relevancy of the selection, maintaining the historical tradition of a given faith community, or, at best, a blending of musical styles. This rather narrow local focus in congregational song, differing widely among local congregations even within the same denomination, is reflected in the great diversity currently found in many hymnals and hymnal supplements. The "Hymn Analysis Checklist" provided in Harry Eskew's and Hugh T. McElrath's *Sing with Understanding*[2] has for several years provided a very helpful aid for analyzing hymns from Western traditions. While it is one of the most comprehensive guides available, however, I would argue that it does not adequately take into account the inherent structure and function of shorter forms of congregational singing found especially in songs from the world Church—i.e., congregational songs beyond the Euro-North American singing traditions and shorter forms such as those in Contemporary Christian Music (CCM), music sung in the Taizé Community, and some of the genres used in the African American community.

This article, therefore, proposes to look beyond the style of the music to the deeper structures that integrate musical style and text in the belief that a clearer understanding of the deeper structures of congregational song may provide clues for incorporating the people's voice in liturgy more extensively. Beyond this, an examination of the varied structures of congregational song may suggest ways to respond to the creative stylistic diversity available to the Church today and, in the process, help us sing together. In particular I will address what I regard as the fundamental question in this debate, namely, how musical structures shape the ritual behavior of congregations. In attempting to answer this question, I will focus on the fundamental characteristics and ritual uses of two musical/textual forms—sequential and cyclic—with reference to hybrid structures derived from both of these.

Characteristics of Sequential Musical Structures

As is the case with many Protestants, I was nurtured in worship through the singing of hymns. By hymns, I am referring to metered poetry set in stanzas. The sequential structure of classic Western hymnody is usually evident in the development of a theological theme over several stanzas. A basic theological concept or scriptural pericope comes to light in stanza 1. Stanza 2 develops this theme or continues the scriptural paraphrase, and so on, until the hymn climaxes in a concluding stanza that draws all of the points together into a whole. A doxological formula, an eschatological reference, a cosmic allusion, a petition, or a strong hermeneutical application may strengthen the climax of a hymn. A hymn tune sustains the sequential progression of the poetry by being recycled for each stanza.

Skillful organists provide a musical interpretation of the text by careful phrasing and varied articulations of the melody, and by choosing appropriate registration and dynamic levels for each stanza according to the text. An exceptional organist may modify the harmonies discreetly from stanza to stanza in the hope of furnishing the text with a more interesting musical foundation. Hoping to realize both poetic and musical climax, organists may employ a variety of musical strategies, especially on the final stanza. These may include an increased fullness in organ registration, the use of an alternate harmonization (implying that the congregation should sing in unison), or a change in tonal center, usually ascending through a modulation following the penultimate stanza to a key a semitone or tone higher than the previous stanzas.

Given the sequential nature of the text, its teleological character is inherent to its performance: a classic Western hymn text is going somewhere. One must note where the text begins and follow carefully the progression of thought through to its conclusion, a process that may take place in as few as two or three stanzas or as many as seven, eight, or even more in some of the classic ballad hymns. A strophic musical structure, repeating in its entirety with each stanza, masks the inherently sequential nature of the text.

How does the singer know when the text has reached a climax? While an organist may provide specific external cues for recognizing the apex of the poem, literary clues internal to the text also may assist the careful singer. In addition to following the content of the text carefully, the singer can see the end of the hymn coming on the printed page, e.g., only two stanzas to go. As a literary structure, the singer should encounter an ultimate thought beyond which any further material would be anticlimactic. For example, consider the final stanza of Isaac Watts's famous hymn, "When I survey the wondrous cross":

Were the whole Realm of Nature mine,
  That were a Present far too small;
Love so amazing, so divine,
  Demands my Soul, my Life, my All.[3]

In previous stanzas, Watts has led the singer through the agony of the crucifixion complete with an invitation to visualize Christ, from top to bottom, on the cross. In the final stanza the singer shifts away from a posture at the foot of the cross to a cosmic perspective focusing on the meaning of Christ's sacrifice. There is nothing more that can be said. The hymn is complete.[4]

Charles Wesley often used an eschatological reference at the culmination of a text.[5] Such is the case in his well-known "Love divine, all loves excelling":

Finish then thy new creation,
  Pure and spotless let us be;
Let us see thy great salvation
  Perfectly restored in thee;

Changed from glory into glory,
  Till in heaven we take our place,
Till we cast our crowns before thee,
  Lost in wonder, love and praise.[6]

If one is truly "lost in wonder, love and praise" in heaven, then there are no further stanzas to sing.

A reference to the triune God is a classic way to bring a hymn to its conclusion. Throughout liturgical history the Church has Christianized the Psalms by adding a *Gloria Patri* at the conclusion as a final stanza. Hymnists continued this tradition. Edward Plumptre concluded his famous processional hymn, "Rejoice, ye pure in heart," with a Trinitarian formula:

Praise God who reigns on high,
  The Lord, whom we adore,
The Father, Son, and Holy Ghost,
  One God for evermore.[7]

Over the centuries, a doxological formula expressing the triune God has become a resting place for prayer, either sung or spoken.

The skilled poet employs many other literary techniques to achieve a sense of climax and conclusion in strophic hymnody. Since there are too many possibilities to list them all here, one final approach must suffice. In addition to those given above, one way of concluding a sequentially-structured hymn text is to end with a petition. Concluding petitions, found throughout the history of Christian song, call to mind the inherent relationship between singing and praying. This is a relationship that is organically connected to the roots of the Judeo-Christian heritage, though not, of course, limited to Christian tradition.[8] Latin verse often ends with a doxological confession. But consider briefly the classic petitions found at the close of many Latin poems. These examples, taken from the sequences approved during the Council of Trent, have served as models for hymnic petitions for many centuries since their conception.

In the final stanza of *Veni, Sancte Spiritus* (attributed to Stephen Langton, d. 1228), sometimes called the golden sequence, the imperative form of the Latin verb *dare* (to give or grant) begins four of the final six lines. The metrical translation by John Mason Neale (1852), though beautiful to the ear, reduces the petitions from four to three and obscures the persistent power of the Latin imperative *da* ("grant") found in the original text.

Da tuis fidelibus	*Fill* thy faithful, who confide
in te confidentibus	in thy power to guard and guide
sacrum septenarium;	with thy sevenfold mystery:
da virtutis meritum;	here thy grace and virtue *send*;
da salutis exitum,	*grant* salvation to the end,
da perenne gaudium.	and in heaven felicity.[9]

Dies Irae (attributed to Thomas of Celano, fl. 1215), concludes with an implied *Kyrie eleison* and the familiar *dona eis requiem*. The metrical translation is by W. J. Irons (1848) as found in the *English Hymnal* (1906):

Lacrymosa dies illa,	Ah! that day of tears and mourning!
qua resurget ex favilla	from the dust of earth returning
iudicandus homo reus,	man for judgment must prepare him;
huic ergo *parce* deus.	*spare*, O God, in mercy *spare* him!
Pie Jesu Domine,	Lord, all-pitying, Jesu blest,
dona eis requiem.	*grant* them thine eternal rest.[10]

In each of the two Latin sequences, the petitions are of such gravity that the hymn ends and waits in eschatological hope for fulfillment. There is no more that we can sing in this earthly life. We must conclude the hymn in the presence of Christ in the fulfillment of time.

Sequential structures are inherently literary in form. Unless they have a refrain or are sung repeatedly so that they are committed to memory, these forms depend upon the eye for participation. Poetic devices in the Euro-North American cultural context, having evolved over the centuries from Greek and Latin poetry, are often dependent upon visual media.[11] This literary quality has many benefits for ritual. Songs suitable for a given liturgical tradition may be gathered into a single collection. Collections may be organized around the performance of the liturgy and specific rites that constitute a valid enactment of the rituals central to that liturgy. Many collections may have a domestic as well as a corporate life, deepening the personal piety of the participant, and enabling a more complete corporate involvement.[12] While the Roman Catholic tradition also had service books such as the *Liber Usualis* and the Sacramentary that supported its rites, the complexity of these books limited their use only to highly educated, literate professional musicians and clergy.[13] The people did not sing from them, so they had no domestic use. Though the Book of Hours was available for private devotions, it was not a formal part of the Mass.[14] Since Vatican II, however, an array of hymnals have provided an option for facilitating the rituals of Catholic liturgy.[15]

Sequential structures use many words in contrast to more melismatic chant settings of other texts for the Mass. Although recent hymn writers vary from classic metrical patterns somewhat, they continue to organize the many words into stanzas structured by a metrical construction and a rhyme scheme. Though guided by the eye on the page, meter and rhyme provide sonorous organizational patterns that aid memory and allow for a more cohesive corporate participation. While mnemonic devices are helpful, sequential written forms lend themselves to literary analysis because of their abundance of words.[16] Because of the visual dimension, the singer is clearly aware of the beginning and may anticipate the conclusion of the hymn by seeing how many stanzas remain. The written text and musical form combine to energize the singer toward the culmination of the hymn. In this sense, it is a relatively closed structure—more or less predictable in length and quality of experience—not likely open to significant textual or musical variation or improvisation. Furthermore, both the music and the text, as contained on the page, may be kept and reread for further reflection or analysis following the singing of the hymn.

Characteristics of Cyclic Musical Structures

It was during my first visit to the Taizé Community in southeastern France that I became aware of the power of cyclic forms.[17] The music that facilitated the corporate prayer used a very different structure than the hymns of my tradition. Brief texts were set in concise musical statements—ostinato, canon, litany, refrain, or response. At first the repetitions seemed like sheer redundancy; but after a time I sensed that repetition was not an accurate description of this musical experience. While on the surface those gathered for corporate prayer might seem to be repeating the same musical mantra over and over, I discerned that theme and variation was a more apt description of the musical and liturgical experience. A brief song, usually eight to twelve measures in length, consisted of a short theme. A single statement of the theme was one cycle. Each time the theme returned, there were variations: a worshipper might become gradually aware of a deeper centering or relaxation of the body after several cycles; a cantor might sing different scriptural or devotional texts above the primary theme on successive cycles; an instrument might provide a variation on the theme; the singer/pray-er might focus on an icon, or hum or sing harmony or become aware of another's harmony. Rather than redundancy, the experience was replete with variation as the main theme or cycle returned again and again.

Teaching in Africa broadened my experience with this form of theme and variation. Once again, I participated in shorter musical forms with a brief text. In this case the musical styles differed radically from the generally meditative sung prayers of Taizé. Though repetition is present, there are also significant modifications: the leader(s) varies the text in a call-response manner; percussion instruments provide subtle variations; dancers interact with the percussion and singing; the intensity seems to gather with each recurrence of the theme. It was not until I spent some time with ethnomusicologist Andrew Tracey in South Africa that I began to understand the broader implications of what he calls "cyclic musical structures."[18]

Cyclic musical structures embrace a variety of musical styles.[19] Regardless of style, the effective presentation of a cyclic structure or the performance of a set ritual in liturgy depends upon establishing a clear distinction between what Ronald Grimes calls boredom and monotony. "Liturgy as a form of work does not surprise, though it may keep us open to the serendipitous moment by its very monotony.... Liturgy is a full emptiness, a monotony without boredom, a reverent waiting without expectation."[20] Tom F. Driver provides further perspective in his discussion of "ritual boredom," in which rituals "have lost touch with the actualities of people's lives and are thus simply arcane; or else the people have lost the ability to apprehend their very need of ritual, do not see what rituals are good for, and thus do not find them even potentially valuable."[21] While popular usage equates "boredom" with "monotony," in this context, a monotonous activity, though repetitive, establishes the safe environment in which a ritual may take place or be performed. By virtue of its repetitive, monotonous character, a ritual may enable the individual to move freely, both cognitively and kinesthetically, within the rule of this safe environment, even to improvise. Monotony has a character of what Driver calls "ritual performance." He indicates that all ritual performances

> require limits....This delineation of what to do and not to do is rooted in ritualization's being, ... a process of channeling and marking, of making pathways for behavior. In order to achieve definite form, ritualization encourages certain acts, *reinforcing them with repetition and slight variation*, while ruling others out. In short, ritual performance requires (and makes) rules of the game, *whether these be known from previous usage or come to be elaborated on the spot.*[22]

Ritual boredom is enervating, causing lack of interest and participation, while monotony facilitates freedom and safe space, i.e., ritual performance. Cyclic structures offer a repetitive ground over which numerous variations may take place. Without these variations, the repetition is subject to boredom. Skillfully performed, musical variations provide enough difference to avoid boredom, but not so much difference to disturb the benefits of monotony.

Other characteristics of cyclic musical structure include this form's essentially oral/aural nature and the effects that this has on kinesthetic response. Books are not necessary for the performance of cyclic structures in the same way that they facilitate sequential musical forms. In fact, books may impede the embodiment of cyclic song. Songs either may be learned orally or, in the case of Taizé chants, may be acquired initially from a score, which is set aside once the short cycle has been internalized. In the case of African music, movement is essential to the performance of the song. Meditative cyclic structures such as Taizé chants also have a kinesthetic dimension as the singer assumes more relaxed postures that encourage centering. Closing one's eyes or focusing on an icon is a traditional way of praying in this manner; holding a book, however, may inhibit the worshipper's ability to achieve a centered state of being. Regardless of mood, cyclic structures encourage a physical response, either toward the ecstatic or toward the meditative, and the use of books ultimately hampers the successful performance of these songs.[23] Jack Goody offers additional insights in his recent study, *The Power of Written Tradition*. Learning through oral means is more intergenerational:

> Oral learning entails a greater amount of showing, of participation. Hence the world of childhood is less segregated from that of adults. Children sit or play around when discussions and performances are taking place, absorbing at least the general atmosphere of these activities and occasionally, if they listen attentively, some of their content as well. Much more learning depends upon the voice, upon face-to-face interaction. Whereas in literate cultures an individual can go off by himself with a book, in oral cultures a partner is needed as narrator or instructor.[24]

The ramifications of this insight for liturgy are significant. Liturgies that are word-centered and literate-based may tend to segregate communities by age and, in the case of visual impairment, disability. If story, narrative, movement, and visual means of stimulation—e.g., symbols, banners, and icons—are absent, large portions of a community may be alienated from full participation. Cyclic musical structures offer some relief from extremely literate liturgies at this point since they allow for easier participation in the liturgy and a minimum use of the written word, if at all.

Musical anthropologist John Blacking brings together this discussion of cyclic structure and the value of monotony in ritual. He suggests that "by releasing the brain from the task of immediate attention to environmental stimuli, [music] stimulates creative thinking by allowing the 'memory surface' of the brain to deal with information for its own sake."[25] Furthermore, "music itself may generate experiences and thoughts that transcend the extra-musical features of the situation."[26] It is perhaps at this point that the mantra-like *ostinati* of the Taizé Community place the singer in a state that allows "creative thinking" or, in this case, prayer to emerge. Through the unity of prayer and song, cyclic structures free the participant from the teleological imperative that dominates much of the western perspective and engages the worshipper in a more timeless experience that transcends the tedium of the situation. The introduction to the United States edition of Taizé music states that the songs "express a basic reality of faith that can quickly be grasped by the intellect, and that gradually penetrates the heart and the whole being."[27] A single thread ties this discussion together. Music with a cyclic structure most often draws upon orality and a sense of monotony for effectiveness more than literary techniques. Monotony opens us to ritual performance, creative thinking, and centered prayer.

The refrain, a hybrid musical form combining sequential strophic stanzas with a recurring cycle, comes in many variations. The chart on page 260 compares the basic characteristics of sequential and cyclic musical structures with refrain forms as a mediating position. At any point along the spectrum, varying musical styles may embody the form, providing a different experience. I propose that sequential structures are primarily content-oriented while cyclic structures are central in forging community. Singing together always enhances a sense of community, regardless of musical structure. The suggestion here is that community formation is a primary motif with cyclic forms, whereas it is a by-product or secondary motif with sequential structures. Note that this is a spectrum with many infinite variations and possibilities at any point. A spectrum also implies that characteristics at one end are also present at the other end, though to a lesser degree.

Musical Structures and Ritual

At the heart of this proposal is the need for worship planners not only to choose appropriate musical styles and textual themes, but also to find the most appropriate musical structure that supports particular rites and rituals in a given faith community. Consider, for a moment, a spectrum of congregational musical forms for use with ritual. At one end is a sequential structure that makes primary use of literate traditions with a focus on textual content. At the opposite end of the spectrum is a cyclic structure that is inherently oral/aural (though text and/or music may be written down at times) and focuses on the shaping of community rather than the communication of content. Refrain and responsorial forms may combine aspects of both.

There are some caveats to such an approach. First, this model proposes a spectrum of possible musical structures rather than a dichotomy between two distinct poles of musical experience. Both sequential and cyclic structures may play a role in most liturgies rather than either one or the other.[28] While I have associated building community primarily as a function of cyclic forms,

Spectrum of Congregational Song Structures
Comparison between Sequential and Cyclic Musical Structures

Refrain Forms
Response
Antiphon
Litany
Epimone

Sequential Structures ◄——►	**Cyclic Structures**
Strophic	Theme and Variation
Textual orientation	Movement orientation
Eye oriented	Ear oriented
Literate tradition	Oral tradition
Predictable performance time	Open-ended performance time
Linear in structure	Episodic in experience
Verbose	Concise
Comments on ritual activity	Participates in ritual activity
Content oriented	Community oriented
Moves toward climax in content	Moves toward total participation and integration of participants

Musical Considerations for Sequential Song

- Includes strophic hymns where the same music is repeated for successive stanzas
- Includes through-composed music and texts where there is no repetition of the music
- May include texts with brief textual repetition (usually on the last line) or epimone
- The essence of the text is essentially monochronic (teleological)
- Harmonic variations, varying instrumentations, and descants may provide musical variety from stanza to stanza

Musical Considerations for Cyclic Song

- Maintains a steady beat once the song begins
- Each repetition of a cycle needs some small variation
- Often uses a soloist (cantor) to sing over the cycle
- Improvisations by soloist over ends of phrases
- Often accompanied by physical response
- Integration of choir and congregation as a unit
- Polychronic (vs. monochronic) sense of time
- Textual improvisations to fit ritual context

sequential musical structures may also bind an assembly together, especially through increased musical familiarity. Likewise, cyclic structures always have content, even if they usually use fewer words and more repetitive oral/aural devices. In specific faith traditions a sequential hymn may, through extensive use, become so familiar that it assumes a cyclic status. In this situation, most participants would not need to use books and would be freer to look up and enjoy a visual as well as aural sense of the gathered community. Goody refers to the process of going back and forth between oral and literate modes as "changing the communicative channel."[29] I propose that communicative channel-switching in worship at appropriate points in the ritual offers the possibility of increased variety and the potential to incorporate more persons into the ritual experience. Congregations that rely solely on literate or oral forms in the United States may not be reaching as diverse a group of participants, nor communicating as effectively, as they otherwise might.

As in any spectrum, there are countless variations between the two poles. For example, refrain forms combine aspects of both sequential and cyclic structures. The stanzas of a hymn with a refrain may provide a sequential component to the experience while the refrain itself functions in a cyclic manner. It is no accident that Roman Catholics focused on refrain and responsorial structures in their efforts to establish congregational singing after the reforms of the Second Vatican Council. Responsorial psalmody blends the structures by chanting the psalm text in its entirety and by either interspersing the text with an antiphon from time to time or concluding with a *Gloria Patri*. A sung litany provides another responsorial form that falls in-between the sequential/cyclic perspectives on the proposed spectrum. Responses (e.g., *Kyrie eleison*, "Lord, hear our prayer," or "Thanks be to God") inserted between appropriate petitions or expressions of thanksgiving add a lyrical quality to the prayers that cannot be achieved by speaking alone. While litanies with brief responses may be written, they may be performed in an aural/oral manner that contributes a fuller sense of praying for the world in the midst of the community rather than offering individual intercessions and petitions.

The liturgical link between sequential and cyclic musical structures is the prayerful quality of the sung word. By prayerful quality, I am not referring to Albrecht Dürer's "praying hands." This early sixteenth-century image suggests a private devotional approach to prayer rather than the prayers of the gathered corporate community. Dürer's print has become an icon for the act of praying that has obscured for many the differences between private and public prayer. As Paul Bradshaw has noted, much that passes for common or cathedral prayer in corporate worship is actually individual or monastic prayer.

The intercessions of common prayer

> . . . should be focused not primarily upon ourselves and our own needs, nor even merely on those of other Christians, but rather upon the needs of the whole world for which Christ died and which he desires to be saved. . . . Instead of this global vision of their vocation, Christians easily lapse into prayer that concentrates upon themselves and those near and dear to them.[30]

The incorporation of music as a vehicle for prayer adds several dimensions to the ritual experience. Singing unifies the body of believers as those gathered integrate their voices and bodies in unified rhythms, melodies, and harmonies. Singing a prayer also adds an element of intentionality to the rite over speaking. By "intentionality" I mean that the act of singing takes more physical effort than speaking. Furthermore, singing together—far more so than merely speaking/reciting together collectively—requires an intentional awareness which simultaneously harbors a potential for promoting greater unity among the gathered body. Singing, too, adds diversity to the soundscape of the liturgical experience. Sung responses may come from various communities in the history of the Church or places around the world. The culturally-specific quality of various musical styles links the prayers of an individual community to worshippers of every place and time. Singing also increases the emotional range of prayer. Rather than being limited to comfortable and predictable emotional responses, the affective aspects of prayer may range from the subtlety of centered prayer in all of its serenity to more ecstatic dimensions of fully embodied prayer enlivened by singing and dancing. The affective power of sung prayer has been addressed by Don Saliers, who states the following:

> At the heart of our vocation as church musicians and liturgical leaders is the question of how we enable the Church to "pray well"—to sing and dance faithfully and with integrity. . . . When we are engaged in sung prayer, we are not simply dressing out words in sound; rather, we are engaged in forming and expressing those emotions which constitute the very Christian life itself.[31]

Thus, the prayerful quality of singing, regardless of musical structure has an ethical dimension. Singing has the power to change faith communities. As Miriam Therese Winter has written, "Who we are is how we pray, and how we pray is who we are becoming. . . . This is essentially why we sing: to express who we are and are becoming."[32]

In conclusion, I will suggest some basic ways that sequential and cyclic musical structures may interact with specific parts of a rite in order to enhance effectively the congregation's participation. This understanding of the integral relationship between musical structure and ritual form is essential for incorporating global song into liturgy with integrity. In general, I propose two principles for choosing between sequential or cyclic musical structures. While each faith community has its own traditions that may modify these principles, they may offer some guidance in a variety of ecumenical settings. Sequential musical structures generally work better when sung following a ritual action. Employing the long-established educational prescript of mystagogical catechesis—doing should precede explaining[33]—it follows that the significance of ritual actions (e.g., procession of the Word, sacramental actions) are reinforced and intensified with a sequential hymn following the action. Sequential hymns offer a lyrical theological explanation for what has been observed and experienced by those assembled. *In general, sequential structures forge unity in the community through singing a common understanding of a ritual following a ritual action.*

In contrast, cyclic musical structures unite organically with ritual actions themselves as they are taking place. One practical reason for this is the fact that the assembly is not as dependent upon holding books or reading texts when participating in cyclic structures. Worshipers may observe and join in through singing and, when appropriate, dancing as the ritual transpires. For example, in many faith communities it is common practice, while receiving the Eucharist, to move forward toward stations or to kneel at a communion rail to accept the bread and wine. Singing by the community enhances this ritual action in many ways. However, it has been my experience that singing lesser-known sequential hymns frustrates those assembled in that they must hold books in their hands if they are to sing effectively. This presents a dilemma. On the one hand, the quality of the singing diminishes considerably without the use of books. On the other hand, taking a book forward inhibits the reception of the communion elements. What does one do with a hymnbook or order of worship while taking communion? The singing generally is less effective since a high percentage of those participating cannot sing as they move forward. Perhaps even more important to the experience is that a congregation, when singing a less-familiar sequential form during a ritual action, may be denied the benefits of becoming more fully aware of both aural and visual representations of community. In this setting it is important to change the communicative channel from that of a written script to total embodiment. *In general, cyclic structures forge unity in the community by embodying the ritual itself through singing, praying, and moving together.*

Cyclic structures allow all present the opportunity to participate more wholly through singing, whether in the pews or while moving forward. Since cyclic songs are primarily transmitted through oral means (even if initially read from a page as an aid to memory), the assembly may look up and sense their participation in the totality of the ritual. Specific styles of music drawn from other cultures (both historical and contemporary) remind the community that the Lord's Supper is set at a table that transcends all times and places. Thus cyclic musical structures emphasize the corporate nature of this ritual more than individual piety. While communion may focus appropriately on individual piety during specific seasons of the Christian year—e.g., on Maundy Thursday or Good Friday—I am encouraging as normative a Eucharistic (thanksgiving) sense of communion where the entire assembly gathers in gratitude rather than only in penitence. The oral character and kinesthetic potential inherent in cyclic music has a quality of *valence*—that is, the quality to unite, interact, react, or merge with other aspects of the environment. It is perhaps this quality that prompted the following statement on sacred music in the *Constitution on Sacred Liturgy*:

> The musical tradition of the universal Church is a treasure of inestimable value, greater even than that of any of other art. The main reason for this preeminence is that, as sacred song closely bound to the text, it forms a necessary or integral part of the solemn liturgy.[34]

It is the quality of valence that allows those assembled, in the language of the Second Vatican Council, to become "full, conscious and active" participants in the drama suggested by the ritual rather than passive observers.

In summary, a focus on musical styles rather than structures disguises the underlying function and foundation that congregational singing provides within liturgy. Musical style at its best is an aural representation of how the people in varying places and times have responded to the established (biblical and traditional) texts and cultural circumstances of their congregations. Variations in musical style remind us of the myriad ways that the Incarnation has been made manifest among us, and of the diversity through which the Holy Spirit moves throughout the Church. Congregational musical structures, however, may be embodied in a wide range of musical styles. An appropriate use of musical structures speaks to the inherent quality of valence in liturgy—how music relates organically to the established rites and rituals of the faith community. An understanding of the role of musical structure and how it interacts with liturgical ritual is therefore essential for those who serve as musical presiders. Congregational song in the twenty-first century is much more varied. Methods of analysis need to respond not only to classic hymn forms, but also to cyclic structures used in world song, contemporary Christian music, African American worship, and the Taizé Community. The structure of these songs provides effective ways for congregations to participate more fully in worship and, hopefully, sing together in the future as a world Christian Church.

NOTES

Aspects of this article appeared as "Form and Ritual: A Comparison between Sequential and Cyclic Musical Structures and Their use in Liturgy," in *Anáil Dé: The Breath of God; Music, Ritual and Spirituality,* ed. Helen Phelan (Dublin: Veritas Publications, 2001), 37–54. It has been updated and broadened for inclusion in this Festschrift.

1. "Editor's Introduction," *Cantate Domino: An Ecumenical Hymnbook,* Melody Edition, 4th ed., ed. Erik Routley (London: Bärenreiter, 1974), xii. Also in Full Music Edition, 1980, ix. This unidentified comment made at one of the editorial meetings in preparation of *Cantate Domino* (was it Routley himself?) is characteristic of the provocative, challenging, stimulating, and terse remarks made by Routley both in writing and in person.

2. See Appendix 2 in Harry Eskew and Hugh T. McElrath, *Sing with Understanding,* 2nd ed., revised and expanded (Nashville: Church Street Press, 1995), 329–330.

3. Selma L. Bishop, *Isaac Watts: Hymns and Spiritual Songs 1707–1748* (London: The Faith Press, 1962), 353.

4. A stanza not usually included in modern hymnals, "His dying Crimson like a robe . . ." adds to the device of hypotyposis employed by Watts. Watts placed it as the penultimate stanza, however, not as the final one.

5. The eschatological character of Charles Wesley texts has recently been highlighted in Teresa Berger, *Theology in Hymns?*, trans. Timothy E. Kimbrough (Nashville: Kingswood Books, 1995), 137–142.

6. *The Works of John Wesley,* ed. Albert Cook Outler, vol. 7, *A Collection of Hymns for the Use of the People Called Methodists,* eds. Franz Hildebrandt and Oliver Beckerlegge (Nashville: Abingdon Press, 1983), 547.

7. Carlton Young, ed., *The United Methodist Hymnal* (Nashville: United Methodist Publishing House, 1989), 160.

8. The Jewish heritage of prayer stresses the unity of prayer and song. Music in the early synagogue functioned in three ways according to Eliyahu Schleifer: "psalmody, cantillation of Scripture, and the liturgical chant in which the statutory prayers were recited by a local worship leader. . . ." See Eliyahu Schleifer, "From Bible to Hasidism," in *Sacred Sound and Social Change: Liturgical Music in Jewish and Christian Experience,* eds. Lawrence A. Hoffman and Janet R. Walton (Notre Dame: University of Notre Dame Press, 1992), 24. Although Christianity has its musical roots in this Jewish ethos, evidence suggests that early Christians developed new songs and forms for their embryonic worship. Unlike much of our worship today, Edward Foley suggests that "there was . . . no sharp distinction between the sung and the spoken, no clear division between what we might call the musical and the non-musical, nor any denial of the fundamental lyricism of Christian worship." See Edward Foley, *Foundations of Christian Music: The Music of Pre-Constantinian Christianity* (Washington, D.C.: Pastoral Press, 1992), 84. Liturgical scholar Paul Bradshaw states, "It is often . . . difficult to determine when the New Testament authors are citing topical prayer-forms with which they are familiar and when they are not, *or even to separate hymns from prayers, since both may employ a similar construction.*" Italics mine. See Paul Bradshaw, *The Search for the Origins of Christian Worship* (New York: Oxford University Press, 1992), 43.

9. From Erik Routley, *A Panorama of Christian Hymnody*, expanded and rev. by Paul A. Richardson (Chicago: GIA Publications, 2005), 138.

10. Ibid. Routley notes (136) that the English versification is at best a noble attempt that allows the singer the opportunity to sing the gist of the text with the original melody. His literal translation is as follows: "Oh, what a day of tears and lamentation, when man, waiting for judgment, rises from earth's ashes: spare him in that day! Kind Lord Jesus, give them rest!"

11. For a brief reference tool of poetic devices, see Austin C. Lovelace, *The Anatomy of Hymnody* (Chicago: G.I.A. Publications, 1965), 91–102. For a much more extensive understanding of the literate hymn tradition, see J. R. Watson, *The English Hymn: A Critical and Historical Study* (Oxford: Clarendon Press, 1997).

12. Among Protestants, inexpensive collections by eighteenth-century hymn writers like Isaac Watts and Charles and John Wesley set the trend in this regard. The Wesleys were particularly concerned that their collections should be affordable to the poor. Since these collections were individually owned, they were used at Society meetings in corporate contexts and in domestic settings as well. These brief collections were theologically or seasonally organized. See the following facsimile reprints by the Charles Wesley Society: *Hymns on the Lord's Supper* (Bristol, 1745); *Hymns for Our Lord's Resurrection* (London, 1746); *Hymns for Ascension-Day and Hymns for Whitsunday* (Bristol, 1746); *Hymns for the Nativity of Our Lord* (London, 1745).

The Book of Common Prayer serves a dual domestic/corporate use for many Anglicans as well. Many faithful Anglicans bring their own copy to worship, but refer only minimally to it because of their intimate familiarity with the book. In the Reformed tradition, John D. Witvliet notes the roles of the Genevan Psalter in shaping both domestic and corporate spirituality. See "The Spirituality of the Psalter: Metrical Psalms in Liturgy and Life in Calvin's Geneva," *Calvin Theological Journal* 32 (1997): 273–97, for a thorough explanation of the dynamic of the Genevan Psalter between home and church.

13. Jack Goody points out in *The Power of Written Tradition* (Washington: Smithsonian Institution Press, 2000), that written works such as these serve several purposes. They provide the possibility of canonization of a body of material, something impossible in oral cultures where there "is no evidence of a fixed utterance existing over long periods of time. . . . In other words, canonization is virtually impossible . . ." (126). While this allows written works, especially of a religious nature, to "establish relatively stable internal norms over large areas" (44), written works can also inhibit diversity of opinion and possess a "hegemonic force" that promotes a dominant perspective. Of course, other writings can in time destabilize such forces for "countercultural, revolutionary, or critical purposes" (130). The fact that the *Liber Usualis* was controlled by an educated male clergy within a largely illiterate social context made destabilization much less likely.

14. For more detailed information on pre-Vatican II rites and music, see John Harper, *Forms and Orders of Western Liturgy from the Tenth to the Eighteenth Century* (Oxford: Clarendon Press, 1991).

15. Other options include seasonal missalettes that usually remain at the church and are not used at home. Recent Catholic hymnals in the United States range from

Worship, 3rd ed. (Chicago, G.I.A. Publications, 1986) and *Gather* (Chicago: G.I.A. Publications, 1988) for traditional Anglo congregations to *Lead Me, Guide Me* (Chicago: G.I.A. Publications, 1987) for African American congregations, and *Flor y Canto* (Portland, Ore.: Oregon Catholic Press, 1989) for Spanish-speaking congregations. *Hymnal for the Hours* (Chicago: G.I.A. Publications, 1989) is for use with daily offices, and *By Flowing Waters* (Collegeville, Minn.: Liturgical Press, 1999) uses only plainsong style for the liturgy. *Ritual Song* (Chicago: G.I.A. Publications, 1996) combines aspects of several of the English-language hymnals. This sampling, while not complete, explores the various genres of Roman Catholic hymnals available in the United States.

16. I am referring here to work done by Walter J. Ong in *Orality and Literacy: The Technologizing of the Word* (London and New York: Methuen, 1982; rep. ed., New York: Routledge, 1988), 38–41.

17. There are many sources that speak of Taizé prayer. For a concise introduction, see Brother Jean Marie, "Prayer and Song in Taizé: Opening the Doors to an Inner Life," *Ecumenism* 31 (December 1996), 16–18. A visit to the Taizé Web site http://www.taize.fr/ also provides additional background.

18. Tracey discusses the nature of cyclic musical structure in "Transcribing African Music in Pulse Notation," a monograph published by the International Library of African Music, Rhodes University, Grahamstown, South Africa, in 1997.

19. For example, the Praise and Worship phenomenon in the United States, highly influenced by charismatic worship practices, makes extensive use of cyclic structures or variants thereof.

20. Ronald Grimes, *Beginnings in Ritual Studies* (Lanham, Md.: University Press of America, 1982), 44.

21. Tom F. Driver, *The Magic of Ritual* (New York: HarperCollins, 1991), 7.

22. Ibid., 100, emphasis added.

23. The charismatic-influenced songs of the contemporary Praise and Worship style often project the text onto an overhead screen, freeing the hands to clap or the body to sway. In practice, even this projection becomes unnecessary as the cycles repeat and the song is internalized. The oral (vs. literate) nature of these songs is further evident in that they are often learned by means of CDs or cassette tapes rather than through musical scores. Compact discs have become the electronic prayer books for Pentecostal and charismatic groups.

24. Goody, *The Power of Written Tradition*, 24.

25. *Music, Culture, and Experience: Selected Papers of John Blacking*, ed. Reginald Byron (Chicago: University of Chicago Press, 1995), 152.

26. Ibid., 153.

27. *Songs & Prayers from Taizé* (Chicago: G.I.A. Publications, 1991), 29.

28. Daily prayer offices often benefit from a unified musical style and structure due to their brevity. Fuller services of Word and Table, by contrast, usually benefit from a diversity of musical styles and structures due to the greater length of the liturgy and the complexity and variety of ritual actions needed to sustain the liturgy.

29. Goody, *The Power of the Written Tradition*, 57.

30. Paul F. Bradshaw, *Two Ways of Praying* (Nashville: Abingdon Press, 1995), 65.

31. Don Saliers, "The Integrity of Sung Prayer," *Worship* 55, no. 4 (July 1981), 291–93.

32. Miriam Therese Winter, "Catholic Prophetic Sound," *Sacred Sound and Social Change: Liturgical Music in Jewish and Christian Experience*, eds. Lawrence A. Hoffman and Janet R. Walton (Notre Dame: University of Notre Dame Press, 1992), 153.

33. For example, in the early Christian Church, catechumens did not receive an explanation for the ritual of baptism before they participated in its mysteries. The principle of mystagogical catechesis employed the concept of entering first into the baptismal act followed by a detailed explanation. Examples of mystagogical catechesis may be found in St. Cyril's (ca. 348) writings as well as others. See "St. Cyril of Jerusalem's Lectures on the Christian Sacraments," trans. R. W. Church, in *Documents of Christian Worship*, by James F. White (Louisville: Westminster/John Knox Press, 1992), 158–160, for representative examples by Cyril (158), Ambrose of Milan (158–59), and John Chrysostom (159–60).

34. "Constitution on the Sacred Liturgy" (1963), *The Liturgy Documents: A Parish Resource* (Chicago: Liturgy Training Publications, 1991), article 112. "Valence" is a term primarily associated with chemistry. It refers to "the combining capacity of an atom or a radical determined by the number of electrons that it will lose, add, or share when it reacts with other atoms." *The American Heritage Electronic Dictionary*, 3d ed., Ver. 3.0A (Novato, California: Wordstar International, 1993).

IV.

Bibliography of Hugh T. McElrath's Works

Hugh T. McElrath

BIBLIOGRAPHY OF PUBLISHED WORKS
with Select Unpublished Works, Arranged by Genre in Chronological Order with Annotations

DAVID LOUIS GREGORY AND WILLIAM JEFFREY JONES

Editors' note: In addition to the works listed below, a large number of sound recordings of recitals and lectures as well as unpublished written materials by Professor McElrath may be found in the Music and Audio-Visual Library at the James P. Boyce Centennial Library, The Southern Baptist Theological Seminary, Louisville, Kentucky. A catalogue is available online at: http://library.sbts.edu/.

Books/Monographs

Keith, Edmond D., and Hugh T. McElrath. *Sing From Your Hearts*. Nashville: Convention Press, [1964].

This text was designed for use as a church study course. The initial chapter provides a general rationale for singing hymns. Each of the subsequent chapters examines two hymns in detail, with Keith discussing their origins and McElrath providing the meaning of each hymn.

12 Devotional Programs Based on the 1967–68 Hymns of the Month. Nashville: Church Music Department, Baptist Sunday School Board, 1967.

This pamphlet offers a supplement to the "Hymns of the Month" published in *The Church Musician* during the 1967–1968 church school year. Each month offers a brief suggested order of worship designed to be used in Sunday school assembly sessions and devotional services. A variety of scripture passages, written prayers, commentary, and poetic verse are presented to provide insight into the respective hymns. Some performance suggestions are also given.

How to Use a Hymnal: A Training Union Special Study Unit. Nashville: Baptist Sunday School Board of the Southern Baptist Convention, 1968.

One of several booklets designed as study courses for laypersons in the Church. McElrath divides this work into six sessions, each dealing with some aspect of hymnal organization or some related aspect of hymnology. McElrath discusses the musical, literary, theological, and spiritual aspects that make up a hymnal. He traces historic influences from the Old Testament to the twentieth century with special emphasis on the contributions of Baptists. He looks at the practical matters associated with understanding and using a hymnal, followed by a unit focused on using the resources in a hymnal creatively.

Great Hymns of Praise. Nashville: Convention Press, 1977.

This book was designed as a text for the Church Study Course series and intended to be used within the educational program of a church. Each of the ten chapters deals comprehensively with a single hymn. McElrath provides the historical background for the origins of each text and tune and a thorough, line-by-line exegesis of the texts as he examines each hymn and hymn tune with a focus upon participatory singing. An LP recording of the same name accompanies this text, with McElrath singing the hymns discussed in the text: Hugh T. McElrath, bass, *Great Hymns of Praise,* Sunday School Board of the Southern Baptist Convention, 5127–03, 1977.

Eskew, Harry, and Hugh T. McElrath. *Sing with Understanding: An Introduction to Christian Hymnology*. Nashville: Broadman Press, 1980.

A comprehensive textbook designed for use in colleges, universities, and seminaries as an introduction to hymnology. Discussion and analysis of hymns reference five hymnals: *Baptist Hymnal* (1975); *Lutheran Book of Worship* (1978); *The Methodist Hymnal* (1964); and *Ecumenical Praise* (1977). The work is divided into three major sections. In section one, "The Hymn in Perspective," the authors examine the components of a hymn—literature, music, Scripture, and theology. Section two, "The Hymn in History and Culture," traces the major streams of hymnody from the early Church through present day. A unique feature in this text is its consideration of the hymns from a cultural perspective (chapter 9). Section three, "The Hymn in Practice," discusses the various uses of a hymn in the life and work of the Church; evangelism, worship, education, and ministry are considered and developed in this section. Appendixes include: (1) an outline for a hymn festival on the hymns of Isaac Watts; and (2) a hymn analysis checklist. A twenty-eight page classified bibliography is also included.

Eskew, Harry, and Hugh T. McElrath. *Sing with Understanding: An Introduction to Christian Hymnology*. 2nd ed., rev. and expanded. Nashville: Church Street Press, 1995.

Updated and keyed to more recent hymnals from a variety of Protestant denominations: *The Baptist Hymnal* (1991); *Hymnbook 1982* (Episcopal); *Lutheran Book of Worship* (1978); *The United Methodist Hymnal* (1989); and *The Presbyterian Hymnal* (1990). The section on cultural perspectives has been updated to examine a broad range of hymnic traditions. Also includes a completely new section dealing with current trends and issues in hymnody. Again, there are helpful appendixes, and the indexes have been greatly expanded and improved from the first edition.

McElrath, Hugh T. and Carol Doran. *An Outline of a Brief Course in Hymnody.* Boston: The Hymn Society in the United States and Canada, 1998.

This text grew from the collaboration of Doran and McElrath for a course on hymnody taught in conjunction with the annual meeting of The Hymn Society. Essentially, this text was designed to accompany a "mini-course" in hymnology, and, despite its brevity, it is amazingly complete and useful.

Hymnals and Hymnal Companions

Reynolds, William J., ed. *Baptist Hymnal.* Nashville: Convention Press, 1975.

McElrath was a member of the Theological and Doctrinal Evaluation Subcommittee for this hymnal. Contains "We praise Thee with our minds, O Lord."

Forbis, Wesley L., ed. *The Baptist Hymnal.* Nashville: Convention Press, 1991.

McElrath served on the Theology/Doctrine Committee for this hymnal. His largest contribution on a hymnal committee is in this hymnal. Contains "We praise You with our minds, O Lord."

Adams, Jere V., ed. *Handbook to* The Baptist Hymnal. Nashville: Convention Press, 1992.

McElrath served as coordinating editor for this handbook and contributed 160 articles for inclusion in it. Keyed to *The Baptist Hymnal* (1991).

Articles and Essays

"The Case for Hymnology." *Review and Expositor* 57 (1960): 184–98.

This published essay is a version of McElrath's inaugural address originally given on September 15, 1959, entitled "The Services of Hymnology to the Broadening of Understanding between the Music and Non-Music Ministries." The focus of this writing, like the original address, champions the role of hymnology and its importance in the seminary community and especially within the local church. This published version is more refined—lacking certain aspects of the dialog and illustrations used in the original speech—but maintains the integrity of the work as a whole.

McElrath addresses the historic conflicts of music in the Church, highlighting the growth and development of music in worship, and its influence and impact as documented in history. He juxtaposes the artistic role of music with the pragmatic role of service to God, contrasting the role of the musician's ministry with the nonmusical ministries of the Church.

Ultimately the author forges the concept that hymnology is one possible solution to the conflicts of the Church, for in hymnology one finds that a variety of interests and disciplines intersect. He then goes on to examine hymnology from various angles with attention to theology, music, education, and worship.

"How Music Helps Men Worship." *Brotherhood Journal* 34, no. 4 (October/November/December 1964): 11–14.

McElrath develops three arguments why music is important in worship: (1) music gives the individual a means to participate actively in worship; (2) music allows the individual to proclaim faith and teach Christian truths to others; and (3) music provides an opportunity for fellowship. He asks why congregational singing among men is weak and follows this inquiry with a helpful response.

"God, Man, and Redemption in Modern Music." *Review and Expositor* 61 (1964): 179–90. Jointly authored with Jay Wilkey.

In this dense musical and theological discourse the authors explore the role of contemporary "art" music in redemption. Allowing that art has the ability to communicate a modicum of truth, and that music is the most universally used art form in the Church, McElrath and Wilkey examine the European musical developments of the first half of the twentieth century from a Christian perspective. The authors trace the significant composers and composition styles associated with each: Arnold Schoenberg with atonal and twelve-tone composition; Alban Berg, his more traditional student; Anton Webern, the more forward-looking student of Schoenberg; and Béla Bartók with the influences of Hungarian folk songs. The modern influence of jazz is also treated in this writing. In the final analysis they conclude: "Only that music which truly expresses man's contemporary situation can hope to portray man's redemption within that situation" (189). Therefore, they determine that the music of Alban Berg is best suited to meet this criteria.

"We Proclaim Our Beliefs Through Congregational Song." *The Church Musician* 16, no. 12 (December 1965): 6–7.

In this short essay McElrath gives a three-part rationale for singing hymns based on the physical, mental, and spiritual well-being of the individual. Although McElrath makes no mention of it, this essay appears to parallel the structure of his hymn, "We praise thee with our minds, O Lord," published one year earlier and popularized in subsequent Baptist hymnals.

"Praise and Worship." *Review and Expositor* 62 (1965): 293–306.

Wrestling with semantics, McElrath draws a clear distinction between "praise" and "worship." He sets forth a scriptural and theological understanding of music in worship and uses this discussion as a launching pad for the primary focus of his article: hymns in worship. In the remainder of the article he examines the salient qualities of hymns, both musical and literary, that make them acceptable vehicles for congregational use.

"Hymns of Concern." *The Church Musician* 18, no. 10 (October 1967): 4–6.

A forward-looking article in which McElrath places great emphasis on the social aspect of worship. He observes that the Baptist tradition has many hymns addressed to others, primarily focused on evangelism or spiritual nurture, but few hymns make a reference to living out the life of Christ with regard to social concerns. He suggests more hymns of this nature would protect worship from becoming a completely internal affair.

"The Oldest Christian Hymn." *The Church Musician* 18, no. 4 (April 1967): 14–15.

This brief article appears to be a predecessor of the "Hymn-of-the-Month." Here McElrath examines the text, "Shepherd of tender youth," attributed to Clement of Alexandria. McElrath's objective is to find ways that hymns from the past such as this one can have contemporary meaning and purpose. To that end McElrath makes timely and timeless observations about a hymn borne out of adversity and its implications for modern humanity.

"Hymns and Hymn-Singing in the Twentieth Century." *The Youth Musician* 3, no. 2 (Second Quarter 1968): A-12, A-13, and A-18.

In this brief essay geared to the youth culture of the 1960s, McElrath expresses empathy for the needs of young people for generationally-relevant language in their hymnody. He produces a short list of trends he perceives in hymnody, encouraging young people to see their hymnic tradition from a new perspective. He also encourages them to put their faith expressions into verse and thereby contribute to hymnody in their own contemporary language. Examples of hymns written by youth are given.

"What's Happened to the Bible in Baptist Congregational Music?" *Music Journal of the Southern Baptist Church Music Conference* 3, no. 3 (January 1970): 18–28.

McElrath declares this article to be primarily a "plea for the restoration of the Bible, and especially the Psalter, to Baptist musical worship" (18). He argues for the importance of the Psalter in contemporary worship claiming that the singing of Scripture, especially the Psalms, will help to combat biblical illiteracy, and that biblical hymnody will encourage Bible study. A classic expression of McElrath's passion for Scripture and hymnody.

"Music in the History of the Church." *Review and Expositor* 69 (1972): 141–59.

In this article McElrath seeks to provide an "appraisal" of music history in the Church from a contemporary perspective. He examines the significant events throughout the history of church music in a detailed, yet succinct summary. Although divergent streams are acknowledged, his goal is to trace the elements of church music history that have strong connections to contemporary evangelical worship and church music and that uphold a high view of music in worship. Salient points from each of the major historical periods throughout the development of church music are cited to support his case.

"Music, Worship, and Congregational Involvement." *Music Journal of the Southern Baptist Church Music Conference* 6 (1974): 1–29.

Originally presented at the SBCMC conference held in Dallas, Texas. Presented on the heels of the release of the 1975 Baptist hymnal, with its primary focus on hymnody as a means of involving the congregation in worship. McElrath starts with a biblical rationale for congregational involvement, reminding the reader that we are a "priesthood of believers" with responsibilities and biblical mandates to sing to God and to each other. McElrath states the need for more congregational involvement in planning worship and in leading worship always with an emphasis on the congregation's need to sing. He provides some creative ways to involve people in various aspects of worship and upholds the Kierkegaardian model as the ideal to which Baptists should ascribe. Also in condensed form in *The Hymn* 26, no. 1 (January 1975): 15–24.

"A Tribute to Three Great Southern Baptist Musicians." *Search* 5, no. 3 (Spring 1975): 16–21.

McElrath begins by putting forth the criteria he uses in determining "greatness" among three famous Southern Baptist church musicians: Isham Emmanuel Reynolds, Baylus Benjamin McKinney, and Claude Marion Almand. McElrath provides basic biographical information and succinctly examines their salient contributions to music in the Southern Baptist tradition.

"Musical Resources for the Study of Hosea." *Review and Expositor* 72 (1975): 503–06.

A concise article in which the author compiles a list of helpful resources related to the Old Testament book of Hosea. McElrath highlights two principal themes: God's faithfulness and patience, and God's call to return to him in a spirit of repentance. McElrath then offers suggested anthems, solos, and congregational hymns appropriate to each theme. The literature list is given as representative and by no means exhaustive, designed only to be a starting point for the student of this unique narrative.

"Perspectives in Public Worship in the 1970s." *Review and Expositor* 75 (1978): 361–70.

In this survey of current trends McElrath begins by challenging those in the Free Church tradition who have the responsibility to plan and lead worship. He then explores the transition of public worship in an age of innovation and experimentation. He briefly examines the similarities in ecumenical worship brought about by the return to historic principles, the subjective and objective aspects of celebration and the impact of "humanizing" worship, the diversity of experience of lay leadership which contributes a pluralism to worship, and the additional creativity that occurs when pastors rely on gifted lay persons and realize the necessity for interdependence.

"HSGBI Manchester 1978." *The Hymn* 29, no. 4 (October 1978): 245–47.

McElrath reviews the annual meeting of The Hymn Society of Great Britain and Ireland in this article. McElrath attended this conference and was the official representative for The Hymn Society of America.

"Hymnody Among Southern Baptists." *American Organist* 14, no. 5 (May 1980): 19.

A brief historical survey of the role of hymn singing in the Southern Baptist tradition from a sociological perspective.

"Music—the Healer." *Search* 11, no. 2 (Winter 1981): 42–52; rep. in *The Church Musician* 47, no. 1 (October 1995): 8–10.

McElrath begins with a series of quotations regarding the healing power of music. This essay provides a historical approach to understanding the basic tenets of present-day music therapy. The author examines the ancient practices of magic and the relationship of the medicine man, music, and rhythm in the healing rituals of primitive cultures. He examines the historic Greek philosophies of music connected with the gods of mythology. McElrath places the healing aspects of music in a Christian context—first examining music historically in the Church, in light of relevant scriptures, and then looking at the present-day role of music and its ability to minister to the basic needs of the individual. The article does not attempt to address the specific principles or methods of music therapy, but rather, examines the role of music and its general therapeutic values.

"A Charles Wesley Hymn Service." *The Church Musician* 34, no. 1 (October 1982): 24–5.

A hymn service highlighting the hymns of Charles Wesley, including a concise and insightful commentary for the transition points within the service.

"Go South, Young Man!" *The Church Musician* 33, no. 6 (March 1982): 45–7.

In this concise article devoted to music missions, McElrath recounts the circumstances that led to his work at The Southern Baptist Theological Seminary and his personal interests in training men and women for foreign music missions. McElrath details the events connected with the first "practicum in music missions," a Southern Seminary field experience in which McElrath and his wife, Ruth, took a group of students to Venezuela to work with missionaries for three weeks in 1981.

"HSGBI Durham 1983." *The Hymn* 34, no. 4 (October 1983): 248–50.

McElrath summarizes the events of the annual meeting of The Hymn Society of Great Britain and Ireland meeting in Durham in 1983.

"Koreans Launch a New Hymnal." *The Hymn* 35, no. 2 (April 1984): 119.

A short summary of events associated with the publication of a Korean hymnal.

"Turning Points in the Story of Baptist Church Music." *Baptist History and Heritage* 19, no. 1 (January 1984): 6–16.

This article, spanning four centuries, highlights significant turning points in Baptist church music, beginning with the contributions of Benjamin Keach as found in Keach's *Spiritual Melody*. It then documents the texts of Isaac Watts, the tunes found in John Rippon's *Selection of Psalm and Hymn Tunes,* the influence of both the Wesleyan Revival and the Great

Awakening, and the position of Baptists on musical issues. It briefly explains the Charleston and Sandy Creek traditions and, in a helpful summary, enumerates the effects of the Great Awakening. McElrath traces two divergent streams of Baptist church music present during the Civil War era, highlighting use of *The Psalmist* in the North and *The Sacred Harp* in the South. He discusses the installation of the first organ in a Baptist church in 1834 and the effect it had in such a strongly-rooted Calvinistic tradition. Gospel songs and their role are also discussed. The work makes no claim to be inclusive, but offers glimpses of a variety of influences thought to be important in the history of Baptist church music.

"Bethlehem, 1985 International Conference on Hymnody." *The Hymn* 36, no. 4 (October 1985): 36–40.

In-depth coverage of hymnological conference, Bethlehem, Pennsylvania. McElrath details the events of this joint meeting of The Hymn Society of Great Britain and Ireland, the Internationale Arbeitsgemeinschaft für Hymnologie, and The Hymn Society of America.

"Church Music at Southern." *Review and Expositor* 82 (Winter 1985): 101–10.

In this article McElrath traces the historical development of The SBTS School of Church Music from the early influences of Manly and Broadus through the death of President Fuller. He discusses three key issues that were influential on the direction of church music at Southern Seminary: First, he examines the contributions of Manly and Broadus and their early emphasis on training ministers in the area of hymnology. Second, McElrath discusses the founding of the SCM and the early debates surrounding whether a seminary should have a music school. Third and finally, he deals with opposing philosophies present in the churches (the Charleston versus the Sandy Creek traditions) and the efforts of the SCM to provide leadership and guidance as it strives to keep balance between these two contrasting traditions.

"A Lesson from a Gaggle of Geese!" *The Church Musician* 40, no. 5 (February 1989): 42.

McElrath details his personal account with a gaggle of geese in this editorial. He uses this image as a springboard to encourage dialogue within the SBCMC.

"Some Reformation Resources for Worship from John Calvin and His Circle." *Review and Expositor* 86 (1989): 65–75.

McElrath focuses on Calvin's Geneva rites as a means for Baptists to examine their heritage as they rethink the possibilities of incorporating historical worship forms of the Reformed tradition. Calvin's order of worship is provided along with a number of prayers appropriate to a variety of worship experiences. McElrath also highlights the importance of psalm singing in the Reformed tradition and then offers a list of psalms and psalm-based hymns found in *Baptist Hymnal* (1975), providing a helpful resource for those desiring to explore both the history and the present boundaries of their worship tradition.

"Tune Your Hearts . . ." *The Church Musician* 40, no. 7 (April 1989): 20.

This is McElrath's follow-up to his president's address delivered to the SBCMC in 1988. He begins with a call to membership by highlighting the purposes of the conference. Then he uses this format to encourage dialogue in the midst of diversity and urges members to continue to work together to strengthen the conference and the ministry of the Church throughout the denomination.

"Chamber Music . . . in Church?" *The Church Musician* 41, no. 11 (August 1990): 41–2.

In this editorial, McElrath seeks to explain church music in terms of chamber music. Much of the article reflects the influence of Augustine Smith as well as that of Erik Routley, in particular Routley's essay in *Music, Sacred and Profane* entitled "Music and Churchmanship."

"The Hymnbook as a Compendium of Theology." *Review and Expositor* 87 (1990): 11–31.

McElrath identifies theological weaknesses in the Baptist tradition, taking a firm stand on issues of worship and hymnody. The anticipated arrival of *The Baptist Hymnal* (1991) provided the motivation for this article. Having served on the Theology/Doctrine Committee for this hymnal, McElrath is well-equipped to examine the various aspects of theology addressed in this article. McElrath emphasizes a need for balancing hymns with gospel songs, always with a major focus on what the hymns say. He explores several key theological issues significant in the criteria for preparing *The Baptist Hymnal* (1991), including trinitarian hymns, hymns focusing on the work of the Holy Spirit, and the use of sexist and militant language.

Contributions to Larger Works

Abingdon Dictionary of Living Religions. Nashville: Abingdon, 1981.

Articles include "Bay Psalm Book," (93–4); "Gospel Songs," (284); "Gregorian Chant," (285); "Music, in Christianity," (503–06); and "The Sacred Harp" (637). In "Music, in Christianity," he offers a well-organized, historical overview of the major developments, seminal events, and traditional and folk sources which have influenced the Church and its music.

"Anniversaries of Hymns, Hymn Writers, and Composers." Annual series, 1984–1997. In *The Ministers* [sic] *Manual (Doran's)*, ed. James W. Cox. San Francisco: Harper Collins/Jossey Bass, 1925—.

In 1984, Cox became the editor of this historic and much-used minister's manual, and he enlisted McElrath to note important hymnic anniversaries. Given in twenty-five-year increments, this annual notation is a hymnological study in and of itself. By his own design, McElrath's contribution to this annual changed in 1998; see "Sermon Suggestions: Congregational Music" below.

"Spirituality and Worship." In *Becoming Christian*, ed. Bill J. Leonard, 46–58. Louisville: Westminster/John Knox Press, 1990. Jointly authored with Bill J. Leonard.

McElrath's contribution to this jointly-authored chapter consists of the final four pages. McElrath begins by addressing "Spirituality and the Music of Worship." Here he finds biblical precedence for the uses of music and discusses the intangible quality of this "language of the soul." He continues in the next section to address "The Contradictory Nature of Church Music." In this section, McElrath discusses issues related to familiar and unfamiliar music and the responsibility of the mature worshiper to make music and to listen to music with an openness that celebrates this creative and imaginative art. Finally, McElrath, as a promoter of congregational song, encourages "Praying the Hymns." That is to say, hymn singing can and should be a prayerful act in which the entire congregation participates.

"Hugh T. McElrath, Church Music 1949–1992 (1992–)." In *How I Have Changed My Mind: Essays by Retired Professors of The Southern Baptist Theological Seminary*, ed. John D. W. Watts, 116–123. Louisville: *Review and Expositor*, 1993.

McElrath reflects on the good fortune that has been afforded him throughout his life as a Christian and an educator. He reminisces about his childhood, early family life, and educational experience, acknowledging the providence of God in autobiographical writing. He then focuses on aspects of his teaching career that have undergone significant change over the years, particularly his ideas concerning American music, ministering to congregations, and new directions in teaching methods. This article gives clear insight into the life of one who is grateful for his heritage, thankful to his Creator, and always open to growth and new opportunities.

"Hymnody, Baptist." In *Dictionary of Baptists in America*, ed. Bill J. Leonard, 148–9. Downers Grove, Illinois: InterVarsity Press, 1994.

Historical overview of significant figures who have contributed to the core of Baptist hymnody in their roles as authors, composers, and hymnologists.

"'Sermon Suggestions: Congregational Music.'" Annual series, 1998–2003. In *The Minister's Manual*, ed. James W. Cox. San Francisco: Harper Collins/Jossey Bass, 1925—.

McElrath shifted emphasis for his annual contribution to *The Minister's Manual* in 1998, which he continued until 2003. Hymnic suggestions are given for each Sunday of the lectionary year, with brief information about each hymn provided.

Hymns by Hugh T. McElrath

"We praise thee with our minds, O Lord." © 1964 Broadman Press (SESAC).

"We praise You with our minds, O Lord." Revised. © 1964 Broadman Press (SESAC).

"To our God we lift our voices." © 1976 Hugh T. McElrath.

"Great God, all power is yours in heav'n and earth." © 1985 Hugh T. McElrath.

"O God of might, through golden years of light." © 1995 Hugh T. McElrath.

"Sound the Word and share God's love." © 1997 Broadman Press (SESAC).

Hymn Tune SAMOHT. Tune by Hugh T. McElrath, arranged and harmonized by Ronald Turner. © 1997 Broadman Press (SESAC).

Published Lectures and Addresses

"A Philosophy of Church Music for Training Church Musicians by Our Seminary Schools of Church Music." *Proceedings of the Southern Baptist Church Music Conference* (1968): 13–16.

In 1968 McElrath, serving as the coordinator for a symposium of the SBCMC, presented "A Philosophy of Church Music for Training Church Musicians by Our Seminary Schools of Church Music." He acknowledged the growing interest in the field of church music and the need to provide quality education designed to produce well-equipped church musicians prepared to meet the challenges of music ministry in the local church.

"La Teología de la Adoración." *Diálogo Teológico* 14 (1979): 7–38.

A Spanish translation of a series of lectures that McElrath presented at an annual pastor's conference in Buenos Aires, Argentina, September 26–30, 1977.

"Seven Vignettes: Church Musicians in Southern Baptist Life and History." *Proceedings of the Southern Baptist Church Music Conference* (1985): 13–21.

A historical glimpse at the developing role of professional music ministry in the Southern Baptist tradition related through the lives and experiences of various individuals, including the author's own. Highly autobiographical at points, giving great insight into McElrath's development and growth as a church musician and educator.

"The Minister of Music in Southern Baptist Life." *Baptist History and Heritage* 21, no. 3 (July 1986): 9–20.

This article, originally an address, was presented in April 1986 at a meeting of the Historical Commission of the SBC and the Southern Baptist Historical Society. It was later republished in *The Church Musician* 38, no. 8 (May 1987): 4–7, 38–40. McElrath, ever the historian, briefly traces the origin of the music minister, laying the foundation with scriptural justification before highlighting early developments which led to the Reformation. Then, after he connects Baptists with the influence of John Calvin, McElrath proceeds to outline the development of the position of music minister in the Southern Baptist tradition beginning in the early 1900s. This in-depth article follows the stages of development within the Church that established the need for the professional minister of music. After tracing the growth and development of the position through most of the century, he tackles issues of education, training, and ordination. He then offers a thorough list of observations, emphasizing the role and the positive effects of the minister of music in the evolving life of Southern Baptist congregations.

"President's Address: With One Voice." *Proceedings of the Southern Baptist Church Music Conference* (1988): 61–74.

Printed form of the address that Hugh T. McElrath gave at the SBCMC held in San Antonio, Texas, in 1988. McElrath used this occasion to call for unity among Southern Baptists; his lengthy, detailed address is essentially a plea for the conference to hold together despite the conflict over worship styles. He provides a thorough list of reasons for unity as he seeks to be sympathetic and understanding to both sides.

"President's Report." *Proceedings of the Southern Baptist Church Music Conference* (1989): 49–51.

A brief report filed on the "State of the Church" in which McElrath reports in the final year of his tenure as president of the SBCMC that the conference is stable. He urges further dialogue at this crucial juncture in the history of the conference and offers a word of hope, looking expectantly to the future.

"The Use of Music: A Prepared Statement." In *On the State of Church Music*, III (papers presented on February 21, 1995, at the Center for Church Music), 37–41. Jefferson City, Tenn.: Center for Church Music, Carson-Newman College, 1995.

Here McElrath describes (and makes clear that he is not defining) worship. He addresses the controversial theme, "Making Worship Attractive," and concludes that this is not our responsibility. He builds a solid argument for his position and then briefly discusses the role of "participation music" in worship. He offers his opinion on the use of three types of music frequently associated with worship: (1) popular music, (2) familiar music, and (3) worship music. With an affinity for the latter, McElrath stresses the importance of educating worshipers and moving away from a passive approach to more active participation.

"How Knowledgeable of the Psalter was William Walker, A. S. H.?" Forthcoming in *Hymnology in the Service of the Church: Essays in Honor of Harry Eskew*, ed. Paul R. Powell.

Lecture honoring the retirement of Harry Eskew as professor of music, New Orleans Baptist Theological Seminary, New Orleans, Louisiana, 2001.

Select Unpublished Lectures and Addresses

"Valedictory: An Appreciation and a Warning." Address to the School of Church Music Graduating Class of 1952, The Southern Baptist Theological Seminary, Louisville, Ky., May 3, 1952.

"The Central Business of the Church." First Baptist Church Choir Banquet, Owensboro, Ky., June 16, 1955, *et alia tempora et loca.*

"Songs of Bondage and of Freedom." Beechwood Baptist Church, Louisville, Ky., September 28, 1958.

"The Services of Hymnology to the Broadening of Understanding between the Music and Non-Music Ministries." Inaugural address, The Southern Baptist Theological Seminary, Louisville, Ky., September 15, 1959.

"The Modern 'Recovery of Worship' and Its Effect on Our Baptist Worship." Address on Missionary Day, The Southern Baptist Theological Seminary, March 28, 1962.

"The Call to Hymnic Pilgrimage: 'Sing unto the Lord a New Song.'" Chapel Address, The Southern Baptist Theological Seminary, October 31, 1962.

"The Praise of God—Our Beginning, Middle, and Ending." First Baptist Church, Beaufort, S. C. , October 11, 1964 (on the occasion of the choir's dedication).

"The Excellence of Our Calling." Address before the Kentucky Church Music Directors' meeting, November 11, 1964.

"Music and Worship." Regent's Park College, Oxford University, United Kingdom, October 16, 1970.

"Music's Parable for Our Living & Service." Immanuel Baptist Church, Lexington, Ky., September 28, 1973, *et alia tempora et loca.*

"Hymns in the Reform Tradition." John Knox Presbyterian Church, Louisville, Ky., September 7, 1975, *et alia tempora et loca.*

"A Singing Look at *The Baptist Hymnal*: Something Old . . . Something New . . . Something Borrowed . . . Something Blue . . . ." St. Matthews Baptist Church, Louisville, Ky., September 28, 1975.

"The Place of the Gospel Song in Today's Church Worship." Crescent Hill Baptist Church, Louisville, Ky., October 28, 1975.

"Creative Uses of the Hymnal." Two Lectures at the Stetson University Church Music Institute, Deland, Fla., January 11–12, 1977.

I. "Creative Use of the Hymnal: A Textual Approach."
II. "Creative Approaches to Hymns and Hymn-Singing: A Musical Approach."

"Some Aspects of the Theology of Worship." Five lectures given at the Annual Conference and Pastor's Retreat Under the Auspices of the Seminario Internacional Teológico Bautista, Buenos Aires, Argentina, September 26–30, 1977.

I. "The Nature of Christian Worship as Response."
II. "The Nature of Christian Worship as Dialogical Action."
III. "The Nature of Christian Worship as Sacrificial Offering."
IV. "The Nature of Christian Worship as Celebrative Play."
V. "The Nature of Christian Worship as Drama."

"Hymns in the Revival Experience." Georgia Baptist Church Music Conference, Tift College, Forsyth, Ga., October 14, 1978.

"Grow in Grace and in Knowledge: 200th Anniversary of *Olney Hymns* (1779)." Lecture for the Louisville chapters of The Hymn Society of America and the American Guild of Organists, Louisville, Ky., September 8, 1979.

"God's Seven Freedoms Promised in Psalm 23." St. Matthews United Methodist Church, Louisville, Ky., October 14, 1979.

"What's Going On in Hymnody?" Louisville Baptist Conference, Airport Road Baptist Church, Louisville, Ky., August 31, 1981.

"O Sing unto the Lord a New Song." For the Fellowship of United Methodist Musicians, Frankfort, Ky., May 15, 1982.

"Hymns—The People's Sacrifice of Praise." Douglass Boulevard Christian Church, Louisville, Ky., August 16, 1982.

"The Significance of the Choir in Leading the People's Song" (the why and how of hymn services). Christ United Methodist Church Choir Retreat, Owensboro, Ky., February 18, 1983.

"The Why, What, and How of Congregational Singing in Worship." Three Lectures for the Church Music Conference in Seoul, Korea, January 9–12, 1984.

"1984—Anniversary Year for Thirteen Hymn and Tune Writers." MacDowell Music Club, Crescent Hill United Methodist Church, Louisville, Ky., May 21, 1984.

"Worshipping with Isaiah Through Jesus Christ." First Baptist Church, Nassau, Bahamas, January 19, 1986.

"Sing with Understanding" (a series of lectures). Smoke Rise Baptist Church, Stone Mountain, Ga., February 4, 1989.

"The Outlook for the Future of *Southern Harmony* Singing." Baptist College Music Faculties, Kentucky Baptist Building, Middletown, Ky., April 1, 1989.

"Singing and Sacrifice." The First Baptist Church, Mt. Healthy, Ohio, August 13, 1989.

"Sacred Harp Singing." Baptist College Faculty Conference, Cedarmore, Ky., September 22, 1989.

"The Shame & the Glory of American Hymns and Hymn Singing." The Southern Baptist Theological Seminary, Louisville, Ky., February 16, 1990.

"The Musical Diversity in the Southern Baptist Convention and How *The Baptist Hymnal* (1991) Speaks to It." Colgate Baptist Church, Clarksville, Ind., September 14, 1991.

"An Introduction to the New Presbyterian Hymn Book—*Hymns, Psalms, and Spiritual Songs.*" Highland Presbyterian Church, Louisville, Ky., September 22, 1991.

"Hymn Singing and the Dramatic Dialog of Worship." First Baptist Church, Taylorsville, Ky., February 16, 1992.

"Let's Get Acquainted with *The Baptist Hymnal* (1991)." Calvary Baptist Church, Madison, Ind., June 17, 1992.

"Donald Winters: The Contributions of a Musical Churchman." Founder's Day address presented in chapel at The Southern Baptist Theological Seminary, Louisville, Ky., February 5, 1991.

"The Theology of Worship." Two lectures presented at the Seminario Internacional Teológico Bautista, Buenos Aires, Argentina, September 8, 1992.

I. "Christian Worship: Trinitarian in Shape."

II. "Christian Worship: Christocentric in Focus."

"Perspectives on the Fifty-Year History of the School of Church Music of The Southern Baptist Theological Seminary." Address at the fiftieth anniversary banquet, Crystal Ballroom, Brown Hotel, Louisville, Ky., October 18, 1994.

"The Significance of 'Singing Billy' Walker and His *Southern Harmony* (1835)." Address given before the Jacksonville, Florida, chapter of the American Guild of Organists, January 9, 1996.

"Praise and Worship Music: Bane or Blessing?" Symposium paper presented before the Penney Farms Retirement Community, Penney Farms, Fla., April 13, 1998.

"Will There Be Another Baptist Hymnal?" A hymn forum with J. Philip Landgrave, Hugh T. McElrath, and Elmer Martens. Sponsored by the Louisville chapter of The Hymn Society in the United States and Canada at The Southern Baptist Theological Seminary, Louisville, Ky., April 26, 2000.

"The Centrality of the Eucharist in Christian Worship: Various Meanings of Holy Communion Expressed by Hymn-Writers of the Church." Address presented before the Penney Farms Retirement Community, Penney Farms, Fla., June 26, 2000.

"Why Do We Sing Amens at the End of Hymns?" Symposium paper presented before the Penney Farms Retirement Community, Penney Farms, Fla., October 10, 2000.

Published Interviews

McElrath, Hugh T. "An Interview with Hugh T. McElrath." Interview by David W. Music (Northfield, Minn., July 10, 1991). *The Hymn* 42, no. 4 (October 1991): 10–13.

This interview with Hugh T. McElrath took place at the annual meeting of The Hymn Society in 1991. McElrath recounts his long history with

The Hymn Society and discusses aspects of his career as a hymnologist. He responds to questions concerning his teaching, his co-authored textbook *Sing with Understanding*, shape-note singing, his work as coordinating editor of the *Handbook to* The Baptist Hymnal, and his work in music missions.

"A Reporter's Telephone Call." *Young Musicians* 23, no. 2 (January/February/March 1993): 14.

A brief telephone interview with Hugh T. McElrath in which he responds to questions concerning the circumstances surrounding the writing of his hymn "We praise You with our minds, O Lord."

Book Reviews

Stevenson, Robert. *Protestant Church Music in America: A Short Survey of Men and Movements from 1564 to the Present*. New York: W. W. Norton, 1966. In *Review and Expositor* 67 (Spring 1970): 253–4.

Routley, Erik. *The Musical Wesleys*. New York: Oxford University Press, 1969. In *Review and Expositor* 68 (Winter 1971): 148–9.

Habets, Alfred. *Borodin and Liszt*. Translated with a Preface by Rosa Newmarch. Reprint of the 1895 edition published by Digby, Long, & Co., London. New York: AMS Press, Inc., 1977. In *Journal of the American Liszt Society* 12 (December 1982): 122–3.

Leaver, Robin A., ed. *Bibliotheca Hymnologica (1890)*. London: C. Higham, 1981. In *The Hymn* 34, no. 3 (July 1983): 185–6.

Lovelace, Austin C. *The Anatomy of Hymnody*. Chicago: G. I. A. Publications, 1983. In *The Southern Baptist Church Music Journal* 1 (1984): 36.

Johansson, Calvin M. *Music and Ministry: A Biblical Counterpoint*. Peabody, Mass.: Hendrickson Publishers, 1984. In *The Southern Baptist Church Music Journal* 2 (1985): 60–2.

Quillin, Roger T. *Meeting Christ in Handel's Messiah: Lent and Easter Messages Based on Handel's Texts and Music*. Minneapolis: Augsburg Publishing House, 1984. In *Review and Expositor* 83 (Winter 1986): 141–2.

Moloney, Raymond. *Our Eucharistic Prayers in Worship, Preaching and Study*. Wilmington, Del.: Michael Glazier, 1985. In *Review and Expositor* 84 (Summer 1987): 551–2.

Leaver, Robin A., ed. *Ways of Singing the Psalms*. In collaboration with David Mann and David Parkes. London: Collins Liturgical Publications, 1984. In *The Southern Baptist Church Music Journal* 4 (1987): 55–6.

Pass, David B. *Music and the Church: A Theology of Church Music.* Nashville: Broadman Press, 1989. In *The Southern Baptist Church Music Journal* 7 (1990): 54–9.

Clarkson, Margaret. *A Singing Heart.* Carol Stream, Illinois: Hope Publishing Company, 1987. In *Review and Expositor* 88 (1991): 298–9.

Warren, James I., Jr. *O For a Thousand Tongues: The History, Nature, and Influence of Music in the Methodist Tradition.* Grand Rapids, Mich.: Francis Asbury Press of Zondervan Publishing House, 1988. In *The Southern Baptist Church Music Journal* 8 (1991): 59–60.

Wicker, Vernon, ed. *The Hymnology Annual: An International Forum on the Hymn and Worship.* Volume 1. Berrien Springs, Mich.: Vande Vere Publishing, 1991. In *The Southern Baptist Church Music Journal* 9 (1992): 75–7.

Batastini, Robert J. and John Ferguson, ed. *Hymnal Supplement 1991.* Supplement to the *Lutheran Book of Worship* (1978). Chicago: G. I. A. Publications, 1991. In *The Hymn* 44, no. 1 (January 1993): 50.

Harper, John. *The Forms and Orders of Western Liturgy from the Tenth to the Eighteenth Century: A Historical Introduction and Guide for Students and Musicians.* Oxford: Clarendon Press, 1991; and White, James F. *Documents of Christian Worship: Descriptive and Interpretive Sources.* Louisville, Ky.: Westminster/John Knox Press, 1992. Joint review in *The Southern Baptist Church Music Journal* 10 (1993): 57–58.

Johansson, Calvin M. *Discipling Music Ministry: Twenty-first Century Directions.* Peabody, Mass.: Hendrickson Publishers, 1991; and Milligan, Thomas B., ed. *On the State of Church Music.* Jefferson City, Tenn.: Center for Church Music, Carson-Newman College, 1993. Joint review in *The Southern Baptist Church Music Journal* 11 (1994): 77–86.

Studwell, William E. and Dorothy. E. Jones. *Publishing Glad Tidings: Essays on Christmas Music.* New York: Haworth Press, 1998. In *The Hymn* 50, no.1 (January 1999): 54–6.

Hymn Stories

"Stand Up, Stand Up for Jesus." *Accent* 6, no. 1 (October 1975): 12.

"Ye Christian Heralds, Go Proclaim." *Accent* 6, no. 2 (November 1975): 12.

"Tell It Out with Gladness." *Accent* 6, no. 3 (December 1975): 10.

"Christ is the World's True Light." *Accent* 6, no. 4 (January 1976): 24.

"Christian Men, Arise and Give." *Accent* 6, no. 5 (February 1976): 24.

"Spread, O Spread the Mighty Word." *Accent* 6, no. 6 (March 1976): 6.

"Ye Servants of God." *Accent* 6, no. 7 (April 1976): 10.

"God of Mercy, God of Grace." *Accent* 6, no. 8 (May 1976): 14.

"O Zion, Haste." *Accent* 6, no. 9 (June 1976): 7.

"Soldiers of Christ, in Truth Arrayed." *Accent* 6, no. 10 (July 1976): 6.

"Savior, Teach Me Day by Day." *Accent* 6, no. 11 (August 1976): 17.

"Thou, Whose Almighty Word." *Accent* 6, no. 12 (September 1976): 24.

"Spirit of God, Descend Upon My Heart." *The Church Musician* 32, no. 4 (January 1981): 8–12.

"Lord, I Want to Be a Christian." *The Church Musician* 32, no. 5 (February 1981): 12–15.

"Lead Me to Calvary." *The Church Musician* 32, no. 6 (March 1981): 16–21.

"Christ the Lord is Risen Today." *The Church Musician* 32, no. 7 (April 1981): 4–9.

"The Lord's My Shepherd." *The Church Musician* 32, no. 8 (May 1981): 18–22, 48–49.

"O God, Our Help in Ages Past." *The Church Musician* 32, no. 9 (June 1981): 12–17, 23.

"Awake, Awake to Love and Work." *The Church Musician* 32, no. 10 (July 1981): 15–19.

"All Hail the Power of Jesus' Name." *The Church Musician* 32, no. 11 (August 1981): 18–23.

"Victory in Jesus." *The Church Musician* 32, no. 12 (September 1981): 12–17.

"Glorious Is Thy Name." *The Church Musician* 33, no. 1 (October 1981): 41–7.

"We Gather Together." *The Church Musician* 33, no. 2 (November 1981): 40–5.

"O Sing a Song of Bethlehem." *The Church Musician* 33, no. 3 (December 1981): 4–9.

"Break Thou the Bread of Life." *The Church Musician* 33, no. 4 (January 1982): 20–5.

"Somebody's Knocking at Your Door." *The Church Musician* 33, no. 5 (February 1982): 19–23.

"The Solid Rock." *The Church Musician* 33, no. 6 (March 1982): 17–21, 28.

"The First Lord's Day." *The Church Musician* 33, no. 7 (April 1982): 4–7, 28.

"Jesus! Name of Wondrous Love." *The Church Musician* 33, no. 8 (May 1982): 40–3, 49–50.

"The Old Rugged Cross." *The Church Musician* 33, no. 9 (June 1982): 18–24.

"His Gentle Look." *The Church Musician* 33, no. 10 (July 1982): 18–21, 49.

"To God Be the Glory." *The Church Musician* 33, no. 11 (August 1982): 40–6.

"Jesus! What a Friend for Sinners." *The Church Musician* 33, no. 12 (September 1982): 40–4.

"Praise the Lord Who Reigns Above." *The Church Musician* 34, no. 1 (October 1982): 19–23.

"Come, Ye Thankful People, Come." *The Church Musician* 34, no. 2 (November 1982): 10–14, 47.

"Good Christian Men, Rejoice." *The Church Musician* 34, no. 3 (December 1982): 4–8.

"O God of Our Fathers." *The Church Musician* 34, no. 4 (January 1983): 22–28, 47.

"I Stand Amazed in the Presence." *The Church Musician* 34, no. 5 (February 1983): 40–5.

"For Me." *The Church Musician* 34, no. 6 (March 1983): 12–16.

"Rejoice, the Lord is King." *The Church Musician* 34, no. 7 (April 1983): 9–11, 45–6.

"Send Me, O Lord, Send Me." *The Church Musician* 34, no. 8 (May 1983): 20–5.

"My Country, 'Tis of Thee." *The Church Musician* 34, no. 9 (June 1983): 40–4.

"Like a River Glorious." *The Church Musician* 34, no. 10 (July 1983): 40–4.

"Day by Day." *The Church Musician* 34, no. 11 (August 1983): 21–5.

"Tell the Good News." *The Church Musician* 34, no. 12 (September 1983): 40–4.

The following hymn articles are taken and adapted from *Handbook to* The Baptist Hymnal (Nashville: Convention Press, 1992):

"God, Our Author and Creator." *The Church Musician* 44, no. 2 (January/February/March 1993): 79. Jointly authored with Harry Eskew.

"Your Love, O God, Has Called Us Here." *The Church Musician* 44, no. 3 (April/May/June 1993): 90. Jointly authored with Paul A. Richardson.

"Lord, Here Am I (Master, Thou Callest)." *The Church Musician* 45, no. 1 (October/November/December 1993): 89.

"Would You Bless Our Homes and Families." *The Church Musician* 45, no. 3 (April/May/June 1994): 89–90. Jointly authored with Harry Eskew and Paul A. Richardson.

"And Can It Be." *The Church Musician*, 45, no. 4 (July/August/September 1994): 89. Jointly authored with Scotty W. Gray.

"Fill the Earth with Music." *The Church Musician* 45, no. 4 (July/August/September 1994): 88–9. Jointly authored with David W. Music.

"For the Fruit of All Creation." *The Church Musician* 46, no. 1 (October/November/December 1994): 49. Jointly authored with Donald C. Brown.

"A Servant of the Least." *The Church Musician* 46, no. 2 (January/February/March 1995): 50. Jointly authored with Milburn Price.

"I've Come to Tell." *The Church Musician* 46, no. 3 (April/May/June 1995): 52.

Unpublished M.S.M. Thesis and Ph.D. Dissertation

"The Improvement of Baptist Worship Through Music." M.S.M. thesis, The Southern Baptist Theological Seminary, 1948.

This youthful and ambitious work is McElrath's earliest extant attempt to present the philosophical ideals that were beginning to shape his thinking regarding church music in general and hymnology in particular. This writing displays his passion for the ongoing ministry of the Church—strongly encouraging change in several identified areas of corporate Baptist worship. The format for the seven chapters is as follows:

1. Worship in General—explores the biblical and historical roots of worship with application made to Baptist worship in particular;
2. Major Factors in Worship Improvement;

3. The Place of Music in Worship;
4. The Worship Uses of Hymns and Hymn Singing;
5. The Organ—An Instrument of Worship;
6. The Choir and Its Ministry in Worship; and
7. Training in Worship.

"A Study of the Motets of Ignatio Donati with Transcriptions." Ph.D. diss., University of Rochester, Eastman School of Music, 1967.

A lengthy scholarly work in two volumes. Volume one places the Italian composer in historical context and examines his "few-voiced motets" in great detail. Volume two contains transcriptions of the motets in modern notation.

Dissertations and Theses Written with Professor McElrath's Guidance

Doctoral Dissertations Supervised by Professor McElrath

Warren, Jerry Lee. "The *Motetti à Voce Sola* of Mauritio Cassati." D.M.A. diss., The Southern Baptist Theological Seminary, 1967.

Crouse, David L. "The Work of Allen D. Carden and Associates in the Shape-Note Tune-Books *The Missouri Harmony, Western Harmony,* and *United States Harmony.*" D.M.A. diss., The Southern Baptist Theological Seminary, 1972.

Wingard, Alan Burl. "The Life and Works of William Batchelder Bradbury 1816–1868." D.M.A. diss., The Southern Baptist Theological Seminary, 1973.

Hammond, Paul G. "Music in Urban Revivalism in the Northern United States, 1800–1835." D.M.A. diss., The Southern Baptist Theological Seminary, 1974.

Downs, Cleamon Rubin. "A History of the Southern Baptist Church Music Conference, 1957–1973." D.M.A. diss., The Southern Baptist Theological Seminary, 1976.

Stevenson, George William. "The Hymnody of the Chocktaw Indians of Oklahoma." D.M.A. diss., The Southern Baptist Theological Seminary, 1977.

Wilhoit, Melvin Ross. "A Guide to the Principal Authors and Composers of Gospel Song of the Nineteenth Century." D.M.A. diss., The Southern Baptist Theological Seminary, 1982.

Landes, William Daniel. "A Hymnal Supplement for Use in the Chapel Services at The Southern Baptist Theological Seminary." D.M.A. diss., The Southern Baptist Theological Seminary, 1983.

Brown, Cynthia Clark. "Emma Lou Diemer: Composer, Performer, Educator, Church Musician." D.M.A. diss., The Southern Baptist Theological Seminary, 1985.

Carle, David Norman. "A History of the School of Church Music of The Southern Baptist Theological Seminary, 1944–1959." D.M.A. diss., The Southern Baptist Theological Seminary, 1986.

Measels, Donald Clark. "A Catalogue of Source Readings in Southern Baptist Church Music: 1828–1890." D.M.A. diss., The Southern Baptist Theological Seminary, 1986.

Howard, John David. "A Profile of the Current State of Music Used in Worship in the Churches of the Northwest Yearly Meeting of Friends." D.M.A. diss., The Southern Baptist Theological Seminary, 1988.

Poole, Thomas Daryl. "Toward an Integration of Music and Theology: Suggestions for the Construction of a Theological Definition of Music." D.M.A. diss., The Southern Baptist Theological Seminary, 1988.

Raley, J. Michael. "Johannes Ockeghem's *Gaude Maria virgo*." D.M.A. diss., The Southern Baptist Theological Seminary, 1988.

Rogers, Rhonda Speich. "The Life and Work of Donald Paul Hustad." D.M.A. diss., The Southern Baptist Theological Seminary, 1988.

Seel, Thomas Allen. "Toward a Theology of Music for Worship Derived from the Book of Revelation." D.M.A. diss., The Southern Baptist Theological Seminary, 1990.

Gregory, David Louis. "Southern Baptist Hymnals (1956, 1975, 1991) as Sourcebooks for Worship in Southern Baptist Churches." D.M.A. diss., The Southern Baptist Theological Seminary, 1994.

Hostetler, Harold Rutherford, Jr. "The Establishment of a United Baptist Choir for Trinidad." D.M.M. diss., The Southern Baptist Theological Seminary, 1994.

Dissertations Read and Approved by Professor McElrath as Committee Member

Quinn, Eugene Francis. "A Survey of the Principles and Practices of Contemporary American Nonliturgical Church Music." D.C.M. diss., The Southern Baptist Theological Seminary, 1962.

Washburn, Seaton Alfred. "Activity Teaching in Younger Children's Church Choirs." D.M.A. diss., The Southern Baptist Theological Seminary, 1973.

Shadinger, Richard Cole. "The Sacred Element in Piano Literature: A Historical Background and an Annotated Listing." D.M.A. diss., The Southern Baptist Theological Seminary, 1974.

Hawn, Charles Michael. "Implications and Adaptations of Piaget's Theory of Play for Preschool Curriculum." D.M.A. diss., The Southern Baptist Theological Seminary, 1975.

Smith, Robert Carl. "Creative Motion as a Technique: Four Sample Analyses and a Live Demonstration." D.M.A. diss., The Southern Baptist Theological Seminary, 1976.

Johnson, Norman Gary. "Healey Willan (1880–1968): His Life and Influences Important to Music." D.M.A. diss., The Southern Baptist Theological Seminary, 1979.

Richardson, Paul Akers. "A Guide for the Study of Solo Song Literature in the English Language by Selected Composers of the 20th Century." D.M.A. diss., The Southern Baptist Theological Seminary, 1979.

Rightmyer, James Robert. "A Documentary History of the Music Program of Second Presbyterian Church, Louisville, Kentucky: 1830–1980." D.M.A. diss., The Southern Baptist Theological Seminary, 1980.

Renfroe, Anita Boyle. "Emil von Sauer: A Catalogue of His Piano Works." D.M.A. diss., The Southern Baptist Theological Seminary, 1981.

Roberts, Maynard Wesley. "An Introduction to the Literature for Two Pianos and Orchestra, 1915–1950." D.M.A. diss., The Southern Baptist Theological Seminary, 1981.

Ganey, Janelle. "A Pedagogical Analysis of Solo Piano Sonatinas by North and South American Composers, 1963–1983." D.M.A. diss., The Southern Baptist Theological Seminary, 1985.

Davidson, Paul O. "The Extra-Liturgical *Geistliches Lied* 1800–1915: A Survey with Musical and Theological Analyses of Fifty Selected Works." D.M.A. diss., The Southern Baptist Theological Seminary, 1989.

Roby, Billy Andrew. "A Performer's Guide to the Songs of Henri Duparc." D.M.A. diss., The Southern Baptist Theological Seminary, 1991.

Smoak, Jeff C., Jr. "An Annotated Catalogue of Articles on Vocal Literature from Selected American Periodicals." D.M.A. diss., The Southern Baptist Theological Seminary, 1991.

Kim, Youngmi Song. "A Performer's Study of *Tabulatura Nova* (1624) by Samuel Scheidt." D.M.A. diss., The Southern Baptist Theological Seminary, 1992.

Moir, Walton Alexander. "An Affirmation and Enrichment of Baptist Spirituality in a Canadian Context." D. Min. research project, The Southern Baptist Theological Seminary, 1992.

Berger, Joy Susanne. "Music as a Catalyst for Pastoral Care within the Remembering Tasks of Grief." D.M.A. diss., The Southern Baptist Theological Seminary, 1993.

Campbell, John Wert. "The Role of Plainchant in the Choral Music of John Rutter." D.M.A. diss., The Southern Baptist Theological Seminary, 1993.

Hill, Carol Wilson. "The Birth of a Brazilian Baptist Hymnal: A Church Music Drama." D.M.M. diss., The Southern Baptist Theological Seminary, 1994.

Walworth, Roger William. "The Hymnological Contributions of Robert Lowry (1826–1899)." D.M.A. diss., The Southern Baptist Theological Seminary, 1994.

Cherrix, Vernon Twilley. "Maurice Hinson: An Annotated Bibliography of His Writings." D.M.A. diss., The Southern Baptist Theological Seminary, 1997.

Combs, Barry Lynn. "Peter Cornelius's Choral Settings with Religious Texts and Pre-Existing Music." D.M.A. diss., The Southern Baptist Theological Seminary, 1997.

Howell, Edward Neal. "An Approach to Expressive and Creative Interpretation of Hymns for Worship." D.M.M. diss., The Southern Baptist Theological Seminary, 1997.

Tillman, Beverly Vaughn. "A Program for Enhancing the Role of Music in Worship at the First Baptist Church, Salem, Indiana." D.M.M. diss., The Southern Baptist Theological Seminary, 1998.

Master's Degree Theses Supervised by Professor McElrath

Kirby, Linnie Sue. "The Influence of John Calvin and His Circle on Present-Day Hymnody." M.S.M. thesis, The Southern Baptist Theological Seminary, 1955.

Hammond, Paul Garrett. "A Study of *The Christian Minstrel* (1846) by Jesse B. Aikin." M.C.M. thesis, The Southern Baptist Theological Seminary, 1969.

Pope, Mary Bhame. "The Sacred Choral Works of John S. Duss." M.C.M. thesis, The Southern Baptist Theological Seminary, 1971. (G. Maurice Hinson supervised final stage of the thesis owing to a sabbatical leave by McElrath).

Carson, Bobby Joe. "A Study of *The Social Harp* by John G. McCurry." M.C.M. thesis, The Southern Baptist Theological Seminary, 1973.

Sharrock, Barry Roger. "A Survey of the Texts and Music of Representative New Hymns as Found in Selected American Protestant Hymnals." M.C.M. thesis, The Southern Baptist Theological Seminary, 1975.

Smoak, Alfred Merril, Jr. "William Walker's *The Southern Harmony* (1835)." M.C.M. thesis, The Southern Baptist Theological Seminary, 1975.

Webb, George Eliga, Jr. "William Caldwell's *Union Harmony* (1837)." M.C.M. thesis, The Southern Baptist Theological Seminary, 1975.

Williams, Melanie Gillett. "A Study in the Parody Techniques of Tómas Luis de Victoria." M.C.M. thesis, The Southern Baptist Theological Seminary, 1975.

Steiner, Stephen Merritt. "The Contributions of A. B. Simpson to the Hymnody of The Christian and Missionary Alliance." M.C.M. thesis, The Southern Baptist Theological Seminary, 1976.

Loftis, Deborah Carlton. "The Hymns of Georgia Harkness (1891–1974)." M.C.M. thesis, The Southern Baptist Theological Seminary, 1977.

Allen, Pamela Payne. "A Programmed Approach to Worship Study for Older Children in Protestant Church Choirs." M.C.M. thesis, The Southern Baptist Theological Seminary, 1980.

Barker, George Stanley. "An Historical Survey of Black Baptist Hymnody in America." M.C.M. thesis, The Southern Baptist Theological Seminary, 1981.

McDuffie, Dennis Vernon. "*The Baptist Hymnal*, 1883: A Centennial Study." M.C.M. thesis, The Southern Baptist Theological Seminary, 1983.

Mullinax, Allen Bruce. "Martin Bucer and the *Strasbourg Song Book*, 1541." M.C.M. thesis, The Southern Baptist Theological Seminary, 1984.

Chaney, Margo Eileen. "The Textual Legacy of Davisson's *Supplement to Kentucky Harmony*." M.C.M. thesis, The Southern Baptist Theological Seminary, 1985.

Dennis, Pamela Richardson. "A Manual for the Use of the Computer as an Instructional Tool in the Private Piano Studio." M.C.M. thesis, The Southern Baptist Theological Seminary, 1986.

Green, Franklin Pasco, Jr. "The Life and Works of Edwin Gershefski with Analysis of Two Choral Compositions: *The Lord's Controversy with His People* and *There Is a Man on the Cross*." M.C.M. thesis, The Southern Baptist Theological Seminary, 1987.

Gregory, David Louis. "Psalmody in the Mid–Nineteenth Century Southern Baptist Tradition." M.C.M. thesis, The Southern Baptist Theological Seminary, 1987.

Hall, Stephen Frederic. "The Christian Folk Musical: A Foundational Study." M.C.M. thesis, The Southern Baptist Theological Seminary, 1987.

Moore, Carolyn Paulette. "The Marian Carols of Trinity Roll O.3.58 and Ritson MS. 5665." M.C.M. thesis, The Southern Baptist Theological Seminary, 1989.

Scudder, Karen G. "Daniel Pinkham's Vocal Solos with Biblical Texts: A Descriptive Guide with Suggestions for Performance." M.C.M. thesis, The Southern Baptist Theological Seminary, 1990.

Iga, Carolyn Sanae. "A Study of the History of Hawaiian Music in Relation to the Development of the Christian Faith." M.C.M. thesis, The Southern Baptist Theological Seminary, 1991.

Master's Degree Theses Read and Approved by Professor McElrath as Committee Member

Glover, John V., Jr. "A Study of Selected Church Cantatas of Johann Kuhnau (1660–1722)." M.C.M. thesis, The Southern Baptist Theological Seminary, 1969.

Martin, Phillip R. "An Analysis of Benjamin Britten's *Noye's Fludde*." M.C.M. thesis, The Southern Baptist Theological Seminary, 1969.

Hornbuckle, William R. "The Southern Baptist Church Musician as Conductor." M.C.M. thesis, The Southern Baptist Theological Seminary, 1969.

Shepard, Paul Dean. "An Analysis of the Music Offerings of Selected Undergraduate Christian Church Colleges with Implications for Improved Church Music Curricula." M.C.M. thesis, The Southern Baptist Theological Seminary, 1969.

Boertje, Wendell Lee. "A Philosophy of the Conductor's Purpose and Role." M.C.M. thesis, The Southern Baptist Theological Seminary, 1970.

Miller, Marian Elaine. "Practices of American Baptist Churches in Indiana Concerning the Ministry of Music." M.C.M. thesis, The Southern Baptist Theological Seminary, 1970.

Harden, Timothy Don. "A Comparison and Analysis of the Identity and Roles of Southern Baptist Ministers of Music and Combination Ministers." M.C.M. thesis, The Southern Baptist Theological Seminary, 1974.

Barker, John Sidney, III. "Organ Design in Selected Southern Baptist Churches, 1960–1974." M.C.M. thesis, The Southern Baptist Theological Seminary, 1975.

McCarty, Rex Byron. "A Documentary History of the Music Ministry of Baptist Tabernacle, Louisville, Kentucky." M.C.M. thesis, The Southern Baptist Theological Seminary, 1976.

Beecher, David I. "A Comprehensive and Sequential Hymn Study Model for Older Children in Church Choirs." M.C.M. thesis, The Southern Baptist Theological Seminary, 1979.

Fiske, Judy Mayberry. "An Analysis of the Solo Organ Works of Daniel Pinkham." M.C.M. thesis, The Southern Baptist Theological Seminary, 1979.

Pedde, Dennis R. "An Analysis of Johann Ludwig Krebs's Eight Chorale Preludes for Organ with Trumpet or Oboe." M.C.M. thesis, The Southern Baptist Theological Seminary, 1981.

Roberts, Dorothée Sida. "*Louange et Prière* et *Coeurs Te Chantent*: A Comparative Analysis." M.A. thesis, The University of Louisville, 1981.

About the Contributors

Louis Ball, dean emeritus of fine arts at Carson-Newman College, served on the editorial committee for *The Baptist Hymnal* (1991) and is a past president of the Tennessee Association of Music Executives in Colleges and Universities, as well as of the Knoxville Music Teachers Association. He has been honored as Teacher of the Year by the Knoxville KMTA, Distinguished Faculty Member of Carson-Newman College, Distinguished Alumnus of The Southern Baptist Theological Seminary, and Outstanding Music Educator in Baptist Colleges by the Church Music Department of the Baptist Sunday School Board.

A. L. "Pete" Butler served the First Baptist Church of Ada, Oklahoma, for twenty-three years (1960–1983) as minister of music before relocating to Kansas City, Missouri, to begin a new program in church music at Midwestern Baptist Theological Seminary. Active as a composer of choral works for adults and children, Professor Butler also composed four hymn tunes found in *The Baptist Hymnal* (1991). Although he officially retired in 2000 (and as senior professor in 2003), he continues to teach courses in hymnology and to serve as guest lecturer.

Paulette Moore Catherwood holds an M.C.M. degree from The Southern Baptist Theological Seminary and a D.Phil. from New College, University of Oxford. Today she maintains a private music studio and lectures in early music history for the University of Cambridge Institute of Continuing Education. She is an authority on the fifteenth-century polyphonic English carol and the author of articles in *Die Musik in Geschichte und Gegenwart* and *Blackwell Encyclopedia of Medieval, Renaissance and Reformation Christian Thought.*

Esther Rothenbusch Crookshank has served since 1994 on the faculty of The Southern Baptist Theological Seminary, where she teaches hymnology and musicology as the Ollie Hale Chiles Professor of Church Music in the School of Church Music and Worship. Her areas of research include nineteenth-century gospel hymnody in the United States and Germany, Baptist hymnody, the hymns of Watts, and the music of the Praise and Worship Movement.

Carl P. Daw, Jr., is the executive director of The Hymn Society in the United States and Canada, a position he has held since 1996. He is in constant demand as a speaker at conferences and retreats, and has published many journal articles dealing with church music, liturgy, and theology of worship. His hymns have appeared in nearly all North American hymnals published since the mid-1980s, as well as in recent hymnals in the United Kingdom, Australia, and Japan, and in numerous supplements and small collections.

Harry Eskew taught at New Orleans Baptist Theological Seminary for thirty-six years. He served on the hymnal committees for the Baptist hymnal in 1975 and 1991 and for eight years edited *The Hymn* (1976–84). He is coauthor (with Hugh T. McElrath) of *Sing with Understanding: An Introduction to Christian Hymnology* (1980; 2nd ed., 1995), and also (with David W. Music and Paul A. Richardson) of *Singing Baptists: Studies in Baptist Hymnody in America* (1994). The Baptist Church Music Conference presented him with the Hines Sims Award in 2002, the same year in which he was also made a fellow of The Hymn Society.

Janelle Ganey served as professor of music for fourteen years at The Baptist Theological Seminary of South Brazil, where she founded the seminary's master of sacred music program and served as the chair of the instrumental division. From 1988 through 1991 she was a member of the commission which produced Brazilian Baptists' new hymnal, *Hinário Para o Culto Cristão*, to which she contributed the hymn tune CORO INFANTIL. She also assisted in research for the recently published *Notas Históricas*, companion to the *Hinário*. Currently she is an Orff music specialist with the Memphis City Schools and church pianist at the First Baptist Church, Memphis, Tennessee.

David Louis Gregory is the music and audio-visual librarian of the James P. Boyce Centennial Library and an adjunct professor in the School of Church Music and Worship at The Southern Baptist Theological Seminary, Louisville, Kentucky. Dr. Gregory also serves as minister of music at Ballardsville Baptist Church, Crestwood, Kentucky. He has published reviews in *The Church Musician Today* and *The Southern Baptist Church Music Journal*.

Paul Hammond is dean of the Warren M. Angell College of Fine Arts at Oklahoma Baptist University. He taught at Ouachita Baptist University (Arkansas) from 1973–1986. He has published articles in *The Hymn*, *American Music*, and *The New Grove Dictionary of American Music*, and was a joint author of *Handbook to* The Baptist Hymnal (1992).

C. Michael Hawn has been a professor in church music at Perkins School of Theology, Southern Methodist University, since 1992 and became director of the Sacred Music Program in 2005. Prior to this he taught at two Southern Baptist seminaries and served churches in Kentucky, Georgia, North Carolina, and Texas as minister of music. His research of late has focused upon congregational song in Africa, Asia, and Latin America, and in cross-cultural worship in the United States. Professor Hawn's recent books include *Halle, Halle: We Sing the World Round* (1999), *Gather into One: Singing and Praying Globally* (2003), and *One Bread, One Body: Exploring Cultural Diversity in Worship* (2003).

Hal Hopson is a full-time composer and church music clinician with over fifteen hundred works in print composed in virtually every conceivable church music genre. Displaying a special interest in congregational song, he continues to contribute to the repertoire of new hymn tunes and responsorial psalm settings. In 1976 his cantata, *God With Us*, was selected to be placed inside the bicentennial capsule at the Kennedy Center, Washington, D.C. (scheduled to be opened again at the Tricentennial in 2076) as representative of twentieth-century American choral composition.

Donald P. Hustad is senior professor of church music at The Southern Baptist Theological Seminary in Louisville, Kentucky; previously he served as director of the Sacred Music Department, Moody Bible Institute, Chicago, and as a musician with the Billy Graham Evangelistic Association. He is the author of *Jubilate II: Church Music in Worship and Renewal* (1993) and *True Worship: Reclaiming the Wonder and Majesty* (1998).

William Jeffrey Jones is the minister of music at the First United Church of Christ, Congregational, in Milford, Connecticut. He previously served as the minister of music/organist for the Presbyterian Church at Danville, Kentucky, where he also was the college organist and an adjunct instructor at Centre College. An active member of the American Guild of Organists, Jones has been a finalist in several organ competitions and has performed numerous recitals in Atlanta and throughout central Kentucky.

Deborah Carlton Loftis is professor of church music at Baptist Theological Seminary at Richmond, in Virginia. In that post she has established a music concentration within the master of divinity degree. Prior to joining the faculty in Richmond in 1999, she served as associate minister of music at Riverchase Baptist Church in Birmingham, Alabama, and was music librarian at the Birmingham Public Library. A member of The Hymn Society in the United States and Canada, she annually indexes its journal, *The Hymn*.

Austin C. Lovelace is a past president and fellow of The Hymn Society. He has composed over seven hundred compositions in a wide variety of genres and has published articles in *The Diapason, The Hymn, Journal of Church Music*, and *The American Organist*. He has served as the minister of music in Baptist, Presbyterian, and Methodist churches. He has been the organizing chair for the Fellowship of Methodist Musicians and served on the Hymnal Committee for *The Methodist Hymnal* (1964), chairing its subcommittee on tunes.

William N. "Mac" McElrath worked for thirty years as a Baptist missionary in Indonesia, where his major assignment was writing and editing materials in the Indonesian language and training others to do the same. Mac has written more than sixty books, equally divided between the English and Indonesian languages. These include *A Bible Dictionary for Young Readers* (1965), a popular favorite, and *Ways We Worship* (1997), which helps teachers, parents, and young readers to understand more about the beliefs and practices of major world religions.

Milburn Price has been dean of the School of Performing Arts at Samford University in Birmingham, Alabama, since 1993. Prior to this, he served as dean of the School of Church Music at The Southern Baptist Theological Seminary in Louisville (1981–1993), and as chair of the Music Department at Furman University (1972–1981). Dr. Price has written text and music for several hymns, some of which may be found in *Baptist Hymnal* (1975), *The Worshipping Church* (1990), and *The Baptist Hymnal* (1991). He is coauthor (with Gary Furr) of *The Dialogue of Worship* (1998), and, together with David W. Music, he has published a revised and expanded edition of *A Survey of Christian Hymnody* (4th edition, 1999).

J. Michael Raley presently teaches in the History Department at Northeastern Illinois University in Chicago. He has served churches in Kentucky, Georgia, and Indiana as pastor and as director of music. His articles and reviews have appeared in *Anuario Musical, The Southern Baptist Church Music Journal*, and *Journal of Southern Religion*. He has been the recipient of research fellowships from the Newberry Library (Chicago), the Max Planck Institute for European Legal History (Frankfurt, Germany), and the Herzog August Bibliothek (Wolfenbüttel, Germany).

Paul A. Richardson is professor of music and assistant dean for graduate studies in music in the School of Performing Arts at Samford University in Birmingham, Alabama. A past president of The Hymn Society in the United States and Canada and a contributing editor to its journal, *The Hymn*, Dr. Richardson has recently completed a revised and expanded edition of Erik Routley's *A Panorama of Christian Hymnody* (2004). His articles and reviews have appeared in a variety of periodicals related to hymnology, church music, and worship.

Rae E. Whitney, a native of England, first taught in rural schools, then for two years worked in London as resident co-secretary of the Fellowship of St. Alban and St. Sergius, an international society devoted to better understanding between Eastern and Western churches. Beginning in the 1970s, she focused upon writing hymns. Her moving texts have now found their way into about a dozen denominational hymnals. In 1995, the Selah Publishing Company issued *With Joy Our Spirits Sing*, which included 230 of Rae's texts. In the fall of 2006, Seleh has scheduled the release of *Fear Not, Little Flock*, a new collection of her texts set to music by various contemporary composers.

Mel R. Wilhoit is chair of the Music Department at Bryan College in Dayton, Tennessee, where he has taught music and fine arts for twenty-five years. He has published widely in the area of gospel hymnody and other musically related subjects. His works have appeared in *The Church Musician, International Trumpet Guild Journal, The Hymn, American Music*, and *Wesleyan Theological Journal,* as well as in standard reference works such as *The New Grove Dictionary of American Music, The New Grove Dictionary of Music and Musicians,* and *Encyclopedia of American National Biography,* in addition to numerous Festschrifts and popular works.

Donald Eugene Winters is professor of church music and voice at the Winters School of Music (named in honor of Dr. Winters's parents, Donald and Frances Winters), William Carey College, Hattiesburg, Mississippi. In addition to his tenure at the college (since 1979), he has served churches in Mississippi, Indiana, and Florida as minister of music. Dr. Winters coauthored (with his mother, the late Frances W. Winters, L.L.D.) *Vocal*

Pedagogy: A Guide to Singing Skills (1984). He has also composed several sets of art songs and continues to write hymns and carols. His most recent endeavor is a collection entitled *Embracing the Light: 20 Advent and Christmas Carols* (forthcoming).

Brian Wren is the John and Miriam Conant Professor of Worship at Columbia Theological Seminary, Decatur, Georgia, and is a Minister of the Word and Sacraments of the United Reformed Church (United Kingdom). He has written the lyrics of more than two hundred hymns and has entries in most recent denominational hymnals in the United States, Canada, Britain, Australia, and New Zealand. Six of his hymn lyrics were translated into Japanese and published in *Hymnal 21* (1997, United Church of Christ in Japan). His other works include *Education for Justice* (1977), *What Language Shall I Borrow? God-Talk in Worship: A Male Response to Feminist Theology* (1989), and *Praying Twice: The Music and Words of Congregational Song* (2000).

Carlton R. Young, professor emeritus of church music at the Candler School of Theology at Emory University, has the unique distinction of having served as the editor of two revisions of Methodist hymnals: *The Methodist Hymnal* (1966) and *The United Methodist Hymnal* (1989). He is a music consultant and editor for *Global Praise* projects of the United Methodist General Board of Global Ministries and of *Companion to* The United Methodist Hymnal (1993), *My Great Redeemer's Praise: An Introduction to Christian Hymns* (1995), and *Music of the Heart: John and Charles Wesley on Music and Musicians* (1995).